Exam	Prentice Hall Title	MCSE Certification Credit	MCSE + Internet Certification Credit	MCDBA Certification Credit	MCSD Certification Credit	MCP + Site Building Certification Credit	MCP + Internet Certification Credit
70-079	*MCSE: Implementing and Supporting Microsoft Internet Explorer 4 by Using the Microsoft Internet Explorer Administration Kit*, Dell, 1999	1 of 2 Elective Requirements	1 of 7 Core Requirements	NA	NA	NA	NA
70-081	*MCSE: Implementing and Supporting Microsoft Exchange Server 5.5*, Goncalves, 1998	1 of 2 Elective Requirements	1 of 2 Elective Requirements	NA	NA	NA	NA
70-085	*MCSE: Implementing and Supporting Microsoft SNA Server 4*, Mariscal, 1999	1 of 2 Elective Requirements	1 of 2 Elective Requirements	NA	NA	NA	NA
70-086	*MCSE: Implementing and Supporting Microsoft Systems Management Server 2*, Vacca, 1999	1 of 2 Elective Requirements	NA	NA	NA	NA	NA
70-087	*MCSE: Implementing and Supporting Microsoft Internet Information Server 4*, Dell, 1999	1 of 2 Elective Requirements	1 of 7 Core Requirements	1 of 1 Elective Requirements	NA	NA	1 of 3 Requirements
70-088	*MCSE: Implementing and Supporting Microsoft Proxy Server 2*, Ryvkin, 1999	1 of 2 Elective Requirements	1 of 2 Elective Requirements	NA	NA	NA	NA
70-098	*Core MCSE*, Dell, 1998	1 of 4 Core Requirements	1 of 7 Core Requirements	NA	NA	NA	NA
70-175	*MCSD: Designing and Implementing Distributed Applications with Microsoft Visual Basic 6*, Houlette, 1999	NA	NA	1 of 4 Core Requirements and 1 of 1 Elective Requirements	1 of 1 Elective Requirements	NA	NA
70-176	*MCSD: Designing and Implementing Desktop Applications with Microsoft Visual Basic 6*, Holzner, 1999	NA	NA	NA	1 of 1 Elective Requirements	NA	NA

MCSE:
IMPLEMENTING AND SUPPORTING MICROSOFT® PROXY SERVER 2.0

ISBN 0-13-011248-8

MICROSOFT CERTIFIED SYSTEMS ENGINEER SERIES

KOSTYA RYVKIN
DAVE HOUDE
TIM HOFFMAN

MCSE: IMPLEMENTING AND SUPPORTING MICROSOFT® PROXY SERVER 2.0

Prentice Hall PTR
Upper Saddle River, New Jersey 07458
http://www.phptr.com

Library of Congress Cataloging-in-Publication Data

Ryvkin, Kostya.
    MCSE. Implementing and supporting Microsoft Proxy Server 2.0 / Kostya Ryvkin, Dave Houde, Tim Hoffman.
        p.   cm. -- (Prentice Hall series on Microsoft technologies)
    ISBN 0-13-011251-8
    1. Electronic data processing personnel--Certification. 2. Microsoft software--Examinations Study guides. 3. Microsoft Proxy Server.
  I. Houde, David. II. Hoffman, Timothy. III. Title. IV. Series.
  QA76.3.R98   1999   99-38993
  005.7'13769--dc21   CIP

Editorial/production supervision: *Vincent Janoski*
Acquisitions editor: *Mary Franz*
Marketing manager: *Lisa Konzelmann*
Developmental editor: *Jim Markham*
Technical editor: *Kirky Ringer*
Manufacturing manager: *Alexis R. Heydt*
Editorial assistant: *Noreen Regina*
Cover design director: *Jerry Votta*

Published by Prentice-Hall PTR
Prentice-Hall, Inc.
Upper Saddle River, NJ 07458

Prentice Hall books are widely used by corporations and government agencies
for training, marketing, and resale.

The publisher offers discounts on this book when ordered in bulk quantities.
For more information, contact: Corporate Sales Department, Phone: 800-382-3419;
Fax: 201-236-7141; E-mail: corpsales@prenhall.com; or write: Prentice Hall PTR,
Corp. Sales Dept., One Lake Street, Upper Saddle River, NJ 07458.

Use of the Microsoft Approved Study Guide Logo on this product signifies that it has been
independently reviewed and approved in complying with the following standards:

- acceptable coverage of all content related to Microsoft exam number 70-088, entitled
  Implementing and Supporting Microsoft Proxy Server 2.
- sufficient performance-based exercises that relate closely to all required content; and
- technically accurate content, based on sampling of text.

All products or services mentioned in this book are the trademarks or service marks of their
respective companies or organizations. Screen shots reprinted by permission from
Microsoft Corporation.

Printed in the United States of America
10 9 8 7 6 5 4 3 2

ISBN: 0-13-011248-8

Prentice-Hall International (UK) Limited, *London*
Prentice-Hall of Australia Pty. Limited, *Sydney*
Prentice-Hall Canada, Inc., *Toronto*
Prentice-Hall Hispanoamericana, S.A., *Mexico*
Prentice-Hall of India Private Limited, *New Delhi*
Prentice-Hall of Japan, Inc., *Tokyo*
Prentice-Hall Singapore Pte. Ltd., *Singapore*
Editora Prentice-Hall do Brasil, Ltda., *Rio de Janeiro*

To Giulia, Sandy, and Tatiana, for cheerfully providing support and enduring the loneliness while we developed this book.

CONTENTS

3

Planning Proxy Server   25

4

Installing Proxy Server   45

5

Proxy Server Administration   77

6

Packet Filtering 155

Networks with Multiple Proxy Server Computers   175

Administering Proxy Clients   207

11

Troubleshooting   295

Kostya Ryvkin, MCSE +I, MCT is a consultant, trainer, and network engineer. He recently co-authored the MCSE study guide *Internetworking with Microsoft TCP/IP on Microsoft Windows NT 4.0* His solid programming and application development background has helped with the development of several utilities in a variety of programming languages. He provides customers with network installation, sophisticated web design and messaging system integration, and advanced technical support.

As a Microsoft Certified Trainer, he has taught these skills in classes over the last few years and is adept at developing courseware, student and trainer kits, lab manuals, and test questions.

Dave Houde, MCP is a consultant, trainer, and network engineer. He recently co-authored the MCSE study guide *Internetworking with Microsoft TCP/IP on Microsoft Windows NT 4.0* and has multiple certifications. He wrote and delivered an advanced SQL 7.0 course and consistently provides advanced messaging solutions such as data recovery programs for customers.

Dave retired from the US Air Force where he had been involved with information technology as a programmer/analyst and operating system/network support engineer in the early seventies. As a programmer, Dave delivered mainframe and microcomputer software ranging from simple accounting and database software to complex navigation and modeling applications. His work with the Internet spans many years.

As a trainer, he has taught an array of Microsoft BackOffice classes for the past two years. He is equally adept at developing courseware, student and trainer kits, presentations, lab manuals and test questions.

Tim Hoffman, MCP, MCSE, MCT, PSS is the president of the Alida Connection and he recently co-authored the MCSE study guide *Internetworking with Microsoft TCP/IP on Microsoft Windows NT 4.0* He has attended specialized military training in troubleshooting, multichannel signals processing, off-line cryptography, high speed cryptographic secure systems, and satellite communications.

His professional career dates from 1969. He has telecommunications and computer expertise including systems analysis, protocol definition / information transfer (X.25 and TCP/IP), network modeling, certification and accreditation of sites, networks and systems, and systems test. He regularly provides troubleshooting and analysis on networks, messaging systems and data repositories. He has provided server and workstation maintenance and repair, configuration management for multiple networks, on-site, on-line and telephone consulting, which included level three technical support. He provides training in the hardware and software installation, configuration and integration. He also authors courseware, trainer materials, presentations, lab manuals, and test questions.

ACKNOWLEDGMENTS

Knowledge is truth. Be relentless in your search for knowledge. This book is for the technical student. The work of several dedicated professionals is what got this book completed, reviewed, and coordinated.

The authors, Kostya, Dave, and Tim want to acknowledge the guidance, patience, support and watchful eyes of the team at Prentice Hall: Acquisitions Editor Mary Franz, Technical Editor Sean Geist, and our task master, Development Editor Jim Markham.

Together we encourage the student to learn as much as possible about the technology and wish you well with your certification exam.

#	Implementing and Supporting Microsoft Proxy Server 2.0 (Exam 70-088) Requirement	Chapter	Syllabus/Paragraph Number	Question(s)
1.	Planning: Choose a secure access strategy for various situations. Access includes outbound access by users to the Internet and inbound access to your Web site. Considerations include: **Translating addresses from the internal network to the Local Address Table (LAT).**	4	4.2	10
2.	Planning: Choose a secure access strategy for various situations. Access includes outbound access by users to the Internet and inbound access to your Web site. Considerations include: **Controlling anonymous access.**	5	5.6	1
3.	Planning: Choose a secure access strategy for various situations. Access includes outbound access by users to the Internet and inbound access to your Web site. Considerations include: *Controlling access by known users and groups.*	5	5.3, 5.6	4
4.	Planning: Choose a secure access strategy for various situations. Access includes outbound access by users to the Internet and inbound access to your Web site. Considerations include: *Setting protocol permissions.*	5	5.3, 5.4	2,3,4,7
5.	Planning: Choose a secure access strategy for various situations. Access includes outbound access by users to the Internet and inbound access to your Web site. Considerations include: *Auditing protocol access.*	5	5.4	25
6.	Planning: Choose a secure access strategy for various situations. Access includes outbound access by users to the Internet and inbound access to your Web site. Considerations include: *Setting Microsoft Windows NT® security parameters.*	4	4.1	5
7.	Planning: Plan an Internet site or an intranet site for stand-alone servers, single-domain environments, and multiple-domain environments. Tasks include: *Choosing appropriate connectivity methods.*	3	3.2	6
8.	Planning: Plan an Internet site or an intranet site for stand-alone servers, single-domain environments, and multiple-domain environments. Tasks include: *Choosing services .*	2	2.1	1–7

9.	Planning: Plan an Internet site or an intranet site for stand-alone servers, single-domain environments, and multiple-domain environments. Tasks include: ***Using Microsoft Proxy Server in an intranet that has no access to the Internet.***	10	10.5	17
10.	Planning: Plan an Internet site or an intranet site for stand-alone servers, single-domain environments, and multiple-domain environments. Tasks include: ***Choosing hardware.***	3	3.1	7
11.	Planning: Choose a strategy to balance Internet access across multiple Proxy Server computers. Strategies include: ***Using DNS.***	7	7.5	1,9
12.	Planning: Choose a strategy to balance Internet access across multiple Proxy Server computers. Strategies include: ***Using arrays.***	7	7.1, 7.2	1,4,7,8,10
13.	Planning: Choose a strategy to balance Internet access across multiple Proxy Server computers. Strategies include: ***Using Cache Array Routing Protocol (CARP).***	7	7.2	2
14.	Planning: ***Choose a rollout plan for integrating a Proxy Server with an existing corporate environment.***	3	3.3	2,3,4,6,7
15.	Planning: Choose a fault tolerance strategy. Strategies include: ***Using arrays.***	7	7.1	4,7,10
16.	Planning: Choose a fault tolerance strategy. Strategies include: ***Using routing.***	7	7.4	3,5
17.	Installation and Configuration ***Create a LAT.***	4	4.2	4, 10
18.	Installation and Configuration: Configure server authentication. Authentication options include: ***Anonymous logon.***	5	5.6	1
19.	Installation and Configuration: Configure server authentication. Authentication options include: ***Basic authentication.***	5	5.6	5
20.	Installation and Configuration: Configure server authentication. Authentication options include: ***Microsoft Windows NT Challenge/Response authentication.***	5	5.6	5
21.	Installation and Configuration: ***Configure Windows NT to support Microsoft Proxy Server.***	4.	4.1	1-3
22.	Installation and Configuration: ***Configure the various Proxy Server services.***	5	5.3, 5.4, 5.5	6

	Objective			
23.	Configure Microsoft Proxy Server for Internet access. Situations include: ***Configuring Proxy Server to provide Internet access through a dial-up connection to an ISP.***	5	5.2	21,22
24.	Configure Microsoft Proxy Server for Internet access. Situations include: ***Configuring Proxy Server to act as an IPX gateway.***	8	8.3	2
25.	Configure Microsoft Proxy Server for Internet access. Situations include: ***Configuring multiple Microsoft Proxy Servers for Internet access.***	7	7.3/7.4	3,4,7,9,10
26.	Configure Microsoft Proxy Server for Internet access. Situations include: ***Configuring multiple Proxy Servers spread across several different geographic locations.***	7	7.1	3,4,5,7
27.	Installation and Configuration: ***Select and use software configuration management tools (for example, Control Panel, Windows NT Setup, Regedt32).***	5	5.1	13, 17
28.	Installation and Configuration: ***Configure auditing.***	5	5.3	9, 10
29.	Installation and Configuration: ***Given a scenario, decide which user interface to use to perform administrative tasks.***	5	5.1, 5.2, 5.3, 5.4	12, 13, 16
30.	Installation and Configuration: ***Identify the licensing requirements for a given Proxy Server site.***	4	4.1	13
31.	Installation and Configuration: ***Configure Proxy Server arrays.***	7	7.3	6,7,10
32.	Installation and Configuration: ***Configure arrays to provide fault-tolerance for Web Proxy client requests.***	7	7.1	4,7
33.	Installation and Configuration: Use packet filtering to prevent unauthorized access. Tasks include: ***Using packet filtering to enable a specific protocol.***	6	6.1	2, 3, 4, 5, 7
34.	Installation and Configuration: Use packet filtering to prevent unauthorized access. Tasks include: ***Configuring packet filter alerting and logging.***	6	6.2	1, 6
35.	Installation and Configuration: ***Configure hierarchical caching.***	7	7.1-7.4	5
36.	Setting Up and Managing Resource Access: ***Grant or restrict access to the Internet for selected outbound users and groups who use the various Proxy Server services to access the Internet.***	5	5.3, 5.6	2, 3

37.	Setting Up and Managing Resource Access: *Grant or restrict access to specific Internet sites for outbound users.*	5	5.2	11, 19
38.	Setting Up and Managing Resource Access: *Choose the location, size, and type of caching for the Web Proxy service.*	4	4.1	6
39.	Setting Up and Managing Resource Access: *Configure active caching and passive caching.*	5	5.3	15, 20
40.	Setting Up and Managing Resource Access: *Implement Web publishing to enable reverse proxying.*	5	5.3	24
41.	Setting Up and Managing Resource Access: *Back up and restore Proxy Server configurations.*	5	5.2	23
42.	Setting Up and Managing Resource Access: *Implement reverse hosting.*	5	5.3	24
43.	Integration and Interoperability *Use the Proxy Server client Setup program to configure client computers.*	4	4.3	7,9,12
44.	Integration and Interoperability: Configure Proxy Server and Proxy Server client computers to use the Proxy Server services. Configurations include: *Microsoft Internet Explorer client computers.*	8	8.1	3
45.	Integration and Interoperability: Configure Proxy Server and Proxy Server client computers to use the Proxy Server services. Configurations include: *Netscape Navigator client computers.*	8	8.1	1
46.	Integration and Interoperability: Configure Proxy Server and Proxy Server client computers to use the Proxy Server services. Configurations include: *Macintosh® client computers.*	8	8.1	6
47.	Integration and Interoperability: Configure Proxy Server and Proxy Server client computers to use the Proxy Server services. Configurations include: *UNIX client computers.*	8	8.1	1
48.	Integration and Interoperability: Configure Proxy Server and Proxy Server client computers to use the Proxy Server services. Configurations include: *Client computers on an IPX-only network.*	8	8.1	2
49.	Integration and Interoperability *Configure a RAS server to route Internet requests.*	9	9.1	2
50.	Integration and Interoperability *Write JavaScript to configure a Web browser.*	8	8.2	4
51.	Integration and Interoperability *Change settings in Mspclnt.ini.*	8	8.4	7

52.	Monitoring and Optimization: *Configure Proxy Server to log errors when they occur.*	5 10	5.3 10.4	9,10 (ch 5) 1 (ch 10)
53.	Monitoring and Optimization *Monitor performance of various functions by using Microsoft Windows NT Performance Monitor. Functions include HTTP and FTP sessions.*	10	10.2	2
54.	Monitoring and Optimization: Analyze performance issues. Performance issues include: *Identifying bottlenecks.*	10	10.2	3
55.	Monitoring and Optimization: Analyze performance issues. Performance issues include: *Identifying network-related performance issues.*	10	10.2	4,6
56.	Monitoring and Optimization: Analyze performance issues. Performance issues include: *Identifying disk-related performance issues.*	10	10.2	5,6
57.	Monitoring and Optimization: Analyze performance issues. Performance issues include: *Identifying CPU-related performance issues.*	10	10.2	5,6
58.	Monitoring and Optimization: Analyze performance issues. Performance issues include: *Identifying memory-related performance issues.*	10	10.2	5,6
59.	Monitoring and Optimization: Optimize performance for various purposes. Purposes include: *Increasing throughput.*	10	10.2	7,12
60.	Monitoring and Optimization: Optimize performance for various purposes. Purposes include: *Optimizing routing.*	10	10.5	8
61.	Monitoring and Optimization *Use Performance Monitor logs to identify the appropriate configuration.*	10	10.2	10
62.	Monitoring and Optimization *Perform Internet traffic analysis by using Windows NT Server tools.*	10	10.2	9,16
63.	Monitoring and Optimization *Monitor current sessions.*	5 10	5.3 10.1	18 (ch 5) 11 (ch 10)
64.	Troubleshooting: *Resolve Proxy Server and Proxy Server client installation problems.*	4 11	4.2, 4.3	11, 5
65.	Troubleshooting: *Resolve Proxy Server and Proxy Server client access problems.*	8 11	8.4	5,8
66.	Troubleshooting: *Resolve Proxy Server client computer problems.*	11	11.3	2
67.	Troubleshooting: *Resolve security problems.*	5	5.6	4, 7, 8
68.	Troubleshooting: *Resolve caching problems.*	5 11	5.3 11.4	14, 16 3

69.	Troubleshooting: *Troubleshoot a WINS server to provide client access to Proxy Servers.*	11	11.5	5
70.	Troubleshooting: *Troubleshoot hardware-related problems such as network interfaces and disk drives.*	11	11.4 11.6	3 8
71.	Troubleshooting: *Troubleshoot Internet/intranet routing hardware and software. Software includes Microsoft Routing and Remote Access Service (RRAS).*	11	11.6	6,7

This book is designed primarily for network professionals preparing for exam 70-088: Implementing and Supporting Microsoft® Proxy Server 2.0. When you pass this exam you become a *Microsoft Certified Professional.* You also earn elective credit toward *Microsoft Certified Systems Engineer* certification and elective credit toward *Microsoft Certified Systems Engineer + Internet* certification.

This book will benefit any computing professional who is responsible for the management of Windows NT-based computing environments, particularly in the enterprise where security is important. It is designed to be both a training guide and reference resource.

Who This Book is For

This book is designed to provide concise and comprehensive information about the Microsoft Proxy Server Version 2.0 and is for computer professionals who manage computers running under the Microsoft® Windows NT 4.0 and Windows 95/98 operating systems. Although many aspects of both client and server side are covered, the readers of this book should have a good working knowledge of a Microsoft Windows operating system, such as Windows 95, Windows 98, or Windows NT 4.0.

What You'll Need

Through the use of numerous illustrations and CD-ROM-based training supplements, we have endeavored to make this book as self-contained as possible. Nevertheless, we acknowledge that there is no substitute for hands-on experience. To fully practice the concepts explained in this book, you will need at least three Intel 486/66 (or better) computers with as least 32 Mbytes of RAM (64 Mbytes recommended), 450MB of free hard disk space, two network adapter cards, two mice (or other pointing device), two VGA monitors, CD-ROM drive, and a 1.44MB 3.5-inch floppy diskette drive. Optional equipment includes a modem or ISDN adapter, a printer, and a tape drive. The Proxy Server will only install on a system running Microsoft Windows NT Server 4.0. Client systems can run Microsoft Windows NT Server 4.0, Windows 95/98.

Applicable "hands-on" portions of the text provide advice on how to obtain maximum training benefit from lesser equipment configurations.

How this Book is Organized

This book is divided into 11 chapters, which cover issues such as planning, installation, administration, packet filtering, performance monitoring, testing and troubleshooting. The numbered sections in each chapter correspond to specific MCSE exam requirements, and each chapter concludes with a list of related study questions. Most chapters have hands-on *Study Break* sections that permit you to practice what you learned. Appendix A contains the answers to all review questions, while Appendix B provides additional installation instructions.

Conventions Used in This Book

This book uses different features to help highlight key information.

Chapter Syllabus

The primary focus of this series is to address those topics that are to be tested in each exam. Therefore, each chapter opens with a syllabus that lists the topics to be covered. Each topic directly corresponds to the Level 1 headings in the chapter. So if there are six Level 1 headings in a chapter, there will be six topics listed under the Chapter Syllabus. If a syllabus topic and Level 1 heading are MCSE-specific, they will be accompanied by an MCSE icon (see the following icon description). However, there may be instances when the topics are not exam-specific. In these cases, the chapter syllabus highlights and corresponding Level 1 headings appear without the MCSE icon.

Icons

Icons represent called-out material that is of significance and that you should be alerted to. Icons include:

This icon is used to identify MCSE-specific Chapter Syllabus topics and appropriate MCSE sections in each chapter.

This icon is used to call out information that deserves special attention; one that the reader may otherwise run a highlight marker through.

This icon is used to flag particularly useful information that will save the reader time, highlight a valuable technique, or offer specific advice.

This icon flags information that may cause unexpected results or serious frustration.

Study Breaks

These sidebars are designed to test your knowledge in a practical manner through the use of performance-based exercises. These exercises provide an opportunity to perform actual tasks that will undoubtedly be encountered in a working environment, and simulated in the Microsoft exam.

Chapter Review Questions

Each chapter ends with a series of review questions. These questions are designed to simulate a part of an actual exam and to reinforce what you have just learned. The number of questions will vary depending on the length subject matter of the individual chapter. All of the questions are taken directly from the material covered in the chapter, and the answers can be found in Appendix A.

About the CD-ROM/Web Site

This book is accompanied by a CD-ROM that contains valuable self-paced training material, courtesy of CBT Systems. Please follow the installation instructions on the CD-ROM.

This book is also accompanied by a Companion Web site on which readers can find additional exam preparation aids and updates to the enclosed material. It is located at www.phptr.com/phptrinteractive.

Overview of Microsoft Proxy Server 2.0

As information technology (IT) grows, the "cyberspace" which it has created grows also. Today's network computing environment is a reflection of the world in which it operates. As we operate in cyberspace, we must be mindful of the need for security and efficiency just as we are when performing non-IT activities in the surrounding world. Fortunately, Microsoft Proxy Server is a relatively simple, inexpensive, and effective way to sharply enhance both the security and the efficiency of our computer networks.

Businesses of all sizes, private and not-for-profit companies from "Mom and Pop" to the Fortune 500 giants, all require a mindset that includes the protection of their network assets. The obvious benefits of connecting the corporate network to the Internet are somewhat overshadowed by the unknown threats of the medium.

In this chapter we introduce the features and benefits of Microsoft Proxy Server 2.0. We briefly discuss Proxy Server as a product that provides security by acting as a firewall between your Local Area Network (LAN) and the Internet. By properly configuring the Microsoft Proxy Server you can provide effective protection to your entire network. Proxy Server will actually improve the performance of remote web sites by caching the most often requested information.

At the end of this chapter you will be able to:

- Describe Microsoft Proxy Server 2.0
- Identify the security features of Microsoft Proxy Server 2.0
- Identify the benefits of using Microsoft Proxy Server 2.0

What is Microsoft Proxy Server 2.0?

Microsoft Proxy Server 2.0 is a software product that runs on Microsoft Windows NT 4.0. It takes advantage of the built in New Technology File System (NTFS) security and scalability and creates a network firewall. Microsoft Proxy Server has best been described as an extensible firewall and content cache server. When we introduce the term firewall it is important to distinguish just what a firewall is and what it does. A firewall is typically described as hardware and/or a software product that restricts unauthorized entry to the internal protected resources from the external environment. Although there are many such products, the most functional employ a multiple layered approach that requires any inbound signal to traverse the entire protocol stack through to the Application layer of the OSI model. Other features might include:

- Packet Filtering, which permits only packets destined to or originating from a specific port to pass.
- Alerts, which let the administrator know when some form of attack might be present.
- Performance Monitoring, which permits sizing and timing studies to ensure sufficient bandwidth is present.

When used in this context, a "firewall" is a system placed between two networks. It is used to protect one of the networks—the "internal" network—by preventing unauthorized access from the other network—the "external" network.

A proxy is something that works on behalf of someone. Microsoft's Proxy Server 2.0 is a software server that offers effective Internet security services for LAN users by blocking intruders. It can also block outbound web site requests, as we shall see later.

Content Caching is offered by Microsoft Proxy Server to help improve the efficiency of web requests. This is a relatively new functionality in the world of computers, so an explanation is in order. Bandwidth is a recurring cost, and the speed of network-to-network communications has always been something of an item to study. The higher the speed, the more the cost. Since bandwidth is expensive, it used to be that only the information required to do the job was sent and received. Now, with every user having the ability and yes, even the need, to frequently locate information on the web, we find the existing bandwidth requirements are going through the ceiling. How do we cut down this need for speed? Simple—we improve the efficiency of outbound web requests to frequently visited web sites by storing local copies of the most frequently hit Internet sites and pages. This storing is called caching. Caching speeds performance because users download from a local Proxy Server on the internal network instead of waiting for the graphics and text to download over the Internet link from a remote host.

End to end, the bandwidth is used more efficiently and the network traffic is reduced. Also, the end user gets the images and text much faster because the content is read from local storage.

Firewall capabilities and content caching makes the Microsoft Proxy server a hybrid that can:

- Provide a secure gateway which protects the internal network from the inside or outside.
- Hide the internal addresses.
- Support IPX/IP translation.
- Cache the most frequently used content.

Proxy Server Security Features

When configured as the single point of information transfer between your organization's LAN and the Internet, Microsoft Proxy Server 2.0 is a powerful tool that protects your organization from unwanted intruders. As with the more expensive hardware and software options, you have the ability to protect internal IP addresses by several methods.

- By using a LAN protocol other than TCP/IP you can achieve protocol isolation to provide an even greater level of protection. In this example, you would simply use the IPX/SPX protocol on all client machines and the Proxy Server would be used to convert the inbound TCP/IP to IPX/SPX and the outbound IPX/SPX to TCP/IP for use on the Internet. Using the Proxy Server in this manner stops intruders at another level, making access to your LAN nearly impossible.

- Filtering can be accomplished at the IP Packet Layer, which provides another security feature. You can enable access to inbound and outbound service ports and establish packet filtering.

- Alerts and logs provide information about the security of the Internet connection, and control access to specific Internet sites based on the criteria of your choice.

- Proxy Server is capable of dynamically opening and closing ports to support client requests, which offers an additional dynamic component.

- The logging facility permits the creation of an audit trail for security events that could be useful in troubleshooting and reviewing the security details of a network environment.

Benefits of Using Proxy Server

As the need for connectivity with the Internet has increased, so has the need for security. Although there are several products that provide firewall protection, most are expensive and are difficult to configure without a great deal of training. Microsoft Proxy Server, however, provides a number of significant benefits and is a relatively easy product to install, configure, and troubleshoot. Although troubleshooting Proxy Server is a real challenge, understand that troubleshooting any firewall technology is complex. Microsoft Proxy Server is easier to troubleshoot than most other third party products because Microsoft Windows NT provides several integrated tools that have a familiar interface and operation. In addition, the resulting error messages are found in the Microsoft TechNet CD and the Microsoft Knowledge Base.

The flexible security provided by using Proxy Server includes dynamic packet filtering, which provides protection from unwanted traffic to the environment through specific filters. We will investigate this feature later in the book, but additional security features include virus scanning, ActiveX and JavaScript filtering, and site restrictions. You can choose additional features from third parties and add them as plug-ins based on the Proxy Server's compliance with existing standards.

Integration with Microsoft Windows NT Server and Internet Information Server provides the Proxy Server with a scalable architecture from the start. Microsoft Windows NT—the required operating system for Proxy Server—provides a solid, distributed, replicated, client/server architecture, which permits Proxy Server to scale from the smallest of single-server installations to very large and complex sites. Windows NT 4.0 provides an integrated Performance Monitor tool and Proxy Server objects are easy to find, understand, and monitor. Also, the Network Monitor provides a detailed look at the network, right down to the contents of individual packets. Close integration with the Internet Information Server permits on-screen and remote management of system services and makes for an out-of-box, ease-of-use that is generally unmatched in similar products. By leveraging the operating system features and functionality, and through close integration with the existing application base, Proxy Server achieves a level of coherence that is nearly impossible, and rarely achieved, by other third party products.

Like most other Microsoft products that are relatively easy to learn to manage, the Proxy Server is easy to maintain and administer. With the exception of the the actual Proxy Server configuration, administration tools are built into Microsoft Windows NT 4.0. You will find yourself using the following:

- User Manager for Domains
- Internet Information Server
- Performance Monitor
- Network Monitor
- Server Manager
- Event Viewer
- Microsoft Management Console

You will also be able to perform Web-based administration using HTML, or command line administration using command-line syntax and parameters.

In addition to tight integration with other Microsoft products, Proxy Server provides better bandwidth utilization—a resource goal most large companies often struggle to attain. The ability to block ports or addresses and the automation of the proxy client installation process makes the operation run smoothly even in large environments.

With the Proxy Server reverse proxy feature, Web publishing support is built in, not added on. Web publishing refers to the ability to place resources on a server accessible to the Internet. *Reverse proxy* is the feature of Proxy Server that permits it to impersonate an internal network Web server to the external network. Through the *reverse hosting* feature of reverse proxy, multiple internal Web servers can publish on the external network—the Internet.

■ Summary

This chapter described Microsoft Proxy Server 2.0 and outlined some of its security features and benefits. We learned that a *proxy* is something that acts on behalf of something else. Proxy Server is a server that operates between two networks representing hosts on each network to hosts on the other. We saw that operating in this fashion, Proxy Server forms a scaleable network firewall. In addition to its firewall function, we found that Proxy Server provides extensive Web caching to improve Internet access efficiency.

Microsoft Proxy Server protects your network's internal IP addresses and can be used to filter IP packets to prevent unauthorized intrusion. It can control access based on a number of criteria and can log network activity.

Proxy Server is relatively inexpensive and easy to install and configure. The software runs on Windows NT 4.0 Server and takes advantage of inherent Windows NT and NTFS security features. The product can sharply increase bandwidth utilization and, through reverse proxy, can permit multiple Web servers to publish on the Internet while providing them with greatly enhanced network security.

▲ REVIEW QUESTIONS

1. *What is the term for storing pages from a remote site on the local Proxy Server called?*
   - A. CMOS
   - B. Reverse Proxy
   - C. Caching
   - D. Performance Monitoring

2. *Describe the features of Microsoft Proxy Server 2.0 (select all that apply)*
   - A. Works only in a UNIX environment
   - B. Can cache remote pages
   - C. Can block outbound URL requests
   - D. Can block inbound URL requests
   - E. Can perform packet filtering

3. *To ensure security at the local drive level, Microsoft Proxy Server 2.0 should be installed on a server running:*

    A. Windows 95

    B. Windows NT Workstation

    C. Windows NT Server

    D. Windows NT Server (Enterprise)

Microsoft Proxy Server Architecture

Now that we understand what Proxy Server is and what it can do for us, let's spend some time looking at some of Proxy Server's specific features and services.

At the conclusion of this chapter you will be able to:

- Define how Microsoft Proxy Server operates on the Internet

- List the Proxy Server services

- Explain the features and use of the Web Proxy Service

- Explain the features and use of the WinSock Proxy Service

- Explain the features and use of the SOCKS Proxy Service

- Discuss the use of TCP/IP and IPX/SPX on the LAN in conjunction with the Proxy Server

Proxy Server on the Internet

When functioning properly, the proxy server should be virtually transparent to both the client computer and the Internet. The user at the client should only recognize the existence of the proxy server when he or she attempts an operation which the proxy has been programmed to prevent. The Internet resource interprets requests as coming directly from a network client. Although both parties "think" they're talking to each other, in reality they are each communicating with the proxy which is relaying the information between them as shown in Figure 2.1. This provides the administrator control over what resources may be obtained from the external network by members of the internal network. More importantly, a properly configured Proxy Server will protect members of the internal network from unauthorized intrusion from the external network.

To accomplish its proxy functions, the Proxy Server employs three services which relate to most of the currently available Internet applications and features:

- Web Proxy Service—for CERN compliant applications
- WinSock Proxy Service—for Windows applications using Windows Sockets
- SOCKS Proxy Service—for applications that use SOCKS

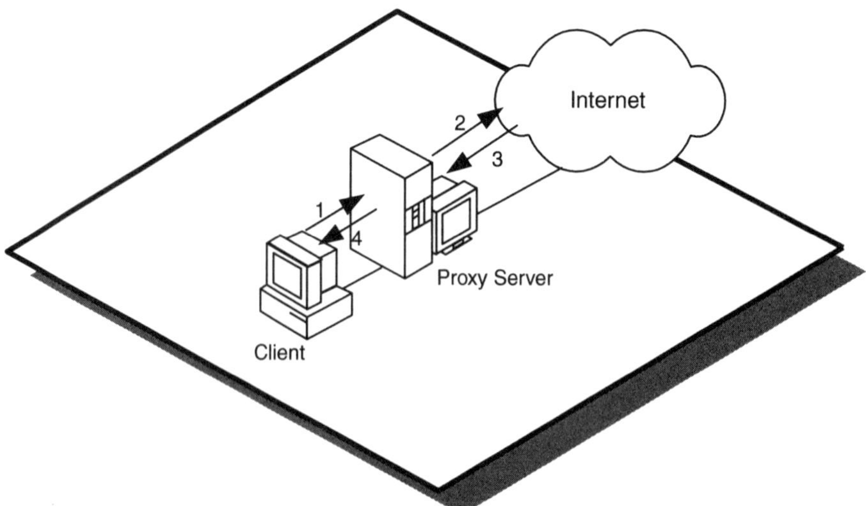

Figure 2.1 *Proxy Server operation.*

The Proxy Server must also be equipped with at least one network adapter for the internal network (the network for which the proxy will provide a gateway to the outside world) and an interface (e.g., network adapter, modem, etc.) to the Internet (or company intranet).

Study Break

What are CERN and SOCKS?

CERN refers to the accepted industry standard for Internet compliant client/server applications. The acronym *CERN* stands for Conseil European pour la Recherche Nucleair (European Laboratory for Particle Physics). This Swiss based organization developed many of the original standards and code libraries that support Hypertext Transport Protocol, World Wide Web, and File Transfer Protocol client/server architecture.

SOCKS is a standard proxy protocol for client/server environments which permits traversing firewalls in a secure and controlled manner The SOCKS server implementation is at the application layer and the SOCKS client library is between the client's application and transport layers. Proxy Server supports SOCKS Version 4.3a. The most recent SOCKS release is Version 5. This release is also known as authenticated firewall traversal (AFT) and is an open Internet standard for performing network proxies at the transport layer. SOCKS Version 5 is covered by RFC 1928. (You can review this and other RFCs at www.cis.ohio-state.edu/rfc/ or http://www.rfc-editor.org)

MCSE 2.1 Proxy Server Services

The three proxy services form the backbone of Microsoft Proxy Server 2.0. We'll describe the services in this chapter and will spend some time learning how to configure them in Chapter 5, "Proxy Server Administration." Although they provide proxy support for distinctly different activities, you'll discover their use and configuration is remarkably similar in most cases!

Web Proxy Service

The Web Proxy Service is designed to support network traffic originating from CERN-compliant browsers (e.g., Microsoft Internet Explorer or Netscape Navigator). Since these browsers run on most of the desktop operating systems currently in use, the Web Proxy Service can respond to requests from a variety of machines to include those running Windows, Macintosh, and UNIX operating systems. The service will support HTTP, FTP, and Gopher protocols. Using the Web Proxy Service, multiple computers can use a single IP address on the outside network. When a Web browser that supports Windows NT Challenge/Response authentication is used, the Web Proxy Service can provide user-level security and secure encrypted logon capability. The Web Proxy service can grant or deny access to selected sites and can provide data encryption through Secure Sockets Layer (SSL) tunneling. The service will, also, log Client Internet request information and will support both active and passive caching to increase the efficiency of use of Internet resources.

While the Web Proxy Service handles client requests from CERN-compliant browsers, many high-end CERN-compliant browsers include helper applications that rely on the User Datagram Protocol. These helper applications are supported by the WinSock Proxy Service (covered next).

The Web Proxy Service runs as an extension to Microsoft Internet Information Server (IIS) Version 3.0 or later—it is dependent on this service. Web proxy is simply a dynamic-link library (DLL) that functions with the Internet Server Application Programming Interface (ISAPI). The two major components of the service are the *Proxy Server ISAPI Filter* and the *Proxy Server ISAPI Application*. These components run within the IIS WWW service and are both found in the Proxy ISAPI application file `W3proxy.dll`

ISAPI FILTER

The ISAPI Filter is called whenever the Web server receives an HTTP request. The filter is designed to *monitor, log, modify, redirect,* or *authenticate* these requests. The filter determines if the call is a standard HTTP request or a CERN-proxy request. (A CERN-proxy request is a request containing a URL complete with protocol and domain name, e.g., `HTTP://www.mydomain.com`.) CERN-proxy requests are routed to the ISAPI Application for processing. (The ISAPI Filter accomplishes this routing by adding additional instructions to the request packets.) Standard HTTP requests are not modified in any way and undergo normal processing through the WWW server.

ISAPI APPLICATION

When it receives the HTTP request, the ISAPI Application performs a number of checks and obtains the requested information if the request meets previously determined criteria.

Client Authentication • The ISAPI Application performs a Client Authentication check to ensure the client is valid and authorized.

Domain Filter Check • Next, the destination Internet domain is checked to verify it is not a domain disallowed by a Proxy Server setting.

Cache Check • If both the client and Internet domain pass their checks, the ISAPI Application examines the Proxy Server cache to see if the requested resource has been cached and is current. If it is, the resource is returned to the client from cache.

Internet Retrieval • If the resource is not found in the cache or if the cached resource doesn't meet predetermined currency requirements, the ISAPI Application will obtain the resource from the Internet and add it to the cache if appropriate. To do this, the ISAPI Application extracts the protocol (HTTP, FTP, Gopher) and domain name from the URL and calls the appropriate Windows Sockets API to process the request. Processing consists of:

- Domain name resolution (through the Domain Name System (DNS) using the DNS cache if possible)
- Connection to the remote site
- Request to the remote site
- Reception of response header from remote site
- Reception of data from remote site
- Relay of data to client
- Caching of data (if appropriate)

It should be noted that this process is fairly time consuming as compared to direct Web access by the client. Additionally, the length of time required to process an Internet request varies depending on how many Internet requests the service is currently processing. The delay in Web processing is offset by the service's caching and *keep-alive* features.

SERVER KEEP-ALIVES

Because Proxy Server runs as an ISAPI application, it can benefit from the enhanced Web performance enjoyed by the Internet Information Server (IIS). IIS will maintain (keep alive) a TCP connection for a specified period of time after completing a request or response. This means that subsequent requests to the same site through the same Proxy Server (regardless of the internal network client making the request) can be made without reestablishment of the TCP connection (provided the request is made within the keep-alive time window).

WEB PROXY CACHING

Local copies of HTTP and FTP objects can be cached to increase efficiency of the overall system. The Web Proxy service performs this function automatically (with some guidance from the administrator) based on a number of factors. Items that change frequently or items that require client authentication are not cached, but many items can benefit from caching and are added to the cache.

To use Web Proxy Caching, the server must have an NTFS partition of at least 5 MB (150MB plus 500k per client is the recommended size). The directory used for caching must have the `Everyone/Full Control` permission. The cache file is named `urlcache`.

Study Break

How does the server know if it should cache an item?

The amount of time an item will be considered "current" in the cache is called its *Time to Live* or TTL. Proxy Server determines the TTL using the following criteria listed in order of precedence:

1. If the web page is marked as "uncacheable" (by its web administrator) it will not be cached.
2. The resource's preset cache TTL (if one exists). This is defined in the resource's HTTP "Expires" header.
3. An explicit TTL set by the administrator for the particular resource (we'll discuss specific procedures for this in Chapter 5.)
4. If none of the above criteria are met, Proxy Server computes the TTL as 20% of the time since the resource was last modified (as specified in its "Last-Modified" HTTP header) with a minimum value of 15 minutes and a maximum value of one day.

To meet the dynamic needs of today's computing environment, proxy server features both *passive* and *active* caching.

Passive Caching • Passive (or "on-demand") caching is Proxy Server's primary caching mode. When Proxy Server services a client request, it first check's the cache. If the requested object is not found in the cache, Proxy Server retrieves the object from the Web, places a copy in the cache (if the object is cacheable) with a Time to Live (TTL), and forwards the object to the client. If the requested object *is* in the cache, Proxy Server checks the

TTL to ensure it is still valid and, if it is, returns the object to the client without making a Web request.

If, in responding to a client request, Proxy Server determines a cached object's TTL has expired, it checks the object to determine if it has changed. If it has not, Proxy Server updates the TTL and returns a copy of the cached object to the client. If, on the other hand, the object has changed, Proxy Server downloads the object, caches a copy, updates the TTL, and passes the object to the client.

When the disk space reserved for the cache is too full to hold new information, Proxy Server will delete older information to make room. Information is deleted using a formula that evaluates age, popularity, and size.

Active Caching • Active caching works like passive caching except Proxy Server doesn't wait for a client request to make sure an object is up to date. Once it has determined an object's use pattern, if active caching is enabled, Proxy Server will generate requests to keep it current based on:

- Popularity—the most requested objects are kept as current as possible
- TTL—Objects with longer TTLs are likely more valuable and are checked more often. Objects who's TTLs are about to expire are also checked for update.
- Server Activity—When Proxy Server is experiencing periods of low server loading, it becomes more aggressive in active caching.

Both active and passive caching are configurable. We'll see how to configure them in Chapter 5 and we'll see how to ensure caching is optimized in Chapter 10.

WinSock Proxy Service

The WinSock Proxy Service provides support for all Windows Sockets-compatible applications as well as TCP/IP and NWLink (IPX/SPX) compatible transports and is compatible with Microsoft Windows-based clients. Through WinSock Proxy, you can control inbound and outbound access by port number, protocol, and/or user or group. Users on the external network can be blocked from accessing resources on the internal network. Additionally, users on the internal network can be blocked from resources on the external network based on Internet domain name, IP address, and/or subnet mask. The WinSock Proxy Service can provide Windows NT Challenge/Response authentication whether or not the client application supports it. Like the Web Proxy Service, WinSock Proxy can provide data encryption through Secure Sockets Layer (SSL) tunneling and can log client Internet request information.

If your network uses browsers which are not CERN-compliant but which can run as WinSock applications, you can run them as WinSock Proxy clients to use the service's security and logging features.

Study Break

What is Windows Sockets?

Windows Sockets is an *interprocess communication* (IPC) mechanism. An IPC is the way applications running on a computer (or on different computers using a LAN or WAN connections) communicate with each other. Windows Sockets defines a set of standard applications programming interfaces (APIs) used in effecting these IPCs.

Windows Sockets is based on communication through "sockets." A socket is a port number combined with a computer address (in the case of sockets over TCP/IP, it's a port number with an IP address, and for sockets over IPX/SPX, it's a port number with an IPX address. In the latter case, an IPX address is simply a network number combined with a MAC address).

Windows Sockets will support both connection-oriented and connectionless communications. Under TCP/IP, connection-oriented communications are accomplished through TCP and the socket is associated with a TCP port number. Connectionless TCP/IP communications are effected through the User Datagram protocol (UDP) and are associated with a UDP port number. (For more information on TCP/IP, see *MCSE: Internetworking With Microsoft TCP/IP on Microsoft Windows NT 4*, Ryvkin, Houde, Hoffman, Prentice Hall, 1999.) Most Internet application protocols (e.g., FTP, HTTP, Gopher) are connection-oriented.

The WinSock Proxy Service (WSP) provides a transparent gateway through which the WinSock Proxy client may access resources on the external network. To do this, the WinSock Proxy Service intercepts the client's Windows Sockets call and issues its own call as depicted in Figure 2.2.

Almost all Windows Sockets 1.1 applications can run remotely through WinSock Proxy. Unfortunately, WinSock Proxy will not support Windows Sockets 2.0 APIs, nor will it allow Windows Sockets 2.0 applications to run remotely

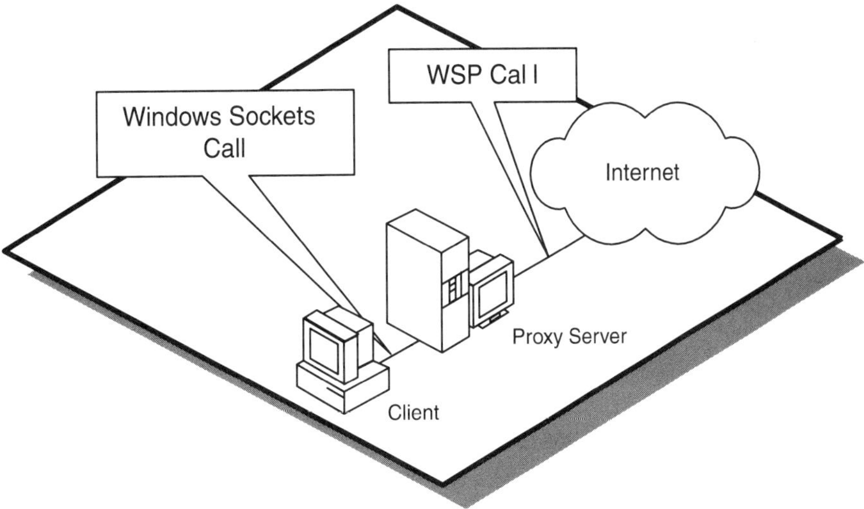

Figure 2.2 *WinSock Proxy Service gateway.*

WINSOCK PROXY SERVICE COMPONENTS

Just as with the Web Proxy Service, the WinSock Proxy Service uses two components. WinSock Proxy depends on a service running on the server and a set of DLLs on each Proxy Server client.

WinSock Proxy Service (on the Proxy Server) • The WinSock Proxy service is installed when Proxy Server is installed. It is a stand-alone service that creates the virtual connections and transfers data between the internal and external networks. If the internal network runs IPX/SPX instead of TCP/IP, the service also functions as a protocol gateway to translate the IPX/SPX call into an Internet compatible TCP/IP call.

WinSock DLLs (on the Client) • Windows Sockets run from DLLs on each Windows computer. (The Windows Sockets DLLs are `Winsock.dll` for 16-bit applications and `Wsock32.dll` for 32-bit applications.) To effect the WinSock Proxy Service, the original DLLs are renamed and replaced with new ones. When the client machine makes a Windows Sockets call, the new DLL receives the call and does one of three things. It may completely process the client request; it may pass the request; to the original (now renamed) DLL; or it may pass the request through the control channel (discussed in the next section) to the WinSock Proxy Service on the Proxy Server. In the case where the new DLL passes the call to the old DLL, it may or may not alter the request before forwarding it.

When the client communicates with resources on the internal network, the calls are referred to the original DLLs and internal network communications proceed normally. (Because the original DLLs are used, this works even when the client is using a third party TCP/IP stack.)

WinSock Proxy Control Channel • A control channel set up between the client and server permits the WinSock Proxy Service to manage various aspects of the service. The channel uses UDP port number 1745 and is established when the WinSock Proxy client DLL is first loaded. Although the channel uses the connectionless User Datagram Protocol, a simple acknowledgement procedure is used to ensure reliable communications over the channel.

The control channel performs four basic functions:

- The channel is first used to communicate the Local Address Table (LAT) to the client. This occurs when the channel is initially established. As we will see later in this book, the LAT contains a list of internal IP addresses and is how the client determines if it is communicating with resources on the internal or external network.

- Another control channel use occurs when the client attempts to connect to a machine on the external network. In this case, the channel is used to establish a TCP connection to the Proxy Server. Once the connection is established, communication through the Proxy Server to the external server progresses as depicted in Figure 2.2, and further use of the control channel for this communication is not required.

- The control channel permits clients to maintain communications with the Proxy Server. The channel is used to send port-mapping information to permit the client to communicate with multiple applications on the external network.

- The control channel is also used to pass Windows Sockets database requests. If, for instance, the client makes a DNS name resolution request, the request is sent to the WinSock Proxy service over the control channel. Once resolution is obtained, the proxy service returns it to the client through the same control channel.

SOCKS Proxy Service

The SOCKS Proxy Service supports the SOCKS standard configuration file and is compatible with all popular client operating systems and hardware

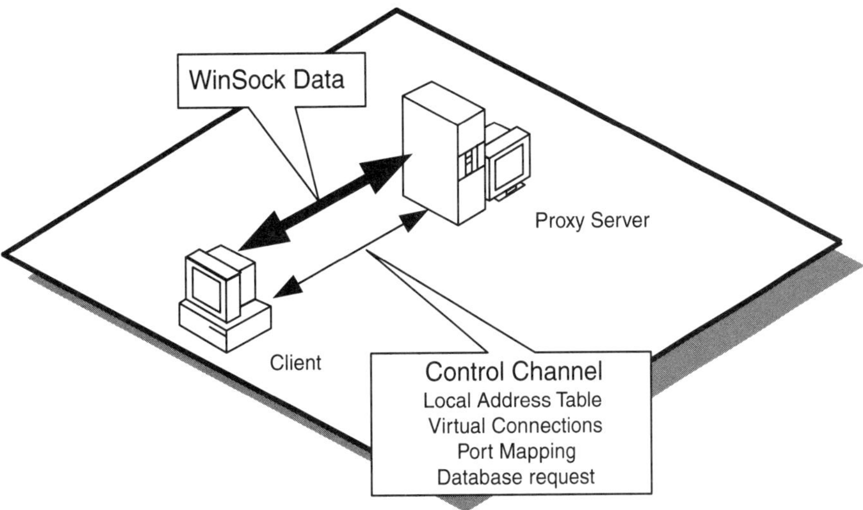

Figure 2.3 *WinSock Proxy control channel.*

platforms. The service supports TCP/IP on the internal network and uses IP authentication to establish a communications channel. It also supports Identification Protocol (Identd) and can log information about client SOCKS requests.

Study Break

What is the Identification Protocol?

> The Identification Protocol (Identd) provides a means to determine the identity of a user of a particular TCP connection. Given a TCP port number pair, it returns a character string which identifies the owner of that connection on the server's system. More information about this protocol can be found in RFC 1413. (You can review this and other RFCs at www.cis.ohio-state.edu/rfc/.)

Proxy Server 2.0 supports SOCKS version 4.3a and permits nearly all SOCKS version 4.0 client applications to run through the SOCKS Proxy Service. Under the SOCKS protocol, a host on one side of a SOCKS server can gain full access to a host on the other side of the server without ever establishing direct IP contact. To do this, SOCKS uses a *Connect* operation and a *Bind* operation.

CONNECT

When it wishes to establish communications with another host, the SOCKS client issues a *connect* request to the SOCKS server. The request contains the SOCKS protocol version number and command code, the target host's IP address and TCP port number, and a client user ID. The SOCKS server processes the request and, if successful, immediately prepares to support two-way communication between the client and external host. The SOCKS server may also return a message indicating the *connect* attempt was rejected or failed. In this case, the connection is immediately closed. The reject or failure message may include a possible cause for the connection fault.

BIND

Once a successful *connect* has been made, the client sends a *bind* request to the SOCKS server when it wants to prepare for an inbound connection from the external host. Similar to the *connect* request, the *bind* request contains the target host's IP address and TCP port number, as well as a client user ID (these must be the same as used in the *connect* request). The SOCKS server processes the request and replies in a manner similar to that used in the *connect* operation. If the *bind* was successful, the client communicates with the external host as if it had a direct TCP/IP connection.

In both the *connect* and the *bind* operation, the server sets a time limit (two minutes in the current implementation). If either process cannot be accomplished within that time, the server closes its connection to the client and takes no further action on the request.

Using Web Proxy and WinSock Proxy Services Together

It is possible to use both the Web and WinSock Proxy services and benefit from the features of each. When properly configured, they can be made to run, essentially, in series to provide a path to the Internet. The key to this involves modifying the Local Address Table (LAT) to indicate the Web Proxy Server's internal IP address is *not* on the local network. Doing so will force the client to use the WinSock Proxy Service to get to the Web Proxy Service. The LAT must be modified to reflect this on all proxy servers on the LAN. In addition to modifying the LAT, the client Internet browser must, of course, be configured to use the Web Proxy server that has been identified as "external" in the LAT, and the client computer must be configured to use a WinSock Proxy server on the LAN. (If the LAN uses only IPX/SPX, no LAT modification is necessary since IPX/SPX communication will be routed through the WinSock Proxy "gateway" anyway.)

When Web and WinSock Proxy services work together, and a client browser makes a Gopher, HTTP, or FTP request, the following sequence takes place:

1. The browser issues a proxy request to the IP address of the Web Proxy Server.
2. The WinSock Proxy DLL on the client intercepts the request. When it checks the LAT for the IP address of the Proxy Server, it finds it is outside the local network.
3. Since the client's WinSock Proxy DLL determines the Proxy Server is remote, it sets up a socket connection between itself and the WinSock Proxy Service, and the WinSock Proxy Service sets up a socket connection between itself and the Web Proxy Service's ISAPI components.
4. The client is now using the Web Proxy service through the WinSock Proxy service and is subject to the configured restrictions of each.

Although the foregoing discussion assumed both the WinSock and Web Proxy Services were running on the same physical server, they could have been operating on different machines as long as the above criteria were met.

USING TCP/IP AND IPX/SPX ON THE LAN

Now that we've seen how Proxy Server operates on the network, let's look briefly at the specifics of how it handles the TCP/IP and IPX/SPX protocols.

TCP/IP on the LAN

When the local network is TCP/IP-based, internal and external communication is handled differently. As you remember, the Local Address Table (LAT) determines which IP addresses are internal and which are external. This information is loaded when the WinSock Proxy client DLL first initializes.

When an application on the client wishes to communicate on the internal network, the WinSock Proxy DLL forwards the request to the original Windows Sockets DLL that was renamed at Proxy client installation. If, however, the communication is with a host on the external network, the WinSock Proxy DLL sets up a socket communication with the WinSock Proxy Service and the WinSock Proxy service sets up a socket communication with the external host.

When the WinSock Proxy client DLL cannot determine if the application is making an internal or external call, it assumes internal. This is the most secure guess because if the target is, in fact, on the external network, an internal call won't be able to transit a properly configured Proxy Server and the communication will fail. While this problem can be caused by a corrupt LAT, it can also be related to a problem in the application itself.

IPX/SPX on the LAN

When the LAN is IPX/SPX-based, the WinSock Proxy server performs as a protocol gateway between IPX/SPX on the internal network and TCP/IP on the external network. The WinSock Proxy server assumes any Windows Sockets over TCP/IP communication from an application is destined for the external network, so no LAT information is required by the WinSock Proxy DLL. The WinSock Proxy control channel will use IPX instead of UDP.

When an application on the internal network attempts a TCP/IP communication, the WinSock Proxy client DLL reformats the Windows Sockets API call to one consistent with IPX/SPX, and the client communicates with the WinSock Proxy server using that protocol. The Proxy Server communicates on behalf of the client on the external network using TCP/IP.

■ Summary

This chapter covered the architecture of the Proxy Server by discussing how the Proxy Server services work in general terms. We saw that a "proxy" is simply something that performs an action on behalf of something or someone else. When properly configured, the Microsoft Proxy Server performs activity on an external network on behalf of its clients on the internal network. The Proxy Server function should be virtually transparent to both internal and external computers. The use of a proxy server provides the administrator control over what resources may be obtained from the external network by members of the internal network. More importantly, a properly configured proxy server will protect members of the internal network from unauthorized intrusion from the external network.

Microsoft Proxy Server employs three services to accomplish its proxy functions: Web Proxy Service, WinSock Proxy Service, and the SOCKS Proxy Service. The Web Proxy Service provides a variety of security features to include the ability to grant or deny access to selected Web sites. It also provides both active and passive caching to increase the efficiency of external network access. The Web Proxy service depends on the operation of ISAPI Filter and ISAPI Application software.

The WinSock Proxy Service supports Windows Sockets communication and can provide a gateway for IPX/SPX on the internal network to TCP/IP on the external network. The WinSock Proxy Service uses the Local Address Table (LAT) to determine if an IP address is internal or external and can provide access control by port number, protocol, Windows NT user or group, Internet domain name, IP address, and/or subnet mask. The WinSock Proxy functions by renaming the client Windows Sockets DLLs and replacing them with its own. The new DLLs call the renamed DLLs for internal communication but refer external communication to the WinSock Proxy Service on the Proxy Server. A WinSock Proxy Control Channel permits the client DLL to communicate with the WinSock Proxy Service.

The SOCKS Proxy Service supports the SOCKS standard proxy protocol version 4.3a. SOCKS uses *connect* and *bind* operations to create communications channels between hosts.

By configuring the LAT to show the Web Proxy Server on the external network, you can use the Web and WinSock proxy services together and use the features of both for your Web activity.

▲ REVIEW QUESTIONS

1. *Sandy has installed a Proxy Server to provide access to the Internet for her local network. All of her users have CERN-compliant browsers and she wants to ensure she can track which Internet URLs her users access. What Proxy Server service would you advise her to install?*
   - A. SOCKS Proxy Service
   - B. CERN Proxy Service
   - C. Web Proxy Service
   - D. WinSock Proxy Service

2. *Bob decides to enable Proxy Server logging to determine which Internet sites are used the most by members on his internal network. His users employ a number of different browsers. For which service(s) should he enable logging? (select all that apply)*
   - A. SOCKS Proxy Service
   - B. CERN Proxy Service
   - C. Web Proxy Service
   - D. WinSock Proxy Service

3. *You've installed a Proxy Server to service Internet requests from your network and want to make use of its content caching features. How must you configure your client computers to take advantage of this capability?*
   - A. Install the Proxy Cache Service
   - B. Add the IP addresses of the client computers to the LAT

    C. Ensure each client computer has a CERN compliant Web browser

    D. Install the SOCKS protocol

4. *One of your users is complaining that he can't access a particular Internet application. You determine that the application depends on the User Datagram Protocol. Which Proxy Server service should you check for proper configuration?*

    A. UDP Service

    B. Web Proxy Service

    C. SOCKS Proxy Service

    D. WinSock Proxy Service

5. *All of Vicky's users access the Internet through a Proxy Server using Internet Explorer. Vicky wants track URLs to determine if anyone is visiting an "adult material" web site during business hours. What is the best way for her to do this?*

    A. Enable WinSock Proxy logging and periodically review the logs

    B. Enable auditing on the Proxy Server and review the audit logs

    C. Enable Web Proxy Service logging and periodically review the logs

    D. Enable SOCKS Proxy logging and periodically review the logs

6. *You have just moved several Macintosh computers to your Windows NT network. Each Macintosh computer runs Netscape Navigator. Your network accesses the Internet via a Proxy Server. Which Proxy Server service(s) will the Macs be able to use? (select all that apply)*

    A. WinSock Proxy

    B. SOCS Proxy

    C. Web Proxy

    D. FTP Service

7. *Your UNIX computer is equipped with a CERN-compliant Web browser that connects to the Internet via the Web Proxy Service. Which protocol(s) can you use? (select all that apply.)*

    A. HTTP

    B. UDP

    C. FTP

    D. None of the above

Planning Proxy Server

This chapter overviews the required hardware to install the Proxy Server software and the items you will need to consider for a Proxy Server rollout. Because there are differences based on the size of your company, we offer scenarios for small, medium, and large companies, and discuss Proxy Server and the Windows NT Domain model issues.

At the conclusion of this chapter you will be able to:

- Determine hardware and software requirements

- Choose the correct hardware configuration for Proxy Server computers

- Identify Proxy Server methods of communication to the Internet

- Identify possible network configurations

- Choose appropriate connectivity methods based on office size

- Integrate Proxy Server with Windows NT Domains

Proxy Server implementation must start with planning. Installing Proxy Server without knowing every detail of your environment and correctly planning will most likely lead you to a mad scramble because most, if not all, connectivity will cease working as soon as the Proxy Server is installed. What you should know about your environment includes: connection methods, size of server(s), integration with Windows NT domains, protocols used, use of Domain Name Servers (DNS), and automated services such as Windows Internet Naming Service and Dynamic Host Configuration Protocol. Used correctly, these will all ease the workload. As you know from your Internet experience, name resolution is, arguably, the most critical piece in the network communication puzzle. You must be intimately familiar with your LAN, and plan the protection you'll need.

Proxy Server presents a barrier to the Internet if it is properly configured but can prevent outbound client connections to the Internet if improperly configured. The network administrator must ensure connectivity and security when and where needed. Microsoft Proxy Server is an excellent tool to protect the company's network from the threats of the outside world and ensure appropriate client connections as necessary. Although the Proxy Server requires time and attention to install and configure, other products do not afford the same ease of configuration and security at such a low cost.

Planning a Proxy Server environment is two separate processes: planning Proxy Server itself and planning your network. Planning a Proxy Server implementation includes determining necessary hardware and software requirements, analyzing optimum proxy settings, and calculating proper configuration parameters, such as name space resolution, for the specifics of your environment. Choices can include when to use single, chained, or arrayed Proxy Servers, and how to balance load and provide redundancy for Internet access across multiple Proxy Server computers.

Network planning for Proxy Server implies careful analysis of your client side, such as types of protocols being used and client software settings. You will be faced with determining the number of Proxy Servers your network needs and whether the Proxy Servers should cooperate. The chapter focus is on a single Proxy Server environment, but we will identify some of the considerations for the cases where multiple Proxy Servers might exist. Networks with Multiple Proxy Server computers are covered in more detail in Chapter 7.

MCSE 3.1   Hardware Requirements

Hardware recommendations for Proxy Server installations depend greatly on the expected number of clients that the Proxy will serve and the office configuration. Gather the information. Who needs access? What type of access is needed? Where are the client machines located? How large is the organization? Have you planned on expansion? These questions will need to be answered to have a good idea of what is needed for a Microsoft Proxy Server implementation.

Initially Proxy Server has the same hardware requirements as Windows NT Server. However, for improved performance you should plan the necessary hardware to meet the expected load. The hardware recommendations are applicable to a single server computer running Proxy Server only. The actual requirements can differ based on number of users to be served, amount of usage, access speeds, LAN connectivity, and the use of other NT services or other software products on the Proxy Server machine. The Proxy Server software requires 10MB of free space for Microsoft Proxy Server after Windows NT 4.0 and SP3 has been installed. Table 3.1 below summarizes the recommended hardware configurations.

To estimate an adequate amount of free disk space for the Proxy Server cache, you should use the following formula: 100 MB + N*0.5 MB, where N is the number of Web Proxy service clients you expect. For example, if your company has 1000 Web clients that need to gain access to the Internet through the Proxy Server, you should reserve 100+1000*0.5=600 MB of disk space for the Web Proxy service cache. Note that this formula provides an adequate amount of cache space. Depending on the actual Internet use, you may ultimately need to double or triple this number. We'll see how to better "tune" the cache later in this book.

Cache size can be changed later with the IIS Administrator program.

Table 3.1 *Proxy Server Hardware Recommendations*

Expected load	Processor	RAM
Minimum	Intel 486 or faster	24 MB* (32MB for RISC)
Up to 300 Clients	Intel Pentium 133-MHz	32 MB*
Up to 2000 Client or more	Intel Pentium 166 MHz	64 MB*
2000 Clients or more	Intel Pentium 200 MHz	128–256MB*
ISP with 1,000 dialup Users	Alpha AXP 300MHz or Intel Pentium Pro 200MHz or faster	256–512MB*

*At least this amount will be required for proper operation

MCSE 3.2   Proxy Server Hardware Configuration

During Proxy Server installation you will be asked to supply not only the total size of the Proxy Server cache, but also specify which of the disks on the system will be used for caching. The use of multiple disk drives is recommended, because breaking a large cache into smaller pieces and distributing them to several disks can provide faster access to cached objects. The effect in a large environment is more dramatic.

If you want to use the advantages of Microsoft Proxy Server 2.0 caching features, you must have a computer that has at least one NTFS partition with the appropriate amount of free disk space. This is a change from Proxy Server version 1.0, where you could use FAT volumes for caching. Microsoft Proxy Server version 2.0 places its cache on NTFS volumes only and this might be a problem if your current disk volume is formatted with FAT. To solve this problem, you can convert the FAT partitions to NTFS without loosing any data by using the `convert` utility. For more information on using the `convert` utility type `convert /?` at the Windows NT command prompt. Note that converting a drive formatted in FAT to the NTFS file system will require that the machine be rebooted.

You should be aware that Proxy Server version 2.0 uses a different caching format than was found in Proxy Server version 1.0. If you are upgrading from version 1.0 to 2.0, the contents of the old cache is removed during Proxy Server 2.0 installation. The cache deletion is a rather quick process. However, if your existing caches are large the old cache deletion can take quite a bit of time to complete.

NETWORK ADAPTER REQUIREMENTS

Before you install Microsoft Proxy Server on your computer, check the Microsoft Windows NT hardware compatibility list. The adapter card(s) must be listed and you must be familiar with the specific card settings such as: IRQ, DMA, base I/O, and shared memory address (if applicable).

Typically, Proxy Server requires one network interface connected to the Internet and one or more network interfaces connected to your internal network. This server is *multihomed*, which means that it has two or more separate interfaces used to connect to the networks you are working with. One or more interfaces are used for the LAN and one interface connects to the external network (the Internet). Once you have installed the new network adapters, it's a good idea to check that there are no device conflicts, such as identical memory base I/O addresses or IRQ levels. Instead of an external network interface card, you can use other hardware devices such as a modem, an ISDN adapter, or higher speed terminal equipment.

You have flexibility in choosing the external network adapter and must keep in mind the needs of your company when choosing the connection type. You will need to determine the number of users that need access and the speed and type of access that they will need. If real-time processing is required, consider this in your decision making process. Obviously, the more users, the higher the connection speed you will need to the Internet.

Although you may install Proxy Server on a multihomed computer, it is NOT a router and should not be thought of that way. A router is a hardware device that connects one network segment to another. It can be as basic as a computer with two network cards or as large and complex as any military equipment. A router serves to pass the packets from one segment to another while Proxy Server works to interrupt the packet flow as necessary to do its job. Routers have their own network addresses, and if you are using an IPX/SPX router it may have its own network name. Routing and Remote Access Services functions as a demand-dial router and makes the dial out connection to the ISP.

Arranging the Connection to the Internet

Most ISPs offer a range of connectivity choices and the type of service you choose will be based on the size of your company, the needs of the users, and the specific services available from the ISP. The costs will be directly related to the speed of connection and how often you will connect. A dedicated connection (24 × 7) will usually cost more than an unscheduled dial up service. A dedicated connection means that you will have a telephone number and port dedicated to your company so that you won't get busy signals. Most ISPs can offer dial-up analog service, dedicated analog service, ISDN, fractional T-1 or full T-1, and higher speeds. Each category of service will require that you know exactly what users need and what the company can afford.

Hardware planning will depend on the size of the company and data needs. Devices such as analog and digital modems or ISDN terminal equipment, routers, CSU/DSU, and other connecting hardware will need to be considered. Internet service providers have a range of services and their prices vary. Some ISPs require lengthy lead time to receive and install hardware. Some require the use of scripts to obtain connectivity. Some have special rate plans for different connectivity options and discounts for educational institutions, and so on. Do you need 24 × 7 or 9AM to 5PM connectivity? What client(s) will you use and how much training will your users need?

Larger companies have Internet connectivity for the most part, but smaller companies are still deploying this valuable asset. Consider the delicate balance between the costs involved and the level of service your users need. You will almost always use every bit of bandwidth available, so plan carefully. Let's discuss the most frequently available choices you will be faced with when establishing an Internet connection:

- **Modems**. Modems are often used where a high-speed permanent connection to the Internet is not required. Dial-up Analog Line modems are used with "Plain Old Telephone Service," also known as the Public Switched Telephone Network, which is the way to say the ordinary phone system using big words. Modems are suitable for the very small offices that require outbound access for Web browsing or handling of light e-mail traffic. Modems operate at comparatively low speeds, usually up to 56Kbs. Most often, modems use Serial Line Internet Protocol (SLIP) or Point-to-Point Protocol (PPP) to connect to the Internet Service Provider for access. If you are using modems, you must install Remote Access Service (RAS) or Routing and Remote Access Service (RRAS) to manage connections to the Internet.

- **ISDN adapters**. Integrated Services Digital Network (ISDN) works over copper wires and is a high-speed, fully digital telephone service that requires the customer to be no more distant than 3 miles from the central telephone office. ISDN is found in cities and, being digital, is more capable to handle higher speeds than analog telephone lines. The terminal equipment and ISDN setup can cost several hundred dollars. There are two standards of ISDN lines that provide different bandwidths or speed of service. The Basic Rate Interface (BRI) is made up of two data channels that are rated for 64kbps and a signaling channel of 16kbps. The two data channels can be used together to carry data at speeds of 128kbps. Primary Rate Interface (PRI) provides 24 channels of 64kbps data and a signaling channel of 16kbps for a combined service rate of up to 1.544Mbps. In addition to the costs for the terminal equipment, ISDN service in some locations includes additional charges known as metered rates, which may make this option cost prohibitive. Be sure to check on this before purchasing the terminal equipment.

- **56Kbps leased lines,** T1/E1 lines, and other types of digital communication connections like frame relay, or fiber cables and terminal equipment, are used for high-speed communications. 56Kbps Data Service Unit/Channel Service Unit (DSU/CSU), T1/E1 terminal equipment and other high speed equipment is expensive in comparison to ISDN or modems, but it provides very high speed transmission. Typically 56kbps or higher is used by organizations that require continuous or dedicated rates of data transfer between remote sites. Each end of the connection requires terminal equipment and the speed of a full T-1 is at a rate of 1.544Mbps, which provides 24 channels of 64Kbps each. Leasing one or more channels on a T-1 is referred to as fractional T-1.

At higher speeds the costs are greater, so keep in mind that the Web Proxy Server service offers caching capabilities that can significantly increase performance and reduce bandwidth requirements. In most scenarios, Microsoft Proxy Server should have two or more network adapters, but the Proxy Server can work with only one network adapter. For example, when you set up a Proxy server that will offer caching functions only, it is possible to follow the scenario illustrated in Figure 3.1.

In this scenario, the desktop machines using Microsoft Internet Explorer are configured to use Proxy Server. When the users need to browse the Internet, the Web Proxy service cache is checked first and, if the requested document is not found in the cache, it is downloaded from the Internet. If the document is in the cache, the reply is returned faster than a connection with the Internet could provide; this is especially beneficial when multiple clients repeatedly request the same document. The speed of the

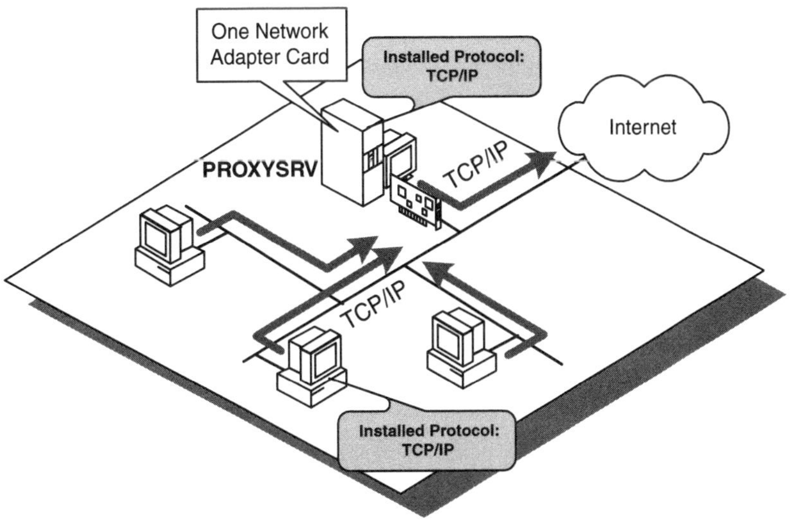

Figure 3.1 *Caching-only Proxy Server with a single network card.*

connection on the LAN is going to be much faster than the speed of a demand dial interface.

Another typical situation to use only one network interface card is when you plan to use Proxy Server behind a firewall, behind another third-party proxy server, or with no Internet access whatsoever. In this case, only an internal network adapter is required for connection to your internal network. The use of an intermediate firewall provides additional security, but caution must be used to properly configure the interface for operation. Using the Microsoft Proxy Server as a caching-only server will improve intranet access speed for users if your network includes many dial-up links.

MCSE 3.3   Identifying Possible Network Scenarios

Although the network scenarios can vary, there are common threads that need to be taken into consideration, such as the amount of data transfer that a network must support, the size of the network (number of computers), and anticipated growth. Proxy Server can provide an excellent measure of security and speed up access when all factors have been considered and the product is properly configured. We will focus on size-based categories such as:

- Small office network
- Branch office or medium-size office networks
- Large corporate network

Your network configuration can be different from what is shown, but the basic concepts, planning, and implementation considerations will remain the same. The specifics of integrating your Proxy Server with existing corporate network servers are covered more fully in Chapter 9.

Small Office Network

A small office network can be depicted as follows:

- Fewer than 250 client computers
- A single LAN segment
- Typically uses NetBEUI or IPX network protocol
- Demand-dial connectivity to an Internet service provider (ISP)

Here, a single Proxy Server computer is used to provide Internet connectivity and network security for the entire office, as shown in Figure 3.2.

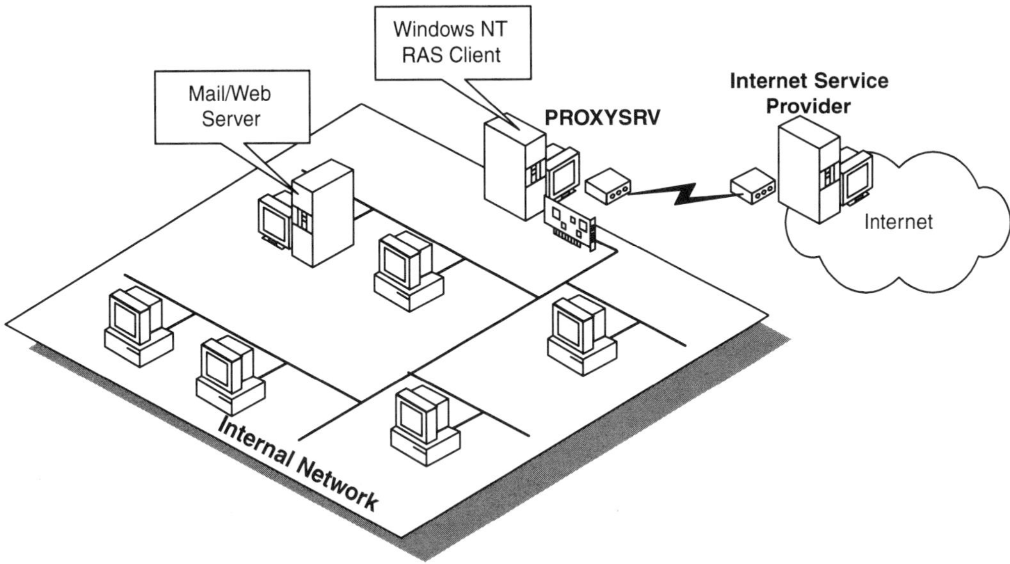

Figure 3.2 *Small office network scenario.*

For the smallest offices, dial-up modem connectivity is appropriate. As the office grows to 100 users, either ISDN or higher speed direct connectivity with the Internet is usually necessary to keep up with the demands of the users.

Proxy Server has the Auto Dial Feature, which uses a RAS Phonebook entry to offer demand-dialing to the Internet. This requires that the Proxy Server computer be configured as a Windows NT RAS client. The Proxy Server uses the modem or ISDN adapter to connect to the Internet and a network adapter card to connect to the internal network. The Local Address Table must be built to identify the internal network.

Proxy Server can provide caching, which can speed up access to the most frequently used URLs by providing a locally stored copy. Enabling this feature will reduce the likelihood that you will have the constant need to dial out to the Internet Service Provider. You will be able to identify the most frequently visited sites and store a local copy and use the active caching feature to automatically obtain the most frequented URLs. Other features such as password authentication, user permissions, protocol definitions, domain, cache, and dynamic packet filtering can all be used to offer a reasonable level of network security with Internet access.

Protocol support planning will be necessary if you have only installed NetBEUI. Here you will need to plan on changing, or at least adding to, your network protocol choices. TCP/IP or IPX/SPX can be added and the introduction of TCP/IP will enable you to use reserved IP address ranges. This requires a small amount of additional planning, as does the use of IPX/SPX, which enables interoperability with Novell NetWare.

Microsoft uses NetBIOS name resolution. Windows Internet Name Service (WINS) on a Microsoft Windows NT Server on the LAN will automate the resolution of NetBIOS computer names. The use of the Domain Name System (DNS) service on Windows NT will provide host name resolution. Although you can install DNS on Microsoft Windows NT Server 4.0, smaller office environments without an administrator will find DNS a burden, as all entries must be made manually. For the smallest offices it is likely that the ISP will remain both primary and secondary DNS.

Medium-Size Office Network

A medium-size office is usually found in a company with fewer than 1,000 computers, and their network can be depicted as:

- The central office with multiple LAN segments
- One or more branch offices with single LAN segments
- Demand-dial connectivity from the branch office to the central office
- Dedicated-link connectivity from the central office to an ISP
- Use of the IP or IPX network protocol

For a single central office with multiple LAN segments, a single Proxy Server at each of the branch offices can be used to offer local caching, local administration of access control, and connectivity to the corporate headquarters. At the main office, several Proxy Server computers can be placed in an array to offer redundancy, distributed caching, and dedicated Internet connectivity. This provides for centralized security to the organization (see Figure 3.3).

The Headquarters Office Network

As the size of an organization grows, so does its need for access and data flow. The headquarters office should use a Proxy Server array to provide distributed caching, fault tolerance, and load balancing. The Proxy Servers each need to be configured with two network interfaces so that they can connect to the internal and external networks—high-speed connectivity and backup connectivity planning will be required. You should also plan for a secondary method of connecting to the ISP or perhaps two ISPs. Usually a T1/E1 line with an ISDN dial-up is present. Each Local Address Table for the Proxy

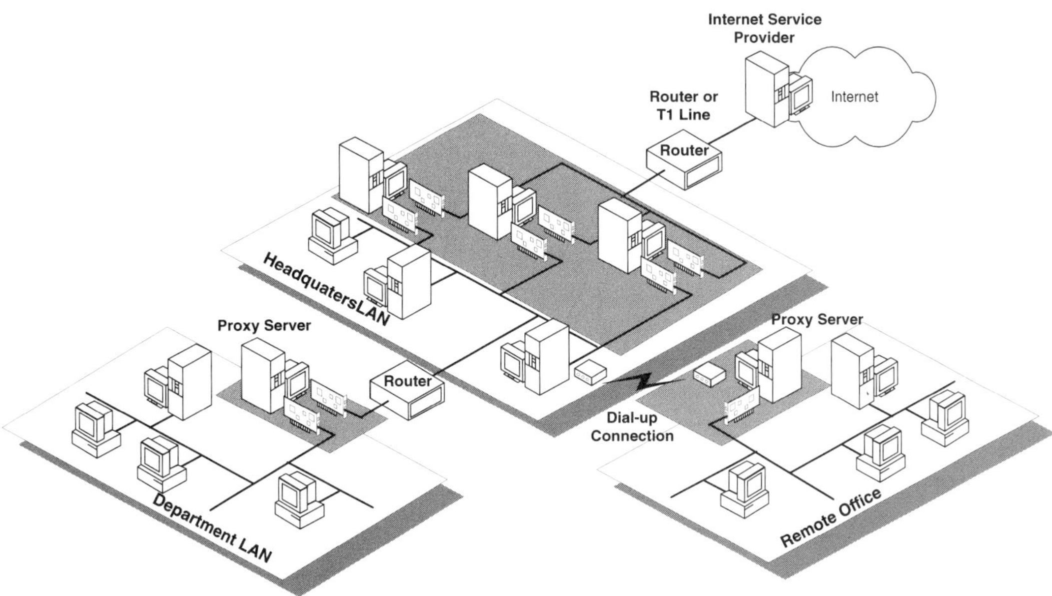

Figure 3.3 *Medium-size office network scenario.*

Server will be built with identical information and it will contain all of the network IP addresses for all branches and the headquarters locations. The external IP address of each computer will be excluded from the LAT.

Remote Access Services (RAS), used to support inbound requests from the branch offices to the main office, can be installed on a separate computer. All requests for Internet access or web pages are the responsibility of the Proxy Server array. Active caching can be set up to pull the most frequently visited URLs and a copy can be placed locally. This saves bandwidth on the WAN links and provides a significant improvement in performance. The client does not have to initiate the process. The whole company can have a global security policy by setting it up at the headquarters, and you can use user permissions, protocol definitions, password authentication, cache filtering, and static (or manual) filtering for increased network security. The administration of the servers is covered in Chapter 5. This scenario uses a single array and your configuration changes would be done on one server and established at all the other members of the array. By the time an organization has grown to have many offices at different locations and applied for its own domain name, the need for DNS services will be evident. WINS will also help by automating the resolution of NetBIOS names (friendly or computer names).

THE BRANCH OFFICE NETWORK

The larger offices will use a dedicated link or WAN connection to the headquarters or main office. Most smaller or satellite offices will use dial-up connections. The Proxy Server incorporates an Auto Dial feature that will use a RAS Phonebook entry to provide demand-dialing to the headquarters, which would use the Proxy Server array and go on out to the Internet if the URL was not found in cache. To make this work properly, the Proxy Server computer at the branch office must be configured as a Windows NT RAS client. The headquarters will have a separate RAS server with multiple inbound lines to support the inbound requests from the branch offices.

Proper setup of the Proxy Server computer includes two network interfaces: one network adapter card to connect to the local area network at the branch, and a modem or ISDN adapter to connect to the remote network at the headquarters. The Local Address Table (LAT) is built with a comprehensive network IP address space for the branch and headquarters offices.

All external (Internet) IP addresses must be excluded to ensure there is no breach of security. Name services by providers such as DNS, WINS, or DHCP should be installed at the satellite or branch office to permit local name resolution. The branch office name server will need to be set up to perform replication of the name space with the headquarters central name servers such as that found with WINS Push-Pull partners.

When you use multiple Proxy Server computers on an internal network with DNS services, you must configure at least one entry for each computer. Each entry indicates an IP address to be searched for on the local network that provides DNS domain name resolution. In some cases, you will want to have a secondary DNS server address to search for and use if the first DNS server is not available.

DNS round-robin offers load balancing for multiple Proxy Server computers and for all client DNS name lookup requests; any of the Proxy Servers that are available can respond. DNS would cycle through the IP addresses for every request. As a result, the load on the Proxy Server computers is divided evenly. To accomplish the load balancing in this way, configure the client configuration file on each client computer appropriately.

At the branch office you will enable caching and reduce the use of demand-dialing so as to reduce the company's long distance telephone bills. Caching will be configured to keep a copy of the most frequently used sites on dedicated local disk drives, but active caching should not be used, as it is set up at the headquarters office. Planning the installation in this manner reduces the work done by the headquarters and provides another measure of load balancing.

Other options such as password authentication, user permissions, protocol definitions, domain filtering, and cache filtering are used to provide network security.

Proxy Server at the satellite office will not have an external interface so packet filtering is not enabled. No direct connection with the Internet will exist, so all client requests are routed to the Proxy Server array at the headquarters office.

LARGE CORPORATE NETWORKS

Large corporate networks with more than 2,000 client machines can be described as follows:

- The headquarters office with a backbone LAN and several LAN segments
- Many branch offices, each with a single LAN segment
- Use of both IP and IPX network protocols
- High speed dedicated-link connectivity to an ISP

Here, a Proxy Server array is the central security provider on the backbone LAN and a Proxy Server computer is used to service each departmental LAN. Proxy Server's excellent scalability can be shown through the introduction of an array at the ISP. Although the introduction of the Proxy Server at the ISP is not necessarily considered part of the Corporate network structure, it serves a valid function of showing how extensive the Proxy Server use can be and how to effectively deploy Proxy in several locations for maximum benefit (see Figure 3.4).

For the branch office networks, a configuration identical to the medium-size office network discussed earlier is what would be needed. The Proxy Servers at the department level are set up the same as the branch office Proxy Server computer. Each has two internal network adapters: one to connect to the specific department LAN, and the other to connect to the backbone LAN.

Each department should be set up to have its own caching Proxy Server. If web Proxy client requests are received that cannot be handled, they are routed upstream to the array.

The large business model requires great attention to detail and takes more time to implement. All of the configuration issues are similar to those discussed for a medium-sized Proxy Server implementation. DNS, WINS, and DHCP are almost a certainty as they provide additional automated configuration, which the network administrators use to their advantage.

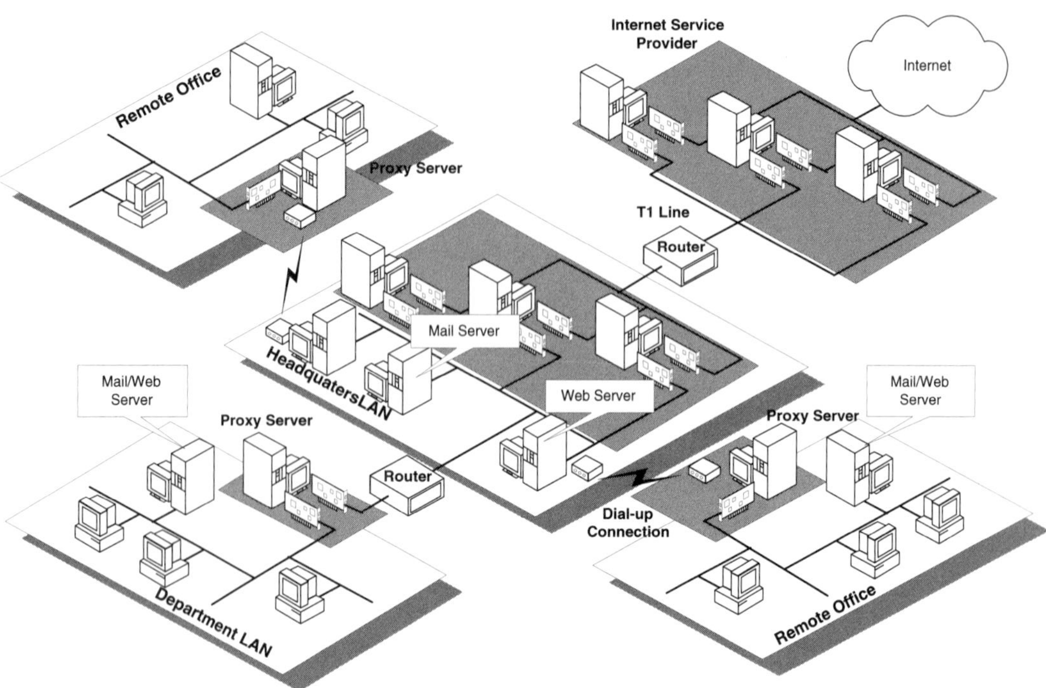

Figure 3.4 *Large corporate network scenario.*

In all of the scenarios above, installing Microsoft Proxy Server permits you to use TCP/IP or IPX/SPX protocols to communicate to the network clients. If you already have installed either of these, you will have little difficulty choosing a network protocol.

Proxy Server and Windows NT Domains

Before installing Microsoft Proxy Server, it's a good idea to plan how it fits into existing NT domain environment. The Proxy Server software on Windows NT 4.0 Server takes advantage of inherent Windows NT and NTFS security features, but what about the different domain models. Some questions to ask: How many domains are there? How many domains are needed? How many domains exist? Does the number of domains need to change for any reason? Why do we need to be concerned with domain security?

For small networks with one domain there is not much to choose or worry about. For larger networks there are security reasons for which it is preferred to install Microsoft Proxy Server as a stand-alone server in your

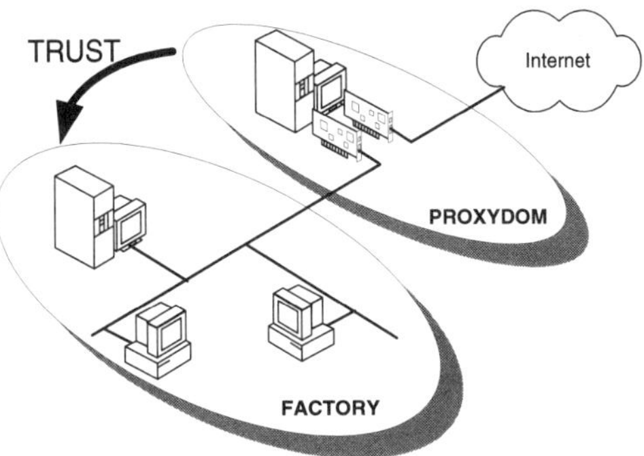

Figure 3.5 *Setting up Proxy Server in a separate domain.*

existing domain. Remember that having multiple domains adds a layer of complexity to the security already present. If your network spans multiple domains you can consider setting up Proxy Server as a Primary Domain Controller within its own domain. In order to regulate the users' access though Proxy Server, the appropriate trust relationships must be established (see Figure 3.5).

In this scenario, the Proxy Server domain (trusting domain) trusts the Factory domain (trusted domain), and an administrator can assign users different permissions on Proxy Server computer including permissions to use protocols. On the other hand, in case of intrusion, having a separate Proxy Server domain will limit unauthorized access to the FACTORY domain, since FACTORY does not trust PROXYDOM.

If other Proxy Servers will be added in the near future they can join the PROXYDOM domain (see Figure 3.6). Remember, Internet domains and Windows NT domain have nothing to do with each other.

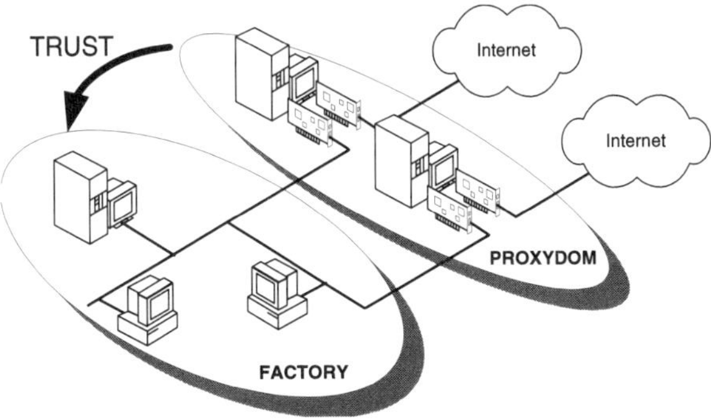

Figure 3.6 *Multiple Proxy Servers on the separate domain.*

■ Summary

This chapter featured a full view of hardware and software planning for Proxy Server. It is critical to remember that understanding the details of your network environment is the most important first step in Proxy Server installation. This understanding must extend to the types of client, name resolution servers, and methods and protocols involved.

We saw that a basic Proxy Server installation has rather modest hardware requirements, but we also saw that the hardware requirements must be interpreted based on the network load. Frequently, the basic requirements won't provide sufficient power for the needs of the installation and should be extended using the guidelines we presented. A major concern when considering hardware is the amount of caching that will be required in your environment. High caching will signal a need for higher capacity, better performing hard drives. Since the Proxy Server computer may act as a conduit to the Internet for a large number of client computers, you must ensure you have network interface cards that can handle the expected load.

If your Proxy Server will provide an Internet link, it is important to understand your requirements so you can properly articulate them to an Internet Service Provider (ISP). You will need to choose a transmission link (e.g., PSTN, ISDN, etc.) to connect to the ISP and also ensure you have an appropriate modem (or other device) to make that connection.

Depending on the actual computing environment, you'll want to select hardware and connectivity methods from the small, medium, or headquarters network. Guidelines in this chapter will help you select the right hardware and connectivity methods for optimum results.

Windows NT Domains will also have an impact on your Proxy Server setup. It is important to understand your network's domain structure and trust relationships to ensure appropriate access to the Proxy Server and network.

▲ REVIEW QUESTIONS

1. *You want to know which clients are using what Internet sites. What feature of Proxy Server do you use?*

    A. Auditing protocol access

    B. Setting protocol permissions

    C. Setting Microsoft Windows NT security parameters

    D. Controlling anonymous access

2. *Your small company wants to secure its existing connection to the Internet. Identify the features of Proxy Server you might want to plan for: (select all that apply)*

    A. Block inbound URL requests

    B. Block outbound URL requests

    C. Use NTFS security

    D. Use File and Print Services for NetWare

    E. Work with multiple domains using trusts

    F. Cache remote pages

    G. Perform packet filtering

    H. Set protocol permissions

    I. Enable auditing

    J. Use DNS, WINS & DHCP

3. *Your company has 15 desktop computers and three modems. The users dial out several times a day to the ISP for mail and one computer remains connected to browse the Internet for research. Which features of Microsoft Proxy Server 2.0 should you consider? (select all that apply)*

    A. Block inbound URL requests

    B. Block outbound URL requests

    C. Use NTFS security

    D. Use File and Print Services for NetWare

    E. Work with multiple domains using trusts

    F. Cache remote pages

    G. Perform packet filtering

    H. Set protocol permissions

    I. Enable auditing

    J. Use DNS, WINS & DHCP

4. *Your company has 250 desktop computers and over 85 modems. The users dial out multiple times a day—several use long distance calls to manufacturers' bulletin boards as well as local calls to the ISP for mail. Most everyone uses the Internet to browse for research. You have a web site on IIS 4.0 with FTP to provide software for 20 remote sales personnel and several engineers. Which feature of Microsoft Proxy Server 2.0 would you choose? (select all that apply)*

    A. Block inbound URL requests

    B. Block outbound URL requests

    C. Use NTFS security

    D. Use File and Print Services for NetWare

    E. Work with multiple domains using trusts

    F. Cache remote pages

    G. Perform packet filtering

    H. Set protocol permissions

    I. Enable auditing

    J. Use DNS, WINS & DHCP

5. *Your company has 3250 desktop computers and over 170 modems. The users dial out multiple times a day—several use long distance calls to manufacturers' bulletin boards. Your mail system is centralized. You have a web site on IIS 4.0 with FTP to provide software for remote sales, marketing and engineering staff. Which feature(s) of Microsoft Proxy Server 2.0 would you choose: (select all that apply)*

    A. Block inbound URL requests

    B. Block outbound URL requests

    C. Use NTFS security

    D. Use File and Print Services for NetWare

    E. Work with multiple domains using trusts

    F. Cache remote pages

    G. Perform packet filtering

    H. Set protocol permissions

    I. Enable auditing

    J. Use DNS, WINS & DHCP

6. *Your company has 3 desktop computers and three modems. The users dial out several times a day to the ISP for mail and one computer remains connected to browse the Internet for research. Your network administrator wants to improve security and just purchased Microsoft Proxy Server. You want to implement the appropriate connection speed. What type of connection should you consider?*

    A. Fractional T-1

    B. T-3

    C. T-1

    D. Analog Modem

7. *Your company has over 300 desktop computers and several use their own modem to dial out for mail and web access. To improve security and lower the telephone line requirements, you purchase Microsoft Proxy Server. What is the minimum acceptable hardware required to install Proxy Server?*

    A. Intel Pentium 200-MHz with 128MB RAM

    B. Alpha AXP 300MHZ with 256MB RAM

    C. Intel Pentium 133-MHz with 32MB RAM

    D. Intel Pentium 166-MHz with 64MB RAM

Installing Proxy Server

This chapter tells about you about installing Microsoft Proxy Server 2.0. We will walk though the setup process and point out the most important issues. We'll examine the Local Address Table creation and Web Proxy cache configuration that occurs during Proxy Server setup. Finally, we'll step through the Proxy client setup.

By the end of this chapter you will be able to:

- Prepare the system for Proxy Server 2.0 installation
- Explain the Proxy Server licensing requirements
- Install Proxy Server and its components
- Install Proxy Server using the unattend setup
- Configure the Local Address Table (LAT)
- Configure the Web Proxy cache
- Install Proxy client software

MCSE 4.1   Before You Install

Now that you understand Proxy Server architecture and planning, it's time to proceed to Proxy Server installation. We need to ensure we have the proper hardware and software requirements and must ensure we're properly licensed to run the product.

Hardware and Software Requirements

Before we actually start installing Proxy Server, however, let's review the hardware requirements, (see Table 4.1).

Remember that hardware requirements can vary greatly depending upon the number of users that Proxy Server will support. Table 4.1 presents only minimum hardware requirements for running the server.

As you may notice, minimum hardware requirements for Proxy Server are the same as for Windows NT Server. Although an additional network interface is often used in Proxy Server environments, it is not necessarily a requirement. Typically, you'll need an additional network adapter to connect your Proxy Server to the Internet. If you plan to use Proxy Server behind a firewall or another third-party proxy server, however, you need only one network adapter (to connect to your internal network).

Another time you'll need only one network adapter is when you're using multiple Proxy Server computers in a chained (cascaded) configuration. In this case, only the most upstream Proxy Server computer requires the second network adapter (or modem) for connection to the Internet (see Figure 4.1).

If you're using Proxy Server as an IP application-level gateway to support internal IPX clients and not for Internet access, only an internal network adapter is required. (See Figure 4.2)

In addition to hardware requirements, we need to meet the following software requirements:

Table 4.1 *Proxy Server Hardware Requirements*

Processor	Intel® 486, or faster
RAM	24 MB for Intel-based systems, 32 MB for RISC-based computers
Disk Space	10MB of free disk space after Windows NT Server has been installed, plus adequate disk space for proxy server cache. Remember, volumes that will contain the cache must be formatted with NTFS.
Network Adapter	At least one is required for connection to the Local Network
Additional Network Interface	A network adapter, modem, or ISDN adapter is required for connection to the external network.

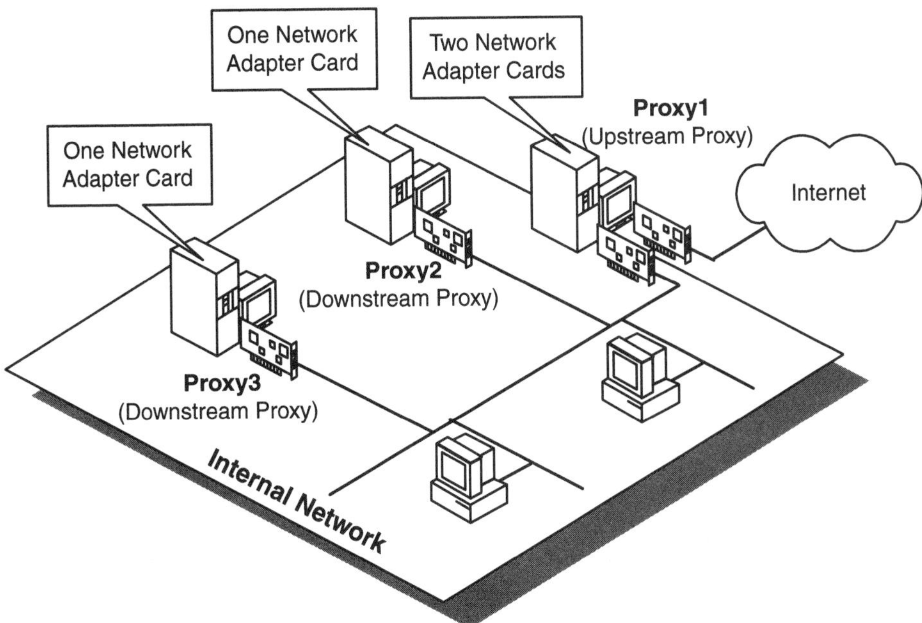

Figure 4.1 *Only the most upstream proxy requires an external network adapter.*

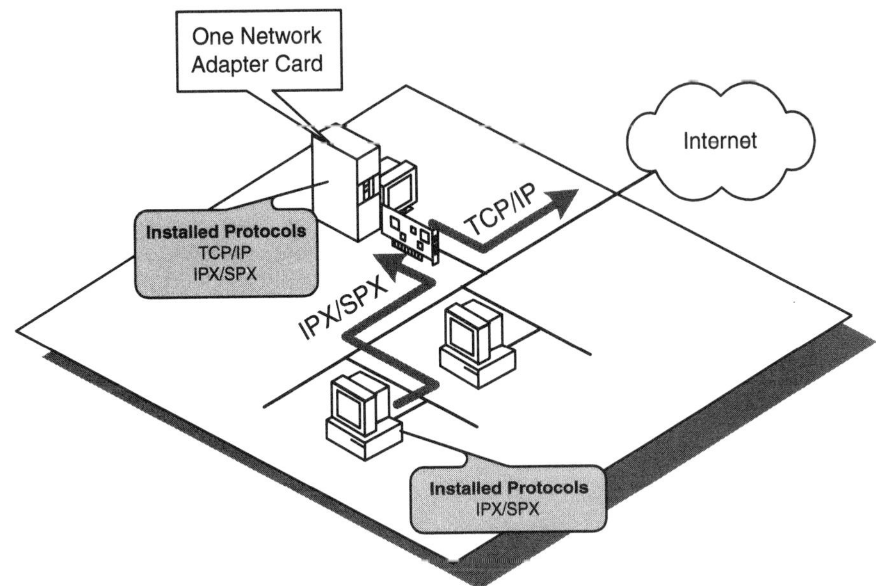

Figure 4.2 *Proxy IPX-to-IP gateway is also able to work with one network adapter.*

- Microsoft Windows NT Server 4.0 (configured and member server, primary or backup domain controller)
- Windows NT Server 4.0 Service Pack 3 or later
- Microsoft Internet Information Server 3.0 or later. Note that when you install Windows NT Service Pack 3 over the Windows NT Server with Internet Information Server 2.0, IIS 2.0 will automatically upgrade to IIS 3.0. Proxy Server 2.0 works well with IIS 4.0 (included in the Windows NT Option Pack).
- TCP/IP protocol suite installed

Before you install Proxy Server on your computer:

- Ensure you have at least one partition formatted in NTFS
- Ensure the internal network interface is properly configured and bound to the protocol(s) in use on the internal network (this may be TCP/IP only, or both TCP/IP and NWLink IPX/SPX compatible transport)
- If your Proxy Server computer uses an external network interface (network adapter, modem, or ISDN card) ensure the interface is properly configured and bound to TCP/IP only
- Ensure you are logged on as a member of the Administrators local group

SETTING UP THE INTERNAL NETWORK ADAPTER

As you already know, you can use TCP/IP or the NWLink IPX/SPX Compatible Transport in your internal network.

If you are using TCP/IP in your internal network you should not use DHCP to assign IP addresses to the internal interface. When setting TCP/IP properties for the internal network adapter, you should enter a permanent reserved IP address (i.e., a static address that is set aside for the Proxy Server) for the Proxy Server computer and an appropriate subnet mask for your local network. When you set the TCP/IP properties, do not enter a **Default Gateway** address for the internal network adapter (only the external interface may have default gateway settings). If your internal network uses DNS or WINS, you may want to configure the internal network adapter to permit Proxy Server to work with these services.

If you are using IPX/SPX on the internal network, you should unbind the NWLink IPX/SPX Compatible Transport from the external network interface for security reasons. IPX/SPX should be bound to the internal network adapter card only. It might seem strange, but TCP/IP must be bound to both the external and internal interfaces, since the Local Address Table must include at least one IP address assigned to the internal network adapter card (see Figure 4.3). You can assign an IP address from a private address space for the internal adapter. Private IP addresses are in the following ranges: 10.0.0.0-10.255.255.255; 172.16.0.0-172.31.255.255; and 192.168.0.0-192.168.255.255. (For more information about private IP address ranges, see RFC 1918. You can review this and other RFCs at www.cis.ohio-state.edu/rfc/.)

If you unbind the TCP/IP protocol from the internal interface, the WinSock Proxy service may not be able to start.

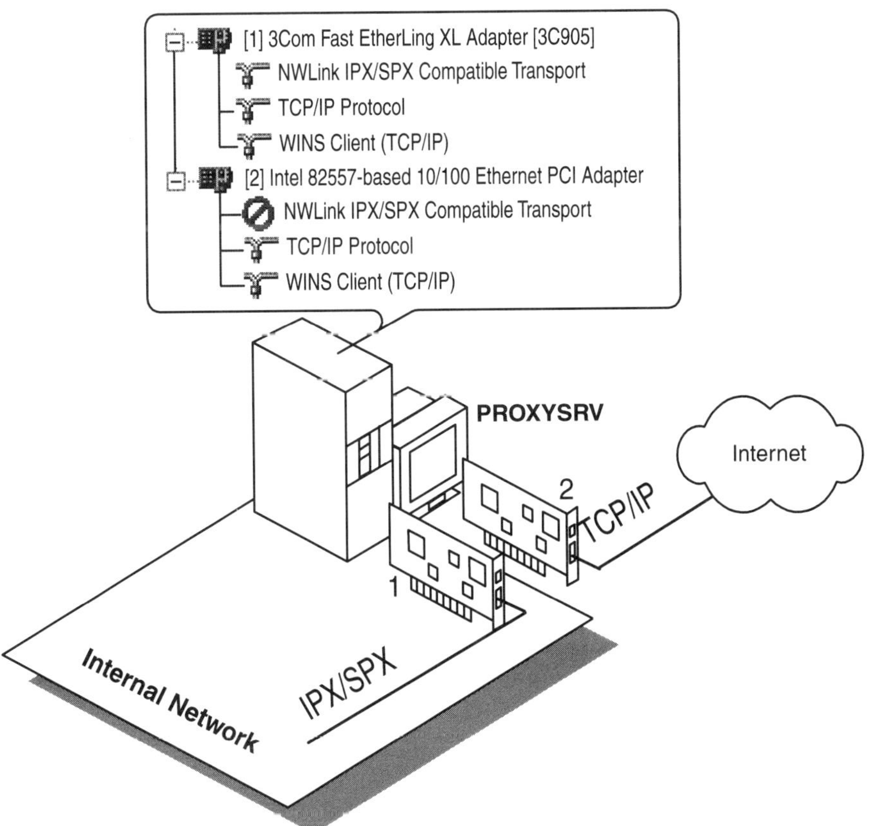

Figure 4.3 *Protocol bindings when internal network uses IPX/SPX only.*

In this figure, Proxy Server has TCP/IP bound to both internal and external interfaces. Note that TCP/IP is not actually used in the internal network. We bind TCP/IP and assign a dummy IP address to the internal interface only to construct a valid Local Address Table (LAT).

Additionally, if you are using IPX/SPX on the Proxy Server computer but the Service Advertising Protocol (SAP) agent is not installed, you should install it before you run Proxy Server setup. The SAP agent is used to advertise the services and server addresses on an IPX/SPX network.

SETTING UP THE EXTERNAL NETWORK ADAPTER

If you are using an external network interface, ensure that it is bound to TCP/IP only. Since the external network can not use IPX/SPX to gain access to the Internet, you should unbind the NWLink IPX/SPX compatible transport from the external interface.

When you configure TCP/IP on the external interface, consult your Internet Service Provider for the correct settings. You need to enter an IP address, subnet mask, and default gateway for the external interface, as well as the IP addresses of the DNS servers that will service your network. Your Internet Service Provider (ISP) may use the Dynamic Host Configuration Protocol (DHCP) to automatically assign TCP/IP parameters to the external interface. In this case be sure that `Obtain an IP address from a DHCP server` is selected for the external interface.

If you plan to dial out to your ISP, install the Remote Access Server (RAS) and configure the RAS client (also known as Dial up Networking). With a RAS client configured, you will be able to use Proxy Server's AutoDial features.

For additional security you may want to unbind the Server service from the external interface in Control panel | Network | Bindings (see Figure 4.4).

Study Break

Reviewing Server Settings

Now that you understand how to prepare your system for Proxy Server, take a few minutes and examine your server's current settings. Refer to the foregoing sections as you explore the `Network` dialog to ensure you're properly configured. If you are doing this exercise on a production network, be sure to talk to your network administrator before changing any settings.

1. Go to the `Start Menu` and select `Windows NT Diagnostics` from the `Administrative Tools (Common)` program group. Check the information on the program's `Version` tab to verify your machine is running Service Pack Three.

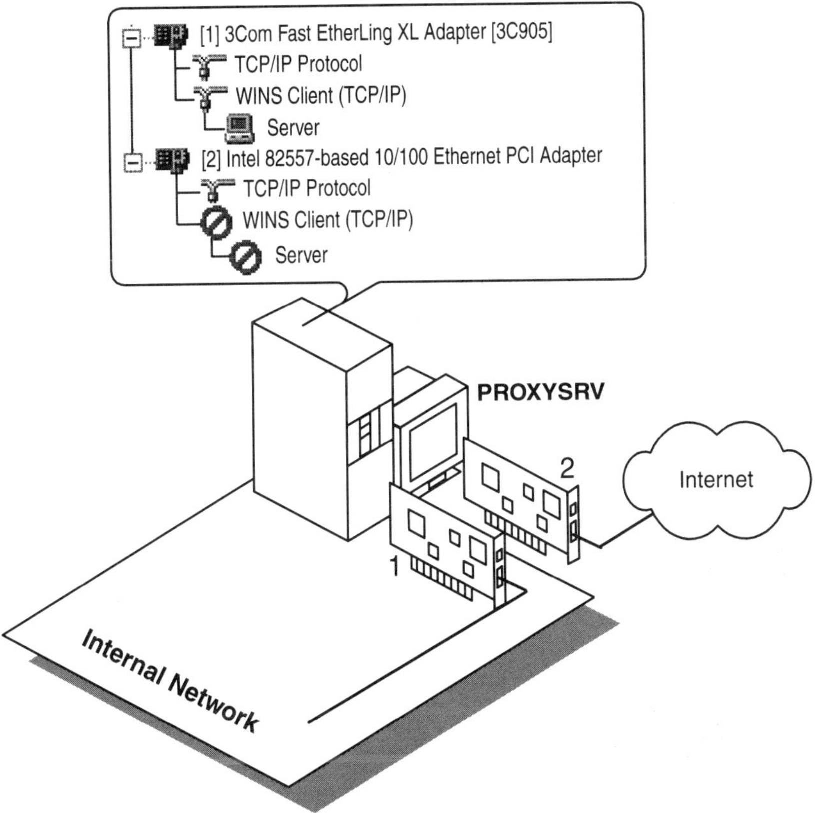

Figure 4.4 *Configuring Proxy Server network interfaces.*

2. Launch the `Network` dialog from `Control Panel`:
   - Select the `Bindings` tab and select `all adapters` in the `Show Bindings for` window. Expand the binding list for each adapter and check the bound protocols. If you see an adapter that has an unnecessary protocol bound to it, highlight it and click the disable button to inactivate it — remember for Proxy Server to work properly, TCP/IP *must* be bound to the *internal* network whether it is used or not. (You may notice that TCP/IP is displayed as two protocols: `TCP/IP Protocol`, and `WINS Client (TCP/IP)`. The former represents the entire TCP/IP protocol binding while the latter represents only the NetBIOS over TCP/IP binding. Disabling only `WINS Client (TCP/IP)` will inactivate only the computer's ability to communicate with other Windows computers using TCP/IP at the NetBIOS level — `Network Neighborhood` and such.)
   - While still in the `Network` dialog, click the `Protocols` tab, highlight `TCP/IP Protocol`, and click the `Properties` button. Verify that static

IP addresses are set for each internal adapter and that no default gateway is set for the internal network adapter(s). If your ISP provides a DHCP address for your external adapter, verify that that option is selected for the external adapter.
- Finally, check the DNS and WINS Address tabs to verify appropriate information has been entered there. (Note that while DNS applies to all adapters, you enter WINS settings for each adapter.)

Proxy Server Licensing Requirements

Licensing for Proxy Server is very simple and straightforward. You may install one and only one server for each Proxy Server license you possess. If you choose to install multiple Proxy Servers in arrays or chains (more on these subjects in Chapter 7), you'll need one license for each Proxy Server computer you'll install. Unlike other server products, however, Proxy Server does not require a client access license (CAL). That means it costs you nothing to connect Proxy Client machines to the Proxy Server machine. Proxy Client software requires no license either. You may install the Proxy Client program on as many machines as you wish.

Don't confuse the Proxy Server client access license with the Windows NT Server client access license. If the client machines connect to the Proxy Server program operating on the Windows NT server but do not use any of the machine's other server features, a Windows NT CAL is not required. If, however, the Proxy Client accesses the Windows NT server running Proxy Server for any other reason (e.g., as a file and print server), you must obtain a Windows NT CAL for each client that will connect to the server for such purposes. Another way to think about this is: if the client had business with the Windows NT server before Proxy Server was installed, then it needs a Windows NT CAL. If, however, the Proxy Server computer will provide only Proxy Server services, no CAL is required.

MCSE 4.2 Running Proxy Server Setup

You have several options for installing Proxy Server. You can simply run server setup by using the Setup program on the Proxy Server compact disk or you can use some command line options to enhance the setup process. You can even run an unattended setup from another computer. In any case, the Setup program will temporarily stop the Internet services on the target computer.

Installing Proxy Server consists of six main steps:

1. Starting Setup
2. Choosing which components to install

3. Setting the Web Proxy cache drives
4. Defining the LAT
5. Configuring client Setup information
6. Setting access control for the Web and WinSock Proxy services

Now let's look at these steps in greater detail as we see how they apply to installation using the setup program, command line options, and unattended installations.

Setup Program

After you launch the setup program from the Proxy Server compact disk and specify the 10-digit CD key, the setup program will ask you for the destination folder in which to install the Proxy Server software. The default folder is C:\msp. You can change the destination folder by clicking the `Change Folder` button (see Figure 4.5).

The folder you choose in this step is the folder for Proxy Server system files and Client distribution files. This folder is *not* used for the Web Proxy Service cache. You will be given a chance to specify the cache location later in the setup program.

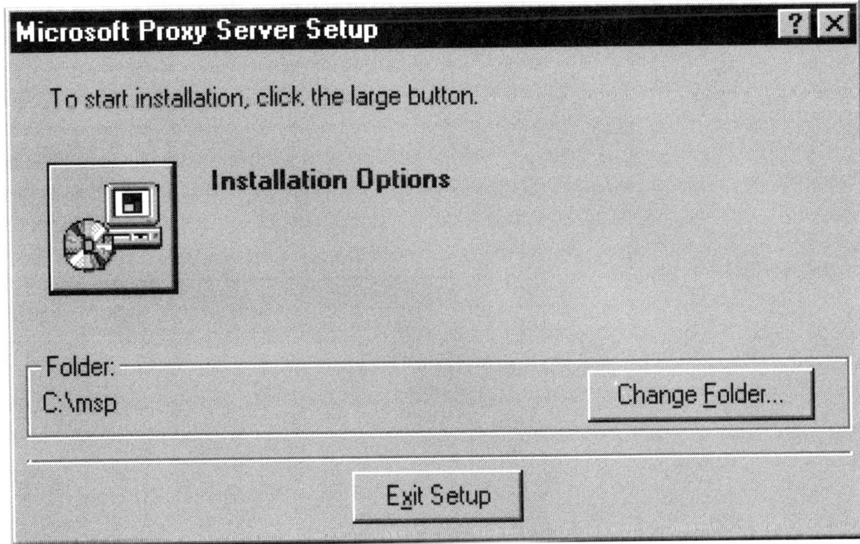

Figure 4.5 *Choosing the destination folder in which to install Proxy Server.*

After choosing the destination folder you can specify what Proxy Server components to install (see Figure 4.6).

To install specific Proxy Server components, select or clear the corresponding checkbox. The setup program will create a directory structure as shown in Figure 4.7.

The Setup program also shares the `Clients` folder with the share name `Mspclnt`.

By default, Proxy client software for Windows 95, Windows 3.x, and Windows NT (for both Intel and Alpha) computers is installed. This software permits WinSock clients to gain access to the Internet through the

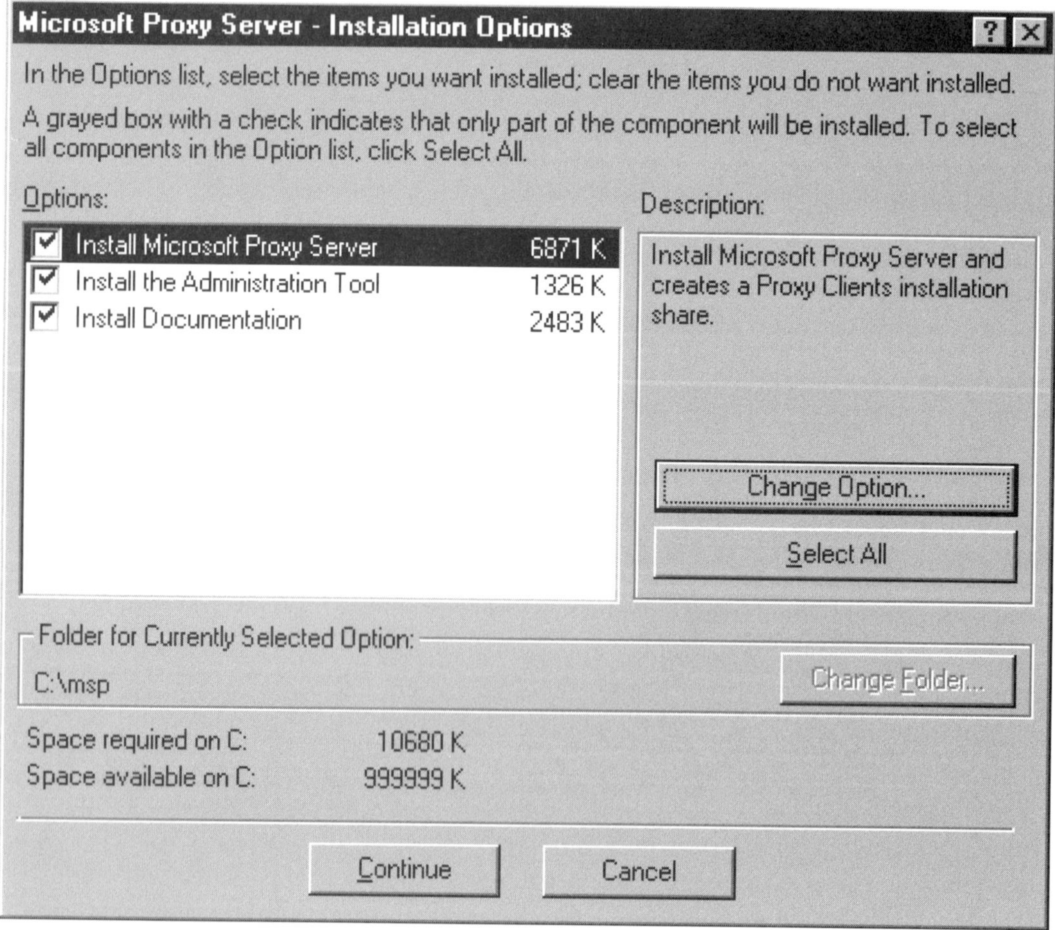

Figure 4.6 *Choosing components to install.*

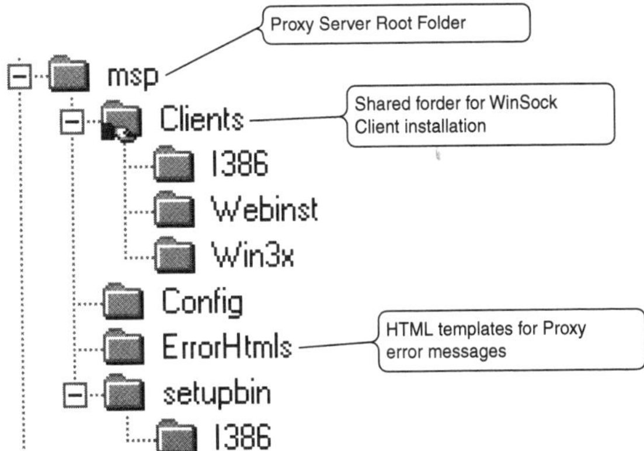

Figure 4.7 *Directory structure created by the Proxy Server installation.*

Proxy Server. It is a good idea to select only the software your network clients will use. If, for example, your network does not have Alpha-based clients, you can save disk space by clearing the `Install NT Alpha Client Share` check box (see Figure 4.8).

After you have chosen the Proxy Server components, you have to specify the location and size of the Proxy Server cache. Check the `Enable caching` checkbox in the `Microsoft Proxy Server cache drives` dialog box to enable Web proxy caching (see Figure 4.9).

Caching is enabled by default and set to 100MB on the drive containing the Proxy Server files.

To assign a disk to store cached data, select the drive letter from the list, specify the maximum size for this disk's cache in the `Maximum Size (MB)` edit window, and click the `Set` button. If you do not want to use the Web Proxy service cache, specify zero as the maximum cache size and press `Set`. Note that you can choose only NTFS formatted disks for caching; FAT volumes will appear dimmed in the dialog box. If you have multiple drives you can spread the Proxy Server cache across several drives. This will increase performance, since different drives can be simultaneously accessed. The minimum cache size on each volume is 5 MB; however, the recommended minimum is higher and depends on the number of Proxy clients.

Remote network drives cannot be allocated for caching.

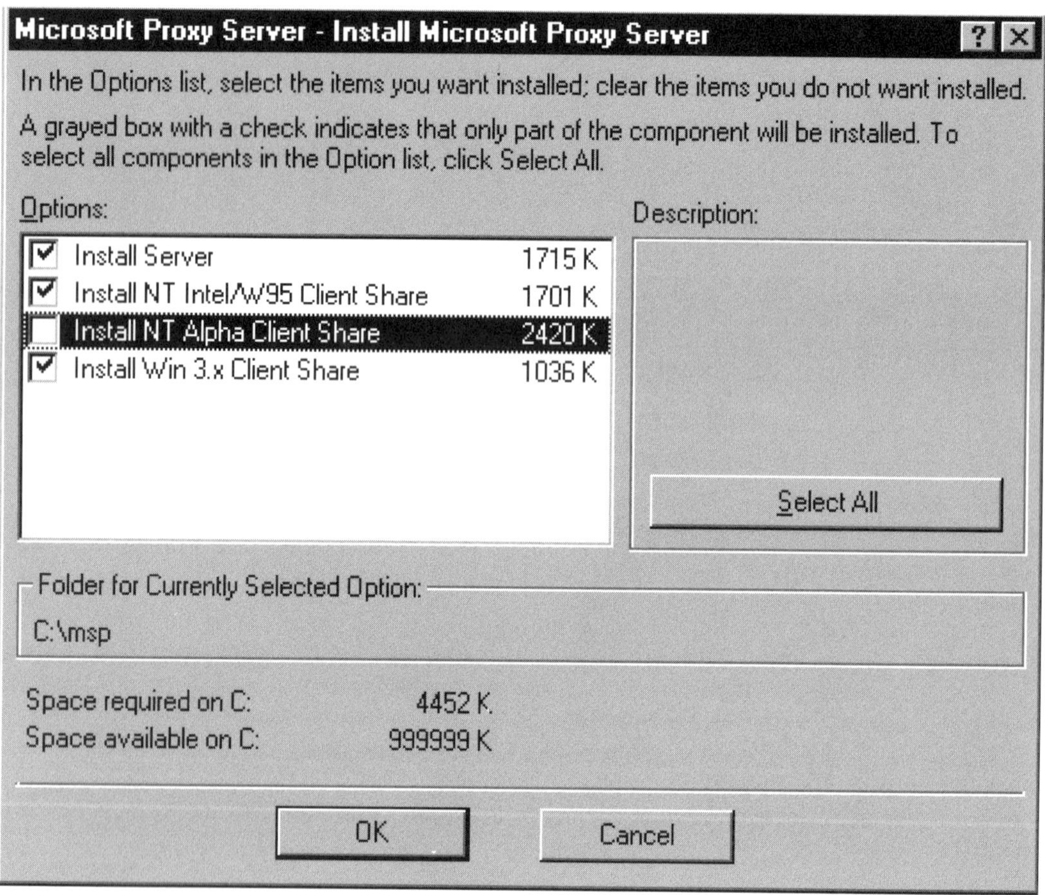

Figure 4.8 *You can save disk space by specifying what client software to install.*

After specifying the cache size and location you must configure the Local Address Table (LAT). You must define all the internal IP addresses on your network and exclude all external IP addresses. The Proxy Server LAT must include at least one IP address assigned to one of the Proxy Server computer's network cards. Use the `Add` and `Remove` buttons to add and remove IP address ranges from the LAT (see Figure 4.10).

You can optionally let the Setup program construct the Local Address Table using information from the local routing table. To have the Setup program construct the LAT, click the `Construct Table` button. After clicking the `Construct Table` button you have to specify what information Setup should use to build the LAT (see Figure 4.11).

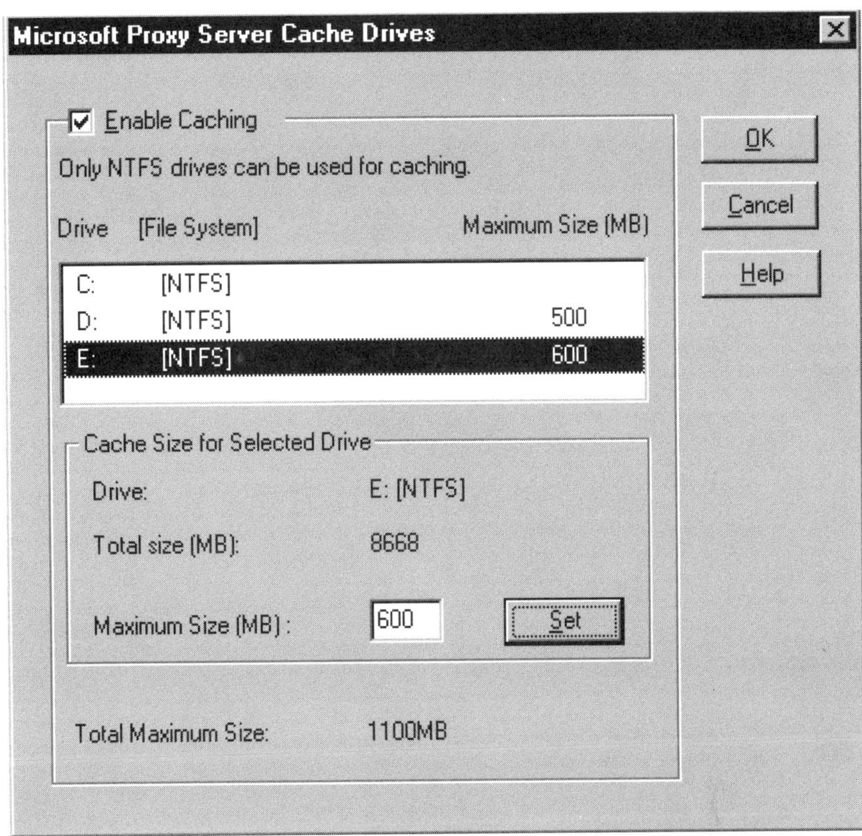

Figure 4.9 *Configuring Proxy Server cache.*

The Setup program can examine the local IP routing table or the IP addresses bound to the local network interfaces to construct LAT. It can even add private address space to the LAT if instructed to do so. Setup is smart enough to add IP addresses of networks not directly connected to the Proxy Server computer by checking the local routing able (see Figure 4.12).

The first three lines in the LAT depicted in Figure 4.12 are private IP address ranges. The fourth line represents Internal Network 1. The fifth line symbolizes the broadcast address that should be also considered local. Finally, the last line describes Internal Network 2 (located across the router). Note that Setup learned about Internal Network 2 by examining the routing table, which contains static routes to other networks.

Even after Setup has constructed the LAT for you, you many want to check that it has not included any external IP addresses. If it has, you'll need

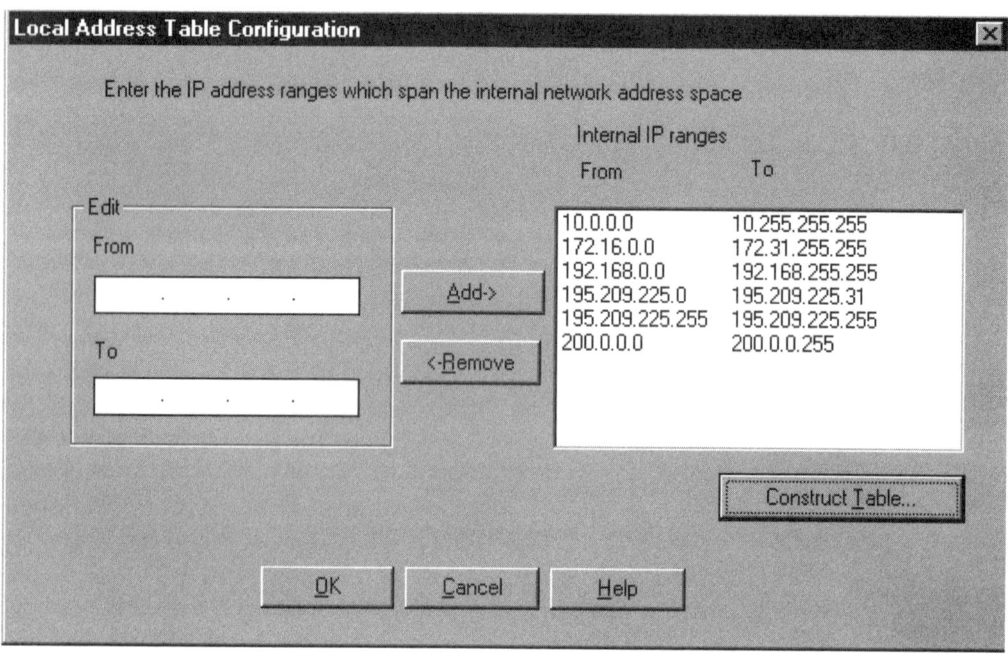

Figure 4.10 *Constructing the Local Address Table (LAT) manually.*

Figure 4.11 *Constructing the LAT automatically.*

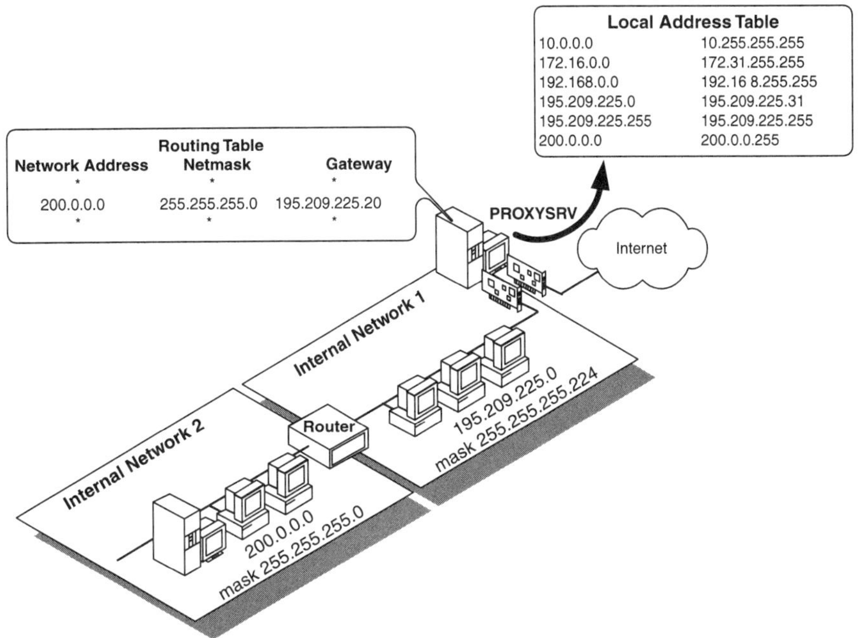

Figure 4.12 *Adding remote internal networks to LAT.*

to delete unwanted IP address pairs. The LAT information is stored in the *msplat.txt* file in the Clients subdirectory. This file is downloaded to client machines during Proxy client installation. The client computer periodically downloads the LAT from the server to ensure it has the most up-to-date information. Proxy clients learn what IP addresses are local (and don't need Proxy Server for packet forwarding), or remote (all packets must go though Proxy Server) from the LAT.

The next step after Local Address Table construction is to configure the client setup. Your settings in the `Client Installation/Configuration` dialog box specify how the client Setup program will configure WinSock clients to be installed from this server (see Figure 4.13). You can configure the WinSock client to connect to the Proxy Server computer by using the computer name or IP address. If you choose to connect by computer name, ensure the name is correct and that name resolution works properly. The third option, `Manual`, is not available during Proxy Server setup. We will learn about it later when we discuss Proxy Server administration.

The Client Setup program looks for any Web browsers installed on the client computer. If a Web browser is found, the client setup program can

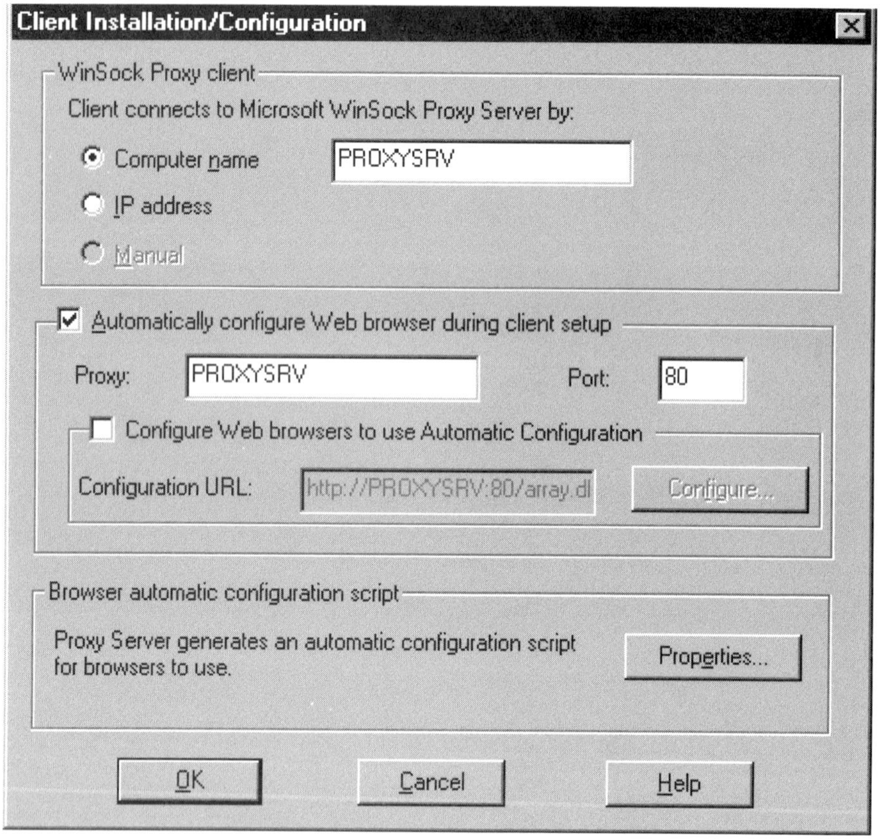

Figure 4.13 *Proxy client settings.*

modify the browser's configuration settings to direct client requests to the Proxy Server computer instead of the Internet. You can control this process by specifying settings in the `Automatically configure Web browser during client setup` box. This is a very powerful feature since it can take hours to manually configure each client Web browser by hand. You can also choose to launch a script to configure Web browsers by specifying a default script or utilizing a custom URL. We will discuss these options as well as the `Browser automatic configuration script` option later in the following chapters.

After you are done with the client configuration dialog box, you have to specify whether to use access control for Web Proxy clients and WinSock Proxy clients (see Figure 4.14).

Access control is enabled by default for both WinSock Proxy clients and Web Proxy clients. If access control is enabled, only those clients that

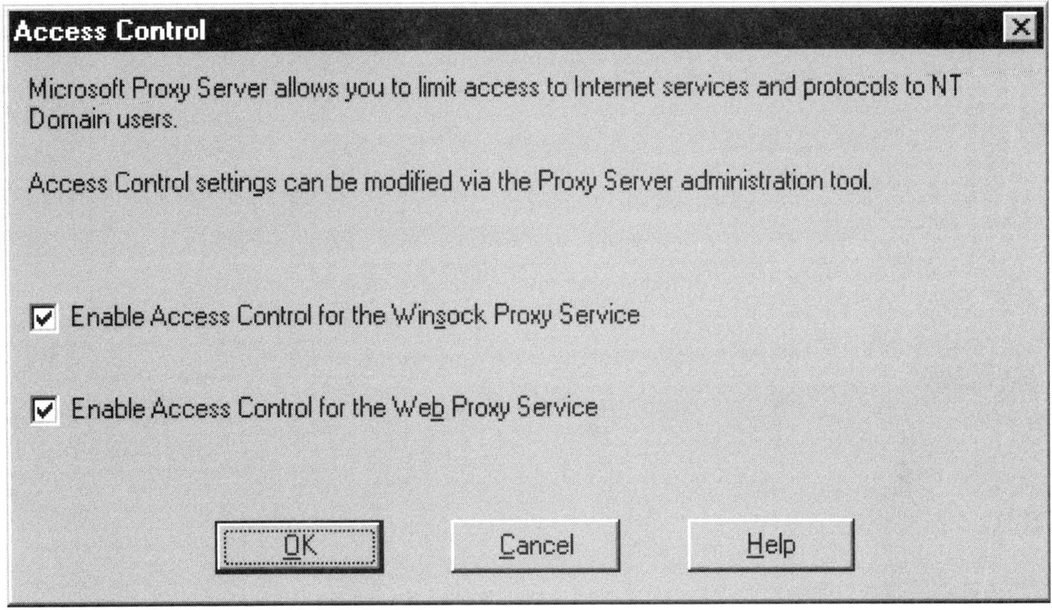

Figure 4.14 *You can limit access to Internet services for Winsock and web Proxy clients.*

have been explicitly assigned permissions are able to use the service. In other words, you must specifically assign permissions to users in the Proxy Server Administrator program before they will be able to use the WinSock or Web Proxy services when the access control checkboxes are checked. If you clear the checkbox, *all* internal clients will be able to use the services. You can change these settings in the Web Proxy and WinSock Proxy property pages.

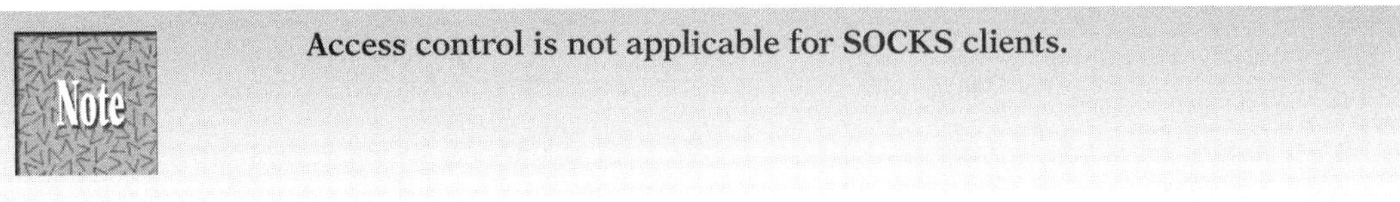
Access control is not applicable for SOCKS clients.

After you specify the access control information you are informed about packet filtering. Initially, packet filtering is disabled and it cannot be controlled from the Setup program. You have to use the Administrator program to enable and control packet filtering. Click OK when prompted. The Setup program will start Internet services and finish the installation.

Note   The Microsoft Proxy Server Setup program creates a log file: C:\Mps-setup.log. If you encounter problems during Proxy Server setup, you can review this file with any text editor.

Let's now summarize what changes are made by the Proxy Server installation (we assume that the complete install was chosen):

- Web Proxy service, WinSock Proxy service, and Socks Proxy service are installed and automatically added to the Internet Service Manager or Internet Management Console (if you have IIS 4.0).
- The HTML based online documentation is copied to the *%system-root%\help\proxy* directory.
- A directory structure for the cache was created on the NTFS volume(s).
- Proxy Server Performance Monitor counters were installed.
- The Local Address Table was constructed.
- The client installation software was copied to the *clients* directory.
- The *clients* directory was shared over the network.

Study Break

Meeting Minimum Software and Hardware Requirements

If you are using IPX/SPX make sure that you have the SAP agent installed (the SAP agent can be installed in Network|Services).

1. Run the Proxy Server setup program from the Proxy Server compact disk.
2. Click `Continue`.
3. Enter the 10-digit CD key and click `OK`.
   You can find this key on the sticker on the back of the CD-ROM case.
4. Click `OK` to confirm the Product Identification information.
   If desired, change the folder to which Proxy Server will be installed by clicking the `Change` button and providing the new destination path.
5. When the `Installation Options` dialog box appears, make sure all components are selected.
   This will install Microsoft Proxy Server, Administration Tool, and product documentation.
6. Click `Continue`.
   The Setup program will temporarily stop the WWW publishing service. The `Microsoft Proxy Server Cache Drives` dialog box appears.
   Is caching enabled by default?   ___________________________

What is the default cache size? ________________________

Note that only partitions formatted with NTFS are available for caching.

7. Accept the default caching size and click `OK`.

The Local Address Table dialog box appears.

8. To construct the LAT for the IP addresses on your internal network, click the `Construct` button.

Note that the default settings for constructing the LAT include private IP address ranges.

9. To select the network interface cards on the server whose IP addresses will be included in the LAT, select the `Load from NT Internal Routing Table` option.

10. Select the internal network cards and then click `OK`.

Ensure the LAT contains only private IP addresses and IP addresses from your internal network. The IP address of the external interface of your Proxy Server computer should *not* appear in the LAT.

11. Remove unwanted IP addresses from the LAT by using the `Remove` button.

12. Click `OK`.

The `Client Installation and Configuration` dialog box appears. Use these choices to specify how the client setup program will configure the WinSock Proxy clients that install from this server.

Note that the `Manual` option is not available at this time.

13. Accept the default settings. Click `OK`.

The `Access Control Dialog` box appears. Accept the default settings. (You can control them from the Proxy Administrator later.)

14. Click `OK`. Proxy Server completes the installation and starts the Internet services.

15. Click `OK` to end the Proxy Setup program.

INSTALLING THE ADMINISTRATION TOOL OR DOCUMENTATION ONLY

You can install *only* the Administration Tool and/or Proxy Server documentation by specifying the appropriate boxes during Proxy Server Setup. By doing this, you can set up a computer inside you network with Proxy Server documentation and the Proxy Server Administration tool and use it to remotely administer Proxy Server (see Figure 4.15). The only requirement in this case would be that the computer for remote administration runs Windows NT Server with Internet Information Server or Windows NT Workstation with Peer Web Services (PWS) installed.

Documentation and Proxy Server Administration Tools are the only portions of Proxy Server that can be installed on Windows NT Workstation. Windows NT Workstation does not support Proxy Server Services. Only Windows NT Server supports Proxy Server Services.

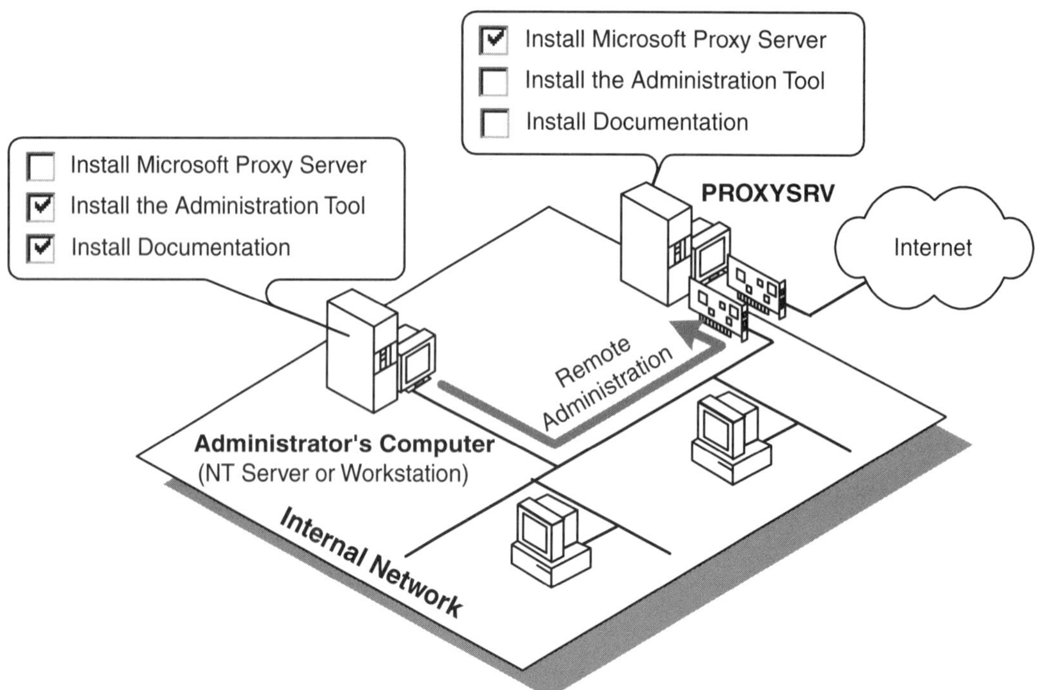

Figure 4.15 *You can administer Proxy Server remotely by installing Administration Tool only.*

Running Server Setup from the Command Line

Alternatively, you can install Proxy Server from a command prompt. Use the following syntax:

```
setup [/r] [/u] [/k] "keynumber"
```

where:

```
/r              reinstalls Proxy Server.
/u              uninstalls Proxy Server but leaves shared
                components.
/k "keynumber"  provides the compact disc key number, with
                keynumber enclosed in quotation marks. The
                keynumber value is the product ID dis-
                played on the Certificate of Authenticity
                provided with the product.
```

Do not enter a dash or a space when you enter the keynumber. If you enter the key number incorrectly, Setup fails without supplying any indication of what the problem is.

Running Unattended Server Setup

There is another option for installing Proxy Server. You can do it from a remote computer by using the unattended setup. The command syntax is as follows:

```
stpwrapp [/sms] /k "keynumber"
```

where:

/sms	is required if you use stpwrapp independent of Systems Management Server
/k "keynumber"	is the compact disk key number enclosed in quotation marks.

When you use *stpwrapp* to set up Proxy Server in the unattended mode, the setup program reads the file named *proxy.ini*. If you are not using unattended Proxy setup, this file has no effect. Table 4.2 presents some important entries in the *proxy.ini* file.

The *proxy.ini* sample file can be found on the Proxy compact disk. You can copy this file to the root of the first hard drive of the computer on which you plan to install proxy server and edit it from there. By default, the Proxy Server unattended installation searches for the *proxy.ini* file on the root of your server's first hard drive.

To better visualize the structure of the proxy.ini file, let's look at the following example:

```
[Proxy Setup Install]
Install Dir = C:\ProxyServer2.0

[Proxy Setup LAT Config]
Include Ranges from all Cards=1
Include Private Ranges=1
Range1=200.0.0.0 200.0.0.255
Range2=195.209.225.0 195.209.225.31
Range3=195.209.225.255 195.209.225.255

[Proxy Setup Client Access Config]
Winsock Proxy Access by IP rather than by Name=1
```

Table 4.2 *proxy.ini Entries*

Entry	Description
Install Dir	Specifies the installation directory for Microsoft Proxy Server. If not specified, the Setup program installs Proxy Server to the first disk drive with enough space. Syntax is *drive:\directory*. This entry is in the [Proxy Setup Install] section.
WinSock Proxy Access Control Enabled	Specifies whether access control for the WinSock Proxy service is enabled. Default is 1 - enabled. This entry is in the [Client Access Config] section.
Web Proxy Access Control Enabled	Specifies whether access control for the Web Proxy service is enabled. Default is 1 - enabled. This entry is in the [Client Access Config] section.
Set Browsers To Use Proxy	If set to 0, prevents the client Setup program from configuring Web clients such as Internet Explorer to use a proxy server. This entry is in the [Client Access Config] section.
Drive	Specifies the disk drive to be used for caching. The drive specified must have at least one NTFS partition. Otherwise, Setup fails. If you not specify this value, Setup will choose the first NTFS partition large enough for adequate caching. This entry is in the [Cache Config] section.
Size	Specifies the minimum and maximum sizes (in megabytes) to be reserved on the drive specified in the *Drive* field for caching. By default the values are 100 100. This entry is in the [Cache Config] section.
Range1, Range2...	This entry defines LAT IP ranges. Syntax is ***Range1**=x.x.x.x y.y.y.y*. For the Setup to be successful at least one entry in this section is required. This entry is in the [LAT Config] section.

```
Winsock Proxy Access Control Enabled=1
Web Proxy Access Control Enabled=0
Machine Name=proxysrv.traincert.com
Set Browsers to use Proxy=0
Set Browsers to use Auto Config=0
WebProxyPort=80
WWW-Proxy=proxysrv.traincert.com

[Proxy Setup Cache Config]
Enable Cache=1
Drive=e:
Size=150 250
```

The proxy.ini file allows you to install Proxy Server to C:\ProxyServer 2.0, configure the Local Address Table, specify access control for Web and WinSock Proxy, manage the Web Proxy service cache, and perform other setup level tasks completely unattended. This means that you are able to install Proxy Server remotely without ever touching the target computer. This could be especially beneficial when the target computer is located a great distance from you.

You can use Remote Command Server (RCMD) to launch programs on remote computers. For more information about remote execution, see the Windows NT Resource Kit documentation.

Reinstalling Proxy Server

You can add new components, remove unneeded components, and restore missing files after Proxy Server has been successfully installed. In order to do so, run the Setup program from the Proxy Server compact disk and follow the on-screen instructions (see Figure 4.16).

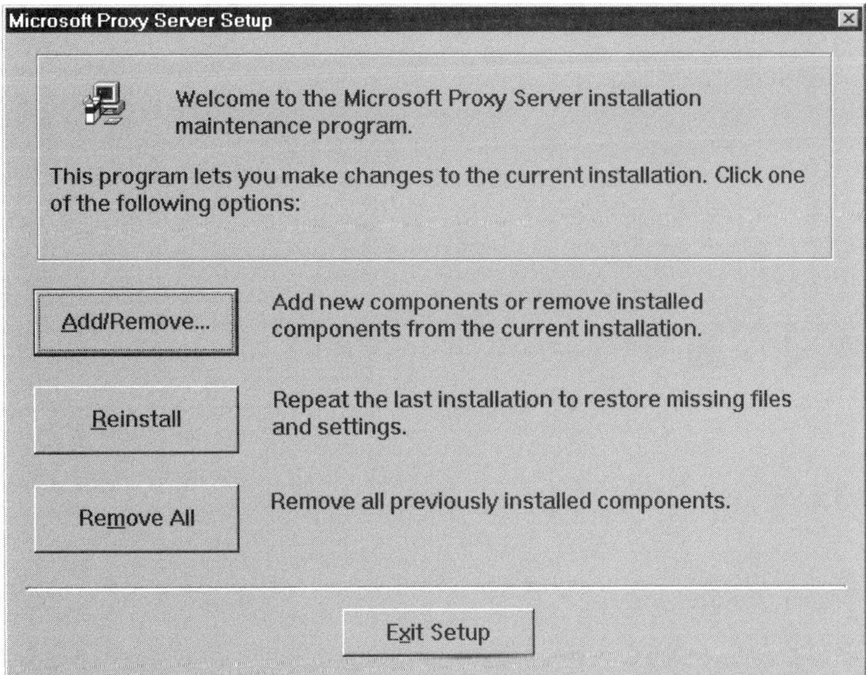

Figure 4.16 *Reinstalling and removing Proxy Server.*

If you want to uninstall Proxy Server from the command prompt, you can do it by typing `setup /qt /u`. This will uninstall Proxy Server silently.

Upgrading the Proxy Server

If you are upgrading Proxy Server from an earlier version (such as version 1.0), simply run the setup program located on the Proxy Server 2.0 compact disk and follow the on-screen instructions. There are, however, some issues you should be aware of. Before upgrading from Proxy Server 1.0 to Proxy Server 2.0, you should verify Windows NT Service Pack 3 or later has been installed and that you have met all other Proxy Server 2.0 prerequisites. If you plan to utilize the Proxy Server 2.0 caching features, ensure that at least one partition is formatted with NTFS. (Proxy Server 1.0 did not require NTFS.) Even if the Proxy Server 1.0 cache was on an NTFS volume, because of differences in content caching procedures, the contents of the cache is deleted during the upgrade and the cache is created anew.

Microsoft Proxy Server 2.0 does not support WinSock Proxy version 1.0 clients. WinSock Proxy 2.0 clients require Microsoft Proxy Server 2.0. After you upgrade the server, you must upgrade the clients as well.

By now you should understand how to install Microsoft Proxy Server 2.0. We discussed three installation methods, including unattended install. Remember the Proxy Server environment is a two-way street. In addition to Proxy Server software, Proxy client software must be properly installed and configured. Let's move on, then, to Proxy client installations.

MCSE 4.3 Proxy Client Installation

We already mentioned that the Proxy Server Setup program creates the *Clients* directory and shares it as *Mspclnt*. The default share permissions are set to `Everyone-Read`. If you look inside the *Mspclnt* share, you will probably notice additional folders containing client-specific files such as Alpha, I386, and Win3x.

Once the network share for the WinSock proxy client is available, you can install the WinSock Proxy client. You can set up the client computer either by using a client Setup program or by using a Web browser. To set up the client computer using the client setup program, connect to the *Mspclnt* share and launch *setup.exe*. You should run the client setup program from the *Mspclnt* share, not from the Proxy Server CD-ROM. This is because the setup program, which you run when you install Proxy Server, modifies some files at the client installation point so that they match the Proxy Server Local Address Table.

The Proxy client setup program configures the client computer as a client of the WinSock Proxy service on the Proxy Server computer. The client setup program will also attempt to configure the Web browser to work with the Web Proxy service if that feature was configured during Proxy Server setup.

The Proxy client setup program makes the following additional changes to the client computer:

- Control Panel is updated with the WinSock Proxy client applet
- The LAT information that is contained in the *msplat.txt* file is copied to the client. (Later on we will see how the client regularly updates this file to keep the LAT information current.)
- The *Mspclnt.ini* file is copied to the client. This file contains configuration settings for Proxy client applications. We'll discuss this file later in the book.
- The *winsock.dll* file is replaced with the Remote Winsock from the WinSock Proxy client. The original *winsock.dll* is renamed to *winsock.dlx*.

As we indicated earlier, you can install the Proxy Client software using a Web browser. In order to do this, connect to the installation page on the server by typing http://*proxyname*/Msproxy (where *proxyname* is the name of the server computer) and follow the on-screen instructions.

Alternatively, you can launch the client setup program from the command prompt by typing:

```
setup [/r] [/u] [/q[1, t]]
```

    where

```
/r      reinstalls Proxy client software (cannot be used
        with 16-bit clients)
/u      uninstalls the WinSock Proxy client application
        but leaves shared components (cannot be used with
        16-bit clients)
/q      runs client Setup in quiet mode. Only progress
        windows are displayed on the screen, but setup
        does not prompt the user to approve or modify in-
        stallation settings.
```

```
/q1      is the same as the /q option, but also hides the
         Setup Completion dialog box.
/qt      is the same as the /q option, but also hides the
         progress windows and the Setup Completion dialog
         box. (This option is not available for 16-bit
         clients.)
```

If you are performing a silent installation of Proxy client software, the setup program looks for a file named *proxy.ini* in the client distribution shared folder. The client *proxy.ini* file has a single section and entry as follows:

```
[Proxy Setup Install]
Install Dir=C:\Mspclnt
```

This entry specifies the folder where the proxy client files must be installed. *proxy.ini* has no effect on the standard (not quiet) Proxy client setup.

Disabling vs. Removing WinSock Proxy Client

After you install the WinSock client, all requests to Internet sites will go through the WinSock Proxy service on your Proxy Server. This is all right as long as the computer can always use the Proxy Server to gain access to the Internet. But what if you have a portable computer that is used both in the office and at home? Suppose you need to have your portable computer to go through the Proxy Server when your are in the office and you need direct connection to your ISP when you are at home? Obviously, installing and uninstalling the Proxy client software each time you switch between office and home will be inconvenient. Fortunately, the Microsoft Proxy client software allows you to disable the WinSock Proxy client (see Figure 4.17).

To disable WinSock client:

1. Go to the Control Panel and clear the Enable WinSock Proxy Client check box.
2. Reboot the computer.

Study Break

Installing a Proxy Client

Find a machine in your network that is not currently a Proxy client. (If all machines are Proxy clients, you can use an existing client. On an existing machine, the installed component search finds the Proxy client software and provides a number of choices. Select "Reinstall" —

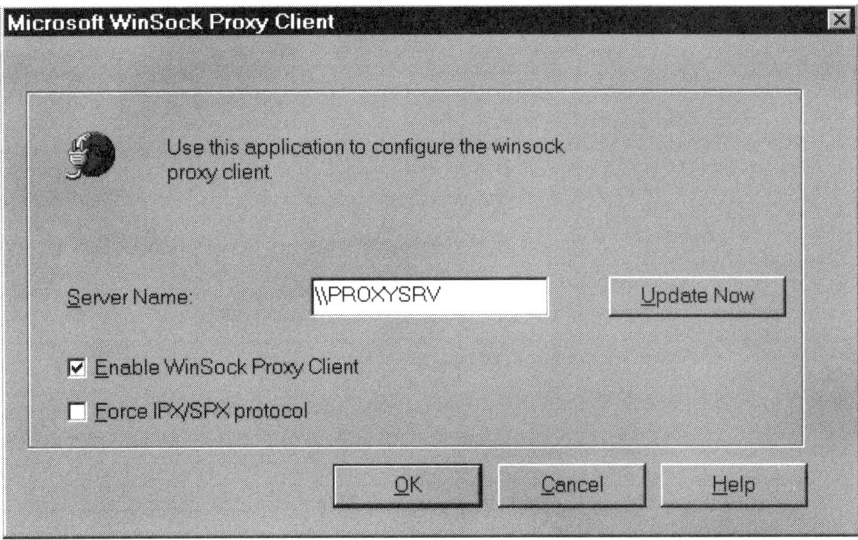

Figure 4.17 *Disabling WinSock Proxy client.*

more on this in Chapter 8.) If you're accomplishing this exercise on a production network, make sure you discuss it with your network administrator before proceeding.

1. From the desktop, click `Network Neighborhood` and select the proxy server machine.
2. Click on the `Mspclnt` folder and launch the `Setup` program.
   - Read and accept the licensing agreement.
   - Verify the client folder location and click the `Start Setup` button.
   - When installation is complete, click `OK` and click the button to restart the computer.
3. When the computer restarts, go to `Control Panel` and verify the existence of the `WSP Client` icon. Double click the new icon to review the Proxy client settings.

■ Summary

In this chapter we learned how to install Microsoft Proxy Server software. We saw that, before installation, we should ensure that the computer meets certain requirements such as running Windows NT Server with Service Pack 3 or later, Internet Information Server 3.0 or later, and the TCP/IP protocol suite. We also pointed out that a Proxy Server computer does not necessarily have to have a second network interface card. Before installing Microsoft Proxy Server, ensure your network adapter card or cards are properly configured. If you are using IPX/SPX on your internal network segment, you should not unbind TCP/IP from the Proxy Server internal network interface or the WinSock Proxy Service will not work. We also said that, for security reasons, it might be beneficial to unbind the Server service from the external interface, so Internet clients would be unable to access shared resources on the Proxy Server computer. It was also recommended to unbind IPX/SPX from the external interface (on networks using IPX/SPX).

This chapter also guided you through the setup process and described how to install specific Proxy Server components. We saw how it might be beneficial to install the Proxy Server Administration Tool and Documentation on an internal computer and use it as an administrator's console. Note that this computer can be either Windows NT Workstation or Windows NT Server. But remember, Microsoft Proxy Server *services* can be installed only on Windows NT Server. We discussed different setup methods and saw that Proxy Server can be installed from the command prompt as well as through the Setup program. We saw that you could even install Proxy Server remotely, without ever touching the target computer.

We discovered how smart the setup program could be in constructing the Local Address Table (LAT). Based on the local routing table, the setup program can learn about internal networks that are not directly connected to the Proxy Server computer, and can use this knowledge for building the LAT. You should always check the Local Address Table after the setup program builds it for you and exclude any incorrect address pairs.

We pointed out that the Proxy Server setup program has settings that allow you to configure Proxy clients that will later be installed from the *\Mspclnt* shared folder. You can configure how proxy clients will connect to the Proxy Server (either by name or by IP address). The client Setup program also looks for Web browsers installed on the client computer and, if a Web browser is found, it modifies the browser's configuration settings to direct client requests to the Proxy Server computer instead to the Internet. You can control this behavior by specifying the appropriate options during Proxy Server Setup.

You also learned that Proxy Client software must be installed from the *\Mspclnt* share, but not directly from the Proxy Server CD-ROM. Finally, we discussed methods of installing Proxy Client software in the unattended mode.

▲ REVIEW QUESTIONS

1. *What are the hardware and software requirements for a Proxy Server computer? (choose all correct answers)*

   A. Intel® 486 processor or faster

   B. 24 MB of RAM for Intel systems, 32 for RISC based

   C. Adequate disk space for Web Proxy cache on a FAT drive

   D. Adequate disk space for Web Proxy cache on a NTFS drive

   E. Internet Information Server 2.0

   F. Internet Information Server 3.0

   G. Internet Information Server 4.0

2. *You are setting up Proxy Server on a computer with one network interface card connected to the internal network and an ISDN adapter connected to the Internet. You want to administer this Proxy Server computer from Administrator's machine on the internal network. You decide to install the Proxy Administration Tool and Documentation on the Administrator's computer. Under what operating system can the Administrator's computer run? (Choose all correct answers)*

   A. Windows NT Server

   B. Windows NT Workstation

   C. Windows 95

   D. Windows 98

3. *You are installing Proxy Server on a network that uses only the NWLink IPX/SPX compatible transport protocol. Your Proxy Server computer has two network adapter cards — one is connected to the internal network and one is connected to the Internet. How would you configure protocol bindings in this situation?*

   A. Bind TCP/IP to the internal adapter only. Bind IPX\SPX to the external adapter.

   B. Bind TCP/IP to the internal adapter only. Bind IPX\SPX to both the external and internal adapter.

   C. Bind TCP/IP to both internal and external adapter. Bind IPX\SPX to the external adapter.

   D. Bind TCP/IP to both internal and external adapter. Bind IPX\SPX to the internal adapter.

4. *You are running Proxy Server Setup and configure the Local Address Table for the Proxy Server computer. Where does the information about LAT get stored?*

   A. MSPLAT.TXT

   B. LOCALLAT.TXT

    C. Proxy Server computer Registry

    D. Nowhere. Local Address Table information cannot be configured during Proxy Server Setup

5. *You are installing Proxy Server on your corporate network. During the Proxy Server Setup you enable the Access Control for the WinSock and Web Proxy services. After Proxy Server is up and running, no one can gain access to the Internet. What could be the most likely reason for this behavior?*

    A. In order for the Access Control for WinSock and Web Proxy Services to work properly, Proxy Server must be configured as a Primary Domain Controller (PDC) for its own domain

    B. In order for the Access Control for WinSock and Web Proxy Services to work properly, you must restart the Proxy Server computer

    C. By default, no one is granted access control to use WinSock and Web Proxy services. You must explicitly grant users access control in the Proxy Server Administration program

    D. You are using FAT volume for Proxy Server caching. FAT volumes do not support access control

6. *You are setting up Proxy Server and you want to allocate 100 MB on drive C: for Web Proxy caching. You launch Proxy Server Setup but when you try to select the C: drive for Web Proxy cache, you are unable to do so. What is causing this problem?*

    A. Drive C: is a boot partition. You cannot use drives that contain Windows NT system files for Web Proxy cache

    B. Web Proxy cache can not be configured during setup

    C. Drive C: is formatted with FAT

    D. You can not allocate 100MB for Web Proxy cache. 500MB is the minimum

7. *You are installing Proxy Client software. Using Windows NT Explorer, you run the Proxy Client setup from the Proxy Server compact disk. The client setup fails. What are you doing wrong?*

    A. Proxy Client software cannot be installed from Windows NT explorer. You need to specify command line parameters in order for the setup to work

    B. Proxy Client software cannot be installed directly from the Proxy Server CD. You need to run the client setup from the *Mspclnt* share

C. Proxy Client software should not be installed on a Windows platform. Only Macintosh and UNIX computers need Proxy client software

8. *You are upgrading Proxy Server 1.0 to Proxy Server 2.0. What happens to the Web Proxy cache contents during the upgrade?*

    A. The cache is preserved

    B. The cache contents are deleted and cache is created anew

    C. The cache contents are preserved only if the Proxy Server 1.0 cache resides on a NTFS volume

    D. Proxy Server 1.0 does not have any caching capabilities

9. *Mary uses a portable computer at home and in the company's office. Her company utilizes Proxy Server to protect the internal network from Internet attacks. In the office Mary installs the WinSock Proxy client on her portable computer and it works fine, but when she tries to connect to the Internet from home using her Internet Service Provider, the connection fails. What would you recommend Mary do to correct the situation?*

    A. Uninstall Proxy Client software

    B. Reinstall Proxy Client software

    C. Install IPX/SPX on her computer

    D. Disable WinSock Proxy Client when she is at home and enable it when she is in the office

10. *Your company is installing Proxy Server at its primary site. The primary site has four class C subnets: 200.0.1.0, 200.0.2.0, 200.0.3.0, and 200.0.4.0. These subnets are located behind Proxy Serve computer. What should be in the LAT?*

    A. 200.0.1.0   200.0.4.0

    B. 200.0.1.0   200.0.4.255

    C. 200.0.0.0   200.0.4.255

    D. 200.0.0.0   200.0.3.255

    E. 200.0.0.0   mask 255.255.252.0

11. *You are setting up Microsoft Proxy Server 2.0, but setup fails. How can you work around this issue?*

    A. Reinstall Windows NT Server

    B. Examine file C:\mpssetup.log

    C. Examine the Security Log

    D. Examine file %systemroot%\system32\proxy.log

12. *What changes are made to the client computer when Proxy client is installed? (Select all that apply)*

    A. Control Panel is updated with the WinSock Proxy client applet

    B. The LAT information that is contained in the msplat.txt file is copied to the client

    C. The Winsock.dll file is replaced with the Remote Winsock from the WinSock Proxy client

    D. The IP forwarding is disabled

    E. The Proxy client setup program attempts to configure Web browser on the client computer

13. *You are currently running one Proxy Server computer in your network but have decided to add three additional Proxy Server computers to form a Proxy Server array. You install the additional computers using the original CD-ROM. Your network currently has 30 Proxy client computers. How many additional Proxy Server licenses do you need to obtain, and how many additional Proxy Server client access licenses should you get?*

    A. No additional licenses are needed

    B. One Proxy Server license and 30 client access licenses

    C. Three Proxy Server licenses and 90 client access licenses

    D. Three Proxy Server licenses and no client access licenses

Proxy Server Administration

This chapter tells you about Proxy Server Administration. You will learn how to configure Proxy Server services using Internet Service Manager, Microsoft Management Console, and command line utilities. We will discuss different Proxy Server settings, including Web Proxy, WinSock Proxy, and Socks Proxy-specific settings. You will know how to configure Proxy Server AutoDial, domain filtering, and security properties. We will discuss concepts such as reverse proxying and reserve hosting, and will outline the key points required to implement them in your network. Finally, we will discuss Proxy Server logging capabilities and how to configure Proxy Server text file and database logging.

At the end of this chapter you will be able to:

- Use Internet Service Manager or Microsoft Management Console to connect to and administer Proxy Server

- Explain and configure a wide variety of Proxy Server settings

- Manage Web Proxy Server-specific settings
- Manage WinSock Proxy Server-specific settings
- Manage SOCKS Proxy Server-specific settings
- Regulate Proxy Server access control

Administration Overview

After you install Microsoft Proxy Server 2.0 and perform basic configuration steps allowed by the Proxy Setup program, you may be interested in how can you administer Proxy Server. You may, for example, want to know how to limit access to Internet sites for certain users or how to manage Proxy Server logging features. We have already mentioned that Internet Information Server 3.0 or higher is a prerequisite for Microsoft Proxy Server. This is because Proxy Server utilizes Internet Service Manager for administering its services. If you have Internet Information Server 4.0 installed, the Proxy Server setup program extends the Microsoft Management Console to provide Proxy Server administration. As you will see, Microsoft Proxy Server closely interacts with Internet Information server and Windows NT and you can develop the administrative configuration that satisfies your needs.

Another method of administering Microsoft Proxy Server 2.0 is through use of the command line. Using command line-based administration you can write scripts and use them to configure multiple Proxy Server computers identically and simultaneously.

Using the Internet Service Manager to Administer Proxy Server

Internet Service Manager, included in the Internet Information Server 3.0, is primarily used to administer the Microsoft Internet Information Server services. Once Microsoft Proxy Server is installed, however, you have the ability to manage Proxy Server services as well. When you choose to install Proxy Server Administration Tools, this does not actually install any additional applications, but adds Web Proxy, WinSock Proxy, and Socks Proxy icons to the Internet Service Manager (see Figure 5.1).

Using the Internet Service Manager you can pause, stop, and start Proxy Server services exactly as you would for the WWW, FTP, and Gopher services. For example, to stop the WinSock Proxy Service, select the WinSock Proxy Service icon and select `Stop Service` from the Properties menu.

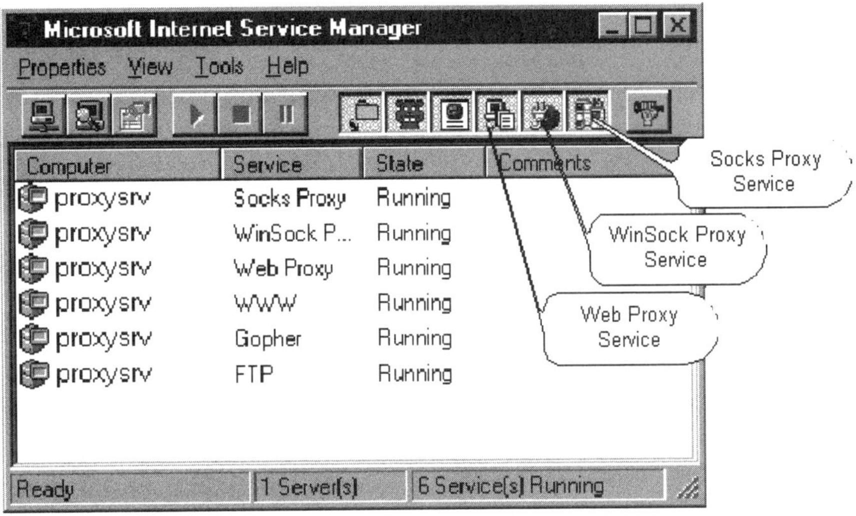

Figure 5.1 *Proxy Setup adds extra icons to the Internet Service Manager.*

SOCKS Proxy service is dependent on the Web Proxy service. If you stop the Web Proxy service, the Socks Proxy service also stops running.

Additionally, you can use the `net start` and `net stop` command to start and stop Web Proxy and WinSock Proxy services. For example, use

```
net stop | start w3svc for the Web Proxy service
net stop | start wspsvc for the WinSock Proxy service
```

There are a number of additional command line tools, which we will discuss a bit later in the section.

If you've used Internet Service Manager before, you certainly know about the Connect to Server feature. This allows you to connect to remote computers, which run corresponding services and administer them remotely. You can also administer Proxy Server services remotely by using the `Connect to Server` option in the `Properties` menu. (See Figure 5.2)

Internet Service manager also allows you to Find All Servers by sending broadcast queries and polling WINS servers. All computers found will appear in the Internet Service Manager.

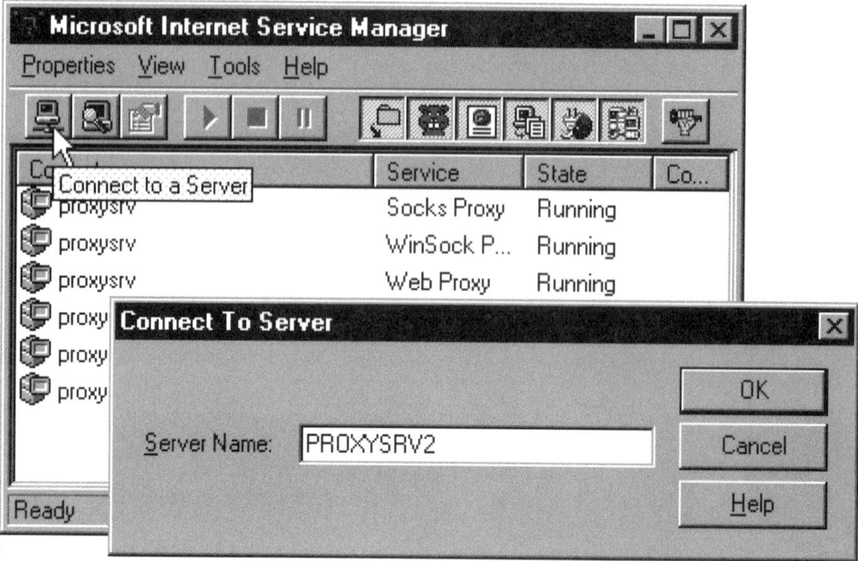

Figure 5.2   *Connecting to remote Proxy Server computers.*

The `Find All Servers` option in the Properties menu that works for WWW and FTP services does not work for WinSock and Socks Proxy services. You have to use the Connect to Server option and specify the name of the computer with WinSock or Socks Proxy services running.

Using the Microsoft Management Console to Administer Proxy Server

If you have Microsoft Internet Information Server (IIS) version 4.0 installed, you will not find Internet Service Manager on your computer. Starting with IIS version 4.0 you should use Microsoft Management Console (MMC) to administer Internet Services. Proxy Server services work well with Microsoft Management Console and can be fully administered from it (see Figure 5.3).

Using the Command Line to Administer Proxy Server

In addition to graphical administration utilities such as Internet Service Manager and Microsoft Management Console, you can administer Proxy Server by using command line utilities. This approach is particularly beneficial if you need to configure multiple Proxy Servers identically or if you want

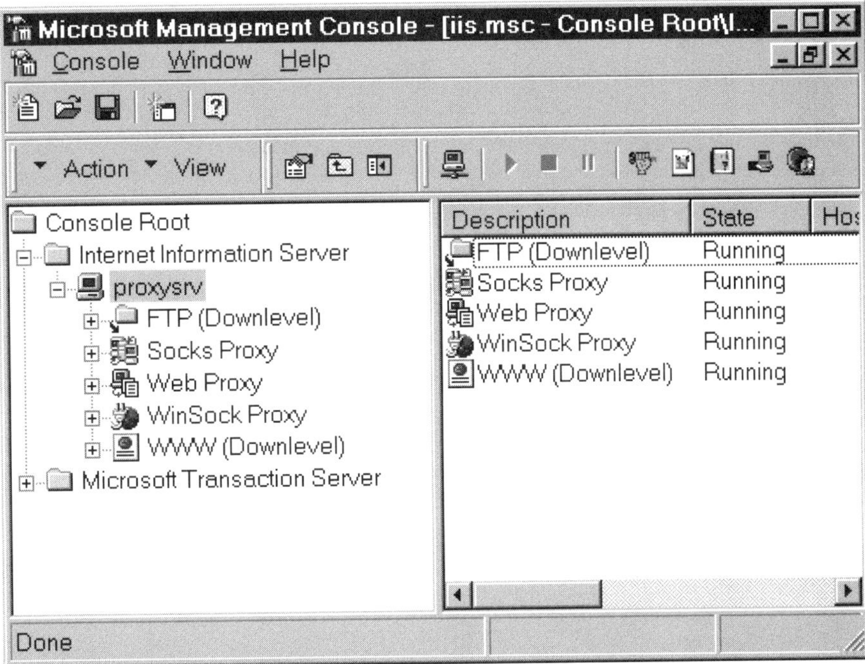

Figure 5.3 *Microsoft Management Console can be used to administer Proxy Server Services.*

to take advantage of scripting. For example, you can create a script using Proxy Server command line utilities and send it to a person without complete knowledge of Proxy Server. This person has only to execute the script and the Proxy Server will be properly configured.

The Proxy Server Setup program installs two command line utilities that can be used to administer Proxy Servers: RemotMsp and WspProto. RemotMsp is primarily used to configure and administer remote Proxy Server computers. You can use the WspProto utility to add, edit, and remove the WinSock Proxy protocol definitions.

The syntax for using the RemotMsp command is as follows (you can see these options by typing the RemotMsp –h):

```
REMOTMSP <common options> <command> <command parameters>
Common options:
-c:<remote computer name> [-v -h]
```

If you do not specify the –c:<remote computer name> the local computer is used.

Commands: can include: START, STOP, or STATUS; SAVE or LOAD; SET; JOIN, REMOVE, SYNC, or STATUS. You can use several command line options, depending on the action you want to take. Let's take a look at some of the most commonly performed tasks.

SERVER SERVICE STATE

To stop, start, or provide status on Proxy Server services, use the following syntax:

```
RemotMsp [common options] START | STOP | STATUS -
SERVICE:service_name
Where service_name can be one of the following:
ALL - for all Proxy Server services
WSP - for the WinSovk Proxy service
WP - for the Web Proxy service
SOCKS - for Socks Proxy service
```

For example, the following command stops the Microsoft Proxy Server Administration service and Proxy Alert Notification service:

```
C:\msp>remotmsp -v STOP -SERVICE:Admin
Stopping mailalrt service
Stopping mspadmin service
Wait for the service to complete the request
Operation completed successfully
```

This command is equivalent to stopping the Microsoft Proxy Server Administration service and Proxy Alert Notification service in Control Panel|Services. When Microsoft Proxy Server Administration is stopped, no one is able to administer Proxy Server using Internet Service Manager or Microsoft Management Console (see Figure 5.4).

The following command starts all Proxy Server services:

```
remotmsp START -SERVICE:all
```

SERVER BACKUP AND RESTORE

In addition to controlling the state of Proxy Server services, you can backup and restore server configuration information. The syntax is:

```
remotmsp [common options] SAVE -FILE:filename
Where filename is the name of the file in which you want
to save the configuration information.
```

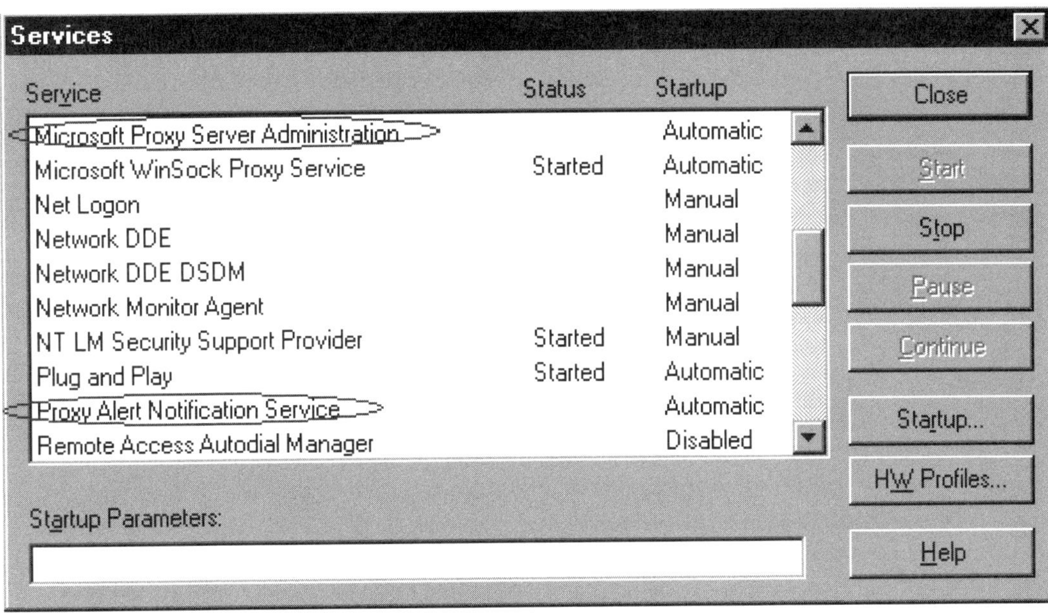

Figure 5.4 *Services applet showing Proxy Server services stopped.*

The `Save` command saves Proxy Server configuration parameters such as authentication options, Web Proxy Service cache parameters, domain filters, protocol definitions, logging options, and many others. You can use the saved information to restore the Proxy Server configuration or use it as a template for new Proxy Server installations.

The `restore (Load)` command retrieves the configuration information from a specified backup file. The -Level parameter is used with the `Load` command to indicate whether the configuration information includes global or computer (machine-specific) configuration parameters. The syntax for the `RemotMsp` utility with the `Load` command is as follows:

```
RemotMsp   [common option] LOAD -File:filename -Level:level
Where:     filename is the name of the configuration file
           level is either Global or Computer
```

For example, the following command will configure the Proxy Server on PROXYSRV using the parameters in the C:\msp\proxy.txt file

```
C:\msp> remotmsp -c:PROXYSRV -v LOAD
  -File:C:\msp\proxy.txt -LEVEL:Global
```

USING `RemotMsp` TO SPECIFY SERVER CONFIGURATION OPTIONS

You can also use `RemotMsp` to enable or disable a variety of server configuration parameters using the following syntax:

```
RemotMsp [common options] SET option=value
Where option is one of the following
WSPAccessControl
W3PaccessControl
EnableDiskCache
ResolveInArray
EnableSynchronization
InternetPublishing
  value is one of the following, except for
EnableDiskCache:
0-to disable.
1-to enable.
  for EnableDiskCache only, value is one of the following:
0-to disable caching.
3-to enable FTP caching only.
5-to enable HTTP caching only.
7-to enable FTP and HTTP caching.
```

For example, the following command disables the access control for WinSock Proxy and Web Proxy services:

```
remotmsp -v SET WSPAccessControl=0 W3PaccessControl=0
```

You can use this feature and write your own scripts to reconfigure Proxy Server services on a scheduled basis for example.

MCSE 5.1   Using ISM or MMC to Configure Web Proxy Server Services

Although command line utilities provide you with a means of configuring Proxy Server, many administrators prefer to use a graphical user interface such as Internet Service Manager (ISM) or Microsoft Management Console (MMC). Using ISM or MMC, you are able to tune and customize the Web Proxy, WinSock Proxy and Socks Proxy Services.

Most of the Proxy Server configuration issues can be performed through *properties* dialog boxes, which can typically be launched by using a context menu and choosing the *Properties* item (see Figure 5.5).

The configuration process is very similar for each of the three Proxy Server services. There are, however, a few differences. Some configuration parameters are service-specific. When you change such a parameter, it affects only one service. Other parameters are common to all three Proxy Server services — changing one of these parameters in any Proxy Server service properties window will affect all Proxy services. It is very important to

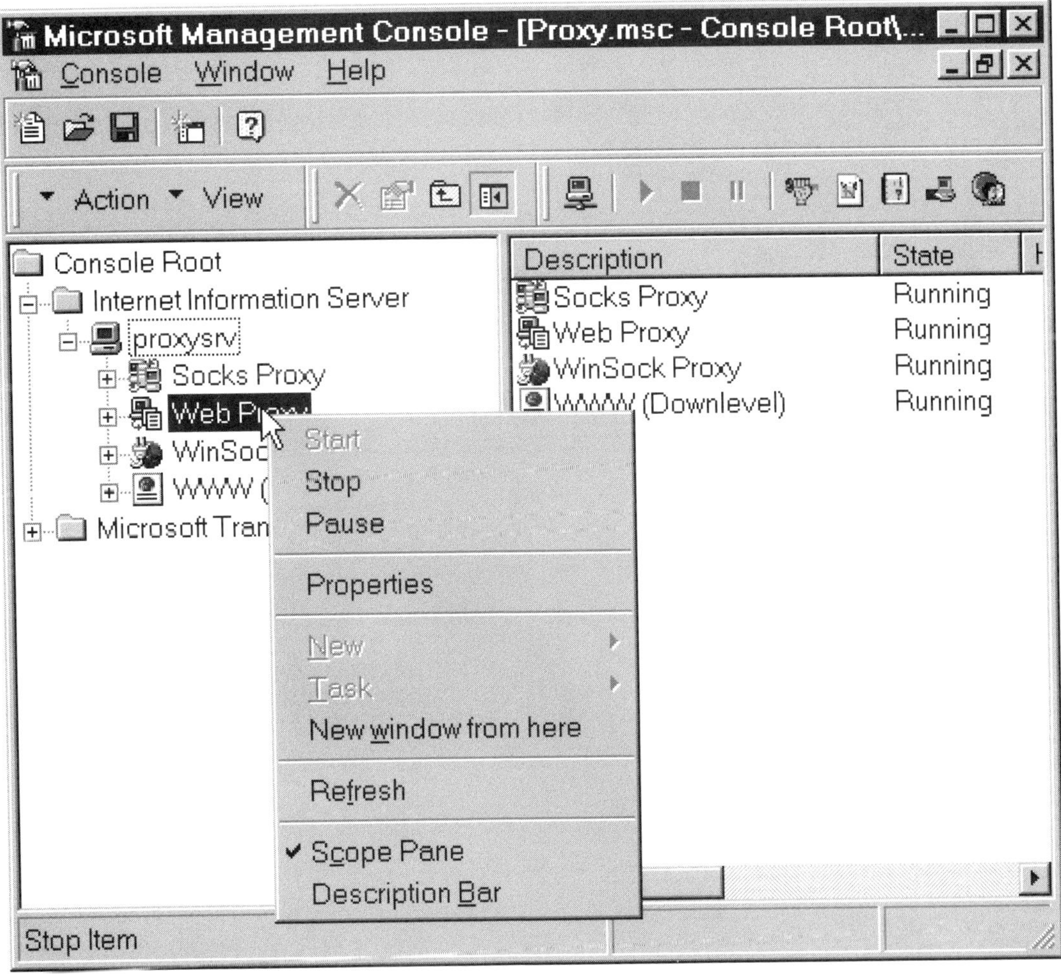

Figure 5.5 *Displaying Proxy Server service properties.*

distinguish between the two types of parameters. Table 5.1 provides a quick reference to which properties can be configured with which services. Properties common to all three Proxy Server services are marked in bold print.

Note Although each Proxy Server service has `Permissions` and `Logging` tabs, these parameters affect only the currently selected Proxy Server service. For example, if you change settings in the `Logging` tab for the WinSock Proxy service this will affect only that service.

MCSE 5.2 Setting Server Parameters

Server parameters are defined as Proxy Server computer-specific parameters that are set for a *computer* running Microsoft Proxy Server (not for a specific *service*) in a stand-alone environment. You can set the following Proxy Server parameters:

- **Auto Dial** — An on-demand dial-out feature of Proxy Server. Auto Dial works with the Windows NT Remote Access Service (RAS) and can be used to schedule dial-out connection times to the Internet through your Internet Service Provider (ISP).

- **Local Address Table (LAT)** — Used by Proxy Server to define your internal network IP address space. If necessary, you can modify or replace the LAT that is stored on the server.

- **Domain filtering** — Used to grant or deny access for specific Internet sites for Web Proxy, WinSock Proxy, and Socks Proxy services.

- **Backing up and restoring a server configuration** — Used to create server backup files that store all server configuration parameters for your server.

Table 5.1 *Proxy Server Services Properties*

Properties	Web Proxy	WinSock Proxy	Socks Proxy
Service	yes	yes	yes
Permissions	yes	yes	yes
Protocols	no	yes	no
Caching	yes	no	no
Routing	yes	no	no
Publishing	yes	no	no
Logging	yes	yes	yes

When you launch the Proxy Server service properties and select the `Service` tab, the dialog box depicted in Figure 5.6 is displayed.

At the top of the `Services` tab there is a `Current Sessions` button. By pressing the `Current Sessions` button, you can view lists of users currently using Proxy Server services (see Figure 5.7).

Select Web Proxy Service, WinSock Proxy Service, or Socks Proxy Service at the top of the Microsoft Proxy Server User Sessions dialog box to view the users connected to the specific service

If you leave the `User Sessions` dialog and return to the `Service` tab, you'll notice below the comment area (where you can add comments about the server), there are two areas: `Shared Services` and `Configuration`. Settings in these areas are not service-specific. Changing configuration parameters in, for example, the Web Proxy service properties dialog box affects

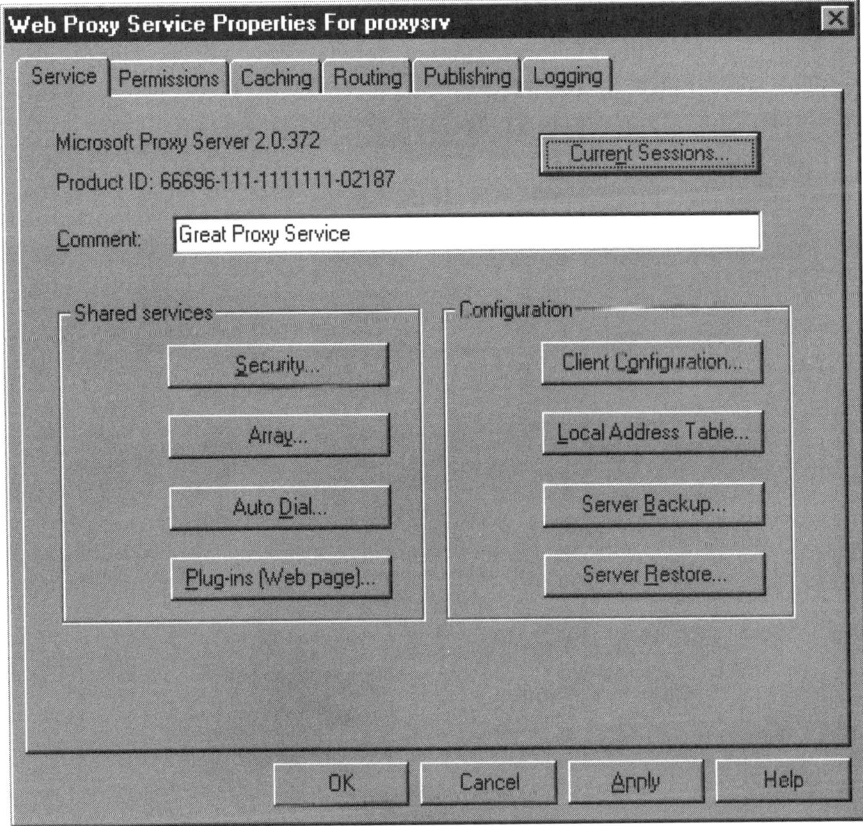

Figure 5.6 *Web Proxy Service properties: service tab.*

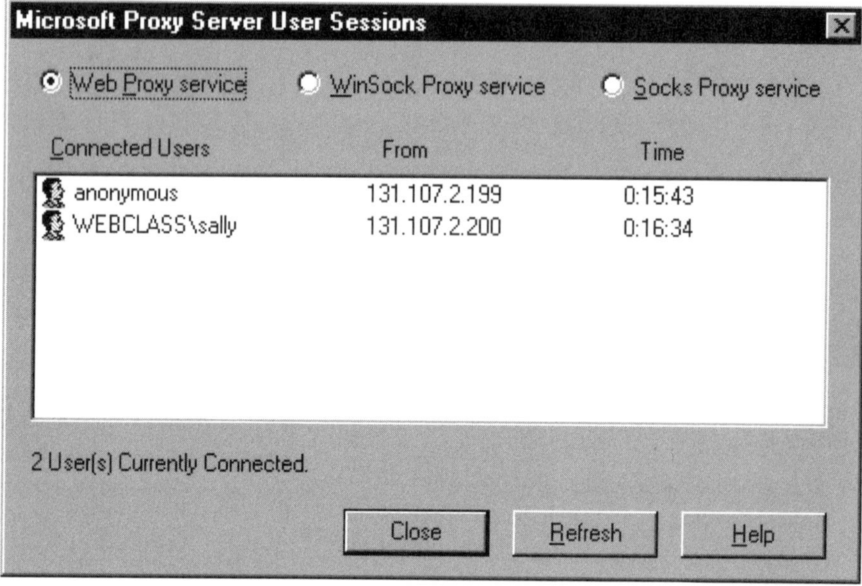

Figure 5.7 *Viewing current sessions.*

Figure 5.8 *Shared services buttons.*

other Proxy Server services also. You can use the buttons in the `Shared Services` and `Configuration` groups to set security parameters (such as packet filtering); modify proxy array membership; configure auto dial properties, configure proxy clients; and perform Proxy Server configuration backup and restore.

Setting Shared Services Parameters

The `Shared Services` area has four buttons: `Security`, `Array`, `Auto Dial`, and `Plug-ins` (see Figure 5.8).

If you press the `Security` button this will open the `Security` dialog box where you can configure packet filters, domain filters, alerting, and packet filter logging. We will discuss domain filters in this chapter and will cover packet filtering, alerting, and logging in Chapter 6.

SETTING DOMAIN FILTERS

The `Domain Filter` tab is used to grant or deny access for specific Internet sites under the Web Proxy, WinSock Proxy, and Socks Proxy services (see Figure 5.9). These can include WWW, FTP, and Gopher sites.

Before implementing domain filtering, you should determine what Internet domain access policy is appropriate for your company. There are two options. The first is more restrictive, provides greater level of security, but leaves less freedom to end-users. It can be called "Everything not explicitly allowed is denied." The second is less restrictive and requires less administrative control. It can be called "Everything not explicitly denied is allowed."

To enable domain filtering, check the box `Enable filtering` in the `Domain Filters` tab of the `Security` dialog box. The general approach to implementing domain filtering is to specify the overall policy by selecting the appropriate option (either `Granted` or `Denied`) and then specify exceptions by using the `Add` button. For example, if you want to restrict your users from accessing sites in the "astalevista.box.sk" domain, you can grant access to all Internet domains and then specify that particular domain will be denied access (see Figure 5.10).

You can specify domain filtering exceptions by using an IP address if you want to exclude a single computer; an IP address and subnet mask pair if you are describing a network; or, as described above, a domain name.

Using Proxy Server domain filtering you can prohibit access to specified sites or allow access to only the sites specified. Domain filtering applies to all users who access the Internet through this server.

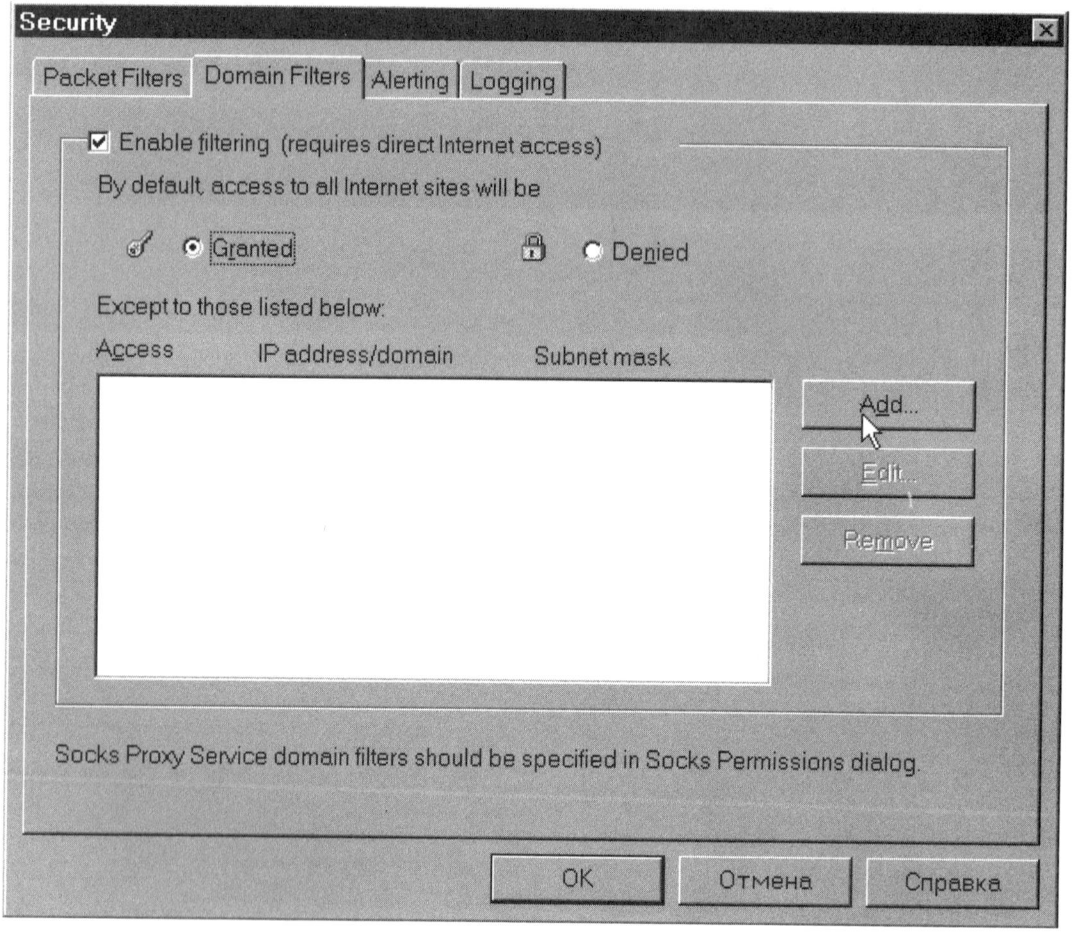

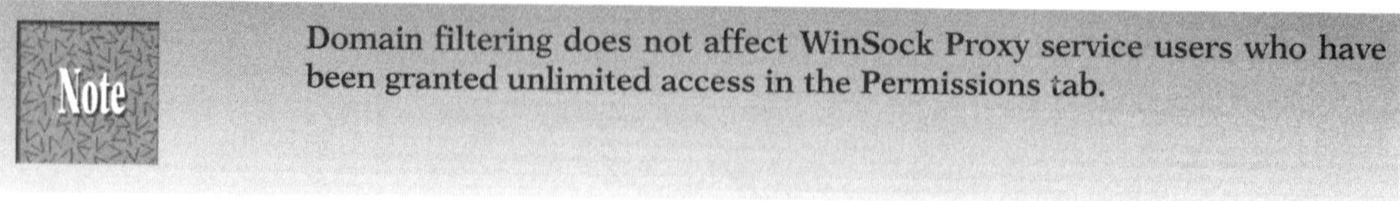

Figure 5.9 *Enabling domain filtering.*

> **Note**
> Domain filtering does not affect WinSock Proxy service users who have been granted unlimited access in the Permissions tab.

The configuration depicted in Figure 5.11 will block your users from accessing any host from the *astalavista.box.sk domain, hacker.com domain, playboy.com domain,* from the network 195.209.225.0, and from the host 131.107.2.200.

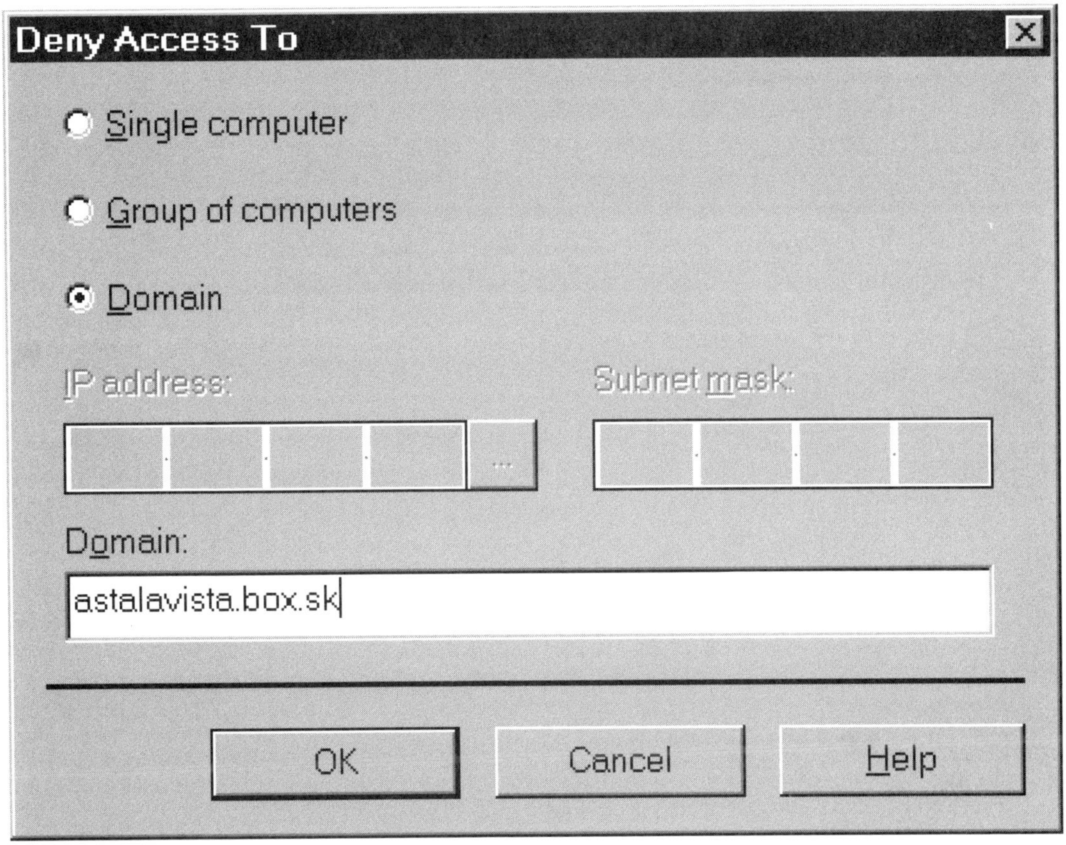

Deny Access To

- ○ Single computer
- ○ Group of computers
- ● Domain

IP address: Subnet mask:

Domain:

astalavista.box.sk

OK   Cancel   Help

Figure 5.10 *Denying access to a domain.*

The most commonly raised question is, "Should you define exceptions by using both the IP addresses and domain names, or is specifying either of them sufficient?" To answer this question, let's see how Proxy Server performs address resolution. For every WinSock or Web Proxy request, Proxy Server tries to perform a standard DNS lookup to resolve the IP address, or a reverse DNS lookup to resolve the domain name. It then compares the lookup results with the domain filtering policy and, if either domain name or IP address are prohibited by the domain filtering policy, Proxy Server blocks the request. In this case, a Web Proxy Client will receive the following message: "The specified URL is denied by the Proxy Server." A WinSock client, on the other hand, simply won't be able to establish a connection. In some cases DNS administrators do not take time to configure reverse DNS lookup. If this is the case, the site is denied by domain name only. A user

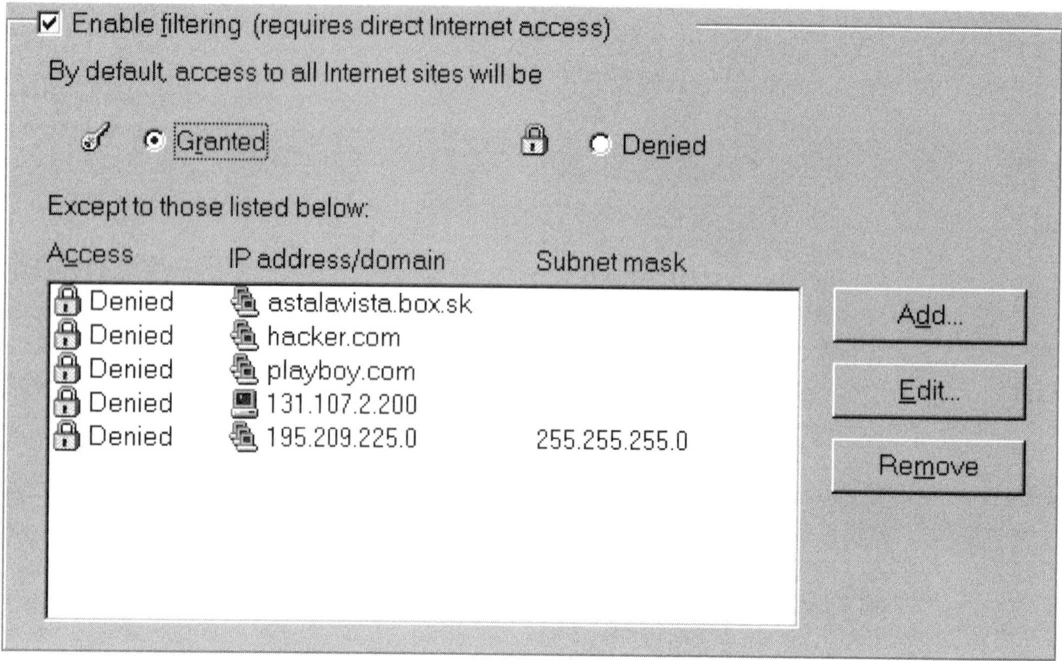

Figure 5.11　*Sample domain filtering configuration.*

who tries to connect using the IP address will be able to do so in spite of the domain filtering policy (see Figure 5.12).

Let's assume you wish to block access to an Internet host located in the *hacker.com* domain. If you configure a domain filter to block only the domain name *hacker.com*, a user who tries to access it by using the domain name will be denied access. When another user tries to connect using the IP address, Proxy Server will try to perform a reverse DNS lookup by issuing the query to a DNS server in the Internet. If no reverse DNS lookup is configured for *hacker.com,* there is no way for the Proxy Server to determine that the requested IP address (209.195.130.87 in Figure 5.12) belongs to *hacker.com.* In this latter case, the client request is passed to the Internet and the user will be able to access the site you attempted to restrict.

If there is no reverse DNS lookup configured for a particular domain, you should specify both domain name and IP addresses for the prohibited site (see Figure 5.13). By doing so, you can ensure restricted Web sites are blocked by their IP addresses even when reverse DNS lookup is unsuccessful.

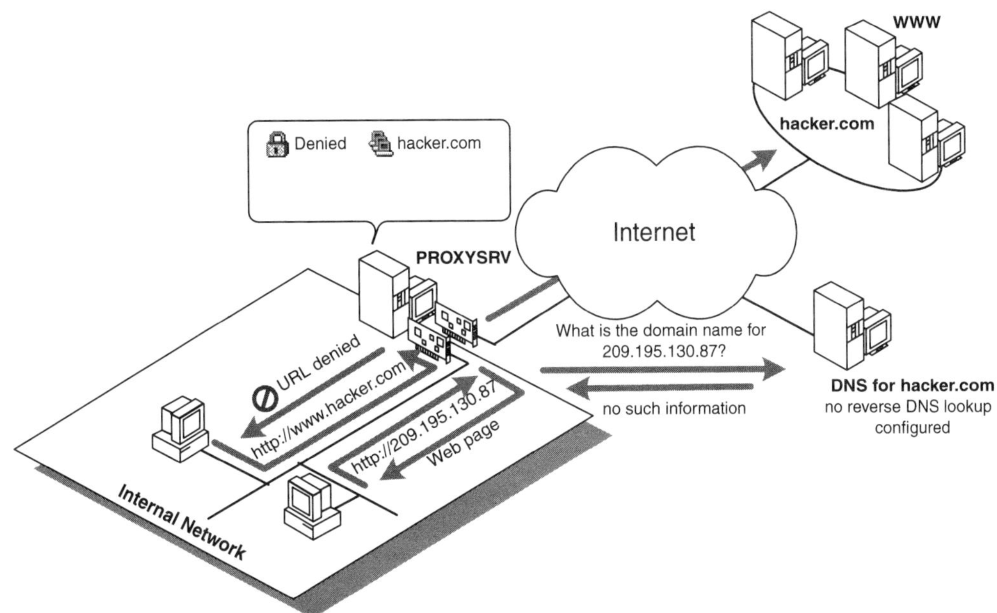

Figure 5.12 *Domain filtering fails when there is no reverse DNS lookup configured for the target domain.*

> **Domain filtering requires the ability to access Internet Domain Name System (DNS) servers. If a chained Proxy Server computer does not have access to DNS, domain filtering is ineffective.**

Configuring AutoDial

If your Proxy Server computer has a modem installed, you can configure it to automatically dial-out to an Internet Service Provider (ISP) to establish a connection. Proxy Server can be set up to dial an ISP only when needed; for example, when a user tries to access a Web page that is not in cache. This feature of Proxy Server is called *Proxy Server AutoDial*.

Proxy Server AutoDial is activated by the Web Proxy, WinSock Proxy, or Socks Proxy service when one of the following events occurs.

- When a requested object cannot be found in a cache (for Web Proxy service)
- When active caching is automatically refreshing cached objects (for Web Proxy Service)

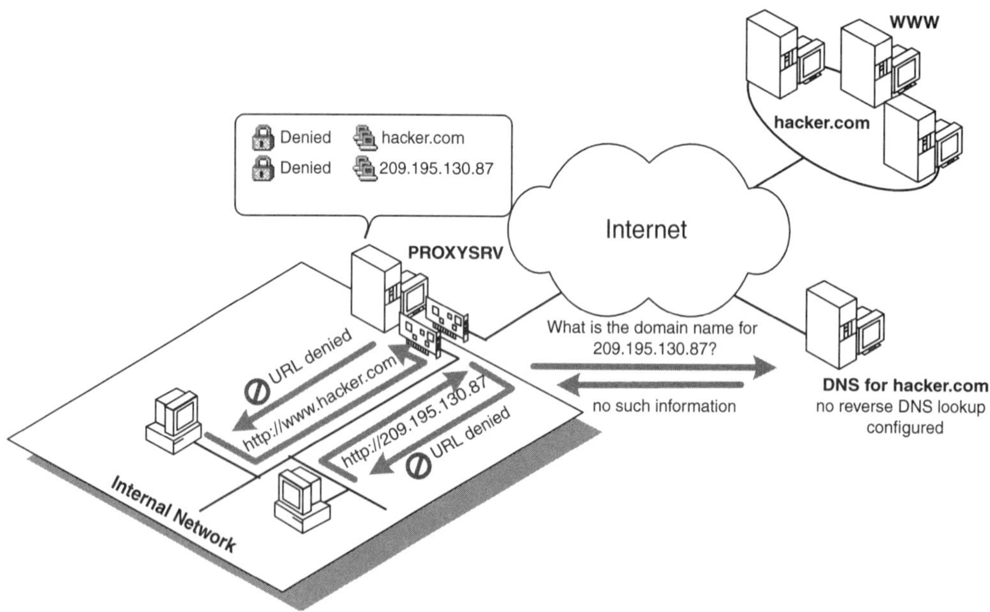

Figure 5.13 *Specifying IP address allows domain filtering to work without reverse DNS lookup on the target domain.*

- When a Client request is received by the WinSock Proxy service WinSock Proxy client requests aren't serviced from the cache and, therefore, must be processed through an external network connection (in this case, by using a dial-up connection).

- When a Client request is received by the Socks Proxy service. As with the WinSock Proxy service, Socks Proxy client requests aren't serviced from the cache and, therefore, must be processed through an external network connection (in this case, by using a dial-up connection).

The Proxy Server AutoDial feature is primarily used to reduce Internet connection time by connecting only when needed. It reduces your company Internet costs when no permanent Internet connection is required. This is especially beneficial for small companies or remote offices when users need Internet access only during normal business hours. During nights and weekends there is no need to pay for an Internet connection.

The AutoDial function can also be used as a backup to provide fault tolerance for an existing permanent Internet connection. For example, if you already have a permanent Internet connection via a T1 link, you can optionally configure the Proxy Server AutoDial feature to dial out to the Internet Service Provider via a modem if the T1 link goes down. Installing Proxy Server AutoDial is a prerequisite for setting up packet filtering if your computer has only a single network adapter and a modem installed. When Proxy Server is first installed, packet filtering is disabled by default. You must first configure AutoDial before you can enable packet filtering. (We will thoroughly discuss packet filtering in Chapter 6.)

Auto Dial works in conjunction with the Windows NT Remote Access Server. To be more specific, Proxy AutoDial uses a Remote Access Service (RAS) Phonebook entry to perform on-demand dial-out connections as a RAS client. To set up Proxy Server AutoDial, complete the following steps:

- Verify that Windows NT Remote Access Server (RAS) has been installed
- Create a RAS Phonebook entry to use with Proxy Server AutoDial
- Configure Remote Access properties to use AutoDial
- Configure user credentials in the Proxy AutoDial settings
- Set dialing services and dialing hours in the Proxy Server AutoDial settings

Study Break

Installing RAS

The first step before configuring Proxy Server AutoDial is to install Windows NT Remote Access Server (RAS) and Dial-up Networking. RAS can be installed either during or after the installation of Windows NT Server 4.0. If you are installing Windows NT and select Remote Access to the network during Windows NT setup, both Remote Access Server and Dial-up Networking will be installed automatically. If Windows NT is already installed, you can add RAS by going into `Control Panel`, double clicking the `Network` icon, and going to the `Services` tab. Click the `Add` button and select the `Remote Access Server` from the list of services. Typically, the following information is required when installing RAS:

- The modem type that will be used
- TCP/IP protocol settings
- Type of access: inbound, outbound, or both.
- Security settings

Your Proxy Server computer should be configured as a RAS client (to dial out only) for use with AutoDial. In order to ensure that, verify that the port usage is set to dial-out only in the `RAS Server properties` in the `Network|Services` dialog box.

For more information about installing and configuring the Windows NT RAS server refer to the Windows NT Product documentation.

After you verified that the RAS is installed and configured to perform as a client, you should configure a phonebook entry that will be used by the Proxy Server. This entry is used to dial your ISP's access number. Before creating a phonebook entry, you may want to check with your ISP for any specific connection settings.

Study Break

Creating a RAS Phonebook Entry

1. On the RAS server, double click the `My Computer` icon on the desktop, and then double click `Dial-Up Networking`.
2. In the `Location Information` dialog box, under `What Country are you in now?`, click the down arrow and select a country.
3. Under `What area (or city) code are you in now?`, type a valid area or city code.
4. Under `If you dial a number to access an outside line, what is it?`, type a valid digit (if applicable).
5. Under `The phone system at this location uses`, click either `Tone dialing or Pulse dialing`, and then click `Close`.
6. In the `Dial-Up Networking` dialog box, if the Phonebook is empty, click `OK` to add a new entry.
7. In the `New Phonebook Entry Wizard` dialog box, follow the on-screen instructions to create a Phonebook entry, and then click `Finish`.
8. In the `Dial-Up Networking` dialog box, select the new Phonebook entry from the drop-down list, click `More`, and then click `User Preferences`.
9. In the `User Preferences` dialog box, under `Enable auto-dial by location`, click to clear the `New Location (the current location)` check box.
10. In `Idle seconds before hanging up`, type `300`.
11. Click `OK`, and then click `Close`.

In order for the Proxy Server AutoDial features to properly function with the Remote Access Server services, some additional RAS configuration is required. You must configure the Remote Access AutoDial Manager and Remote Access Connection Manager services to use Proxy Server AutoDial (instead of RAS AutoDial) to manage dial-up support. To do this, perform the following steps:

- In `Control Panel|Services` stop and disable the `Remote Access AutoDial Manager` service. You can do this by clicking the `Startup` button and selecting `Disabled`.
- In `Control Panel|Services` start the `Remote Access Connection Manager` service and set it to `Automatic`. You can do this by clicking the `Startup` button and selecting `Automatic`.

The last two steps will actually configure the Microsoft Proxy Server AutoDial settings. Configuring Proxy Server AutoDial involves setting up credentials for dialing out, enabling dial-up for Proxy Server services, and restricting times when dial-out connection occurs.

Most Internet Service Providers require additional user information, such as username and password, to be entered when a dial-up connection is made. You can specify these credentials through the `Credentials` tab of the Microsoft Proxy AutoDial dialog box (see Figure 5.14).

If your connection to the ISP requires sending additional information as a part of the logon process, you can use scripts with dial-out. Although Proxy Server AutoDial does not support automated dial-up connections, you can use RAS dial-out scripting options. For more information about RAS scripting capabilities, see the RAS online help.

Another Proxy Server AutoDial setting configures dialing hours. By limiting dialing hours you can regulate dial-out connection times. If your Internet access is billed by connection time, limiting dialing times can reduce you Internet expenses. When dialing hours are cleared, dialing docs not occur and users receive an error message if the information they request must be obtained from the Internet. By default, dialing is enabled for all hours. Figure 5.15, for example, shows a configuration which will permit dial-out access only during normal business hours.

You can control which Proxy Server services may use the AutoDial feature. To permit WinSock and Socks client calls to initiate AutoDial, for instance, select the checkbox `Enable dialing for WinSock and SOCKS proxy`.

When Proxy Server is not allowed to dial out, active caching does not take place. A dial-out connection will not be terminated, however, if active caching is already taking place.

Figure 5.14　*Configuring user credentials for AutoDial.*

If you are setting Proxy Server AutoDial for the first time, or if you clear the Proxy AutoDial Settings, you must stop and restart the Web Proxy, WinSock Proxy, and Socks Proxy services for the changes to take effect. Once the Proxy Server AutoDial has been used at least once, you will not need to follow this procedure.

> **Proxy Server AutoDial does not support multiple RAS Phonebook entries. Auto Dial credentials and dialing hour properties apply only to the RAS Phonebook entry selected at the time Auto Dial changes are applied.**

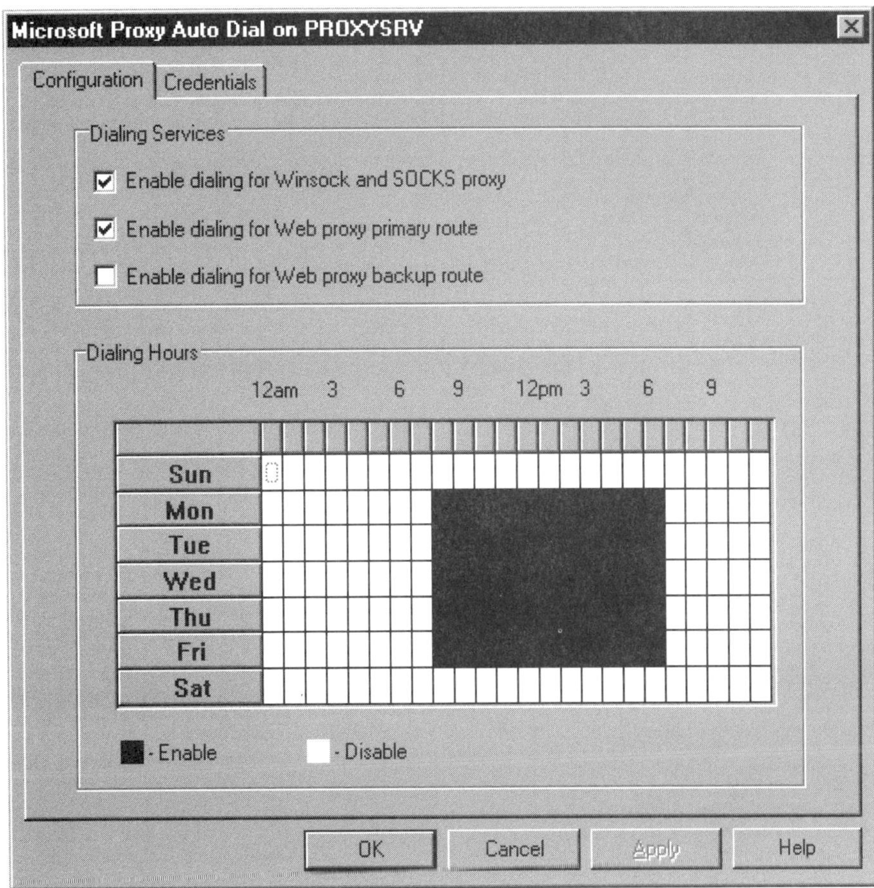

Figure 5.15 *Setting up Proxy AutoDial times.*

After you install Remote Access Server and configure Proxy Server AutoDial, it is recommended to unbind the WINS client from the external interface (dial-up client). This is recommended for security purposes to prevent NetBIOS connections from the Internet to the Proxy Server computer.

Changing the Local Address Table

You may remember that the Local Address Table (LAT) is used to determine whether a requested IP address is located on the internal or external network. The Local Address Table is initially created during Microsoft Proxy Server installation. During setup you provide information about the IP address range for your internal network. The Proxy Server Setup program can also construct the LAT for you based on the local routing table on the Proxy Server computer and the IP addresses of its network interfaces. IP addresses that are external were specifically excluded from the table during the Proxy Server setup. In previous chapters we indicated that LAT information is contained in the `msplat.txt` file on the server (a master copy of the LAT) and is downloaded to client computers.

This approach works until we add additional computers or — perhaps — another IP subnet to the internal network. There may also be a problem if we decide to change the IP addresses of existing computers in the internal network. To permit us to make such changes, we need a method of modifying the Local Address Table to reflect alterations in the network addressing scheme. Fortunately, after Proxy Server installation is complete, the server's copy of the LAT can be modified or completely replaced. This is done through the `Local Address Table` button on the `Service` tab (see Figure 5.16).

MODIFYING THE LAT

You can modify the existing LAT by manually adding or removing IP address pairs. The dialog box used to modify the LAT is exactly the same as you saw during the Proxy Server setup (see Figure 5.17). The method of modifying the LAT was discussed in Chapter 4.

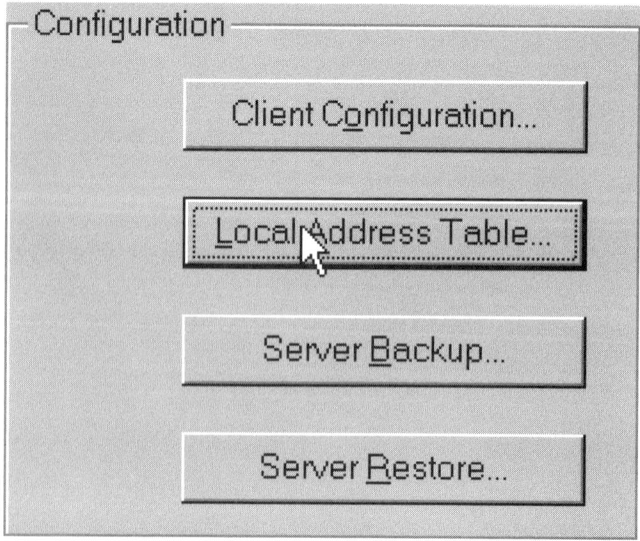

Figure 5.16　*Service tab, local address button.*

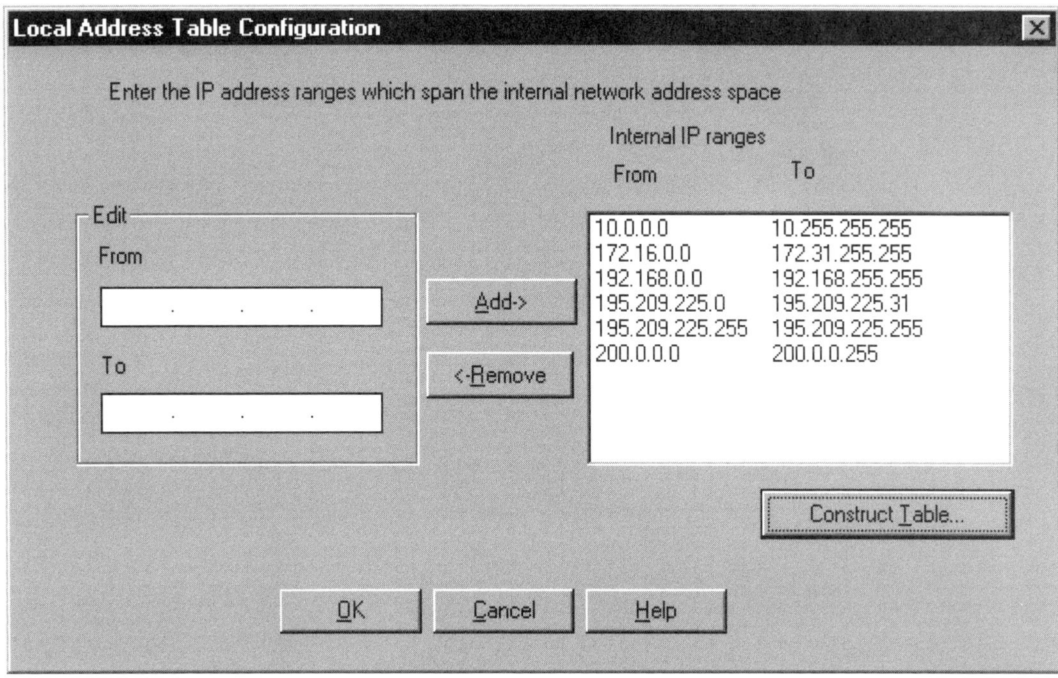

Figure 5.17 *Modifying the Local Address Table.*

You can add IP address pairs until all address ranges of your internal network are defined, and you can remove any IP address pairs that define external (Internet) addresses.

Study Break

Modifying the LAT

1. In Internet Service Manager (if you are using IIS 3.0) or Microsoft Management Console (if you are using IIS 4.0), double-click the computer name next to the Web Proxy, WinSock Proxy, or Socks Proxy service.
2. In the `Service Properties` dialog box, click `Local Address Table`.
3. In the `Local Address Table Configuration` dialog box, review the entries under `Internal IP ranges`. To add or remove IP address pairs, do one or more of the following:
    * To add a range of IP addresses to the list: Under `Edit`, type a pair of addresses in `From` and `To`, and then click `Add`.

- To add a single IP address to the list: Under `Edit`, type the same address in both `From` and `To`, and then click `Add`.
- To remove an IP address or address pair from the list: Select it under `Internal IP ranges`, and then click `Remove`.
4. When you are finished, click `OK`.
5. In Internet Service Manager, stop and restart the Web Proxy, WinSock Proxy, and Socks Proxy services for the changes to take effect on the server.

You can also completely replace the LAT, generating a new list of IP address pairs automatically from the Windows NT Routing Table. Of course, before you replace your LAT, the Windows NT routing table must be set correctly.

Generating a New List of IP Adresses

1. In Internet Service Manager (if you are using IIS 3.0) or Microsoft Management Console (if you are using IIS 4.0), double-click the computer name next to the Web Proxy, WinSock Proxy, or Socks Proxy service.
2. In the `Service Properties` dialog box, click `Local Address Table`.
3. In the `Local Address Table Configuration` dialog box, click `Construct Table`.
4. To add the reserved private IP address ranges to the LAT, select the `Add the private ranges` check box.
5. Select the `Load from NT internal Routing Table` checkbox and do one of the following:
   - If you do not know which of the server's network adapter cards are connected to the internal network, click `Load known address ranges from all IP interface cards`.
   - If you know which of the server's network adapter cards are connected to the internal network, click `Load known address ranges from the following IP interface cards`, select the appropriate internally connected cards, and click to clear the externally connected cards.
6. When you are finished, click `OK`, and review the list of IP address pairs displayed. To add or remove IP address pairs, do one or more of the following:
   - To add a range of IP addresses to the list, under `Edit`, type a pair of addresses in `From` and `To`, and then click `Add`.

- To add a single IP address to the list, under `Edit`, type the same address in both `From` and `To`, and then click `Add`.
- To remove an IP address or address pair from the list, select it under `Internal IP ranges`, and then click `Remove`. When you are finished, click `OK`.
7. In Internet Service Manager, stop and restart the Web Proxy, WinSock Proxy, and Socks Proxy services for the changes to take effect on the server.

Backing Up and Restoring Server Configuration

Once you set all server configuration parameters you may want to back them up, to provide recovery. Additionally once you have the Proxy Server configuration backed up, you can restore it to a different server to provide an identical configuration. We already mentioned that you could backup and restore the Proxy Server configuration parameters using the `RemotMSP` command line utility. You can also back up and restore all server configuration parameters and store them locally in a text file using the graphical user interface.

To back up a server configuration

1. In Internet Service Manager (if you are using IIS 3.0) or Microsoft Management Console (if you are using IIS 4.0), double-click the computer name next to any of the Proxy Server services.
2. In the `Service Properties` dialog box, on the `Service` tab, click `Server Backup`. The Backup Dialog box appears (see Figure 5.18).

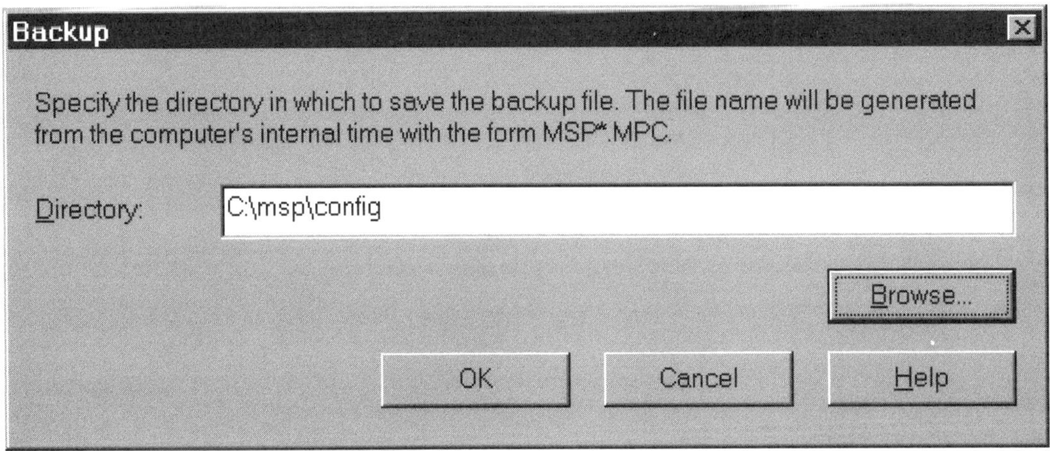

Figure 5.18 *Backing up the Proxy Server configuration.*

3. In the `Backup` dialog box, in `Directory`, type a valid path for the directory to store a new server backup file. Or, click `Browse` to display a listing of the local file system, and select an existing directory path from the list.
4. Click `OK` to start the backup.

By default, the backup file is located in C:\Msp\Config. The name of the file is `MSP`*yyyymmdd*`.mpc`, where *yyyy* is the year, `mm` is the month and `dd` is the day of backup.

You can save your configuration to any directory by specifying an alternative directory name in the Backup dialog box. It is recommended that you save server backup files to an NTFS disk partition for maximum security.

Once you have the Proxy Server configuration backed up, a server may be restored or rolled back to a previous configuration. You can perform partial configuration restore or full restore. A partial restore rolls back only non-computer-specific configuration parameters, such as user permissions or array membership information.

The following configuration parameters are *not* rolled back during a partial restore:

- Size and location of the Web Proxy service cache
- Location for all service logs and the packet filter log
- Packet filtering configuration
- Auto Dial configuration information
- Server alias used in the "Http Via" header for routing
- Server intra-array IP address(es)
- Proxy Server registry keys that cannot be configured through the user interface

During the full restore all configuration parameters that pertain to the server are restored. Note that you can choose to restore any server backup file. That means you can configure several identical Proxy Server computers by backing up one set of Proxy Server configuration parameters and restoring the configuration on another Proxy Server.

To restore a server configuration:

1. In Internet Service Manager (if you are using IIS 3.0) or Microsoft Management Console (if you are using IIS 4.0), double-click the computer name next to any of the Proxy Server services.

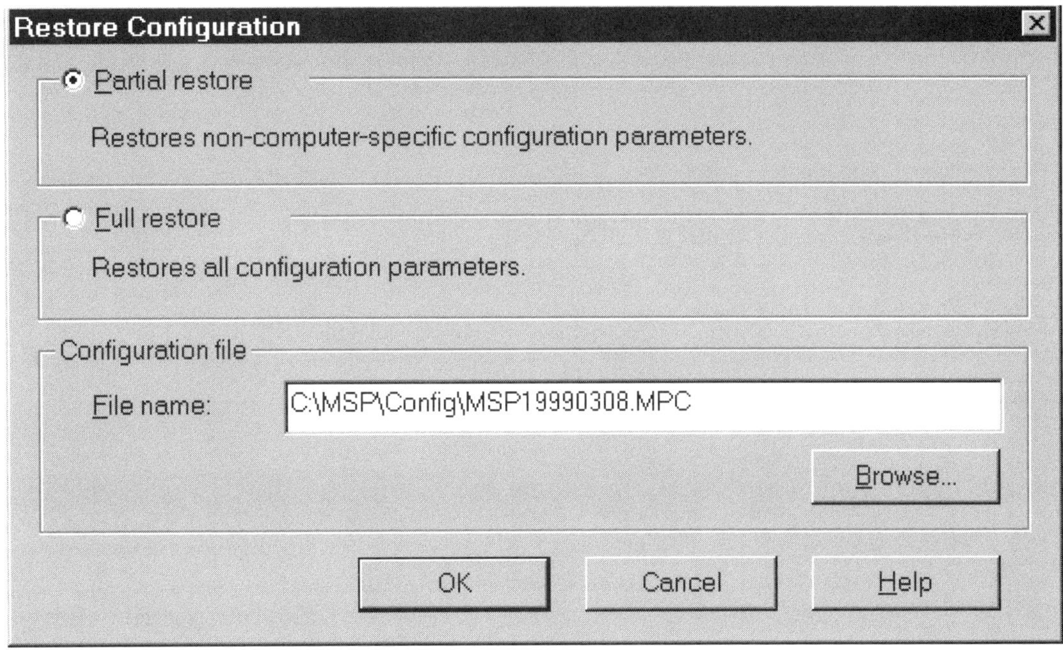

Figure 5.19 *Restoring Proxy Server configuration.*

2. In the `Service Properties` dialog box, on the `Service` tab, click `Server Restore`. The `Restore Configuration` dialog box appears (see Figure 5.19).

3. Do one of the following:

   • To restore only non-computer-specific server configuration parameters, click `Partial restore`.

   • To restore all server configuration parameters, click `Full restore`.

4. Under Configuration file, type a valid path for the location to the server backup file. Or, click `Browse` to display a listing of the local file system, and then select an existing path and file name from the list.

5. Click `OK` to start the restore.

MCSE 5.3   Managing the Web Proxy Service

We have just discussed the configuration parameters that are common for all three Proxy Server services. Now let's proceed to configuration parameters that are service-specific. There are six tabs that are used to configure the Web Proxy service parameters. Table 5.2 briefly explains the purpose of each tab.

Table 5.2 *Web Proxy Service Configuration Tabs*

Tab	Description
Services	Use this tab to specify non-service-specific parameters. Changing the properties on this tab will affect all Proxy Server services.
Permissions	Use this tab to give a user or group permission to use different Internet protocols, such as FTP and HTTP.
Caching	Use this tab to enable or disable the caching feature and to configure caching options.
Routing	This tab is used to configure the routing options if your Proxy Server is a member of Proxy Server chain or array. We will discuss Proxy Server chains and arrays in Chapter 7.
Publishing	Use this tab to configure reverse proxy and reverse hosting. This enables Proxy Server to respond to external requests.
Logging	Use this tab top configure Web Proxy service logging.

Web Proxy Permissions

The Permissions tab allows you to grant permission to use the Web Proxy service to users and groups of users. You can enable and disable permission access control by checking and clearing the `Enable Access Control` checkbox. If the `Enable Access Control` checkbox is cleared, everyone has permission to use the Web Proxy service. If you check the `Enable Access Control` checkbox, you must explicitly configure permissions to allow you users to use the Web Proxy service (see Figure 5.20).

Permissions are configured for each protocol individually. Permissions for the following protocols can be configured from the Permissions tab:

- FTP read
- WWW
- Secure
- Gopher

Note

Permissions for the HTTP and HTTPS protocols are the same. If a user is assigned permissions to the "WWW" protocol, he or she will have access to secure SSL Web (HTTPS) pages as well as to standard HTTP Web pages. If the user does not have permission to use the "WWW" protocol, he or she has access to neither the HTTP nor the HTTPS protocol. Permissions assigned to the "Secure" protocol are reserved for protocols that use secure ports other than port 443 (e.g., Snews).

To grant a specific user or group of users a permission to use a protocol:

1. Select a protocol from the Protocol list.
2. Click the `Edit` button.

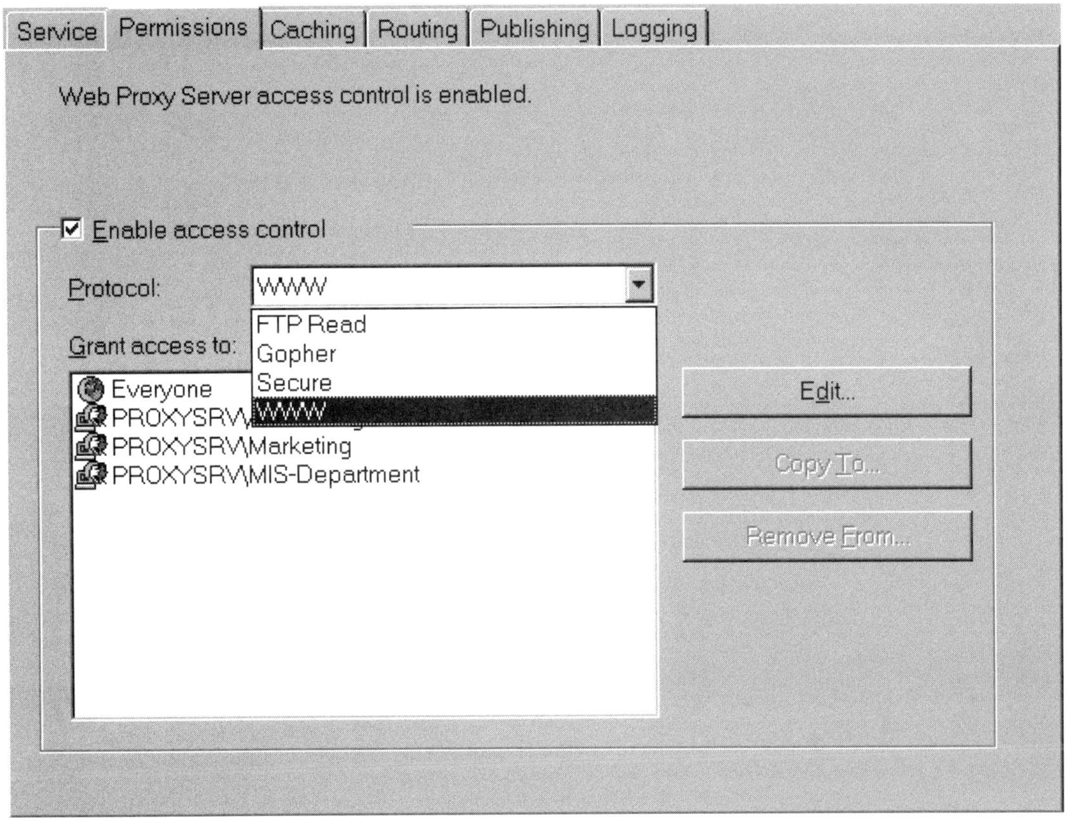

Figure 5.20   *Setting permissions to use Web Proxy Service.*

The `Protocol Permissions` dialog box appears showing you the Access Control List (ACL) (see Figure 5.21).

3. Edit the access control list by adding or removing users and groups from it.

Additionally you can use the `Copy To` and `Remove From` buttons to add the selected user or group permissions to another protocol or remove user and group permissions from the selected protocol.

You can use `User Manager for Domains` to create user groups containing all user accounts that need access to the Internet through the Web Proxy service. Then, for each protocol in the Permissions tab, you could apply permissions only once for the entire group, rather than for individual members. You can then assign access permissions by regulating the groups' membership.

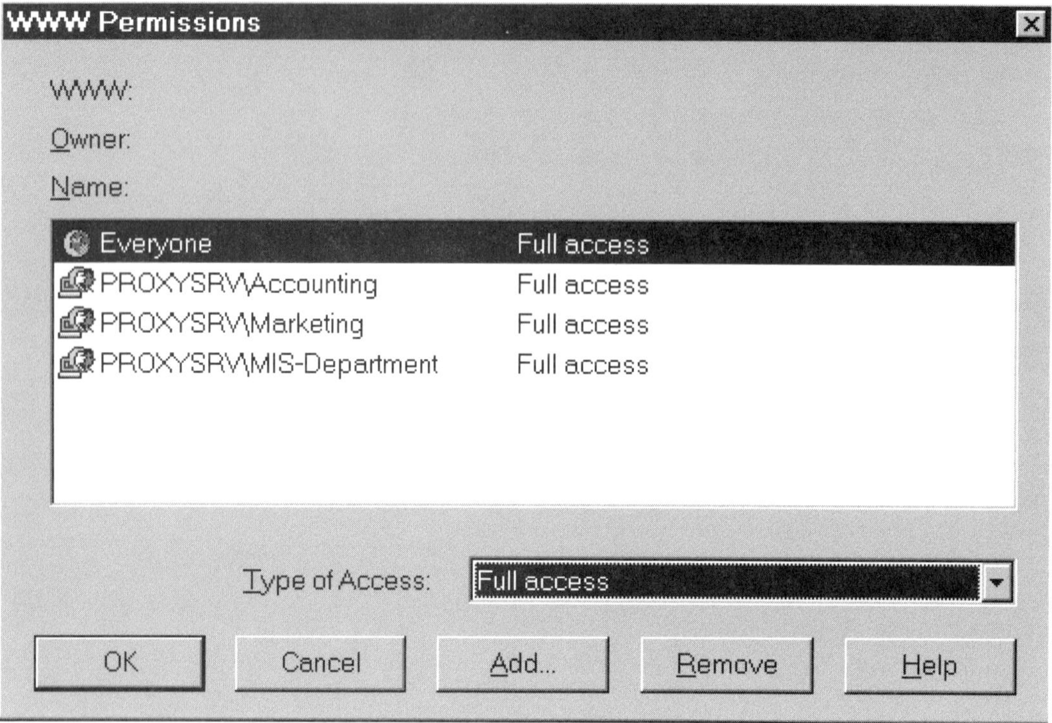

Figure 5.21   *Access control list for a specific protocol.*

Web Proxy Cache

As we discussed in Chapter 2, the Web Proxy service can use caching to store local copies of HTTP and FTP objects. All object types associated with a URL can be cached (except for those that are dynamically generated objects or objects obtained through a secured connection). Subsequent client requests for these objects can be serviced from an assigned cache disk drive rather than issuing a request over the Internet. This reduces bandwidth requirements on your Internet network connection and improves user response.

The Caching tab is used to enable or disable caching and to configure Web Proxy cache parameters. The Web Proxy cache can operate in two modes: active caching and passive caching. You can enable and disable either mode by checking and clearing the corresponding checkboxes in the Caching tab (see Figure 5.22).

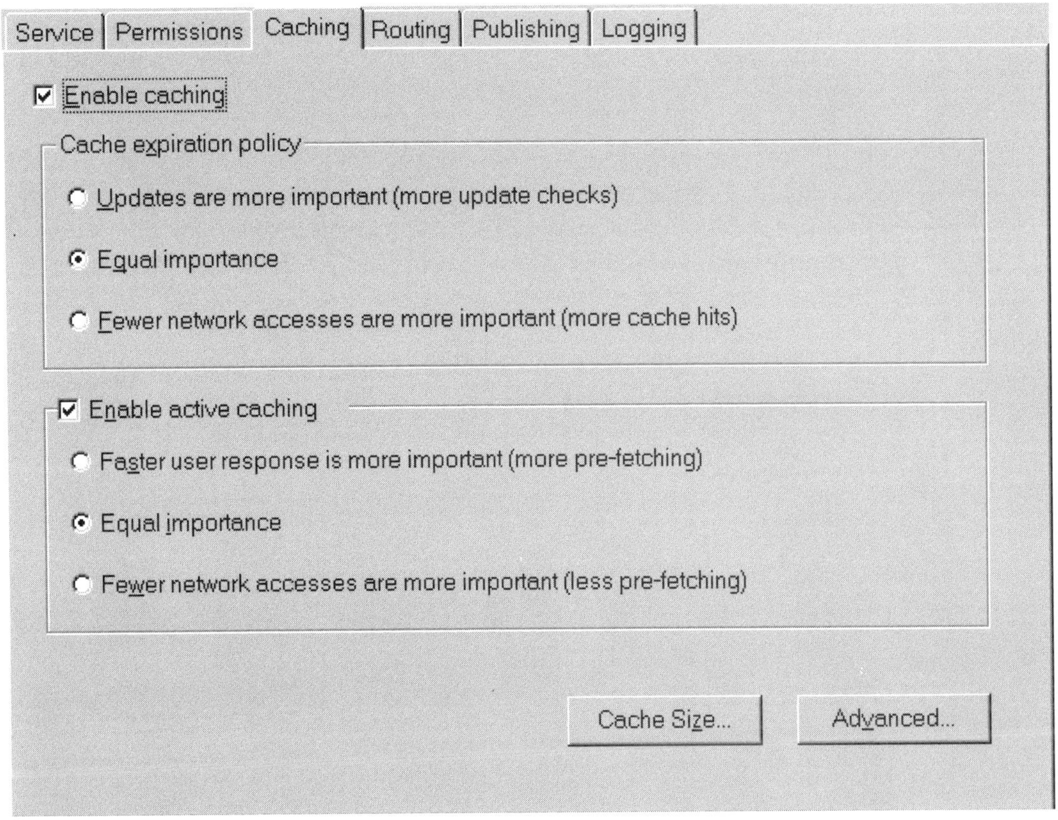

Figure 5.22 *Configuring Web Proxy caching properties.*

Note The controls on the `Caching` tab are unavailable unless you configured at least one disk drive on the server computer as an NTFS partition.

With passive caching, all cacheable objects returned to the Proxy Server by Internet servers are stored in the cache. In Chapter 2, when we discussed Proxy Server architecture, we stated that Proxy Server calculates a Time-To-Live (TTL) for all objects in the cache. When an object's TTL has expired, the next request for the object is serviced from the Internet instead of the cache.

If you enabled passive caching you have an option to select the cache expiration policy which specifies the freshness of objects in the cache. An object's freshness is a measure of how long a copy of an object in the cache is used in place of the object from the original Web site. You can set this option to make Proxy Server perform fewer Internet requests or update objects in cache more frequently.

With active caching, the freshness and availability of popular objects is automatically ensured by Proxy Server. Active caching automatically goes out to the Internet for an object (without client prompting) when the TTL has expired or is near expiration. Proxy Server performs active caching based on the object's popularity. Additionally, the active caching algorithm tries to refresh objects during times of low Proxy Server usage.

If you enable active caching you can customize its behavior. You can request more updates, thus ensuring that users will receive the most up to date information, or you can request fewer network accesses, thus saving the network bandwidth.

Active caching does not always work. If you are using the Proxy Server AutoDial feature, active caching is effectively disabled during the hours when AutoDial is not allowed.

Study Break

Setting Passive Caching and an Expiration Policy

1. In Internet Service Manager (if you are using IIS 3.0) or Microsoft Management Console (if you are using IIS 4.0), double-click the computer name next to any of the Proxy Server services.
2. In the `Service Properties` dialog box, click the `Caching` tab, and make sure the `Enable caching` checkbox is selected.
3. Under `Cache expiration policy`, do one of the following to set the freshness of objects in the cache:
   - To maintain the freshest cache data and therefore increase the amount of Internet traffic that the server generates, click `Updates are more important (more update checks)`.
   - For equal importance between the freshest cache data and the best cache performance, click `Equal importance`.
   - For more cache hits and therefore the best user response, click `Fewer network accesses are more important (more cache hits)`.

To set active caching: Click the `Enable active caching` check box and do one of the following:

- For the best cache performance and therefore the best user response, click `Faster user response is more important (more pre-fetching).`
- For equal importance between the freshest cache data and the best cache performance, click `Equal importance.`
- For the least Internet traffic on your server and therefore the stalest cache data, click `Fewer network accesses are more important (less pre-fetching).`

When you set up Proxy Server, you have the ability to specify the cache size and location. After Proxy Server is installed, the Web Proxy cache contains data and it should be administered only by using Internet Service Manager. Do not use the Proxy Server Setup program to change the cache properties after the Setup is completed. You can change the cache size and location after Proxy Server is installed by using the `Cache Size` button in the Caching tab.

You can increase or decrease the cache size, specify additional drives for caching, or even set the cache size to zero. If you decrease the cache size on a selected drive, some cached data on that drive may be deleted. You cannot control which data will be deleted from the cache. If you set the cache size for a selected drive to zero, all cached data is deleted and the cache is cleared. You can use this option to clear the cache. If you increase the cache size on a drive, there is no effect on the data already cached on that drive.

Study Break

Configuring the Cache Drives

1. In Internet Service Manager (if you are using IIS 3.0) or Microsoft Management Console (if you are using IIS 4.0), double-click the computer name next to any of the Proxy Server services.
2. In the `Web Proxy Service Properties` dialog box, click the `Caching` tab, and then click `Cache Size`.
3. To change the cache size on a particular drive, select the drive from the list, and do one of the following:
   - To increase the cache size, under `Cache Size for Selected Drive`, in `Maximum Size (MB)`, type a new value, and then click `Set`. The new value must be less than the value shown in `Total Size (MB)`.

- To decrease the cache size, under `Cache   Size   for   Selected   Drive`, in `Maximum Size (MB)`, type a new value, and then click `Set`.
- To stop storing cached data on the drive, under `Cache Size for Selected Drive`, in `Maximum Size (MB)`, type `0`, and then click `Set`.

4. Repeat step 3 for each cache drive you want to configure, and then click `OK`.

Each time the Web Proxy service starts, it performs a cache integrity check. This can take some time depending on the size of the cache and the number of objects in the cache. When the cache integrity check is in progress, it is not possible to configure the cache drives or cache size. If you try to do this, Proxy Server displays an error message.

If you click the `Advanced` button you can configure the advanced caching policy. You can, for example, limit the maximum size of cached objects, specify the objects' Time to Live (TTL), and create cache filters (see Figure 5.23).

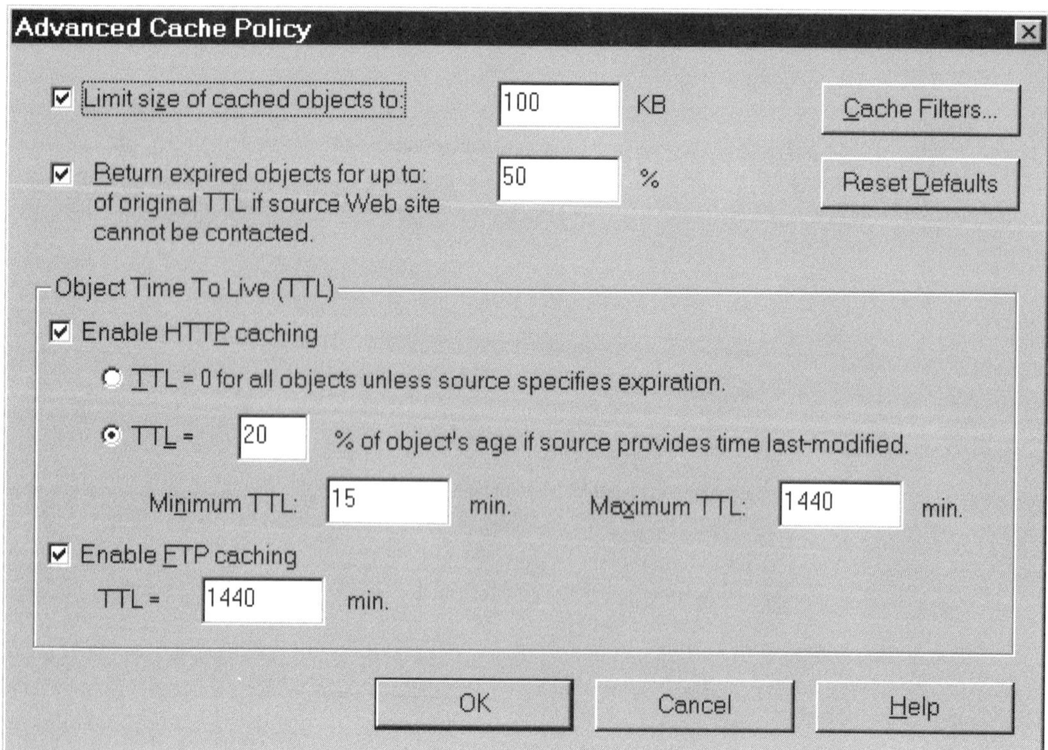

Figure 5.23   *Advanced cache policy.*

You have an option to configure the Web Proxy service to continue to use cached objects that have expired. An object expires when its TTL runs out. You can specify the time beyond an object's expiration that it can still be returned to a client. This can be useful when an expired object cannot be updated because contact can't be established with the source Internet server. Under this option, users will still receive information, but the information can be outdated. If the `Return expired objects for up to:` checkbox is cleared, the client does not receive the cached object if the Internet server is unavailable and the cached object has expired. This feature is enabled by default.

You can specify an object's TTL for both HTTP and FTP objects by checking the `Enable HTTP caching` and `Enable FTP caching` checkboxes.

The option "`TTL = 0 for all objects unless source specifies expiration`" specifies that there is no time limit for object expiration unless the Internet server provides one (i.e., object will not expire). `Option TTL = % of object's age if source provides time last modified` specifies a time span between object updates. If selected, you must enter values for `Minimum TTL` and `Maximum TTL`.

Depending on the values you enter for `TTL%`, `Minimum TTL`, and `Maximum TTL`, **Proxy Server may alter your** `Cache Expiration Policy` **settings (on the** `Caching` **tab) and may even disable the** `Cache Expiration Policy` **radio buttons.**

Another powerful option is to create a list of cache filters. This provides the ability to cache or not cache objects from specific Internet sites. You can specify cache filters by pressing the `Cache Filters` button in the `Advanced Cache Policy` dialog box (see Figure 5.24).

The `URL` column displays the URL to filter and the `Status` column specifies whether objects from the selected URL are cached. If the status is `Cached`, objects from that URL are always cached. If the status is `Not Cached`, objects from that URL are never cached. You can specify, for example, to deny caching of all Internet objects from a site, and then create another filter to re-enable caching of objects from a particular subtree of the site. In the example shown in Figure 5.24, no objects from the *www.microsoft.com* site will be cached except for those from the `train_cert` directory. You can use the `Add`, `Edit`, and `Remove` buttons to modify caching filters.

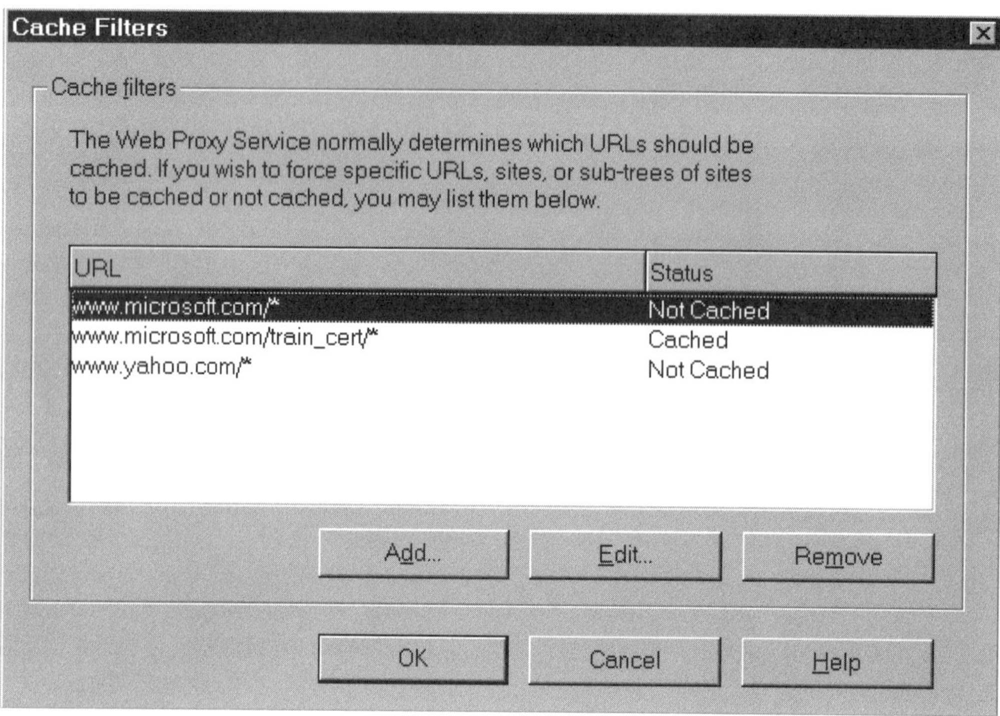

Figure 5.24 *Configuring caching filters.*

Study Break

Building the Cache Filter List

1. In Internet Service Manager (if you are using IIS 3.0) or Microsoft Management Console (if you are using IIS 4.0), double-click the computer name next to any of the Proxy Server services.
2. In the `Web Proxy Service Properties` dialog box, click the `Caching` tab, click `Advanced`, and then click `Cache Filters`.
3. To create a new cache filter, click `Add`. Or, to edit an existing cache filter, select the applicable filter in the list, and then click `Edit`.
4. In the `Cache Filter Properties` dialog box, in `URL`, type a URL to be filtered in one of the required forms.
5. Under `Filtering Status`, do one of the following:
   - To always cache Internet objects returned from the URL entered, click `Always cache`.
   - To prevent caching of Internet objects returned from the URL entered, click `Never cache`.

6. Click OK to return to the `Cache Filters` dialog box.
7. To delete a cache filter, select the applicable filter in the list, and then click `Remove`.
8. Repeat steps 3 through 7 as necessary to build the cache filter list, and then click OK.

Proxy Server also can use a cache distributed across multiple Proxy Server computers, which are connected in arrays and in chains. This can greatly improve client performance and reduce Internet-bound traffic on your network. We will discuss this feature in Chapter 7 when we discuss Proxy Server arrays and chains.

Web Proxy Routing

You can use the `Routing` tab to direct your clients' requests for Internet objects. You can route requests through an array, to upstream Proxy Servers, or directly to the Internet. We will thoroughly discuss these options in Chapter 7.

Web Publishing through Proxy Server

As we said in previous chapters, Proxy Server not only allows internal clients to connect to external servers, but also provides a way to publish information to the Internet. For the purpose of this discussion, the word "publishing" is defined as publishing to external Internet clients. In other words "publishing" refers to placing documents on a Web server so they can be reached by anyone with Web access. When you publish on the Internet using a Web server, you can potentially compromise your network security. Publishing could also increase the exposure of your internal network to Internet.

Instead of exposing your company Web server directly to the Internet and thus compromising your network security, you can configure Proxy Server to respond to incoming requests from external Web clients by discarding the requests or sending them to a local or internal Web server. In this configuration, Proxy Server impersonates an internal Web server to the outside world. You can configure Proxy Server so multiple computers located in your internal network can publish to the Internet.

Although it is possible to have a Web server that publishes information to the Internet running on the same computer with Proxy Server, using the Proxy Server computer for web publishing is not recommended for security and performance reasons. Rather, you should use a computer (or computers) in your internal network to run IIS for Web publishing and let hosts on the external network access it (them) *through* the Proxy Server computer's Reverse Hosting and Reverse Proxy features.

REVERSE PROXYING AND HOSTING

Microsoft Proxy Server 2.0 includes both reverse proxying and reverse hosting as a means of mitigating the concerns associated with publishing to the Internet. The use of these features permit robust Web publishing while not compromising network security or publishing flexibility. You can set up reverse proxying and reverse hosting on the `Publishing` tab (see Figure 5.25).

Reverse proxying is the ability of Proxy Server to listen to incoming requests for an internal Web server computer and respond on behalf of that server. Reverse proxying can be thought of as "inverse chaining," in that a request is forwarded *downstream* to the Web server located behind the Proxy Server computer. The term reverse is used because the Proxy Server forwards requests backwards from the Internet to the internal network, which is reverse of the usual forwarding requests from internal clients to the Internet (see Figure 5.26).

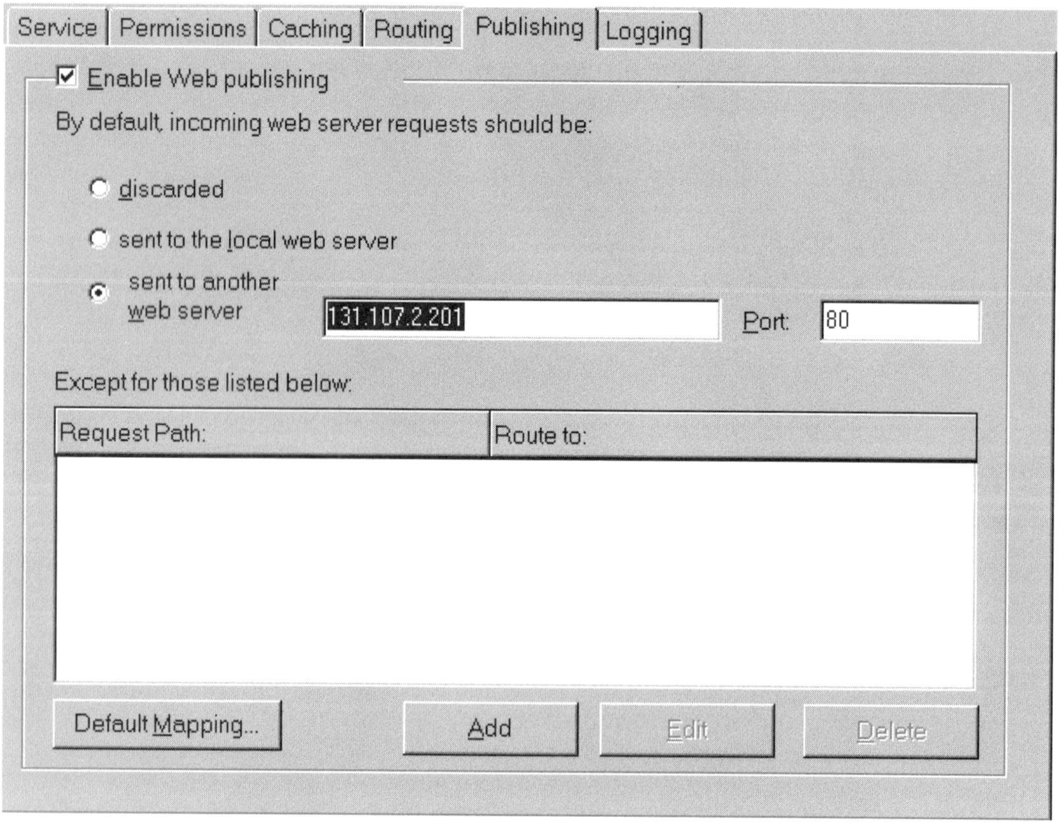

Figure 5.25 *Reverse proxying and reverse hosting is set on the publishing tab.*

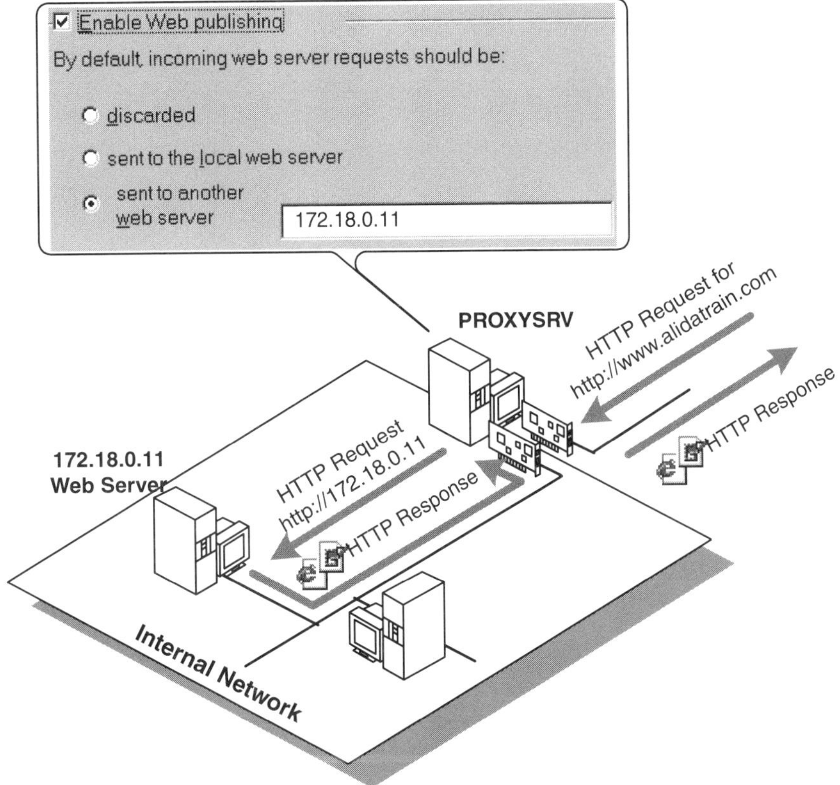

Figure 5.26 *Reverse proxying.*

For example, you configure Proxy Server to provide reverse proxying and set it to forward all incoming Web requests to the local server that has the IP address 172.18.0.11. When an Internet request is received, Proxy Server issues a query to the internal server and requests the document from it. After the document is received, Proxy Server sends it to the Internet client. The client can only see that the document came from the Proxy Server computer, and thus internal network security is not compromised. Additionally, you do not have to reconfigure the internal Web server to participate in reverse proxying. The only requirement is that the internal Web server is able to speak with the Proxy Server. It is important to note that the external client has to connect to the Proxy Server but not to the internal Web server. In the context of Figure 5.26, this means *www.alidatrain.com* should be resolved to one of the Proxy Server's IP addresses (preferably an external one).

Another technology, called reverse hosting, takes publishing to the next logical step by maintaining a list of internal servers that can publish to the Internet. This feature allows Proxy Server to listen and respond on behalf of multiple servers located behind it. In other words, under reverse hosting, Proxy Server maintains a mapping table to allow multiple server computers to securely publish to the Internet by means of a single IP address. As with Reverse Proxying, the process is transparent to the Internet client. There is no indication that the request is being passed to an internal server (see Figure 5.27).

When you configure publishing parameters, set an overall policy first, and then set exceptions to the policy (see Figure 5.28). Exceptions are displayed in the `Except` list.

The listed entries display the incoming URL request and what the URL is mapped to. When Proxy Server receives the request from an Internet

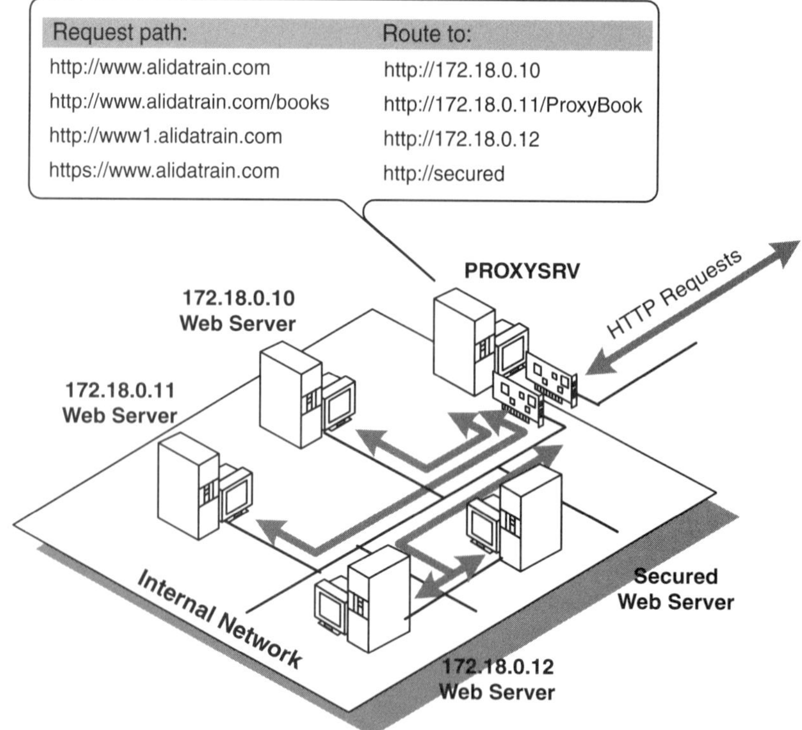

Figure 5.27 *Reverse hosting.*

Figure 5.28 *Reverse hosting configuration.*

client, it evaluates the HTTP header and finds the URL to which the request is destined. Based on the information extracted from the HTTP header URL, Proxy Server uses the exception list to forward the request to the appropriate internal Web server.

Older Web clients might not specify which Web server to request content from. Type the default server name in `Default Local Host Name` (click on the `Default Mapping` button), for clients that do not supply this information.

As in previous Proxy Server areas, in order to make the configuration work properly you must have DNS entries for the internal Web servers pointing to the Proxy Server's external IP address. Doing this ensures the client will request documents from the Proxy Server computer, not directly from the internal Web server.

Study Break

Configuring Publishing Parameters

1. In Internet Service Manager (if you are using IIS 3.0) or Microsoft Management Console (if you are using IIS 4.0), double-click the computer name next to any of the Proxy Server services.
2. In the `Web Proxy Service Properties` dialog box, click the `Publishing` tab.
3. Select the `Enable Web Publishing` checkbox, and do one of the following:
   - To ignore all incoming Web server requests, click `Discarded`.
   - To forward incoming Web server requests to the Proxy Server's Web publishing service and to enable listening, click `Sent to the local Web server`.
   - To forward incoming Web server requests to a specific internal computer, and enable listening on the Proxy Server computer, click `Sent to another Web server`, and type a valid server name and port number.
4. To set the default Web server host, click `Default Mapping`. In the `Default Host` dialog box, type the default host name of the Proxy Server computer, and then click `OK`.
5. To edit a reverse host route, under `Except for those listed below`, select the route, click `Edit`, modify the settings in the `Reverse Host Route` dialog box, click `OK`, and then click `OK` again.
6. To remove a reverse host route, in `Except for those listed below`, select the route, click `Remove`, and then click `OK`.
7. Click `Apply`, and then click `OK`.

You can use the following procedure to create a reverse host route for Web publishing. You create a reverse host route by mapping an incoming URL to a specific internal computer.

To create a reverse host route:

1. In Internet Service Manager (if you are using IIS 3.0) or Microsoft Management Console (if you are using IIS 4.0), double-click the computer name next to any of the Proxy Server services.
2. In the `Web Proxy Service Properties` dialog box, click the `Publishing` tab, verify that the `Enable Web Publishing` checkbox is selected, and then click `Add`.
3. In the `Mapping` dialog box, under `Send Web Server request for`, in `Path`, type a valid URL beginning with http:// or https://.
4. Under `To this URL`, in `URL`, type a valid URL for the Proxy Server to send the request to. Begin the URL with http:// or https://

5. Click OK, click `Apply`, and then click OK again.
   Note that you must have appropriate name resolution methods configured if you are using names instead of IP addresses.

USING THE HTTPS FOR INTERNET PUBLISHING

In some cases you it is necessary to implement secured publishing (HTTPS) from your internal Web server to the Internet. Proxy Server allows you to use the Secured Sockets Layer (SSL) for Internet publishing. You have several options to do this. One of them is reverse proxying.

To implement an HTTPS connection from the Proxy Server to the Internet client you must install a valid SSL certificate on the WWW service of the Proxy Server computer. The reverse proxy connection between the Proxy Server and the internal web server will be still sent in unencrypted form by default (See Figure 5.29)

This is not likely a big concern since you usually trust your internal users. If, however, you wish to have an encrypted connection between the

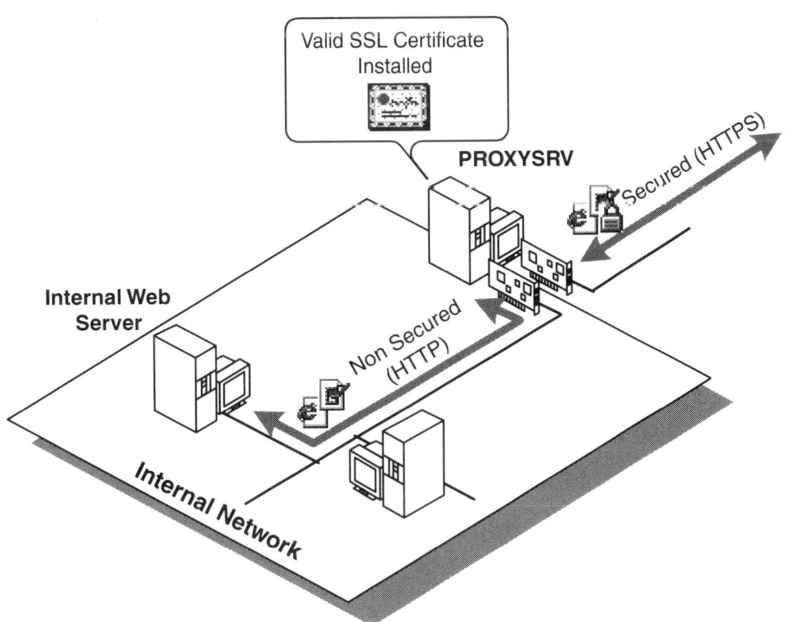

Figure 5.29 *Reverse proxying using HHTPS.*

internal web server and the Proxy Server, you can effect this by installing another SSL certificate on the internal Web server. In this case, the reverse proxy connection must be set to connect to the internal Web server via the secure port 443. This procedure has a very big disadvantage: because the proxy server must decrypt and encrypt transfers on both sides, overhead is significantly increased and performance suffers dramatically.

Finally, if you are using packet filtering with secured publishing, you will have to create a filter for port 443 to enable access. Packet filtering will be discussed in Chapter 6.

Reverse proxying and reverse hosting offer great flexibility and enhanced security. Using these technologies, you can make any computer on your internal network publish to the Internet (provided it is running an HTTP server application, such as Internet Information Server). Security is not compromised because all requests pass through Proxy Server first, which acts like a single point of connection to the Internet. An added bonus to the Internet user is that of enhanced performance. Since Proxy Server caches objects, the next time the same URL is requested, Proxy Server fetches and returns the object from its cache.

If you implement reverse proxying on your Windows NT computer with Service Pack 3 installed, you may notice that caching does not work under reverse proxying. You may need to install Windows NT 4.0 Service Pack 4 to correct this problem. For more information see Knowledge base article Q177906.

Before you implement reverse proxying or reverse hosting in your production environment, you should test all Web publishing content and links to ensure compatibility with Proxy Server 2.0. While Proxy Server is compatible with most Web publishing content, if your content is using the HTTP 302 redirect messages, some of the functions might not work. If this is the case, you can use server proxying instead.

Configuring Logs

Microsoft Proxy Server has three service logs that record events generated by the Web Proxy, WinSock Proxy, and Socks Proxy services. Proxy Server has also a separate log for packet filtering that records network packet traffic-related events. All log information can be written to a text file or in an ODBC-compliant database table (such as Microsoft® Access or Microsoft® SQL Server). Log data contains client information, connection information, server information, and information about objects being accessed.

By default, all information is logged to a text file. After installing Proxy Server, you can set configuration parameters for either logging to a text file or logging to a database. You can also choose between two log formats — regular or verbose. Regular format generates logs smaller in size but these logs will contain a reduced number of information fields for log entries. For the verbose format, all available information is logged. Alternatively, you can turn logging off — but this is considered as an unsecured operating condition. It is recommended that Proxy Server logs are enabled and the logged data reviewed carefully and regularly.

Why would you choose between regular logging and verbose logging? Generally, if you have limited disk space, you should use regular logging. If your disk space is not limited or you are planning to log information to a database for further analysis, use verbose logging. You may want to store log data and the Web Proxy service cache on different disk volumes to prevent the disk from filling up. If you put your logs on the same volume where the Web Proxy cache resizes, the cache may be affected when logs become full.

Web Proxy service log configuration can be done in the `Logs` tab on the `Web Proxy service properties` dialog box (see Figure 5.30).

To enable Web Proxy service logs, check the `Enable logging using` checkbox. By default, the regular logging format is selected. You can select verbose format for verbose logging. To select the log type, choose either `Log to file` or `Log to SQL/ODBC database` option.

LOGGING TO A TEXT FILE

If you chose to log to the text file you can configure the log file directory by selecting the path in the `Log file directory` box. The actual name given to text-file logs depends on how logging is configured. You have an option to configure logging to create a new log each day, week, or month. When a new log file is started, the old log file is closed and you can archive it for future analysis. The text-file logs for the Web Proxy service can take the following forms:

- W3*yymmdd*.log for daily logs
- W3W*yymmw*.log for weekly logs
- W3M*yymm*.log for monthly logs

where:

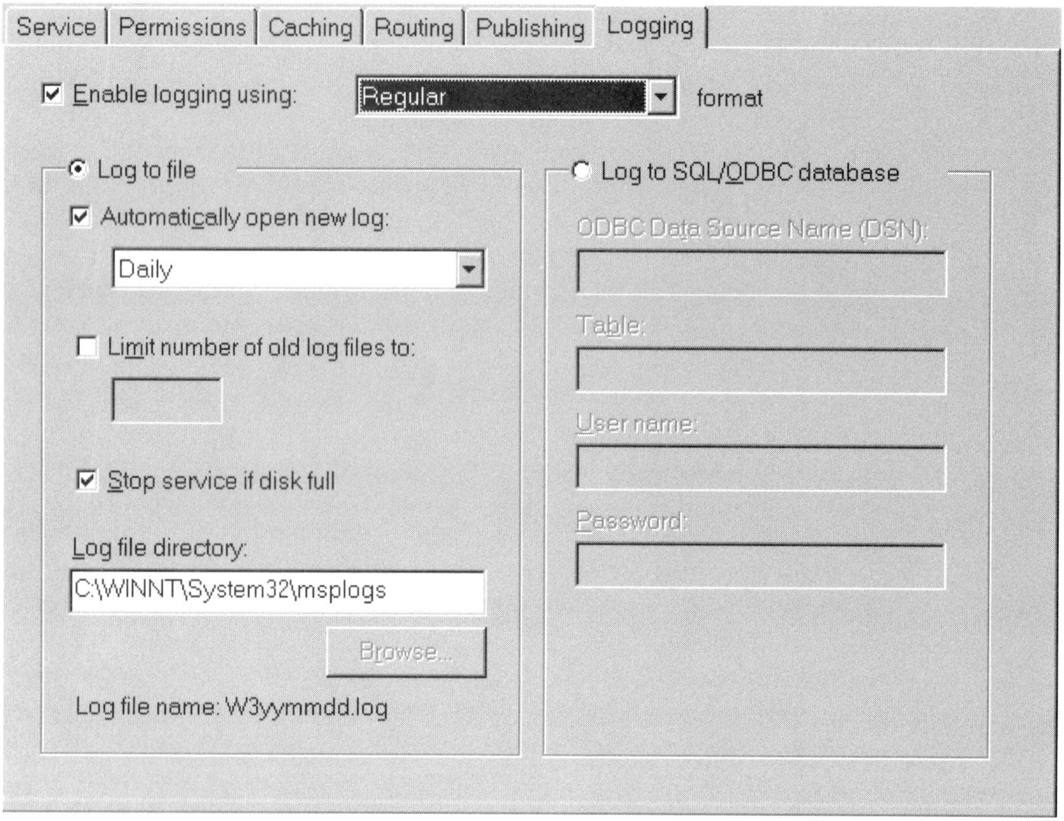

Figure 5.30 *Configuring Web Proxy Server logs.*

yy is a number between 00 and 99 indicating the year.
mm is a number between 01 and 12 indicating the month.
dd is a number between 01 and 31 indicating the day of the month.
w is a number between 1 and 5 indicating the week of the month.

Additionally, you can set the number of log files that are stored on the hard drive by checking the `Limit number of old logs to` box and specifying the maximum number of log files. You can also force the Web Proxy service to stop when the disk with log files becomes full. To do this, check the `Stop service if disk full` checkbox. By doing so, you ensure that no Web Proxy service event will go unnoticed. Once the Web Proxy service is stopped because the log files are full, you may need to remove files from the hard drive before you can restart the service.

You can use different parsing tools and spreadsheet programs such as Microsoft Excel to parse the text logs and create reports. Remember that in the Proxy log files, a single comma separates log fields, so each comma in a log file entry should be used to force a field break to occur.

Study Break

Logging to a Text File

1. In Internet Service Manager (if you are using IIS 3.0) or Microsoft Management Console (if you are using IIS 4.0), double-click the computer name next to any of the Proxy Server services.
2. In the `Web Proxy Service Properties` dialog box, click the `Logging` tab.
3. Make sure the `Enable logging using` checkbox is selected, and click either `Regular` or `Verbose` from the drop-down list.
4. Make sure the `Log to file` option is selected.
5. If you want to use the same Proxy log file continuously, click to clear the `Automatically open new log` checkbox.
6. If you select the `Limit number of old logs to` checkbox, type a numeric value in the box provided.
7. If you want the applicable service to halt if the log disk is full, click the `Stop all services if disk full` checkbox.
8. Review and, if appropriate, change the log file directory in `Log file directory`, and then click `OK`. Or, click `Browse` to display a listing of the local file system, click the path and file name you want, and then click `OK`.

LOGGING TO A DATABASE

As an alternative to storing Proxy Server logs in text files, you can log to any ODBC-compliant database, such as Microsoft SQL Server or Microsoft Access. Open Database Connectivity (ODBC) technology provides a common interface for accessing heterogeneous databases — it provides an open, vendor-neutral way of accessing data stored in a variety of databases

Configuring Proxy Server to log information to the ODBC-compliant database is a little bit more complex than configuring logging to a text file. To set up logging information to an ODBC-compliant database, you must complete the following steps:

1. Install the database application.
2. Install the ODBC driver for the database you are using.
3. Create a system Data Source Name (system DSN) for the database.

4. Create a table in your database application with the necessary fields.
5. Configure the log for the database.

The first step is installing the database application. You can install the database on the computer running Proxy Server or on a remote server. For example, you can use Microsoft SQL Server or Microsoft Access as your database application. See your product documentation for specific installation procedures.

The second step is to install the ODBC driver on the Proxy Server computer. An ODBC driver must be installed before you can use database logging options with Proxy Server. You can use the Internet Information Server Setup to install ODBC drivers.

You can use Microsoft Access to install the Microsoft Access ODBC driver. Proxy Server requires the 32-bit ODBC drivers shipped with Microsoft Office 95 or later, Professional Edition and Microsoft Access for Windows 95 or later. The ODBC driver for Microsoft Access version 2.0 does not work with Proxy Server.

The next step is to create a system DSN. ODBC uses the system DSN as a logical name to refer to the driver. After the ODBC driver for your database is installed, a unique system DSN must be added for database logging. To create the system DSN use the `ODBC32` icon in `Control Panel`.

You can also create a system DSN remotely by using a Web browser and an HTML file provided by Internet Information Server (IIS). For more information, read Internet Information Server documentation.

The next step you should do is to create a database table. Table elements such as data types and field names must be appropriately defined for the database application you are using. Fortunately, there are two sample SQL database table template files provided with Proxy Server. They are installed by Setup to *C:\Winnt\help\proxy\misc* on your Proxy Server computer. The *Msp.sql file* can be used for creating a database table for the Web Proxy, WinSock Proxy, or Socks Proxy services. Another file — *Pf.sql* can be used to create a database table for packet filtering. You can use these template files with Microsoft SQL Server or with Microsoft Access.

You can use the following procedure to create a database table in Microsoft Access using a database template file:

1. Start Access and open the database you previously created for Proxy Server logging.
2. On the `Queries` tab, click `New` to create a new query.
3. In the `New Query` dialog box, on the View menu, click `Design`, and then click `OK`.
4. In the `Show Table` dialog box, on the View menu, click `SQL View`, and then delete any text present in `Query`.
5. Open the template file *Msp.sql* in the notepad and copy and paste the entire contents of the file in `Query`, click `Save`, and then click `OK`.
6. Double-click the query you just saved. Click `Yes` in any pop-up message boxes.
7. Rename the Microsoft Access table for use with a particular Proxy Server service.

The same table format is used for regular and verbose logging formats. When regular logging format is selected, some fields are not used and remain empty.

Finally, when the preceding steps have been completed, you can configure Proxy Server for database logging in the Web Proxy service properties `Logging` tab.

Study Break

Installing an ODBC Driver

1. Click `Start`, point to `Programs`, point to `Microsoft Internet Server (Common)`, and then click `Internet Information Server Setup`.
2. Click `OK`, click `Add/Remove`, and then click `OK` again.
3. Select the `ODBC Drivers and Administration` checkbox, and then click `OK`.
4. In the `Install Drivers` dialog box, click the appropriate driver in `Available ODBC Drivers` (Access, SQL Server, etc.), and then click `OK`.

To create a system Data Source Name:

1. Click `Start`, point to `Settings`, click `Control Panel`, and click the `ODBC` icon.

2. In the `ODBC Data Source Administrator` dialog box, click the `System DSN` tab, and then click `Add`.
3. In the `Create New Data Source` dialog box, click an ODBC driver, and then click `Finish`.
4. In the dialog box specific to your driver, in `DSN`, type the Data Source Name.
5. Type the appropriate information to configure the remaining DSN parameters.
6. Click `Options` and, in `Database Name`, type a database name.
7. Click `OK`, and then click `OK` again.

To set Web Proxy service logging log to a database:

1. In Internet Service Manager (if you are using IIS 3.0) or Microsoft Management Console (if you are using IIS 4.0), double-click the computer name next to any of the Proxy Server services.
2. In the `Web Proxy Service Properties` dialog box, click the `Logging` tab.
3. Make sure the `Enable logging using` checkbox is selected, and click either `Regular` or `Verbose` from the drop-down list.
4. Click `Log to SQL/ODBC Database`.
5. In ODBC `Data Source Name (DSN)`, type the system DSN you created for the database that you will be logging to. In `Table`, type the name of the table that you will be logging to. In `User name` and `Password`, type a user name and password that are valid for the database.
6. Click `Apply`, and then click `OK`.

INTERPRETING THE WEB PROXY LOGS

Logs are useless when you do not review them. Table 5.3 presents the logging table field names and a brief description of each field. Items marked with an asterisk are available in verbose mode only.

Table 5.3 *Log File Field Descriptions*

Field Name	Description
Client IP Address	The IP address name of the client computer initiating a proxy request.
Client User Name	The Windows NT logon account name for the current user on the client computer initiating the service request
*Client Agent	For the Web Proxy service, indicates specialized header information from the client browser to use when processing the proxy request.
*Authentication Status	This indicates whether or not the service request is using an authenticated client connection to Proxy Server. (Y or N)
Log Date	The date the logged event occurred
Log Time	The time the logged event occurred.

Table 5.3 Continued

Field Name	Description
Service Name	The name of the active service being logged. "W3Proxy" indicates Web Proxy service logging, "WSProxy" indicates WinSock Proxy service logging, and "SOCKS" indicates Socks Proxy service logging.
*Proxy Name	The name of the computer running Proxy Server.
*Referring Server Name	In chained Proxy Server configurations, the name of the downstream Proxy Server computer that routed the request to the upstream Proxy Server computer.
Destination Host Name	The domain name for the remote computer servicing the current connection. For the Web Proxy service, a hyphen (-) in this field may indicate that an object was sourced from the Web Proxy Server cache and not from the destination.
*Destination IP Address	The network IP address for the remote computer servicing the current connection. For the Web Proxy service, a hyphen (-) in this field may indicate that an object was sourced from the Web Proxy Server cache and not from the destination.
Destination Port	The reserved port number on the remote computer servicing the current connection. This is used by the client application initiating the request.
*Processing Time	This indicates the total time in milliseconds needed by Proxy Server to process the current connection. It measures elapsed server time from when the server first received the request to the time when final processing occurred on the server (results were returned to the client and the connection was closed). Note that for cache requests processed through the Web Proxy service, processing time measures the elapsed server time needed to fully process a client request and return an object from the server's cache to the client.
*Bytes Sent	The number of bytes sent to the remote computer during the current connection. The use of a hyphen (-) or the use of a zero or negative number in this field indicates that this information was not provided by the remote computer, or that no bytes were sent to the remote computer.
*Bytes Received	The number of bytes received from the remote computer during the current connection. The use of a hyphen (-) or the use of a zero or negative number in this field indicates that this information was not provided by the remote computer, or that no bytes were received from the remote computer.
Protocol Name	Specifies the protocol used for transfer (such as HTTP, FTP, or Gopher).
*Transport	This field is always TCP for the Web Proxy Service because that's what the Web Proxy Service uses (the same field for the WinSock Proxy Service may show TCP/IP, UDP, or IPX/SPX).
*Operation	Specifies the current HTTP method used. Possible values are GET, PUT, POST, and HEAD.
Object Name	For the Web Proxy service, this field shows the contents of the URL request.
*Object MIME	The Multipurpose Internet Mail Extensions (MIME) type for the current object. This field may also be filled with a hyphen (-) to indicate that this field is not used, or that a valid MIME type was not defined or supported by the remote computer
Object Source	Indicates the source used to retrieve the current object, as shown in the following table.
Result Code	This field can be used to indicate either a Windows (Win32) error code (for values less than 100), an HTTP status code (values between 100 and 1,000), or a Windows Sockets error code (for values between 10,000 and 11,004).
Cache Information	Indicates whether the object was cached (1 cached, 0 not cached).

MCSE 5.4   Managing WinSock Proxy Service

From previous chapters you know that WinSock Proxy service is used by Windows applications that use Windows Sockets to communicate. WinSock Proxy service allows an application that is Windows-Sockets-compatible to work as if it were directly connected to the Internet. Windows Sockets applications make an API call in order to communicate with the Internet. The WinSock Proxy client software redirects these APIs to the WinSock Proxy service on the Proxy Server computer, thus establishing a communication to the Internet through the Proxy Server. When a request is made by a WinSock client, the Internet request is accomplished virtually by the Proxy Server, using its external (Internet) IP address as the source IP address.

In addition to what WinSock Proxy service does, you have several options to control its functionality by specifying different settings in the WinSock Proxy service properties dialog box. The WinSock Proxy properties dialog box has four tabs: Services, Protocols, Permissions, and Logging (see Figure 5.31).

The purpose of these tabs is described in Table 5.4.

The Services tab is common to each Proxy Server service. Since we thoroughly covered it in the previous section, we'll not repeat it here. Additionally, the logging tab for the WinSock Proxy service has the same configuration settings as that for the Web Proxy service, which we just discussed. The only logging difference is the WinSock Proxy log file name: WS*yymmdd*.log for daily logs, WSW*yymmw*.log for weekly logs, and WSM*yymm*.log for monthly logs. In this section, we'll study only the WinSock service-specific tabs: Protocols and Permissions.

Configuring WinSock Service Protocols

The Protocols tab is used to configure protocol definitions. Protocol definitions determine which WinSock applications can be used to access the Internet. For each protocol, you can define which ports can be used for outbound and inbound connections. You can configure existing protocol definitions, create new protocol definitions, and delete unwanted protocol definitions. By defining and using WinSock Proxy service protocols, you can regulate WinSock access to the Internet (see Figure 5.32).

Proxy Server Setup installs a large set of predefined protocol definitions for the WinSock Proxy service. In most cases these protocol definitions are enough to provide Internet access for the most popular client applications. You are not limited to these predefined protocol definitions, however,

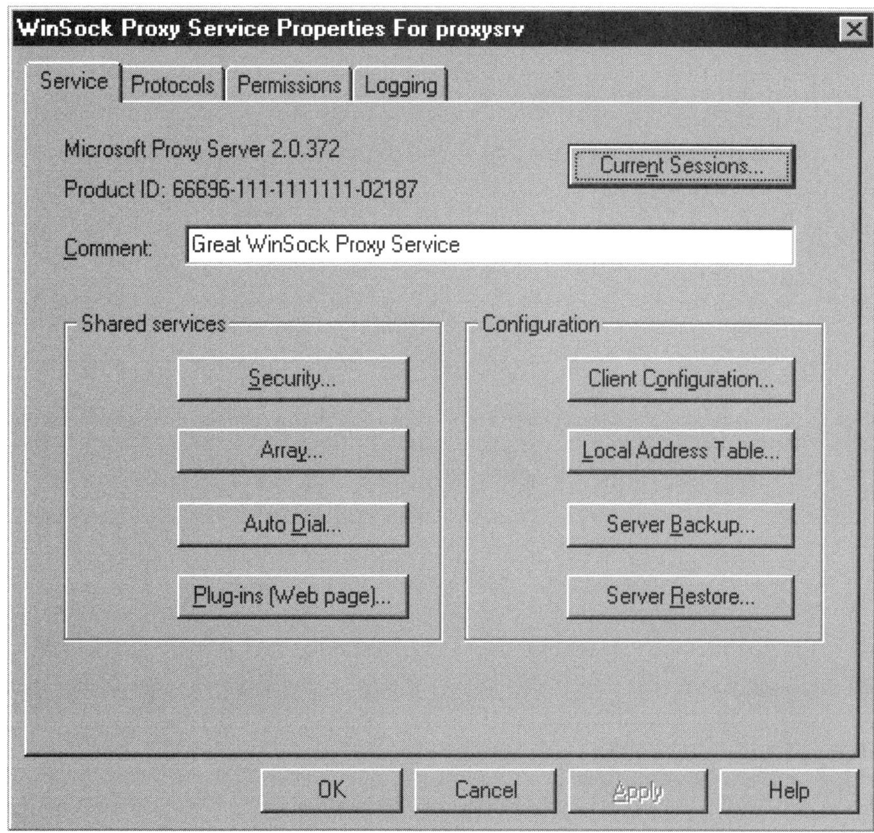

Figure 5.31 *WinSock Proxy service properties.*

Table 5.4 *WinSock Proxy Service Configuration Tabs*

Tab	Description
Services	You can use this tab to specify non-service-specific parameters. Changing the properties on this tab will affect all Proxy Server services
Protocols	Is used to determine which Windows Sockets applications will be allowed access to the Internet through the WinSock Proxy service.
Permissions	Use this tab to give a user or group permission to use different protocols, with the WinSock Proxy service.
Logging	Use this tab to configure WinSock Proxy service logging.

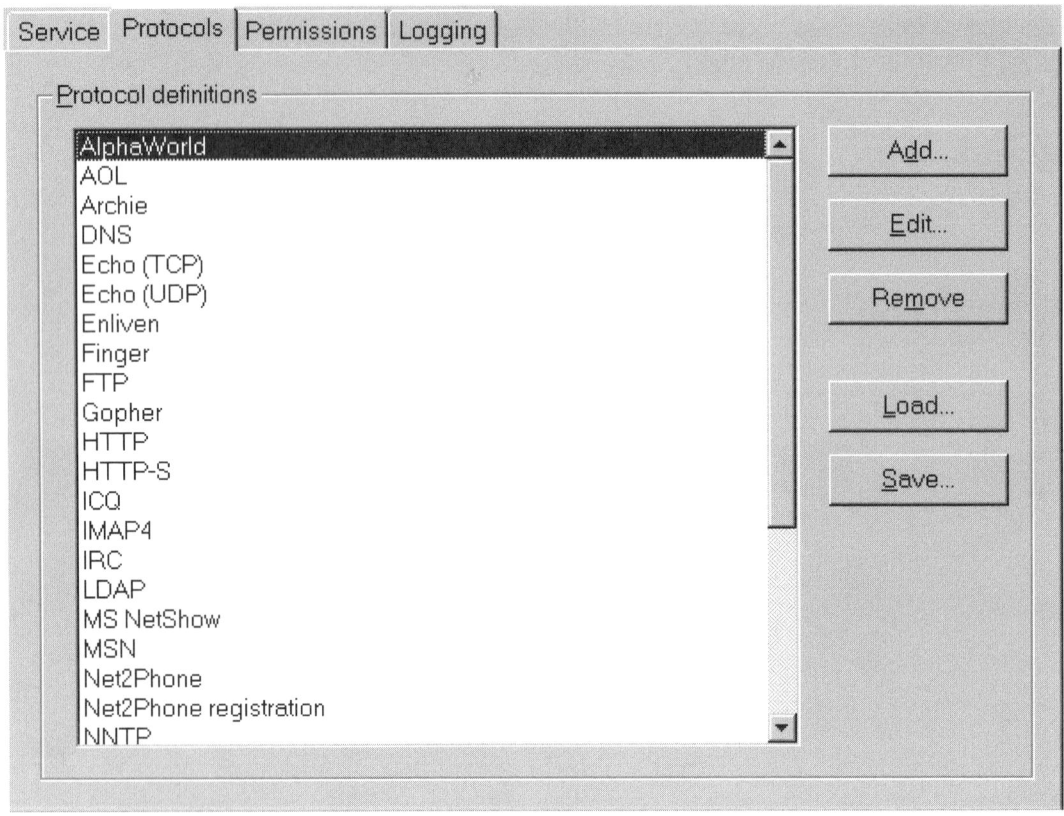

Figure 5.32   *WinSock Proxy service protocols tab.*

nor are you restricted to Windows Sockets applications that work with these predefined protocol definitions. You use the `Protocols` tab to add protocol definitions that support additional Windows Sockets applications.

Use the `Add`, `Edit` and `Remove` buttons to add, modify, and remove protocol definitions. If you press the `Add` button, the `Protocol definition` dialog box appears (see Figure 5.33).

The `Protocol name` box provides a space for you to type the name of a protocol definition to add to the WinSock Proxy service. The `Initial connection` box defines the connection parameters for the WinSock Proxy service. Specify the port number that is used for initial connection, the type of the transport protocol used (TCP or UDP), and the connection direction (inbound or outbound). An inbound connection allows external sites to initiate connections to clients through the selected port. An outbound connection allows internal clients to initiate connections to external sites.

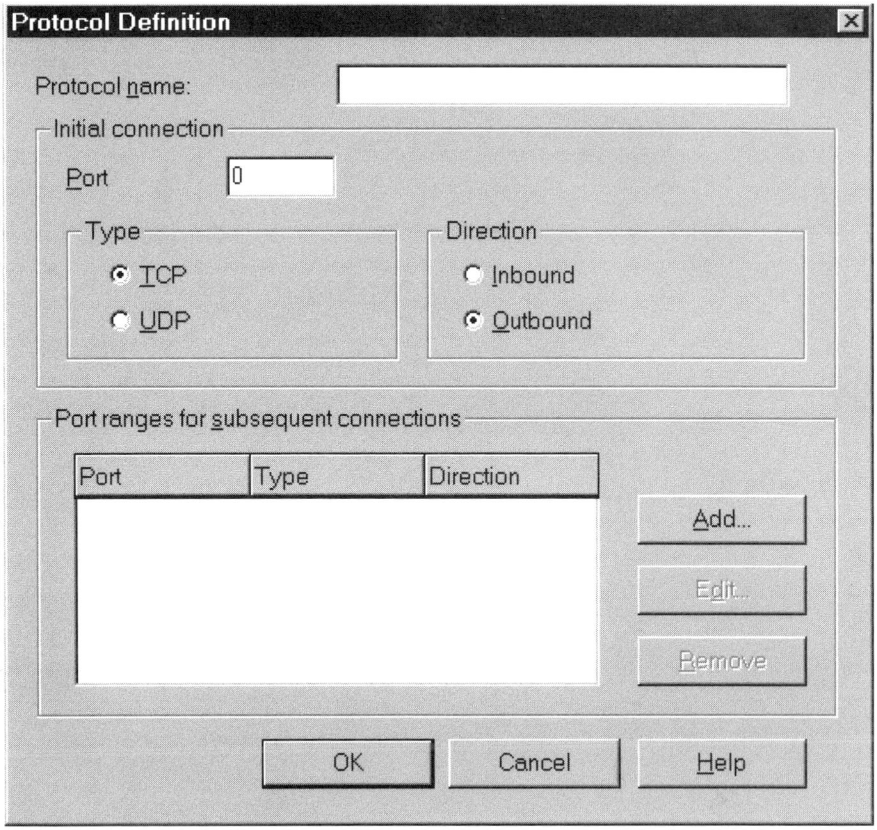

Figure 5.33 *Protocol definition dialog box.*

The Port ranges for subsequent connections box defines how to handle connections or packets that originate after the initial connection is set. You can click the Add button to configure the port, packet type, and direction for subsequent connections. A port range setting of 0 for inbound connections indicates any port, which allows the server to select the port from the range 1024 through 5000.

Let us consider the following scenario: You want to provide inbound access to your internal FTP server. By default, the standard set of protocol definitions provides only an FTP protocol that can be used strictly for initial outbound access. That means that only internal WinSock clients can use the WinSock Proxy service to connect to the Internet. To let an external client connect to an internal FTP server, a new FTP protocol definition must be created (see Figure 5.34).

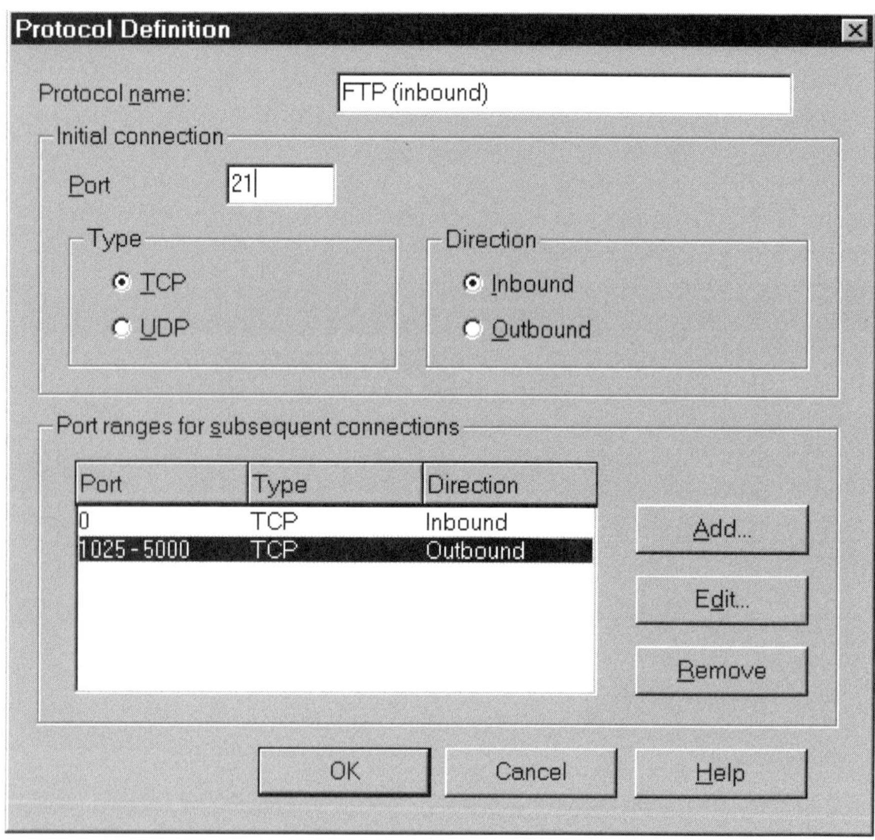

Figure 5.34 *Protocol definition to provide inbound FTP access.*

In addition to defining a protocol, you need to configure the FTP server to act as a Proxy Client. For more information about administering Proxy Clients, see Chapter 8.

Study Break

Creating a New Protocol Definition

1. In Internet Service Manager (if you are using IIS 3.0) or Microsoft Management Console (if you are using IIS 4.0), double-click the computer name next to any of the Proxy Server services.

2. Launch WinSock Proxy service properties, click the `Protocols` tab, and then click `Add`.

3. In the `Protocol Definition` dialog box, in `Protocol name`, type a name for this protocol definition.
4. Under `Initial connection`, in `Port`, type a valid port number that will be used for the initial connection on the server.
5. Under `Type`, click either `TCP` or `UDP`.
6. Under `Direction`, click either `Inbound` or `Outbound`. Click `Inbound` if you want external clients to connect to internal WinSock Proxy client computers. Click `Outbound` to have internal WinSock clients connect to external computers.
7. Under `Port ranges for subsequent connections`, click `Add`.
8. In the `Port Range Definition` dialog box, in `Port or Range`, type a valid port number or a range of port numbers.

A port range setting of 0 for inbound connections indicates any port, which allows the server to select the port from the range 1024–5000.

9. Under `Type`, click either `TCP` or `UDP`.
10. Under `Direction`, click either `Inbound` or `Outbound`.
11. Click `OK`.
12. Click `OK` and verify that the new protocol definition appears under `Protocol definitions`.
13. Click `Apply`, and then click `OK`.

When a new protocol definition is created, you can assign your users permissions to use this protocol in the `Permissions` tab. By default, no users are granted access for the new protocol definition (unless Access Control is disabled). To allow users to use the protocol to access the Internet, user permissions must be granted explicitly.

You have an option to save all protocol definitions to file. To do so, click `Save`, and then complete the `Save Protocol Definition` dialog box. Once the protocol definitions are saved, you can load them to another computer.

Configuring WinSock Proxy Permissions

The `Permissions` Tab in the WinSock Proxy service properties dialog box is used to designate which users or groups can use the particular protocol to access the Internet through Proxy Server. Assigning permissions to WinSock service protocols is very similar to assigning permissions to the Web Proxy service, with the only exception that the set and the number of protocols for WinSock and Web Proxy services are different (see Figure 5.35).

You can see the predefined protocols that Microsoft Proxy Server comes with, as well as custom protocols that you define in the Protocols tab.

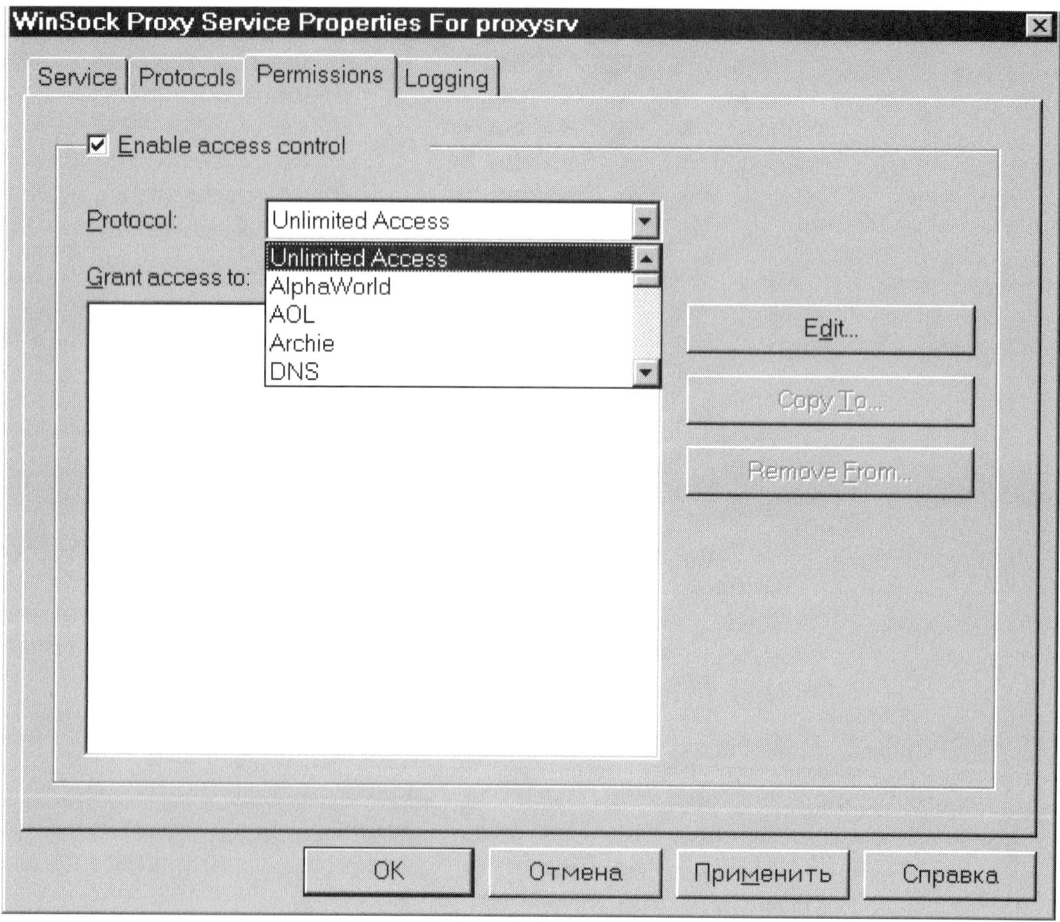

Figure 5.35 *Assigning permissions to the WinSock Proxy service protocols.*

You can set permissions to an individual protocol or to a group of protocols. You can also remove users' permissions from multiple protocols at once.

To set permissions for a single protocol:

1. In Internet Service Manager (if you are using IIS 3.0) or Microsoft Management Console (if you are using IIS 4.0), double-click the computer name next to any of the Proxy Server services.

2. In the `Service Properties` dialog box, click the `Permissions` tab, and then click the `Enable Access Control` checkbox.

3. To grant or to deny a user or group the right to use a protocol to access the Internet, select the protocol from the list in `Protocol`, and then click `Edit`.

4. In the protocol `Permissions` dialog box, select a user or group from the list, and do one of the following:

   - To add a user or group, click `Add`. In the `Add Users and Groups` dialog box, select a user or group from the list, and then click `OK`.
   - To remove a user or group, select the user or group from the list, and then click `Remove`.

5. When all protocols have their permissions set appropriately, click `OK`.

You can copy user permissions from one protocol to one or more other protocols. You can also remove user permissions from several protocols at once.

To set permissions for several protocols:

1. In Internet Service Manager, double-click the server name next to the Web Proxy service or the WinSock Proxy service, and then click the `Permissions` tab.
2. Select a protocol from the list in `Protocol`, and then select one more users and groups in `Grant access to`.
3. Click either `Copy To` or `Remove From` to copy or remove user permissions from the selected protocol.
4. When permissions are set appropriately for the users of the selected protocol, repeat steps 2 and 3 as necessary.
5. When all protocols and users have their permissions set appropriately, click `OK`.

MCSE 5.5 Managing Socks Proxy Service

You may remember that SOCKS is a cross-platform mechanism that establishes secure communications between client and server computers. The Socks Proxy service extends the redirection provided by the WinSock Proxy service to non-Windows platforms. It uses TCP/IP and can be used for many applications, such as Telnet, FTP, Gopher, and HTTP.

Socks Proxy service cannot be used to provide support for applications that utilize the UDP protocol such as RealAudio, streaming video, or NetShow.

There are three tabs available in the Socks Proxy server properties that allow you to configure this service: Service, Permissions and Logging. Table 5.5 describes the purpose of each tab.

Table 5.5 *Socks Proxy service configuration tabs*

Tab	Description
Services	You can use this tab to specify non-service-specific parameters. Changing the properties on this tab will affect all Proxy Server services.
Permissions	Use this tab to give a user or group permission to use different protocols with WinSock Proxy service.
Logging	Use this tab to configure Socks Proxy service logging.

The Service tab is shared with the Web Proxy and WinSock Proxy services — as discussed earlier in this chapter.

CONFIGURING THE SOCKS PROXY SERVICE PERMISSIONS

Socks clients establish an initial connection to the Proxy Server. After the circuit is established, the Socks Proxy service relays application data between the client and the Internet server. The process is similar to that used between WinSock clients and the WinSock Proxy service. Because the Socks Proxy service does not have a client-side component to redirect API calls, however, standard methods of client authentication (such as Windows NT challenge/response) cannot be used. You can control what applications can connect to what Internet computer by specifying rules in the Permissions tab (see Figure 5.36).

The Socks Proxy service security is based on IP addresses, port numbers, and destination hosts.

The Permissions tab displays an ordered list of entries where each entry specifies a source, destination, port number, and whether a request subject to these parameters should be granted or denied. The list of rules is ordered so that the first entry that satisfies a request is applied. By default, all requests are denied, so if no entry is found corresponding to the client request, the request is denied. You can use the `move up` and `move down` buttons to change the order in which the rules are checked.

If you click the `Add` button, the `Socks Permissions` dialog box appears to permit you to specify new rule settings (see Figure 5.37).

The Action drop-down list specifies whether the request will be denied or permitted.

The Source box specifies the origin of the request, by either all computers, an Internet domain of computers, a single computer IP address, or an IP address and subnet mask combination. The Destination box specifies the allowed or denied destination. The Port list specifies the relative range of the port number. It can be equal (EQ), not equal (NEQ), greater than (GT), less than (LT), greater than or equal (GE), less than or equal (LE). The port

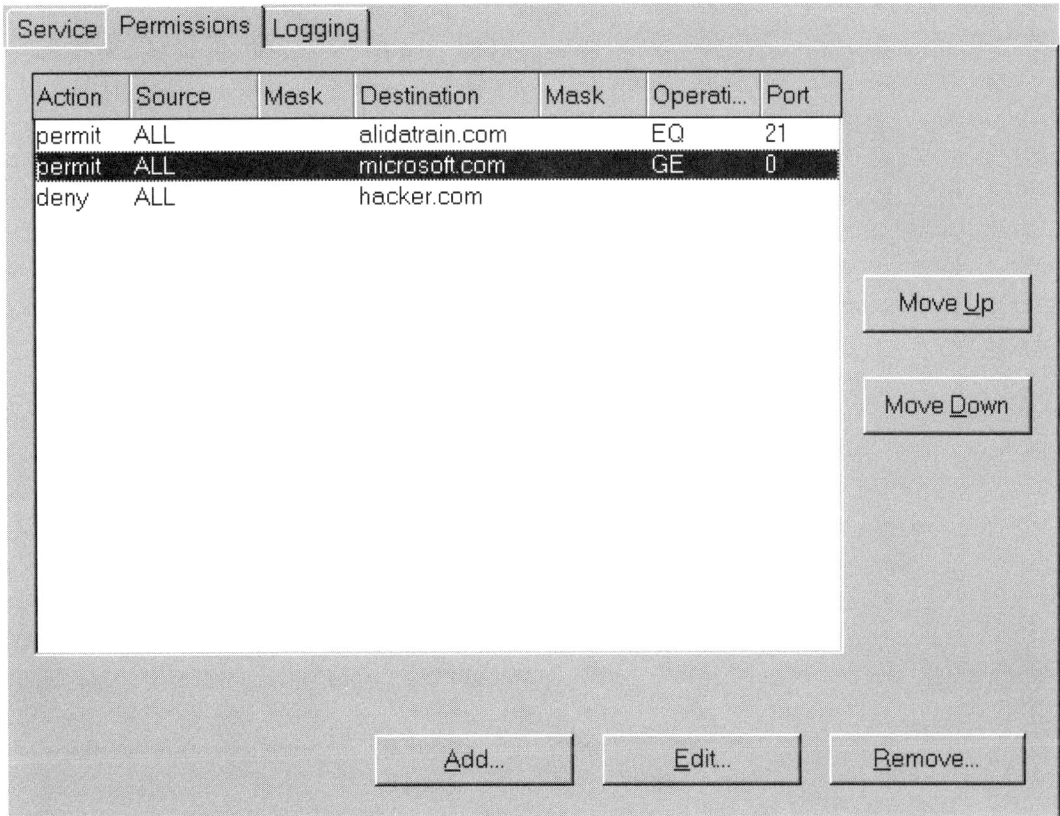

Figure 5.36   *Socks Proxy service permissions.*

number or service name box provides a space for you to type the port number or the service name. The service name can be a valid TCP service name.

As you may have noticed, the Socks Proxy service can open only a primary port for an application (compare it to the WinSock Proxy service); secondary port connections are not supported.

Study Break

Creating a SOCKS Permission

1. In Internet Service Manager (if you are using IIS 3.0) or Microsoft Management Console (if you are using IIS 4.0), select the Socks Proxy service near the computer name, launch `Properties`.

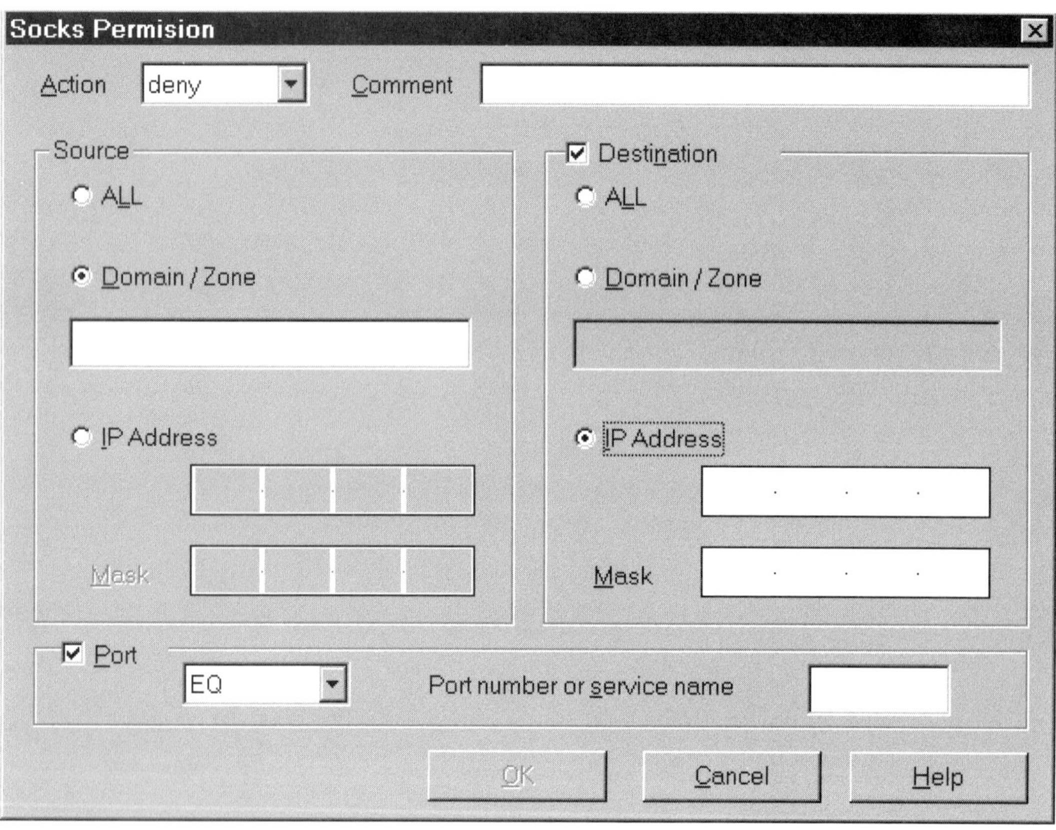

Figure 5.37   *Creating a new rule for the Socks Proxy service.*

2. Click the `Permissions` tab, and then click `Add`.
3. In the `Socks Permission` dialog box, click the down arrow next to `Action`, and select `permission` from the drop-down list.
4. In `Comment`, type a name for the permission being created.
5. Under `Source`, do one of the following:
   • To apply the permission to all computers, click `ALL`.
   • To apply the permission to a domain of computers, click `Domain/Zone` and enter a valid Internet domain or zone.
   • To apply the permission to a single computer, click `IP Address` and type a valid IP address. In `Mask`, type a valid subnet mask.
6. To define a destination definition, select the `Destination` checkbox, and do one of the following:

- To apply the permission to all computers, click `ALL`.
- To apply the permission to a domain of computers, click `Domain/Zone` and enter a valid Internet domain or zone.
- To apply the permission to a single computer, click `IP Address` and type a valid IP address. In `Mask`, type a valid subnet mask.

7. Select the `Port` checkbox, click the down arrow, and select a function from the list. In `Port number or service name`, type a valid port number or service name to apply the function against.
8. When finished, click `OK`.

To modify the SOCKS permissions list:

1. In the `Socks Proxy service properties` dialog box, click the `Permissions` tab.
2. Do one or more of the following:
    - To edit an existing permission, select it, click `Edit`, modify the applicable settings shown in the `Socks Permission` dialog box, and then click `OK`.
    - To change the order of a permission in the list, select it, and click either `Move up` or `Move down`.
    - To delete a permission, select it, click `Remove`, and then click `OK`.
3. Repeat until all permissions are configured appropriately.

CONFIGURING SOCKS PROXY SERVICE LOGS

The Socks Proxy service logging can be configured in the Logging tab. The Logging tab configuration is similar to the Web Proxy and WinSock Proxy Logging tabs — you can configure text file logging or logging to ODBC-compliant database. The file name that is used for the Socks Proxy service begins with SP:

- SP*yymmdd*.log for daily logs
- SPW*yymmw*.log for weekly logs
- SPM*yymm*.log for monthly logs

where:

yy is a number between 00 and 99 indicating the year.
mm is a number between 01 and 12 indicating the month.
dd is a number between 01 and 31 indicating the day of the month.
w is a number between 1 and 5 indicating the week of the month.

MCSE 5.6 Proxy Server Access Control

Earlier in this chapter we indicated that the Web Proxy service and WinSock proxy service can use access control lists to specify what users and groups of users can access the service. Let us now discuss some advanced tasks that allow a Proxy administrator to control access to external networks and protect the internal network from external intrusion.

Securing Web Proxy Service

Web Proxy server can be configured to allow use of HTTP, FTP, Gopher, or Secured protocols on a per-user or per-group basis. In Chapter 2, we mentioned that a Web Proxy client can use different authentication methods to connect to the Web Proxy service.

The Web Proxy service uses the same password authentication methods for client requests as those configured in the WWW service of IIS. The authentication methods used for client-to-Proxy Server communication include anonymous logon, basic authentication, and Windows NT challenge/response authentication. As a Proxy Server administrator you can enable or disable these authentication methods to reflect your network needs.

Use WWW service properties to configure authentication methods for Web Proxy service. If you use Internet Information Server 4.0 on your Proxy Server computer, launch WWW service properties, go to the Directory Security tab, and click the Edit button in the Anonymous Access and Authentication Control box. The Authentication Methods dialog box appears (see Figure 5.38).

Remember that all basic and Windows NT challenge/response authentications are effective only if you enable access control in the Web Proxy service properties Permissions tab. For simplified management of the Web Proxy service, you can disable access control. This is useful if anonymous user access is all that is needed for users on your network. If you want to manage individual users' access, access control should be enabled. This will permit you to fully administer individual security for each user on your network.

ANONYMOUS LOGON

When the Internet Information Server installed, a default anonymous user account named IUSR_*computername* is created, where *computername* is the name of the server computer. This account is used by the Web Proxy service

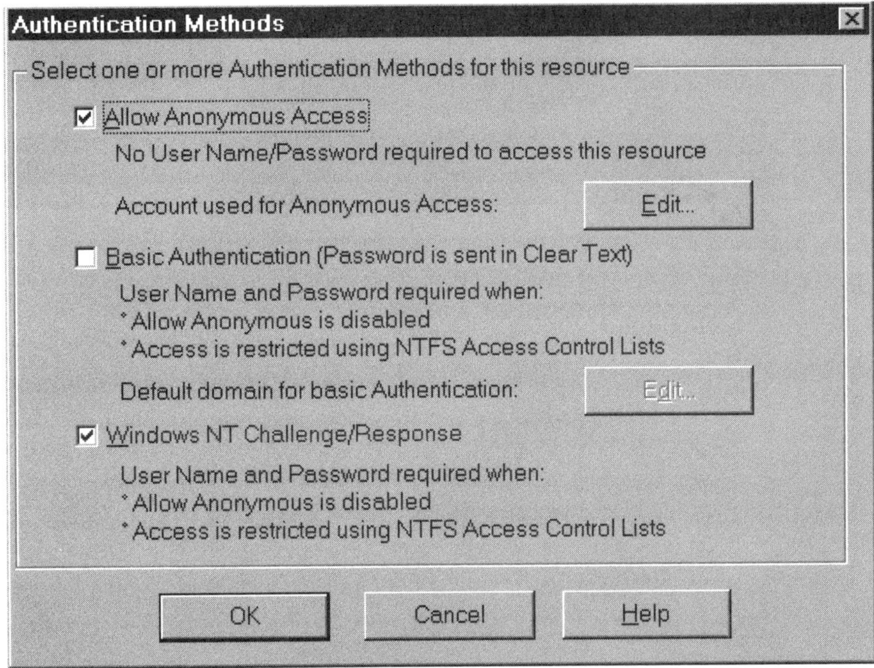

Figure 5.38 *Configuring authentication methods for Web Proxy service.*

to grant permissions — the user does not need to be assigned further user permissions in the Web Proxy service.

If you only select `Allow Anonymous` and do not select one of the other types of authentication, all included items on the Web Proxy service `Permissions` tab are ignored. If you have disabled anonymous authentication in the WWW service and have enabled basic authentication, you must explicitly grant user permissions before users can access the Internet by using the Web Proxy service.

If anonymous logon is allowed, all client applications use it disregarding that other authentication options are set. To force users to log on with an account and password, disable anonymous logon.

Some FTP sites require an e-mail user name as the password for anonymous FTP client access. When a password is required for anonymous access, Web Proxy sends *proxyuser@domain,* where domain is the current Internet DNS domain in the TCP/IP settings.

BASIC AUTHENTICATION

Basic authentication is a standard HTTP mechanism that sends and receives user information as clear text. Passwords and user names are encoded but not encrypted in this type of authentication. This means that anyone using a protocol analyzer can capture packets, decode the packet data using widely available utilities (such as Uudecode), and discover usernames and passwords.

In basic authentication, the client is responsible for prompting the user for his/her user name and password credentials. The credentials are then encoded (not encrypted) and sent to the server. The user name must be an account on the computer running IIS or in a trusted domain of that computer. When using a trusted Windows NT domain account, the user name must contain the domain name in `domain\account` format.

Through most of this chapter, we speak of domains in the context *of Internet Domains*. In this section we're speaking of *Windows NT Domains*. As you're likely aware, the two have only the moniker "domain" in common.

Study Break

Specifying a Default Domain for Authentication

If your user accounts are located in a different Windows NT domain from that of the Proxy Server and basic authentication is enabled, your users will have to specify their credentials using the `domain/account` format. Users typically prefer to log in without specifying a domain. Fortunately, you have an option to specify a default domain in IIS to permit that.

If you are using Internet Information Server 4.0, right click on the Default web site, click on the `Directory Security Tab`, and click `Edit` in the `Anonymous Access and Authentication Control` section. Click `Edit` in the `Basic Authentication` section. Here, you can enter a `default domain` to use or specify a "\" to specify that all trusted domains should be checked for logon validation.

If you use Internet Information Server 3.0, you can only add a default domain by editing the registry. You should add the following value to the registry:

HKEY_LOCAL_MACHINE\SYSTEM\CurrentControlSet\Services\W3SVC
Value Name: DefaultLogonDomain
Data Type: REG_SZ
Value: \\name of the domain controller.

For more information about specifying a default domain, visit *http://support.microsoft.com/support/kb/articles/q168/9/08.asp*

> Registry editing should be done with great caution. The registry is unforgiving—a single wrong change may render the system completely unusable. You should make only changes you understand and double-check them prior to completing your edit. Other precautions, which include running an emergency repair disk update, should also be taken. Registry editing may be accomplished through the utilities `regedt32.exe` or `regedit.exe`.

Basic authentication provides weak security, but for some client types, such as UNIX-based Web clients, basic authentication is the only available means of establishing password-required access to Web-published document files. If you allow access from a Windows-based computer, consider implementing Windows NT Challenge/Response authentication instead.

CHALLENGE/RESPONSE AUTHENTICATION

Unlike basic authentication, which forwards user names and passwords as clear text from client to server, Windows NT challenge/response authentication follows a more complex process that requires multiple communications between the client and server.

Using challenge/response authentication with any Web browser other than Microsoft Internet Explorer version 4.0, however, might result in rejection of client configuration scripts (JScripts), or incorrect display of HTTPS pages that use the Secure Sockets Layer (SSL). Browsers like Netscape Navigator do not support this authentication type at all. You should use Basic authentication if you are using a Web browser other than Microsoft Internet Explorer version 4.0 or newer.

Challenge/response authentication works within the security model to provide a transparent logon procedure for clients. The client computer uses its established user logon information to identify itself to the server. The user is not prompted to enter these user credentials. Instead, the information is available after the user first logs on to a Windows NT-based computer. Windows NT challenge/response authentication only works where the client and server computers are located in the same or trusted domains.

Securing the WinSock Proxy Service

The WinSock Proxy service uses Windows NT challenge/response authentication only to provide secure communication for Windows Sockets applications. The WinSock client application does not have to support the Windows NT challenge/response authentication — authentication is done by the WinSock Proxy service client software.

Controlling Different User Access Times

As we've seen, Proxy Server has a built-in feature that can control proxy access times for all users. You set this up by configuring Proxy Server AutoDial options. This is useful if you want to limit all users to times when they can use the proxy services. Unfortunately, this time limitation is indiscriminate and even affects accounts in the Administrator groups. There is no direct way to configure different access times for different users. There are, however, some workarounds.

You can create a special group ("Proxyusers," for example) and grant the group permission to use Web Proxy, WinSock Proxy, or both. You can then modify the membership in this group dynamically by using, for example, a scheduling program, such as AT, to run a batch script that will add and remove members of the proxy group based on time of day, week, month, etc. You can use the Windows NT Resource Kit utility USRTOGRP.EXE to modify group membership.

■ Summary

This chapter introduces a wide variety of Proxy Server administration tasks and features. We discovered that Proxy Server services can be administered using Internet Service Manager if you are using IIS 3.0, or Microsoft Management Console if you are using IIS 4.0. Proxy Server can be administered through the command line interface using the RemotMsp and WspProto utilities. RemotMsp is primarily used to configure and administer remote Proxy Server computers. You can use the WspProto utility to add, edit, and remove WinSock Proxy protocol definitions.

Service Parameters

We studied in some detail how to configure and tune the Web Proxy, WinSock Proxy and Socks Proxy, services. We discovered that there are some configuration parameters that are service-specific — when you change one of these parameters, the change affects only one service. There were also some parameters common to all three Proxy Server services — and changing these parameters in one Proxy Server service properties window also affects the other Proxy services.

AutoDial and RAS

We discussed the Proxy Server AutoDial feature. AutoDial works with the Windows NT Remote Access Service (RAS) and can be used to schedule dial-out connection times to the Internet through your Internet Service Provider. The Proxy Server AutoDial feature is primarily used to reduce Internet connection time by connecting only when needed. It reduces your company Internet costs when no permanent Internet connection is needed.

Domain Filtering

We introduced Proxy Server domain filtering. Domain filtering is used to grant or deny access for specific Internet sites under the Web Proxy, WinSock Proxy, and Socks Proxy services. Remember that for every WinSock or Web Proxy request, Proxy Server tries to perform a reverse DNS lookup to resolve the IP address to the domain name. It is recommended that you specify domain filtering by both IP address and domain name in case reverse DNS lookup is not configured for the given domain.

Caching

In addition to common configuration parameters, such as AutoDial and domain filtering, Proxy Server has many service-specific settings. For example, for the Web Proxy service, you can configure caching and web publishing parameters. The Caching tab of the Web Proxy service properties dialog is used to enable or disable caching and to configure Web Proxy cache parameters. The Web Proxy cache can operate in two modes: active caching and passive caching. You can enable and disable either mode by checking and clearing the corresponding checkbox on the Caching tab. If you enable passive caching, you have the option to select the cache expiration policy, which specifies the freshness of objects in the cache. You can set this option to make Proxy Server to perform fewer Internet requests or to update objects in the cache more frequently.

With active caching, the freshness and availability of popular objects is automatically ensured by Proxy Server. If you enable active caching, you can customize its behavior. You can request more updates to ensure users will receive the most up-to-date information, or you can request fewer network accesses to save network bandwidth.

When we discussed Web Proxy caching, we said that, after Proxy Server is installed, the Web Proxy cache contains data and should be administered only with the Internet Service Manager. You can increase or decrease the cache size, specify additional drives for caching, and even set the cache size to zero using the Caching tab. If you decrease the cache size on a selected drive, some cached data on that drive may be deleted. In addition to controlling the cache size, you can specify caching filters to control whether or not items from specific Internet sites are cached.

Publishing

Proxy Server not only allows internal clients to connect to external servers, but also provides a way to publish information to the Internet. You can configure Proxy Server to respond to incoming requests from external Web clients by discarding the requests or sending them to a local or internal Web server. This is called reverse proxying and reverse hosting. *Reverse proxying* is the ability of the Proxy Server to listen to incoming requests for an internal Web server computer and respond on behalf of that server. *Reverse hosting* maintains a list of internal servers that can publish to the Internet, thereby allowing Proxy Server to listen and respond on behalf of multiple servers that are located behind it.

Logging

We provided a detailed description of the Proxy Server logging capability. All log information can be written to a text file or to an ODBC-compliant database table (such as Microsoft® Access or Microsoft® SQL Server). Log data contains client information, connection information, server information, and information about objects being accessed. Additionally, you can choose between regular and verbose logging.

WinSock Proxy Service

The WinSock Proxy service can be administered by specifying protocol definitions and assigning permissions to the protocols. Protocol definitions determine which WinSock applications can be used to access the Internet. For each protocol, you can define which ports can be used for outbound and inbound connections. You can configure existing protocol definitions, create new protocol definitions, and delete unwanted protocol definitions.

Socks Proxy Service

Unlike the Winsock Proxy service, the Socks Proxy service has no true permissions feature. Socks Proxy service security is based on IP addresses, port numbers, and destination hosts. The Permissions tab displays an ordered list of entries where each entry specifies a source, destination, port number, and whether the request using these parameters should be granted or denied.

Finally, we discussed three authentication methods that are used by the Proxy Server for client-to-Proxy access. Authentication methods are anonymous logon, basic authentication, and Windows NT challenge/response authentication. The Web Proxy service can use all methods, while the WinSock Proxy service can use Windows NT challenge/response only.

▲ REVIEW QUESTIONS

1. *Which account is used by all anonymous users of the Web Proxy service?*

    A. Windows NT Guest account

    B. IUSR_*Computername*

    C. Everyone

    D. Administrators

    E. No account

2. *You grant user Mary permission to use the WWW protocol in the Permissions tab of the Web Proxy service properties dialog box. What Internet resources can Mary access? (choose all that apply)*

    A. HTTP

    B. HTTPS

    C. FTP read

    D. FTP write

    E. Gopher

    F. Telnet

3. *You want to grant unlimited access for WinSock Proxy protocols to the Administrators group and limit other users to use SMTP and POP3 protocols only. How can you accomplish this?*

    A. Grant each user access to each protocol individually

    B. Grant the Administrators group Unlimited access and Domain Users group access to SMTP and POP3 protocols

    C. Disable access control in the Permission tab

    D. It is not possible, you cannot specify access on per-protocol basis

4. *You want to grant access to a specific port for the WinSock Proxy service to a group called Managers. How can you do this?*

    A. Create a protocol definition and grant Managers access to this protocol

    B. Create a new port range and grant Managers access to this protocol

    C. Select the port number on the Permission tab and grand access to this port to the Managers group

    D. It is not possible to assign port access

5. *What type of authentication can the WinSock Proxy service use?*

    A. Password authentication

    B. Share level security

    C. Basic Authentication

    D. Windows NT Challenge/Response Authentication

6. *Which type of connections are not supported by the Socks Proxy service?*

    A. TCP

    B. UDP

    C. Telnet

    D. HTTP

7. *You want to limit access to certain Internet sites for Web Proxy and WinSock Proxy users. For this purpose you created domain filters by using the fully qualified domain names of the restricted servers. Some users are still able to connect to those servers. What is the mostly likely reason?*

    A. You must specify domain filters to Web Proxy and WinSock Proxy service individually

    B. Some users are granted Unlimited Access in the WinSock Proxy

    C. Only basic authentication has been enabled; for domain filtering to work properly Windows NT Challenge/Response authentication must be enabled

    D. Domain filtering has no effect on WinSock Proxy service

8. *By default, all requests through Socks Proxy service are granted. (True or False)*

9. *What type of logging is enabled by default?*

    A. No logging

    B. Logging to a text file

    C. Logging to a ODBC compliant database

    D. Logging to a SQL database

10. *You want to configure logging to an ODBC compliant database. What steps should you take?*

    A. Install the ODBC driver for the database you are using

    B. Create a system Data Source Name (system DSN) for the database

   C. Create a table in your database application with the necessary fields

   D. Configure the log for the database in the Logging tab of the Proxy Server service

   E. All of the above

11. *The IS manager reports that some of the employees are spending too much time visiting Web sites that are not related to production. You are instructed to block access to these sites. Upon reviewing the Proxy Server logs, you notice most unwanted requests are destined to www.soapopera.com. What is the best way to block access to this site to specific users?*

   A. Implement packet filtering

   B. Implement domain filtering

   C. Create a protocol definition in WinSock Proxy service. Deny access to this protocol to certain users

   D. Deny access to WWW protocol in the Web Proxy service for these users

12. *You want to ensure that all of your Windows NT client computers are able to use the NNTP protocol to access Usenet groups in the Internet. Where can you check this?*

   A. In the Protocols tab in the WinSock Proxy service

   B. In the Protocols tab in the Web Proxy service

   C. In the Protocols tab in the Socks Proxy service

   D. In the *mspclnt.ini* file

13. *You just added a new hard disk to your Proxy Server computer and want to utilize it for caching. How can you do this?*

   A. Run Proxy Server Setup and specify the new cache size

   B. Change the cache size in the Caching tab of the Web Proxy service

   C. Proxy Server will automatically detect the new drive and will use it for caching

   D. You cannot do this. Once the Proxy cache is created, its size can not be changed

14. *Users are reporting that the access to the external Web site, which contains marketing information, is very slow. How can you improve performance?*

   A. Disable caching

    B. Enable passive caching and set the caching filter to not cache the marketing site

    C. Implement packet filtering

    D. Enable active caching and set the caching filter to always cache the marketing site

15. *You are the Proxy server administrator and want to limit caching of large objects that are downloaded through FTP. How can you do this?*

    A. Limit the cache size. Objects that exceed the cache size are not cached

    B. Limit size of cached objects in the cache policy in the Web Proxy service

    C. Do nothing, FTP objects are not cached

    D. You cannot limit caching size of FTP objects — only HTTP objects can be limited for caching

16. *You installed an additional Proxy Server computer and now want to exclude one of two drives from caching on the original Proxy server. How can you do this?*

    A. Delete the folder reserved for caching on one of the hard drives

    B. Launch the Web Proxy service properties, go to the caching tab, and specify the cache size 0 on one of the drives

    C. Launch the Web Proxy service properties, go to the caching tab, and select the `Delete Cache` command

    D. You need to reinstall Proxy Server to do this

17. *What's the purpose of the* `Remotemsp` *utility?*

    A. Configure and administer remote Proxy Server computers

    B. Configure and administer Proxy Client computers

    C. Configure and administer the local Proxy Server computer

    D. Save and restore the Proxy Server configuration

18. *How can you monitor who is currently using Web Proxy service?*

    A. Using security log in the Event Viewer

    B. Using performance monitor

    C. Using `Current Sessions` button in the WinSock Proxy service Properties

    D. None of the above

19. *You want to prevent your users from accessing the domain www.somedo-main.com. You created a domain filter using the fully qualified domain name. What should you do next?*

    A. Enable access control in the Web Proxy service

    B. Enable access control on the WinSock Proxy service

    C. Create a domain filter using the IP address of *www.somedo-main.com*

    D. Enable Windows NT challenge/response authentication or basic authentication in the WWW service properties

20. *How would you configure the Web Proxy service to update objects in cache more frequently?*

    A. In the cache expiration policy for active caching, `select Faster User response is more important`

    B. In the active caching box, select Equal importance

    C. In the Advanced Cache Policy, specify TTL=50% under objects Time to Live (TTL) box.

    D. In the Advanced Cache Policy, specify Minimum TTL=50%

21. *Which of the following are required for Proxy Sever AutoDial? (select all that apply)*

    A. A valid RAS phonebook entry

    B. Proxy Server must be a member of the proxy server array; Auto-Dial works only between array members

    C. Windows NT RAS installed

    D. RAS services configured to work with AutoDial

22. *Your users are using Microsoft Internet Explorer as their Web browser. You want Proxy Server AutoDial to occur each time your users want to browse the Internet. Some users are complaining that when they try to access an external Web server, AutoDial does not work. All other users can utilize the AutoDial feature. What should you check to correct this problem? (Select two correct answers)*

    A. Check that all users have permissions to use Proxy Server Auto-Dial

    B. Check that all users have dial out permission in user manager for domains

    C. Check that AutoDial is enabled for Socks Proxy and WinSock Proxy services

    D. Check that all client browsers are configured to use the Proxy service

23. *What Proxy Server parameters are not rolled back during partial restore?*

    A. Size and location of Web Proxy service cache

    B. Packet filtering configuration

    C. AutoDial configuration information

    D. Proxy Server registry keys that cannot be configured through the user interface

    E. All of the above

24. *You are planning to host multiple Web sites for your customers. Your network is protected by a Proxy Server computer. You want to install customer Web sites in your internal network. How can you implement your plan?*

    A. Implement reverse proxying and assign each internal Web site a valid Internet IP address. Enable IP forwarding on the Proxy Server computer

    B. Implement reverse hosting and assign each internal Web site an IP address from a private address space. Configure Proxy Server computer for Web publishing

    C. Implement server proxying. Make each of the internal Web servers a WinSock Proxy client. Enable anonymous access for the WinSock Proxy service

    D. This cannot be done — you cannot place Web servers behind Proxy Server

25. *The IS manager reports that some of the employees are spending too much time visiting newsgroups. What is the best way to find out which employees are doing this?*

    A. Review Web Proxy logs

    B. Review WinSock Proxy logs

    C. Use Windows NT Event Viewer

    D. Use current session button in the Web Proxy Service properties

Packet Filtering

Now that we've seen how to install and configure the Proxy Server services, it is time to turn our attention to the Proxy Server feature that makes it operate like a firewall — *Packet Filtering*. Packet filtering protects your Proxy Server's external network interface by intercepting packets destined to specific Proxy Server services and passing or blocking them based on your configuration. When a packet is blocked or when suspicious events occur, Proxy Server can record them in a log and/or send an alert via e-mail.

At the conclusion of this chapter you will be able to:

- Describe packet filtering and explain the difference between static and dynamic filtering
- Discuss the effect of packet filtering on the internal network
- Configure Proxy Server to enable specific protocols, ports, and users

155

- Configure packet filter alerting and logging
- Interpret the contents of the packet filter log

Packet Filtering

Packet filtering works just the way it sounds. Under packet filtering, packets are examined and accepted or rejected before they're allowed go to higher protocol layers or to an application. You can configure packet filtering to exclude all packet types except for those you specifically allow. Packet filtering can block packets of a specific protocol and can permit only packets originating from or destined to a particular host. Packet filtering occurs at the external network interface and can be used to block packets destined to any internal network server service (e.g., SOCKS Proxy, WinSock Proxy, Web Proxy, World Wide Web, Simple Mail Transfer Protocol). Packet filtering can reject packets associated with several well-known attacks such as address spoof/SYN and FRAG attacks. When packet filtering is turned on, all packets are rejected except for those that are allowed by the packet filtering exception list (we'll see how to configure this list in the next section).

Study Break

What Are Address Spoof/SYN and FRAG Attacks?

Address Spoof/SYN Attack: An address spoof or SYN attack is designed to overwhelm the computer to make its network services unavailable. The attack begins when a TCP connection request (SYN) is sent to the targeted computer. The packet's source IP address is replaced with an address that is not in use, or one belonging to another computer. The TCP SYN is sent repeatedly and each time the target computer receives it, it returns a SYN-ACK acknowledgement message. Since the source IP address is bogus, it is not answered, and the targeted computer will make five additional transmissions. Each TCP SYN will use the targeted computer's network resources for over three minutes. A barrage of TCP SYNs can prevent the computer from doing anything else. This type of attack fits into a category knows as *Denial of Service.*

FRAG Attack: A FRAG attack is an attempt to gain access to a protected computer by fragmenting the transmitted packets to make them so small they appear uninteresting to the protection software. Since the protection algorithms are not interested in these packets, they are able to "sneak" into the computer.

Static and Dynamic Filtering

Filtering can be static or dynamic. Under dynamic filtering, ports (only those on the exception list) are open only when a valid communication with them is taking place. When the communication is complete, the port is closed. Dynamic filtering can be thought of as a one-way door in the firewall. When an internal client attempts an authorized contact, the door is opened from the inside; when the session is over, the door slams shut and incoming packets are stopped at the firewall. This limits the number of inbound and outbound ports exposed at any given time. With dynamic filtering, you don't need to worry about ensuring that an outbound port is available, since applications on the internal network can open the "one-way door." If you want hosts on the external network to gain access to the internal network, however, you must provide a filter exception to permit their access (under both static and dynamic filtering). If, for instance, you enable dynamic packet filtering and want external clients to obtain access to a web server on the internal network (through the Proxy Server), you must add a filter exception. (Fortunately, there are a couple of predefined filters available for this very purpose, you simply select them and add them to the exception list — we'll see how to do this in the next section.) When dynamic filtering is disabled, the system supports to static filtering only. Under static filtering, outbound ports must be designated on the exception list to permit internal applications to get out to the external network. If you don't employ dynamic filtering, you will need, for instance, to create your own HTTP filter exception to permit internal hosts to reach the Internet.

Static filtering is typically required only when an application (e.g., Microsoft Exchange) is hosted on the Windows NT server that is running Proxy Server. While applications on the internal network can easily get to the network through the Proxy Server services and dynamic filtering, applications on the Proxy Server itself cannot. In this case, you must revert to static filters and create explicit exceptions for each inbound and outbound communication your Proxy Server will allow. (You may need to create *wspcfg.ini* files for applications, such as Exchange Server, running on the internal network. More on this later in the book.)

Remember, under packet filtering, you must provide a packet filter exception to open the appropriate port for every communication that will be *initiated* by a host from the *external* network whether you use dynamic or static filtering.

Impact on Internal Network

Internal network communication is not affected by packet filtering. Since packet filtering applies to the external and not the internal network adapter, Windows NT security functions (e.g., user permissions, password authentications) still work as advertised on the internal network. Note that, while Proxy Server will support multiple *internal* network adapters, it will support only one *external* network adapter.

Event Tracking

As we'll see, Proxy Server can track anomalies detected by the packet filters. It can place them in a Proxy Server log file, write them to the Windows NT System Log, and/or send an e-mail alert. Detected anomalies include dropped packets, packets sent to closed ports, and packets using disallowed protocols.

MCSE 6.1 Using Packet Filtering to Enable Specific Protocols, Ports, and Users

Now that we've talked about how packet filtering works, it's time to actually see how to configure packet filtering on your proxy server. To view packet filtering, select SOCKS Proxy, WinSock Proxy, or Web Proxy service properties and click the `Security` button on the `Service` tab of the properties dialog.

Packet filtering applies equally to all Proxy Server services. Packet filter changes made to any service properties will apply to and appear in the properties for each of the other services also.

Select the `Packet Filters` tab of the `Security` dialog to reveal the dialog shown in Figure 6.1.

Note that the `Enable packet filtering on external interface` checkbox is unchecked by default. To enable packet filtering, check this dialog box. When you check the enable filtering checkbox, note that the `Enable dynamic packet filtering of Microsoft Proxy Server packets` becomes checked also. This is because dynamic filtering is the default once packet filtering is enabled. (If you wish to revert to static filtering, you must uncheck this checkbox.) To enable packet filtering to inspect

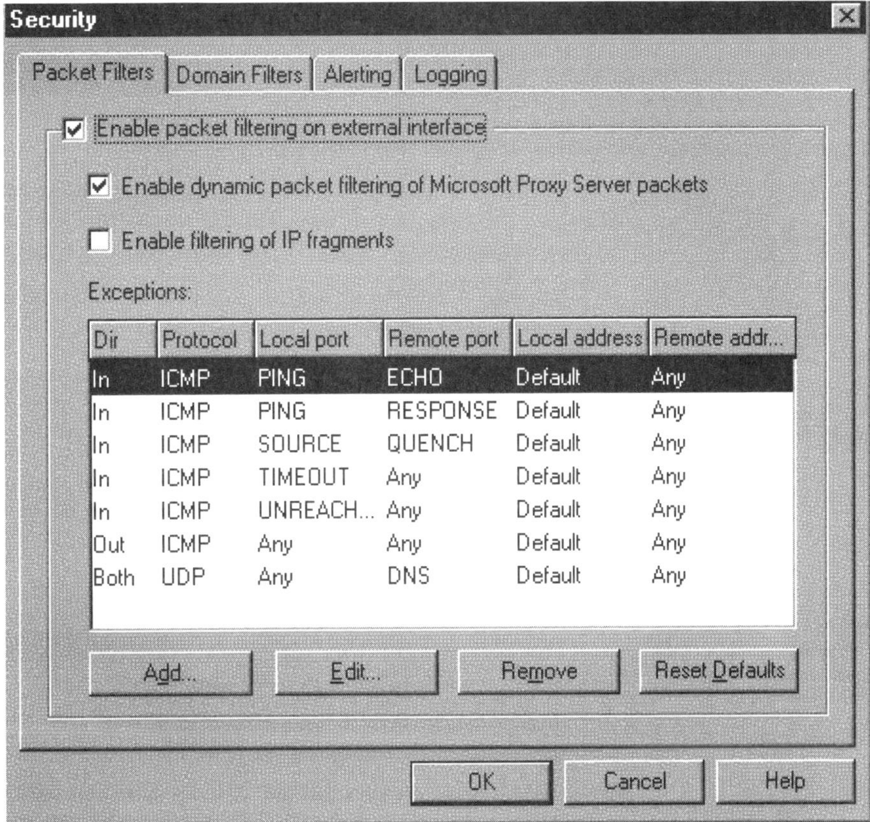

Figure 6.1 *Packet filters tab of security dialog.*

packet fragments and datagrams, you may check the `Enable filtering of IP fragments` checkbox. This setting will protect you from address spoof/SYN and FRAG attacks.

If the Proxy Server is not equipped with an external interface (network adapter card, modem, etc.), you will be unable to activate packet filtering.

Note the items listed in the `Exceptions` window. With packet filtering enabled, these represent the *only* packets that will be allowed to transit the external interface — all others will be blocked. This applies to *all* packets attempting to go through the interface. They can be from the Internet or from a client on the internal network.

When you activate packet filtering, you must review the filters listed in the `Exceptions` window to determine if they meet your needs. Notice that filters define data flow direction, transport protocol, and local and remote ports and IP addresses. You should check all these factors to ensure the predefined exceptions will work for you. The available filter parameters should give you sufficient flexibility to create whatever filtering plan you require. In some cases (such as with the Point-to-Point Tunneling Protocol) you may need to configure multiple filters (actually exception list entries) for proper operation. (For PPTP, these filters–PPT Call, PPT Receive — have been predefined and may be added to the list as defined below.)

Modifying or Creating Packet Filters

If the predefined filter exceptions don't meet your needs, you'll need to modify the existing ones or create some new ones. Note that the `Packet Filters` tab has four buttons at the bottom. The `Add` and `Edit` buttons perform similar functions. The `Add` button will add a new filter exception while the `Edit` button permits you to modify the characteristics of the currently selected filter exception. The `Remove` button will delete the highlighted filter exception (effectively blocking everything that meets the criteria it defined). The `Reset  Defaults` button will restore packet filtering exceptions to the way they were when Proxy Server was first installed.

To create a new packet filtering, click the `Add` button to reveal the `Packet Filter Properties` dialog as shown in Figure 6.2.

If a predefined filter meets your needs, click the `Predefined filter` radio button and select the appropriate filter from the list box (as shown in Figure 6.3). Predefined filters are available for ICMP, DNS, PPTP, SMTP, and POP3. You *must* use the predefined filters for DNS, PPTP, SMTP, and POP3 transports. Microsoft recommends you also use the predefined filter for ICMP. Otherwise, leave the `Custom  filter` button selected and proceed to define the filter in the `Custom filter` area.

If you create your own custom filter, you will need to decide on the filter parameters:

- `Protocol  ID`: Select the appropriate protocol from this drop-down box; you may choose `ICMP`, `TCP`, `UDP`, or `Any`. (Selecting `Any`, of course, will permit this filter to pass any protocol it encounters. It will also prevent you from selecting local and remote ports.)
- `Direction`: Use this drop-down box to determine if your filter will work for *inbound, outbound,* or *inbound and outbound* packets.

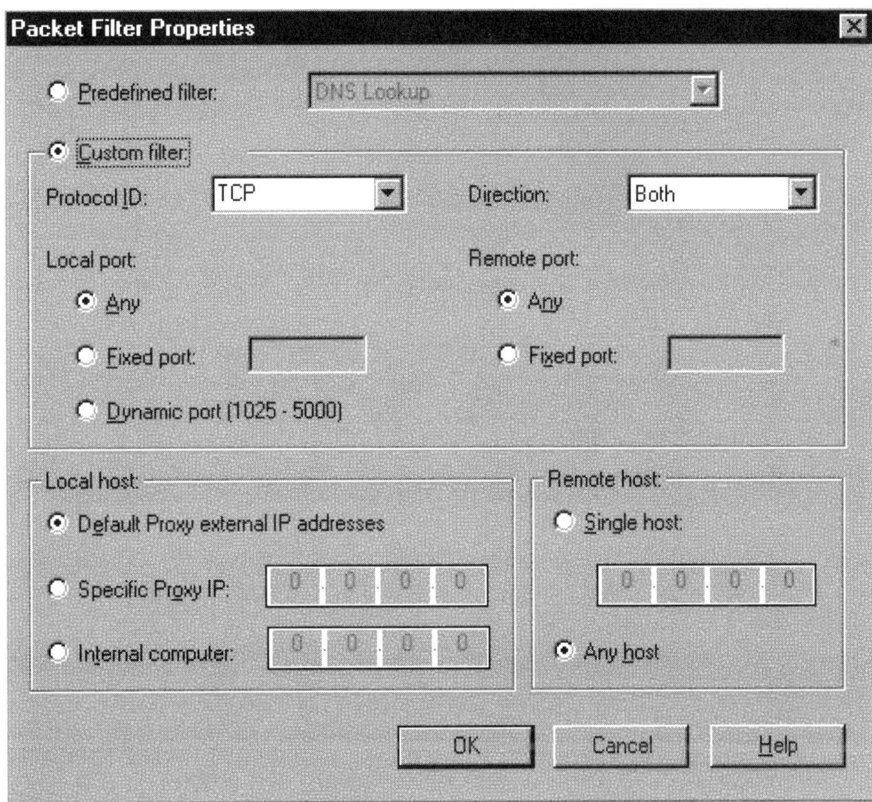

Figure 6.2 *Packet filter properties dialog.*

- `Local Port`: This selects a port number on the local Proxy Server computer. You may choose `Any`, `Fixed Port`, or `Dynamic Port`. Selecting `Any`, of course will permit the filter to work regardless of port. If you select `Fixed Port`, you must enter a port number and that will be the only local port that will work with this filter. Selecting `Dynamic Port` will permit the filter to work with any port number in the appropriate dynamic range — this permits Proxy Server to use the most efficient route.

- `Remote Port`: This selects a port number on the remote host computer. You may choose `Any` or `Fixed Port`. As with `Local Port`, selecting `Any` will permit the filter to work regardless of port and if you select `Fixed Port`, you must enter a port number, which will be the only remote port to work with the filter.

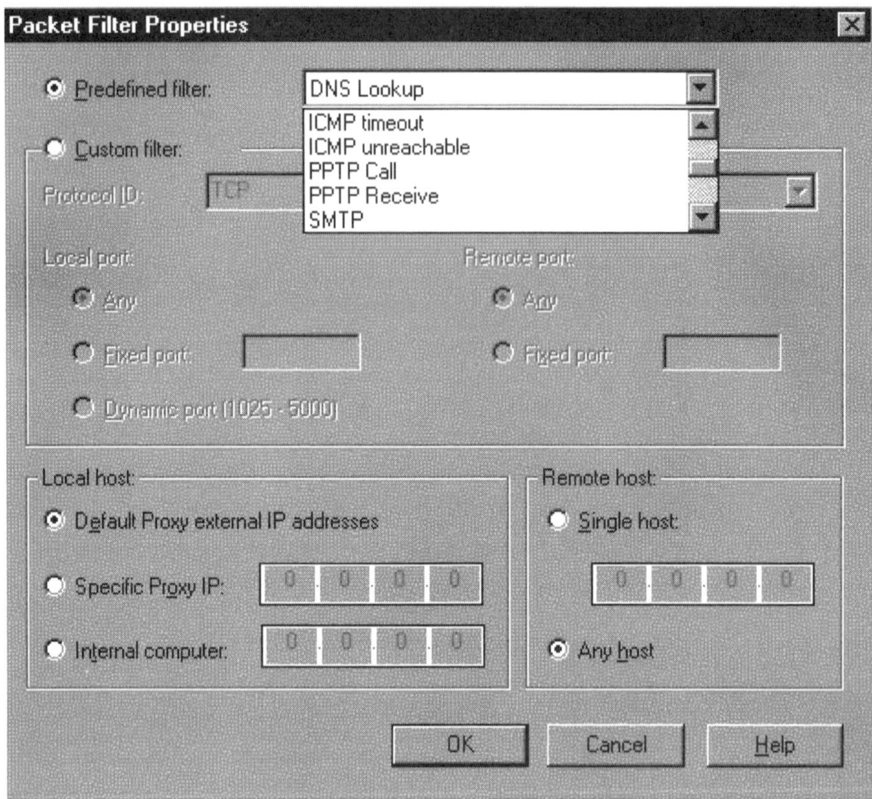

Figure 6.3 *Selecting a predefined filter.*

Whether you use a predefined or custom filter, you can still specify local and remote host information:

- `Local Host`: This refers to the internal computer on your network that will exchange packets with a host on the external network — typically the Proxy Server computer. You can select the `Default Proxy external IP address`, `Specific Proxy IP`, or `Internal computer`. The `Default Proxy external IP address` is the Proxy Server's default external interface IP address (this is the IP address you see when you view the `IP Address` tab of the `TCP/IP Properties` dialog). Selecting `Specific Proxy IP` permits you to enter a specific IP address for the Proxy Server's external interface. (This would permit you to select an additional IP address bound to the Proxy Server's external interface. Additional IP addresses can be bound by clicking the `Advanced` button on the `IP Address` tab of the `TCP/IP Properties` dialog). Entering 0.0.0.0 for the `Specific Proxy IP` enables the filter exception for any IP address bound to the external interface. If you select `Internal computer`, you can enter the IP address of a specific computer on the internal network that will be allowed to exchange packets.

- `Remote Host`: This refers to the computer on the external network that will be permitted to exchange packets with the `Local Host`. You may select `Single Host` or `Any Host`. As you might suspect, selecting `Any Host` allows packets to be sent to or received from (depending on your settings) any computer on the external network. Alternatively, you may select `Single Host` and specify an IP address. In that case, the filter will apply only to packets sent to and/or received from the computer with the specified IP address.

There are a few common reasons for creating new packet filters. When you configure Proxy Servers in a chain, you need to create filters that allow packet exchange with the downstream Proxy Server computer. You will also need to create filters when your Proxy Server runs additional services such as PPTP, DNS, or SMTP.

Study Break

Installing a Packet Filter

Let's assume you wish to host a web server through the Proxy Server and want to also use dynamic packet filtering. Using the steps outlined earlier, find and install the predefined filter exception to permit access by hosts on the external network. Did you find the HTTP Server (Port 80) filter?

MCSE 6.2 Configuring Packet Filter Alerting and Logging

Enabling packet filtering also enables packet filter alerting. Alerting can notify you of:

- Rejected packets — packets dropped by packet filtering
- Protocol violations — packets which don't conform to the allowed protocol structure (viewed by Proxy Server as potentially malicious)
- Disk full — alerts you when the hard disk is full

When any of the above occur, you can configure alerting to write an event to the system log or send an e-mail message to a designated recipient.

Alerting cannot be enabled unless packet filtering is turned on.

Setting Alert Events

To view packet filter alerting, select SOCKS Proxy, WinSock Proxy, or Web Proxy service properties and click the `Security` button on the `Service` tab of the properties dialog.

Packet filter alerting applies equally to all Proxy Server services. Packet filter alerting changes made to any service properties will apply to and appear in the properties for each of the other services also.

Select the `Alerting` tab of the `Security` dialog to reveal the dialog shown in Figure 6.4.

To configure an alert for a particular event, select either `Rejected packets`, `Protocol violations`, or `Disk full` from the event drop-down box as shown in Figure 6.5.

To enable alerting for the event in the `Event` window, check the `Generate system event if more than...` checkbox and enter the number of times per second threshold in the `events per second` edit window. This threshold value is the number of selected events (rejected packets, protocol violations, disk full) that must occur within a second before the alert is triggered. The default value is 20, but you may wish to increase or decrease this depending on your network activity and the degree of responsiveness you desire.

If you would like alerts for this event to be transmitted via e-mail, check the `Send SMTP mail` checkbox. (We'll see how to configure the mail service in the next section.) If you would like the event to show in the System Log, check the `Report to Windows NT Event Log` checkbox. Note the `Delay before next report` edit window near the bottom of the dialog. This represents the minimum amount of time before alerts are "fired." The default of five minutes means you'll receive alerts for this event at no less

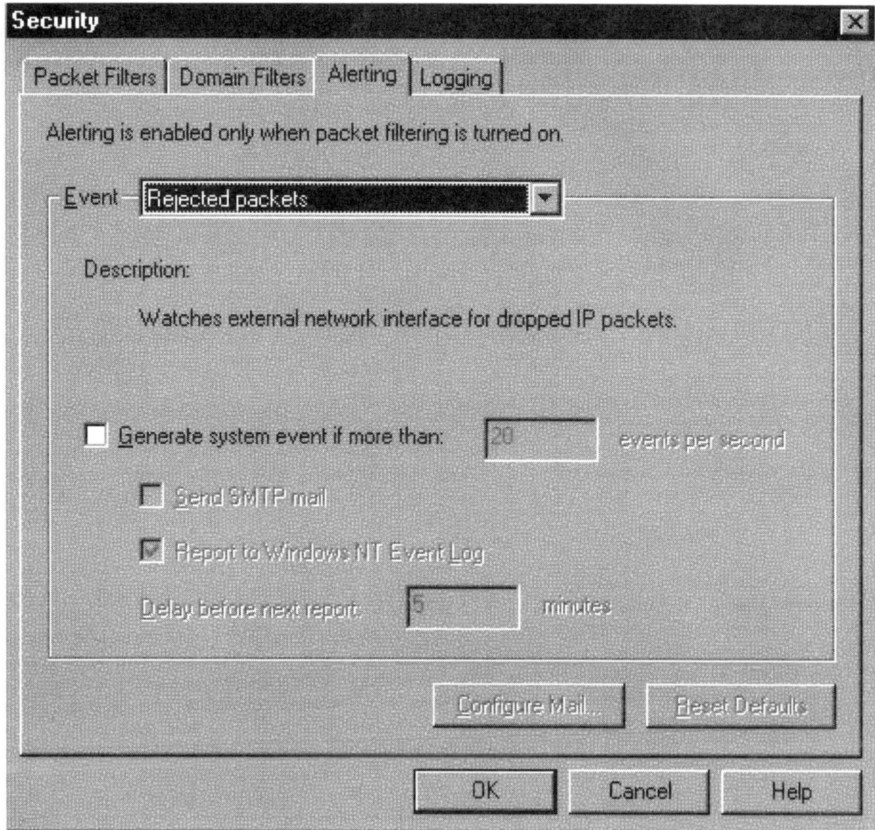

Figure 6.4 *Alerting tab of security dialog.*

than a five-minute interval, even if events that exceed the alerting criteria are constantly occurring. This will prevent you from receiving a flood of messages when a problem occurs. As with the event threshold, you may want to alter this value depending on the responsiveness you desire. The dialog also contains a `Reset Defaults` button. You can use this button to quickly return alerting for the particular event to the default.

Configuring E-mail Alerting

Once you've decided you want Proxy Server to send e-mail alerts, you'll need to configure the mail alerting feature. Before we actually configure e-mail alerting, you'll need to check a few important messaging concerns:

- The e-mail recipient must have a valid SMTP e-mail account. If you'll use a Microsoft Exchange Serve to send mail, the client account must

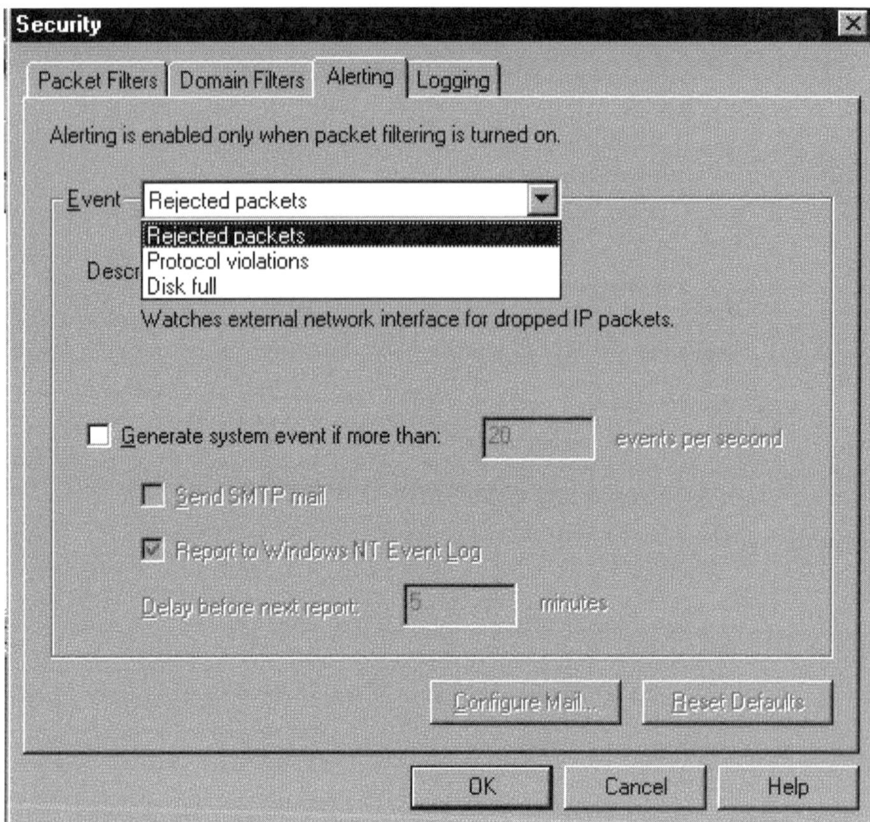

Figure 6.5 *Select event type for alerting.*

be from a legitimate Windows NT domain account. This can be a normal user account; it needs no special privileges.

- You must decide on a mail server through which to send the alert. You should use a mail server on the internal network because using a mail server on the external network would require you to use the path that is generating the alerts. Relying on such a path is tenuous at best.

With the groundwork complete, we can now turn our attention to configuring the e-mail alert. While still on the `Alerting` tab of the `Security` dialog, click the `Configure Mail` button to reveal the `Configure Mail Alerting` dialog depicted in Figure 6.6.

Enter the name or IP address of the mail server you'll route mail through in the `Mail server` edit window and enter the port number the

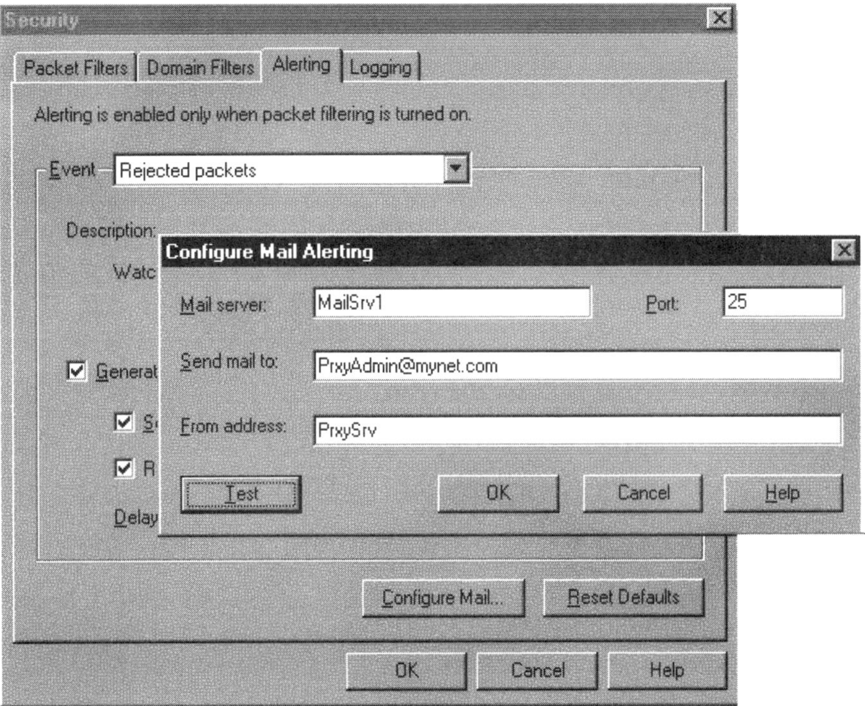

Figure 6.6 *Configure mail alerting dialog.*

mail server uses for SMTP mail in the `Port` window (this is typically port 25). In the `Send mail to` window, enter a valid SMTP address for the individual to whom you wish the alert sent. In the `From address` window enter an address for the Proxy Server computer (while using a valid SMTP address is recommended, you may actually use any name to identify which machine sent the alert). When you have configured all the parameters, click on the `Test` button to send a test message to the recipient you just configured. You may then click `OK` to close the dialog.

If, in spite of the foregoing discussion, you elect to send messages from the Proxy Server computer to a mail server on the *external* network, you must include the SMTP predefined filter exception to permit the Proxy Server to send SMTP mail through the external interface (once packet filtering is enabled).

Configuring Altering

Using guidance in the preceding section, configure alerting to generate a system event for rejected packets for more than one event per second. Have it write to the system event log and, if you have a mail-capable system, configure e-mail alerting also. (If you configure e-mail alerting, use the `Test` button to verify proper operation.) We'll check operation of this feature during the next hands-on section.

Packet Filter Logging

In addition to sending filter information to the Windows NT System Event Log, you may also send information to a dedicated Proxy Server log file that functions just like the logs for the Web WinSock and SOCKS Proxy services. The packet filtering log uses file naming conventions similar to the other logs. Instead of starting with the characters "WS," "W3," or "SP," however, the packet filtering log begins with "PF." Just as with the other logs, you may also elect to route your log entries to a SQL/ODBC database.

The Proxy Server Setup program installs a file called **pf.sql** in the **<systemroot>\help\proxy\misc** directory on the Proxy Server computer. This file provides a template for constructing the database table to receive your log data. The template is for use with Microsoft SQL Server and Microsoft Access databases.

To configure packet filter logging, select SOCKS Proxy, WinSock Proxy, or Web Proxy service properties and click the `Security` button on the `Service` tab of the properties dialog. Select the `Logging` tab of the `Security` dialog to reveal the dialog shown in Figure 6.7. Use the same procedures to configure packet filter logging you used to configure logging for the other services in Chapter 5.

The log file is written, by default, to the `<systemroot>\system32\ msplogs` directory and contains a listing of dropped packets. The text file contains the following comma delimited fields:

1. Date: The date the packet was captured
2. Time: The time the packet was captured
3. SourceIP: The IP address of the computer that originated the packet (may be the local or the remote computer depending on the packet's direction of travel)

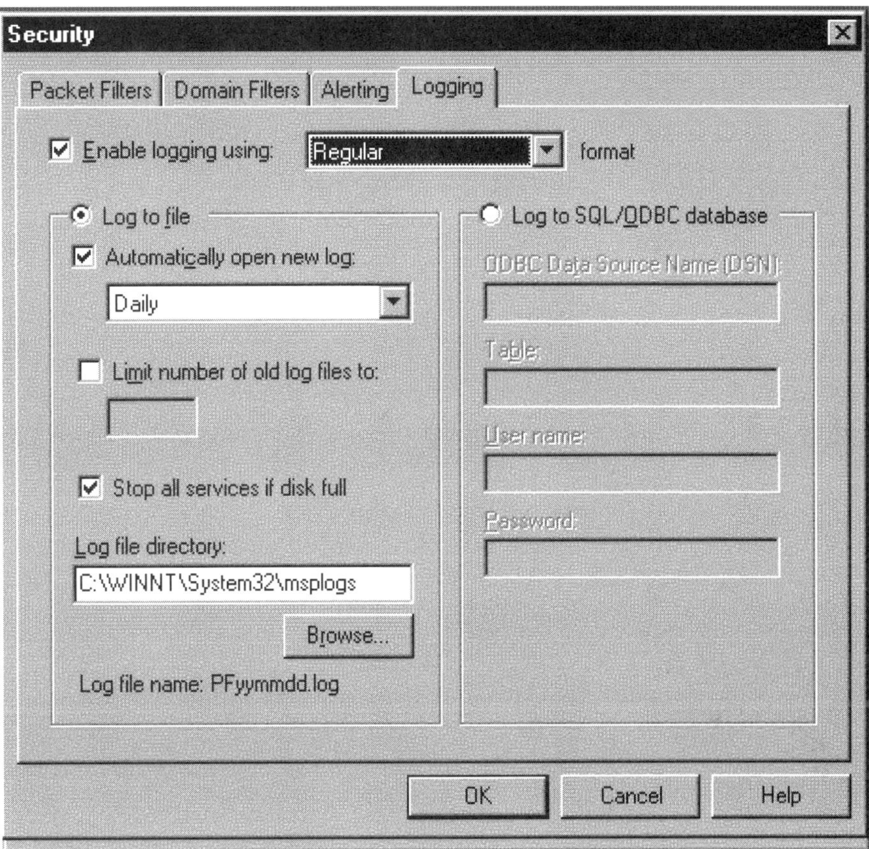

Figure 6.7 *Configure packet filter logging.*

4. TargetIP: The IP address of the computer that was to receive the packet (may be the local or the remote computer depending on the packet's direction of travel)

5. Protocol: The transport level protocol used for the transmission

6. SourcePort: The service port number of the computer that originated the packet (may be on the local or the remote computer depending on the packet's direction of travel). This port is valid only for TCP, UDP, or ICMP packets

7. TargetPort: The service port number of the computer that was to receive the packet (may be on the local or the remote computer depending on the packet's direction of travel). This port is valid only for TCP, UDP, or ICMP packets

8. TCP Flags: Valid only for TCP packets, this field shows the flag value from the packet's IP header:

   - FIN: Final close connection — no more data from sender
   - SYN: Synchronization packet
   - RST: Reset packet — aborts TCP connection
   - PSH: Push — normally used to display data on a client computer without client input
   - ACK: Acknowledge
   - URG: Urgent

9. Action: Zero for drop packet, one for accept packet (since only dropped packets are logged), this will always be zero

10. Interface: IP address of the interface that received the packet (normally the Proxy Server external adapter)

11. Raw IP Header: The IP header of the data packet that caused the alert. This is in hexadecimal format. (This field is written only when logging is configured for the *Verbose* format)

12. Raw IP Packet: The payload from the packet that caused the alert. This is in hexadecimal format. (This field is written only when logging is configured for the *Verbose* format)

You can use packet filter logging to troubleshoot packet filtering problems. Since the log displays dropped packets, it can help you determine what parameters you must select in creating your own filter exception for a particular inbound or outbound communication.

Study Break

Verifying Your Configuration

1. Using the preceding guidance, configure packet filtering logging. Now, disable dynamic filtering and attempt to access a Web site on the external network through an internal network client. Could you? Why not?

2. Check the Proxy Server System Log. Do you have any dropped packet alerts? (If you configured e-mail alerting, did you get an e-mail notification?)

3. Check the packet filter log to determine what packets were dropped and create your own packet filter exception(s) to permit Web access. (Hint: look for dropped TCP packets between a dynamic port on the external interface and port 80 of the Internet host.)

■ Summary

This chapter told us that packet filtering is a way to protect the Proxy Server external adapter by inspecting each packet that transits it. Packets may be filtered by protocol, port, source, or destination. Packet filtering applies to all Proxy Server services and may be either static or dynamic. Dynamic filtering, the default, opens a port when a client on the internal network initiates a communication. Both the client and the host it contacts on the internal network may communicate through the open port. When the client terminates the communication, the port is closed and no external host will be permitted access. To permit access by an external host, a packet filter exception must be created to keep the selected port open for communication. When dynamic filtering is disabled, the system will revert to static filtering. Under static filtering, filter exceptions must be configured for both inbound and outbound communication. Static filtering is normally used only when applications such as Microsoft Exchange Server are hosted on the Proxy Server itself.

Packet filtering can log activity and provide alerts when rejected packets or protocol violations are detected or when the hard disk is full. Alerts can be written to the system log or sent via an e-mail message. A dedicated filter log receives information concerning each packet dropped by packet filtering. The log may be read as a text file or routed to a SQL/ODBC database.

▲ REVIEW QUESTIONS

1. *You have been directed to analyze packets that are rejected by your Proxy Server. How can you configure Proxy Server to notify you when packets are rejected?*

   A. Set an alert in Windows NT Network Monitor

   B. Configure Alerting in the Proxy Server Security properties

   C. Configure packet filter logging

   D. Configure Packet Forwarding

2. *You have just installed a Web server on your internal network. The Web server is configured to operate through your Proxy Server computer's Web Proxy service, which uses dynamic packet filtering. Users on the external network are unable to contact the Web server. What step should you take to permit access to the Web server while ensuring a high degree of internal network security?*

    A. Enable Packet Forwarding on the Proxy Server computer

    B. Disable dynamic packet filtering

    C. Add a packet filter exception for inbound HTTP traffic

    D. Add a packet filter exception for outbound HTTP traffic

3. *You are concerned that users on the external network may be able to view the NetBIOS name table on your Proxy Server computer. What step(s) should you take to ensure this information is secure?*

    A. Delete the NetBIOS name table

    B. Enable dynamic packet filtering

    C. Make the machine a WINS client

    D. Remove the default gateway from the external interface

4. *Your network is protected by a Proxy Server computer using dynamic packet filtering. A user in one of your remote offices needs to access your file server over the Internet. How can you permit her access while maintaining a high degree of internal security? (Select all that apply)*

    A. Switch to static packet filtering

    B. Disable packet filtering

    C. Create an inbound filter exception that permits only the user's computer (by IP address) access to your network

    D. Edit the filter exception to permit access only to the designated file server

5. *You have a Web server on your internal network that is configured to use TCP port 300 for HTTP. Your Proxy Server uses dynamic packet filtering and is configured to permit the internal Web server to use the Web Proxy Service to publish on the Internet. What else is required?*

    A. Add an outbound TCP packet filter exception for port 300

    B. Disable dynamic packet filtering

    C. Add the predefined HTTP packet filter exception

    D. Add an inbound TCP packet filter exception for port 300

6. *You've enabled packet filtering to afford your network additional security from Internet intrusion. What should you configure to ensure you're notified when attempts are made against Proxy Server ports which have been closed by filtering?*

    A. Rejected Packets

    B. Port Violations

    C. Protocol Violations

    D. Filter Violations

7. *What can you do to prevent your Proxy Server computer from listening for RPC requests on the external interface?*

    A. Disable RPC service

    B. Enable Access Control

    C. Disable Access Control

    D. Enable Packet Filtering

Networks with Multiple Proxy Server Computers

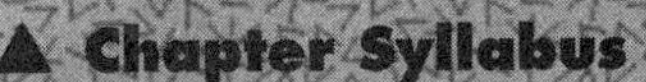

▲ Chapter Syllabus

In many endeavors if a little is good, a lot is better. Such is the case with Proxy Server. By utilizing multiple servers, you can increase your effective cache size, increase your available bandwidth to the external network, permit load balancing, and provide Proxy Server fault tolerance.

At the conclusion of this chapter you will be able to:

- Define Proxy Server Arrays and Chains and discuss the advantages of each

- Explain the Cache Array Routing Protocol and discuss the chief advantage over previous cache routing schemes

- Configure multiple Proxy Server computers to form arrays and chains

- Manually configure WinSock Proxy and Web Proxy gateways

- Employ DNS and WINS to load balance Web Proxy gateways

MCSE 7.1 Multiple Proxy Server Arrangements

Multiple proxy servers can be placed in a network in two configurations: arrays and chains. Each has its own features and set of advantages. Arrays and chains may be combined to offer a hybrid structure combining some of the advantages of both.

Proxy Server Arrays

In an array configuration, Proxy Server computers are arranged in parallel as shown in Figure 7.1. In this configuration, which is also known as *Distributed Proxying*, Proxy Servers can combine their resources to provide load balancing and fault tolerance. In this peer-to-peer arrangement, each array-member must be running Microsoft Proxy Server 2.0. A Proxy array provides fault tolerance because each Proxy Server computer is capable of functioning independently. If one or more machines go down, the remaining Proxy Servers carry the load. The effective Proxy Server cache is increased because all the individual caches are combined to form a single large logical cache.

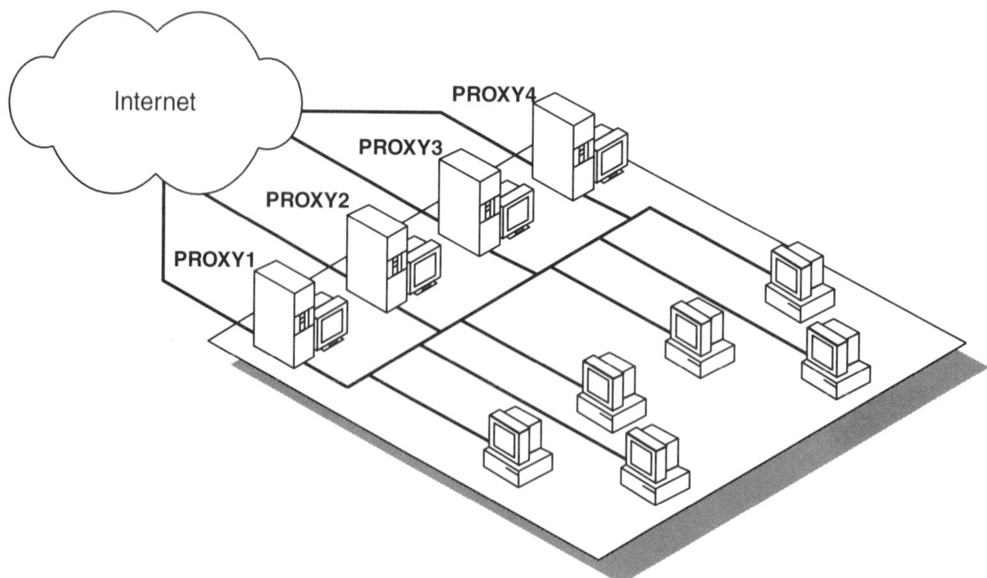

Figure 7.1 *Proxy Server array.*

Even though a Proxy Server array provides excellent fault tolerance, a client that is configured to use a particular Proxy Server computer as a gateway will be unable to access the external network when that computer is down. While other members of the array can provide connectivity, the client must use the configured gateway to gain access to the array.

Each member of a Proxy Server array provides its settings to the other members of the array. Settings are propagated using a synchronization process much like that of *My Briefcase*. Each member is aware of the other members of the array. When a member goes down, the other members know this and listen for the inoperative member's return. The following information is synchronized to ensure each array member has the same settings:

- Standard and advanced Web Proxy Service caching options
- Protocol configuration for Web and WinSock Proxy services
- Web Proxy service publishing and security information
- Web Proxy service upstream routing options
- WinSock Proxy service security information
- Permissions for SOCKS Proxy service
- Client configuration information
- Domain filters
- Service logging information (except packet filtering)
- Local Address Table information

The following information is not synchronized and may be uniquely set on each array member:

- Packet filters, packet filter alerts, and packet filter logging
- Logging directories
- Web Proxy service cache size and directory locations
- Web Proxy Service `Enable caching` (`Enable active caching` *does* synchronize)

SOME IMPORTANT ARRAY CONSIDERATIONS

While Proxy Server arrays can be a significant benefit to our networks, we need to be aware of a number of important factors before we proceed:

- Proxy Server Administration: Since most Proxy Server settings are synchronized with the other array members, configuring more than one server at a time can cause ambiguities. As we'll see, Proxy Server has a method for dealing with these ambiguities, but the best plan is to avoid them by configuring only one arrayed Proxy Server at a time.

- Administrative Permissions: Administrative permissions are required before you can create or join an array. If you will accomplish these tasks, ensure your administrative permissions extend to each array member you plan to administer.

- Domain Accounts: Since Proxy Server arrays encompass multiple machines, it is best to use a domain (not local machine) administrative account to access and manage them.

- Machine Limit: The practical upper limit for a Proxy Server array is about 20 machines.

- Machine requirement: For a large business, at least one Proxy Server array member should be installed for every 2,000 computers.

GATEWAYS

When Proxy Servers are arrayed, they can each provide an Internet gateway, effectively increasing your Internet bandwidth. The Web Proxy service can be configured to permit clients to share these gateways. Alternatively, you can configure groups of clients to use only a single gateway. The choice will depend on usage patterns of your network. The WinSock Proxy service, however, does not permit such alternatives. To balance WinSock Proxy gateway access, you must assign a specific gateway to each client computer. Actual assignments should be based on client usage patterns. We'll see how to configure gateway access a bit later in this chapter.

When we say a Proxy Server array increases bandwidth, it is important to remember the actual amount of available bandwidth depends on the external connection. If, for instance, you have an array of five Proxy Server computers, each with an external interface that *independently* accesses the Internet (through its own modem or T1 line), you will actually increase your bandwidth. If, however, each Proxy Servers external interface accesses the Internet through the same T1 line (which is often the case), your actual bandwidth is set by the bandwidth available from the T1 line — regardless of how many servers you add to the array. In this latter case, we can still say the Proxy Server array increases *available* bandwidth because the more efficient caching obtained with a Proxy Server array will reduce the requirement for Internet access, making more bandwidth available for other uses.

What is Meant by "Usage Patterns?"

Let's say, for example, you have 10 clients that show very light Internet use and six clients that exhibit heavy Internet use. If there are four gateways available, you might put the 10 light users on a single gateway and assign two heavy users to each of the remaining gateways.

Proxy Server Chains

In contrast to Proxy Server arrays, which employ Proxy Servers in a parallel configuration, Proxy Servers may also be combined serially to form a chain, as shown in Figure 7.2. Chaining is also referred to as *Routing, Cascaded Proxying,* or *Hierarchical Proxying.* The caching available from a Proxy Server chain is referred to as *Hierarchical Caching.* As you work your way along the chain, those servers closer to the Internet are known as *upstream* servers while those closer to the client are considered *downstream* servers. This nomenclature is independent of the actual direction of communication. Proxy chains can provide load balancing and improved caching but, because they are serially configured, they provide no fault tolerance. (A measure of fault tolerance may be obtained by configuring a backup route.) If one member of the chain goes down, final access to the outside network fails.

Unlike arrays, Proxy Server chains share no configuration information. Each server remains an independent entity, relying on the others only to complete the route to the external network. Because configuration information is an individual concern, chained Proxy Servers do not all need to run Proxy Server 2.0. A Proxy Server chain may also include Proxy Server 1.0 computers as well as those running third party proxy and firewall products.

When a request is issued to a proxy chain, the most downstream Proxy Server attempts to honor the request from its cache. If it cannot, it will pass the request upstream. If no server can provide the requested information, the query is ultimately passed to the external network. We'll see how to configure Proxy Server chains a bit later in the chapter.

`MCSE 7.2` Cache Array Routing Protocol

If Proxy Server arrays provide a single large effective cache, how do members of the array know exactly where to find cached items? Microsoft Proxy Server 1.0 used the Internet Cache Protocol (ICP) to perform this function.

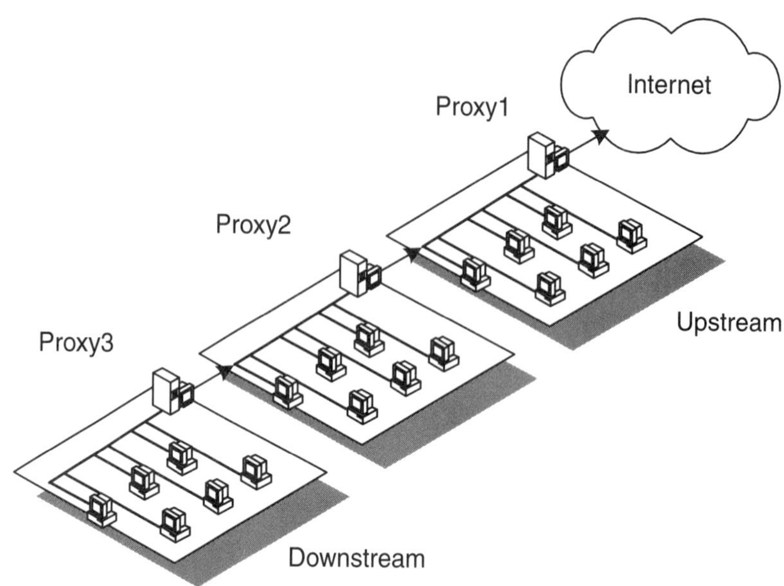

Figure 7.2 *Proxy Server chain.*

Unfortunately, ICP was a query routine, which required a check of each cache until the requested information was found or until the request had to be passed tot he external network. As you may imagine, a few simultaneous queries with the attendant negative or affirmative acknowledgements can sharply increase network traffic. As the network is scaled up, more servers and more clients result in more queries and even more network traffic. To make matters worse, ICP caused the cached information, once located, to be copied to the client's default Proxy Server, which resulted in a great deal of duplication within the caches.

Proxy Server 2.0 introduces the Cache Array Routing Protocol (CARP) to replace the older ICP. Unlike ICP, CARP is *"queryless."* Instead of checking each cache for its contents, CARP goes directly to the correct location and retrieves the data. Because CARP is, essentially, a set of algorithms that function on top of HTTP, it can perform its duties without the introduction of a new "wire protocol." Since CARP can go directly to cached information and since it retrieves the information in-place, it sharply increases the scalability of any Proxy Server array.

CARP performs its magic by computing the location for each cached URL. Since all arrayed Proxy Servers are members of an "array membership list" which is regularly checked (based on time-to-live) for active membership, it is easy to determine the servers with cache resources. To determine where to cache a particular URL, CARP first computes a hash value for each name on the array membership list. Next, CARP computes a hash value for the URL and combines these values using a combination algorithm which takes into account the load handling capability of each server (obviously, a server with greater capacity should get more cached items). The server that attains the highest "score" from this process receives the URL. The retrieval process works exactly the same way. When a URL is to be located, CARP computes a score in exactly the same way (the score will always come out the same) and will go directly to the appropriate server. (Remember, hashed values are combined through a *combination algorithm*; they are not added. A simple add would result in the server with the best scoring name getting all the cached items.)

If the server with the highest score is not available (because it has gone down or been removed from the network), the next highest scoring server will be checked. If it does not contain the cached information, it will query the external network and will cache the information upon receipt. Because the highest scoring available server always gets to cache the information, adding or removing machines from the array causes little impact to the array. New servers pick up items for which they score highest and the previously high scoring servers allow the information they once "owned" to time out and leave their caches. Likewise, when a server is removed, the next highest (now highest) scoring server is queried and obtains the information if required. The fraction of the total number of caches reassigned when a machine is added or removed is approximately $1/n$, where n is the number of active Proxy Servers.

Since every member of the array maintains a copy of the array membership list, any member of the array or any client browser can use CARP to quickly compute the location for any URL without the need for extensive network queries or the maintenance of cache location tables. Because requests are always sent to the highest scoring server, it is not possible to develop a "routing loop" where servers continually query each other for requested non-cached information.

CARP can provide both hierarchical and distributed routing. While most of the foregoing discussion has assumed distributed routing (that is, *within* an array), hierarchical routing permits the forwarding of requests from a single proxy up to an array of upstream proxies.

While ICP was used only on Proxy Servers, CARP may be implemented on clients using the existing, industry standard, client Proxy Auto-Config file (PAC). PAC permits clients, as well as Proxy Servers, to obtain cache resolution through CARP.

Although the first word in CARP is *cache*, CARP functions even when caching is turned off. CARP selects the Proxy Server computer within the array that will retrieve the desired resource. When you access a particular Proxy Server computer, it will use CARP to determine which array member should actually locate the resource and the query proceeds through that computer.

Study Break

What is Hashing?

Hashing, or *hash coding*, is simply a way to compute a location key for a particular data item. A *hash function* is applied to the item to yield a *hash value*, which becomes the item's key or index. Hash functions should result in unique hash values or *hash collisions* will occur when an attempt is made to place more than one item in the same indexed location. Hash functions must be tailored to work with the particular items they'll hash and should compute values based generally on the available number of indexed locations.

When you look a name up in a telephone book, you usually hash that name by extracting the first letter of the last name to give us a general location in which to enter the listing. If that was the extent of CARP's hash function, every server whose name started with the same letter would yield the same value. The CARP hash functions undoubtedly use several factors. Factors such as the value and position of each letter in the server name as well as the total number of letters in the name would be appropriate in this case.

MCSE 7.3   Configuring Proxy Server Arrays

A Proxy Server array is created when the first two machines are linked as array members. At that point, the array is given a name and additional machines may join by using the array name. To configure a Proxy Server array (assuming there are multiple Proxy Server 2.0 computers in your environment) accomplish the following:

1. From Internet Service manager select the SOCKS, WinSock, or Web Proxy service and select Service Properties from the Properties menu. Click the Array button to reveal the dialog shown in Figure 7.3.
2. Click the `Join Array` button and enter the name of another Proxy Server computer on your network as shown in Figure 7.4.
3. Since we're creating a new array, the system next asks us to name the array. Enter a name for the new array as shown in Figure 7.5 and click OK.

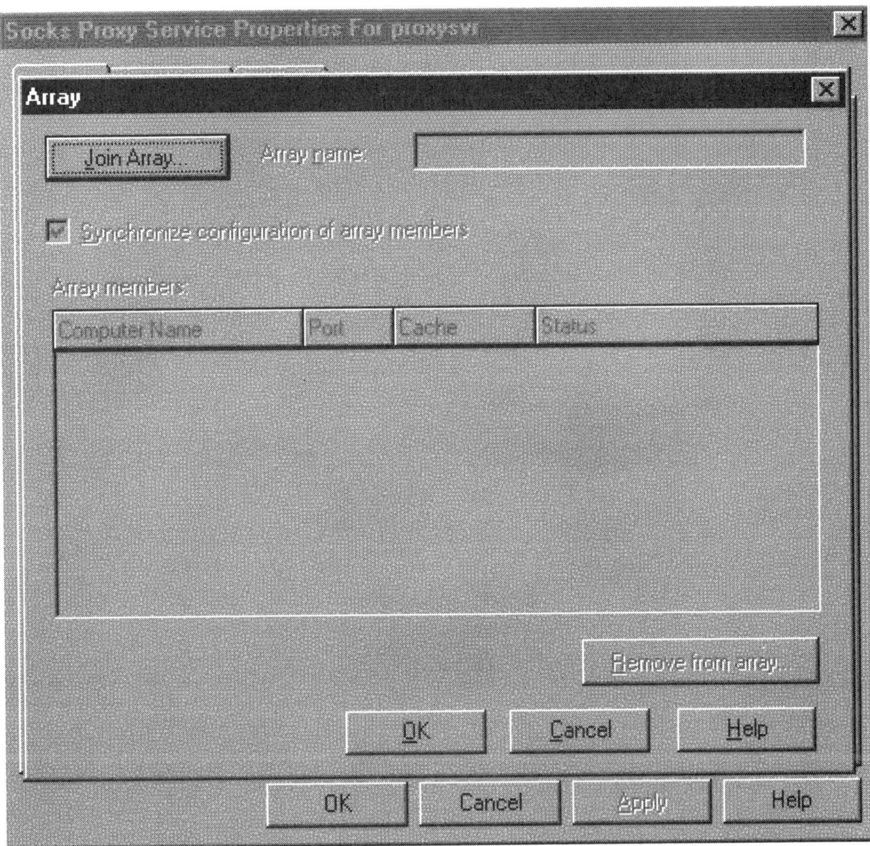

Figure 7.3 *Array dialog.*

4. Click OK to close the Array dialog box and click Apply on the `Service` tab to implement the array configuration.
5. You may now click on the `Array` button once again to display the completed Array dialog shown in Figure 7.6.

Note that array members are configured for automatic configuration by default. You may have also noticed that the `Array` dialog box provides an option to remove any server displayed in the list box by highlighting it and clicking the `Remove from array button`. Additionally, you can cause the local computer to leave the array simply by clicking the `Leave Array` button. When the array consists of only two Proxy Server computers, removing either of them will, of course, terminate the array and cause each machine to operate in a stand-alone mode. When you attempt to do this, you are warned accordingly.

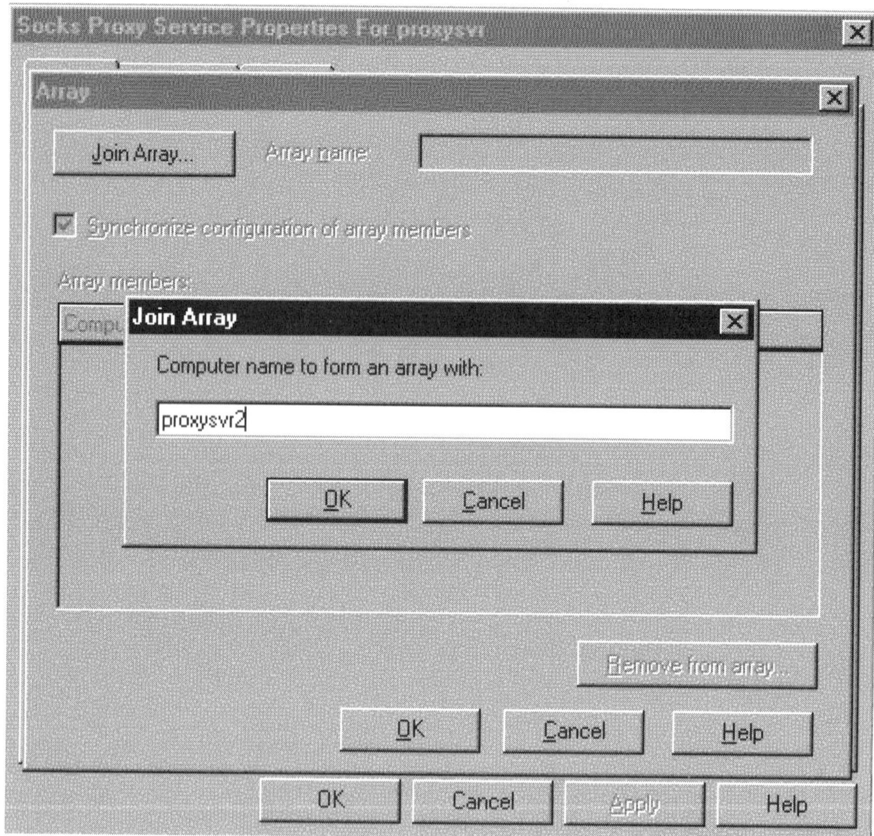

Figure 7.4   *Adding another Proxy Server to the array.*

Configuration Changes and Synchronization

Just as *My Briefcase* becomes confused when changes are made to both copies between synchronization, Proxy Server arrays complain when conflicting changes are made to different Proxy Servers between synchronization periods. When this happens, the administrator making the conflicting change is shown the dialog exhibited in Figure 7.7. Selecting `Refresh` will discard your changes in favor of those made on the other computer. If you select `Overwrite`, on the other hand, your changes will take effect and will replicate across the array.

If you decide to force your changes on the network (with `Overwrite`), you are shown the `Array Configuration Conflict` dialog as depicted in Figure 7.8. This dialog is telling you that other servers have tried to make

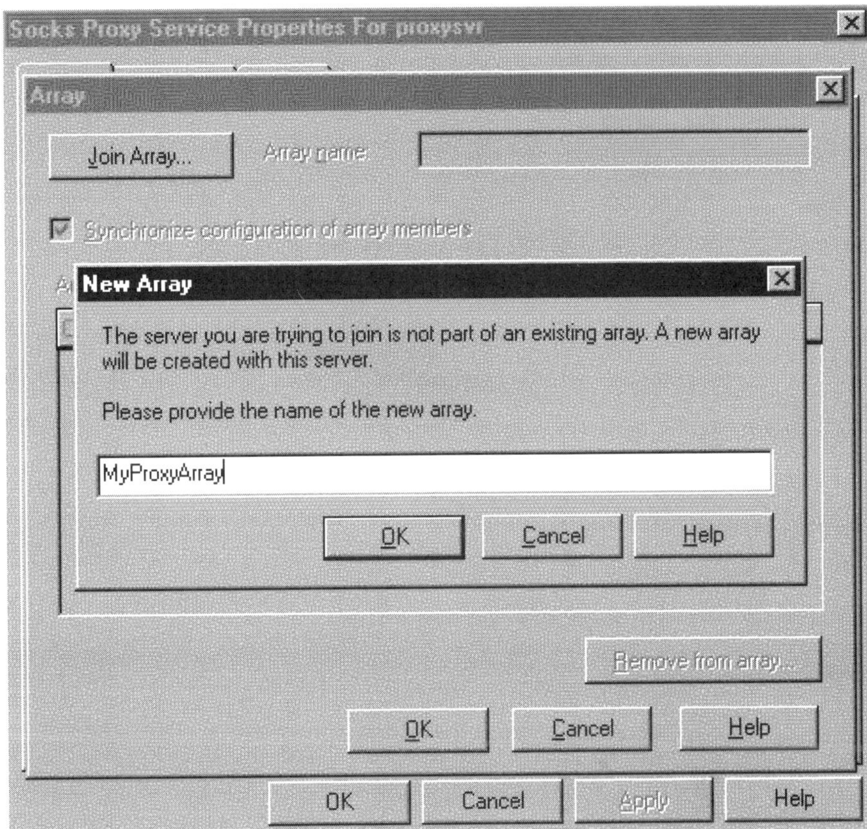

Figure 7.5 *Enter array name.*

changes to parameters at the same time. Select the server whose changes you wish to propagate throughout the array and click `Synchronize Now`. If you select `Cancel`, you return to the Internet Service Manager and array synchronization is not accomplished. Each time you attempt to make a change, you will ultimately be returned to the `Array Configuration Conflict` dialog.

Although, as we've seen, there is a way to resolve configuration conflicts, the best policy is to avoid conflict by updating only one server at a time.

After making configuration changes to a Proxy Server, make sure you stop and restart each Proxy Server service.

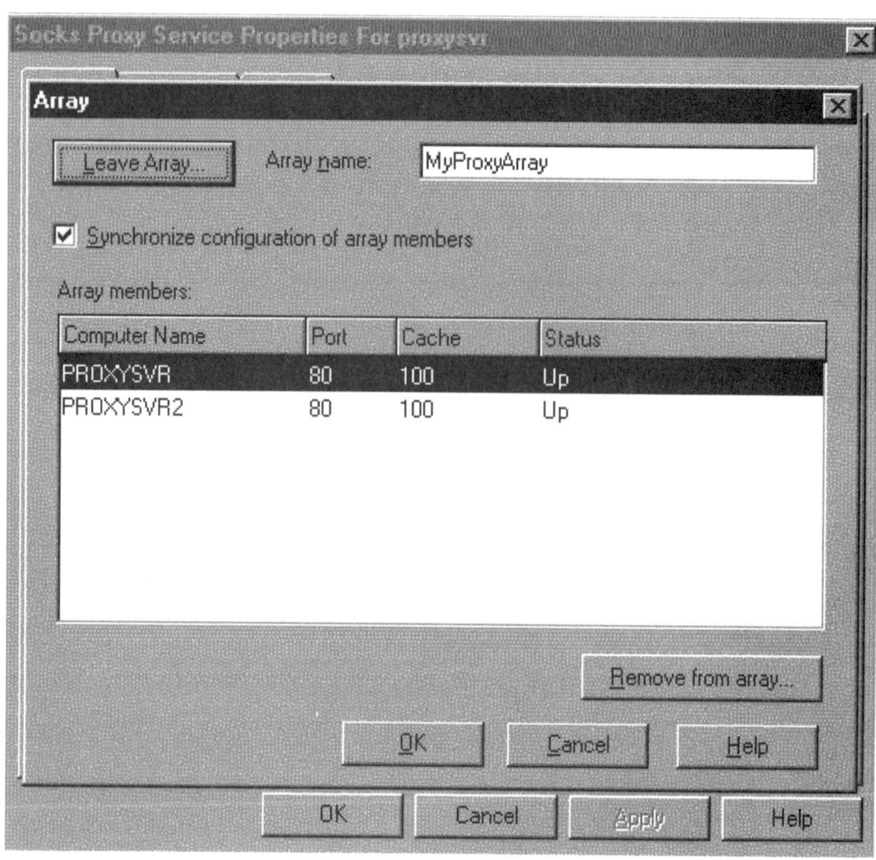

Figure 7.6 *Array dialog showing array members.*

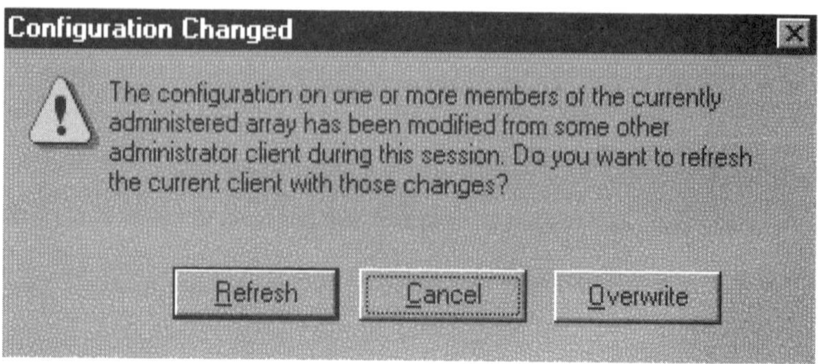

Figure 7.7 *Configuration changed dialog.*

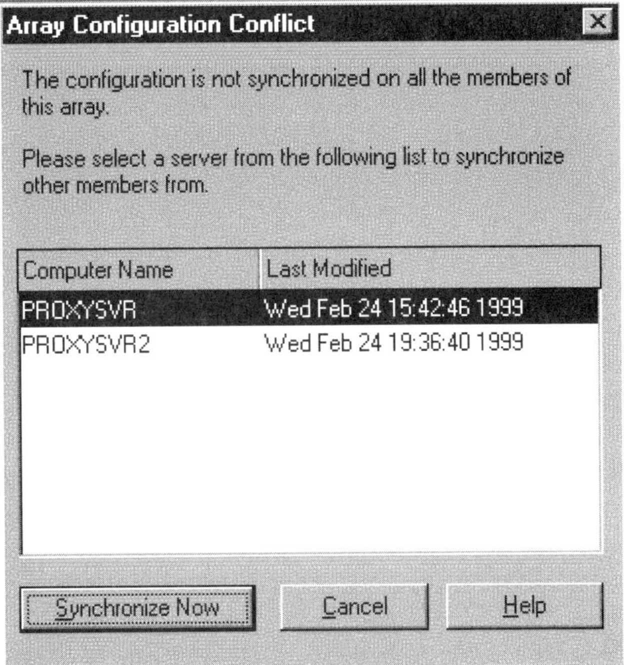

Figure 7.8 *Array configuration conflict dialog.*

Routing Within the Array

If your Proxy Server is a member of an array, you'll likely want it to route client requests within the array before looking for resolution on the Internet or a designated upstream server (we'll see how to designate an upstream server in the next section). While this behavior is the default, it can be configured from the Web Proxy Service's routing tab (see Figure 7.9). If the `Resolve Web Proxy requests within the array before routing upstream` checkbox is not checked, any request that cannot be fulfilled by the local server is routed upstream instead to other array members.

Once the `Resolve Web Proxy requests within the array before routing upstream` checkbox is checked, you have access to the advanced options. Click the `Advanced` button to reveal the `Advanced Array Options` dialog shown in Figure 7.10. From this dialog you may alter the `Table TTL`. It is the `Table TTL` that specifies how often members update their array membership tables. If the volatility of your network warrants a number other than the 50-minute default value, you may change it here. (This property will be propagated to other array members.)

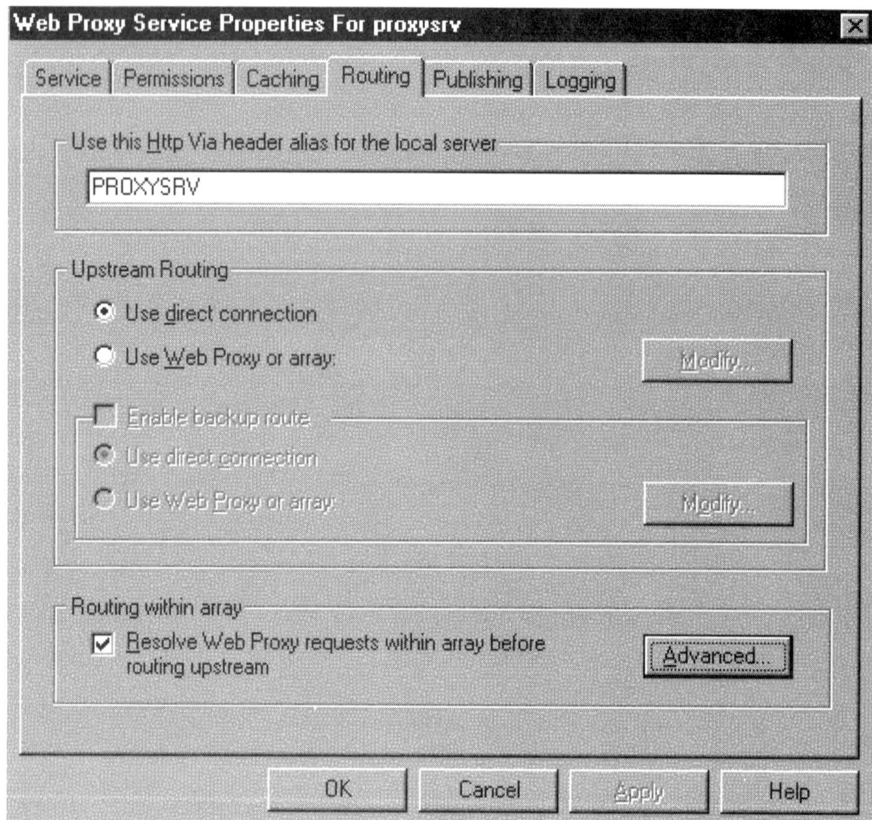

Figure 7.9 *Routing tab.*

Note the `Use credentials to communicate within array` section. This provides account information that may be required to access other members of the array. (This is normally an issue when array members are in different Windows NT domains.)

If authentication with the array members is an issue, check the `Use credentials to communicate within array` checkbox and enter a username and password that will permit a logon to the other array members. If the system supports encrypted authentication (such as in a Windows NT domain), select the `Allow encrypted authentication (NT CR)` radio button. Otherwise, select `Allow basic/clear text authentication`. Ensure the selected user has permission to use HTTP. Since this information

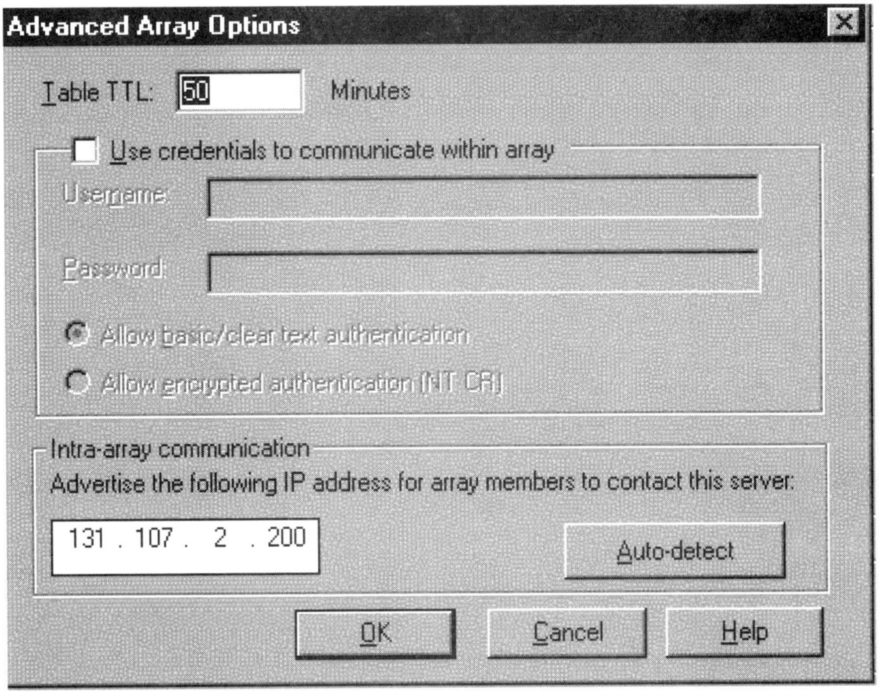

Figure 7.10 *Advanced array options dialog.*

is propagated to all other array members, ensure the account selected will work for all Proxy Servers within the array.

The `Intra-array communication` section permits you to select the IP address the local Proxy Server will use to communicate with the other servers in the array. If the server has only one IP address on the internal network, this will already contain that address. If your server has multiple network adapter cards on the internal network (for instance one for communicating with clients and one for communicating with array members), the system may have made the wrong guess concerning which one to use for the array. When you have multiple internal network interfaces, be sure to check this value to ensure the system has picked the correct one. You may enter the appropriate IP address in the edit window or click the `Auto-detect` button to cycle through the machines internal network IP addresses. When you have completed reviewing this dialog, click `OK` to leave the `Advanced Array Options` dialog and `Apply` to enter your changes.

Study Break

Creating a Proxy Server Array

If you are using a production network for your hands-on training, be sure to discuss the following activities with your network administrator before proceeding. Using the steps outlined in Chapter 4, install Proxy Server on another machine in your network. Once the new Proxy Server is operating, refer to the steps in this section and create a Proxy Server array that consists of your Proxy Server computers.

1. On one of the arrayed computers, change the Active Caching status.
2. Allow a few moments for the array to synchronize and check active caching on the other Proxy Server. Did it change?
3. Experiment with other options and see how they synchronize.
4. Try making conflicting changes to both machines and see how the array responds.
5. When you've completed this exercise, remove one Proxy Server computer from the array to remove the array from the network.

MCSE 7.4   Configuring Proxy Server Chains

Proxy Server chains provide hierarchical caching and are created by designating each downstream Proxy Server to route requests to an upstream Proxy Server. To do this, accomplish the following steps:

1. From Internet Service manager select the Web Proxy service and select Service Properties from the Properties menu. Click the Routing tab to reveal the dialog shown in Figure 7.11

   Under `Upstream Routing`, select `Use Web Proxy` or `Array` and click the `Modify` button to reveal the `Advanced routing options` dialog shown in Figure 7.12.
   Enter the name of the upstream proxy server in the `Proxy` edit window. If you will use an HTTP port other than 80, ensure you enter the appropriate port number in the `Port` edit window. `Auto-poll` is selected by default. This option will prompt your server to automatically poll the upstream server for array properties (use only if the upstream server is actually an array). One of the properties retrieved is the array membership list. (You'll remember the importance of this list from the Cache Array Routing Protocol section of this chapter.) The `Array URL` entry is automatically entered based on the name you enter for `Upstream Web Server`. The format

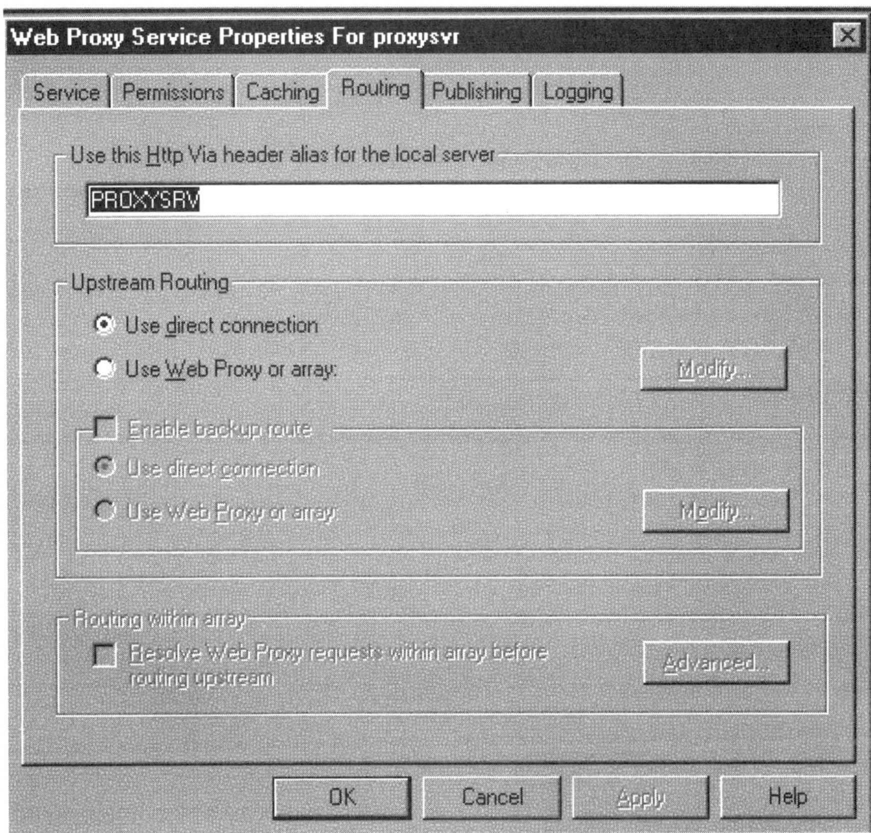

Figure 7.11 *Routing tab.*

is as shown in Figure 7.12. `Proxysvr2` is the name of the upstream server and `80` is the port number it uses for HTTP.

While still in the `Advanced Routing Options` dialog (Figure 7.12), look at the `Use credentials to communicate with upstream proxy/array` section. This provides account information that may be required to access the upstream Proxy Server. (This is normally an issue when the upstream Proxy Server is in a different Windows NT domain.) If authentication with the upstream Proxy Server is an issue, check the `Use credentials to communicate with upstream proxy/array` checkbox and enter a username and password that will permit a logon on the upstream server. If the system supports encrypted authentication (such as in a Windows NT domain), select the `Allow encrypted authentication (NT CR)` radio button. Otherwise, select `Allow basic/clear text authen-`

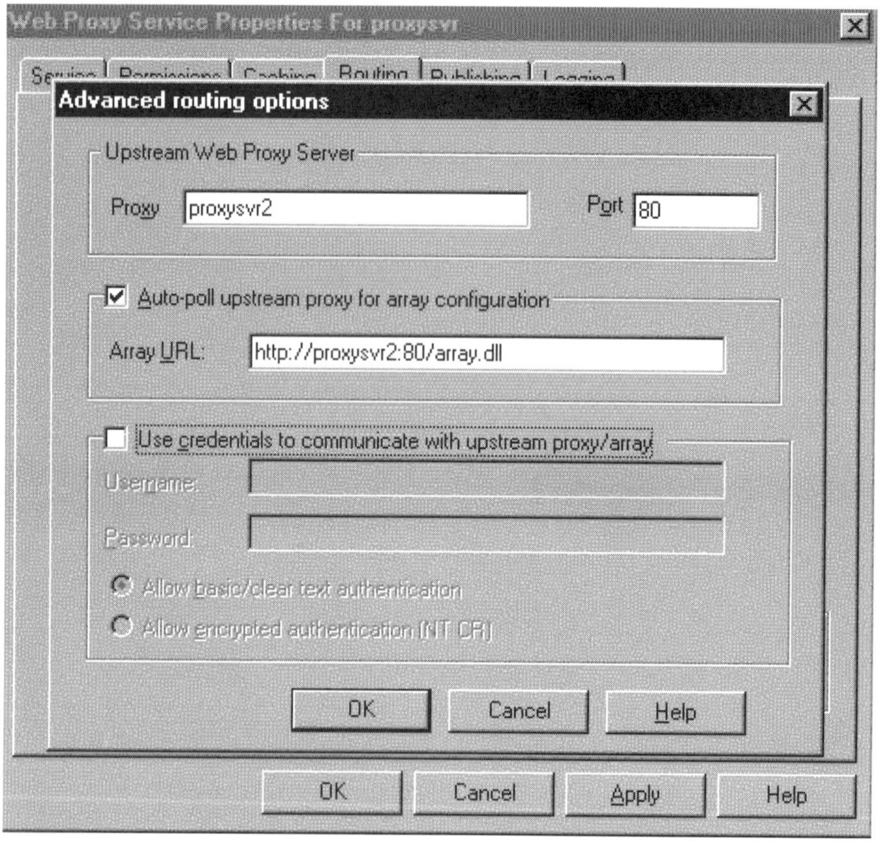

Figure 7.12 *Advanced routing options dialog.*

tication. When you have completed entries under `Advanced Routing options`, click `OK` to return to the `Routing` tab.

If you wish to have a backup route (one that will take effect when the designated upstream server or array is unavailable), check the `Enable backup route` checkbox on the `Routing` tab (see Figure 7.11). You may select `Use direct connection` to allow your Proxy Server to go directly to the Internet when it can't find the upstream server, or you can select `Use Web Proxy` or `array` if you wish to route to an alternate upstream server or array. If you select `Use Web Proxy` or `array`, you'll need to click on the `Modify` button which will reveal a new `Advanced routing options` dialog (see Figure 7.12). Complete this dialog in the same manner used for the initial upstream server but enter information for the desired backup server or array.

Note

Remember, that while Proxy Server arrays apply to all Proxy Server services, chains are applicable to the Web Proxy service only.

Study Break

Viewing the Array Membership List

You may wish to view the array membership list from the command line. The RemoteMSP utility, found in the \msp directory permits you to view the array membership list and the load factor and status of each machine in the array. The syntax for the utility is as follows:

```
RemotMsp status -member:servername -v
```

where *servername* is the array member from which you wish to view the array membership list.
In the following example, we view the membership list from array member *proxysvr*:

```
C:\msp>remotmsp status -member:proxysvr -v
Array configuration information from proxy PROXYSVR

Version 02.00.0372
Proxy Array
Array Name: MyProxyArray
Synchronize Array Configuration: Enabled
Distributed Cache: Enabled

Machine Cache Load Time
Name Status Size Factor Version Stamp
PROXYSVR OK 100 100 (%50) 02.00.0372 36d6f029 36d6f029
PROXYSVR2 OK 100 100 (%50) 02.00.0372 36d6a646 36d6a646
0 machines are down.
The array is syncronized
Operation completed successfully
```

Multiple Proxy Servers, Windows NT Domains, and Trusts

We've discussed the use of credentials for both arrays and chains and indicated they would, typically, be required in a network with multiple Windows NT domains. As you're aware, under Windows NT, permission is required to access resources. In a single domain it is fairly easy to provide access permissions to all resources since everyone has an account on the domain controller. What happens when you need to access a resource in another domain? If you're a Proxy Server and you need to access a Proxy Server in another domain, the "credentials" can permit you that access through an account on the other domain. In Proxy *chains*, since each server needs to access only the next server in the chain, each set of credentials need contain only a username and password valid on the next upstream Proxy Server

When dealing with Proxy Server arrays across multiple domains, however, the plot thickens a bit. Each array member will likely need to contact each other array member on a regular basis. When array members are in different domains, the user name and password entered in "credentials" will need to work properly in each domain. To permit this, trust relationships may need to be set up between domains containing the Proxy Server array members. The number of trusts depends on the number of Proxy Servers and the number of domains. If each proxy server need only contact one other Proxy Server (two-machine array) even when the other machine is in another domain, no trust is required. This is because each machine need only use an account for the other domain. In the case of three Proxy Server computers in three domains, however, you would need a minimum of three one-way trusts with each domain trusting the next. Each Proxy Server could use credentials for one of the other domains and the credentials would work in the remaining domain because of the trust. The situation gets even more complex when some array members share a domain and others don't. In such cases, you'll need to map out the locations of domains and Proxy Server array members to determine where trusts must exist.

Study Break

Configuring a Proxy Server Chain

Use the steps in this section and configure your Proxy Server computers in a chain. If only one of your machines has an external interface, make sure you configure that one as the upstream server. To prove this works, configure your browser to use the downstream Proxy Server. (If the downstream Proxy Server has an external interface disconnect its cable.) Use your browser to access a resource on the external network. If you're successful, your browser went through the downstream Proxy Server, which accessed the external network through the upstream Proxy Server. Once you've proven upstream routing works, reconnect the external interface on your downstream server (if you disconnected it previously) and return your downstream server's upstream routing to `Use Direct Connection`.

MCSE 7.5 Configuring Gateways

As we learned at the beginning of this chapter, Proxy Server arrays can provide a network with multiple gateways. To achieve proper load balancing, it is important to be able to perform the configuration required to ensure balanced access to the available gateways by members of the internal network. Even though the computer that ultimately retrieves a particular resource within the array is determined through CARP, the client enters the array through a designated gateway. It is important to ensure this gateway access is balanced throughout the network. Although we're approaching the subject from the standpoint of gateway balancing for *arrays*, it's important to understand that these techniques will work for multiple Proxy Server computers on an internal network whether they're arrayed or not. In this section we will look at ways to provide both automatic (variable) and manual (fixed) gateway selection.

Configuring WinSock Proxy Gateways

As you will remember, earlier in this chapter we indicated that while the Web Proxy Service can be configured to share gateways, balancing WinSock Proxy gateway access requires that you assign a specific gateway to each client computer. The WinSock Proxy gateway is automatically selected during client installation. After client installation, a new gateway may be selected through the `WSP Client` icon in `Control Panel` to reveal the dialog shown in Figure 7.13. To change the designated gateway, replace the machine name listed under `Server Name`. You should select WinSock Proxy gateways based on the capability of the gateway and the usage pattern of the machine's user. If, for instance, the user of the machine frequently uses applications, such as RealAudio, that utilize greater than average resources, you should assign the user to amore powerful gateway or to a gateway that has fewer other users assigned.

Manually Configuring Web Proxy Gateway

Like the WinSock Proxy gateway, a Web Proxy gateway is automatically installed during client installation. If you wish to manually change the gateway, you may do so through the browser. If you're using Internet Explorer 3.0, select `View|Options|Connection` to reveal the dialog depicted in Figure 7.14. (If you are using Internet Explorer 4.0, select `View|Internet Options|Connection` and click the `Advanced` button to arrive at the same dialog.) From this dialog, you may change the name of the designated Proxy

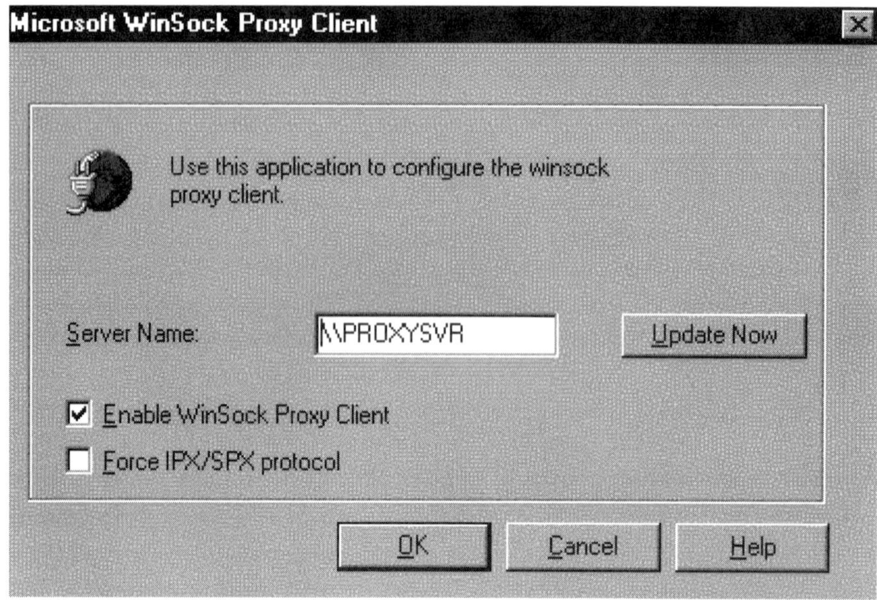

Figure 7.13 *Microsoft WinSock Proxy client dialog.*

Server to a machine you feel more appropriate. If you will employ this manual method (vice the automatic selection of Web Proxy gateways, which we will discuss in the next section), use the load balancing concepts we discussed for WinSock proxy gateways.

Using DNS to Balance Internet Access Across Multiple Proxy Servers

Web Proxy gateway access may be automated through a Microsoft DNS Server placed on the internal network. The *Round Robin* feature of the Microsoft DNS server can cycle through your Proxy Servers to provide the IP address of a different server for each client request. To configure DNS to provide Round Robin service, set it up as shown in Figure 7.15. The two proxy servers in our array are `proxysrv` and `proxysrv2`. You can see the host records (A records) for them in the `Zone Info` window. In addition to the A records, we have included our Proxy Server computers in CNAME records. You can see that we have created a CNAME record for each Proxy Server using the alias `proxyary`. Once the DNS is configured in this way, clients should be configured to access the Proxy Server using the CNAME address (in our case, `proxyary.traincert.com`) rather than the Proxy Server's NetBIOS name.

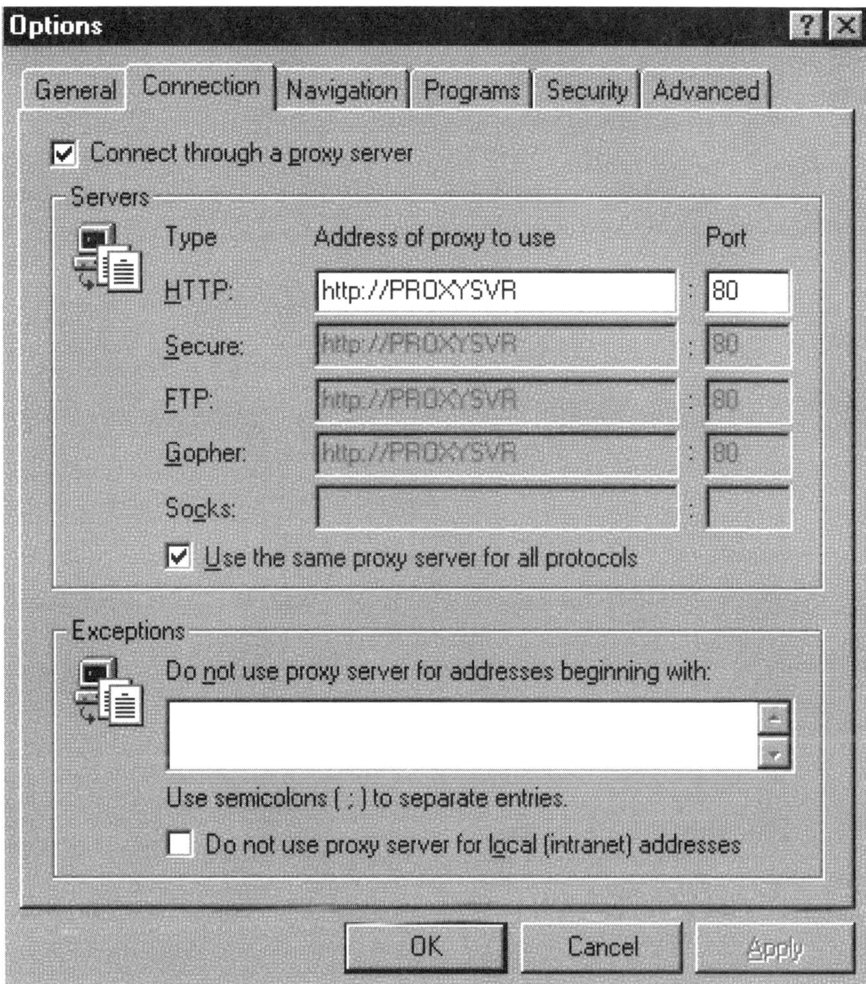

Figure 7.14 *Configuring Web Proxy Gateway in Internet Explorer.*

Study Break

What are A and CNAME Records?

DNS Servers can be configured to provide many different pieces of name resolution information to the network. Of these, the most basic is the *Host Record* (also known as the *A Record*). The Host Record is simply a mapping of a computer's fully qualified domain name to its IP address. Note the A record for the machine `proxycli` shown in Figure 7.15. Since the DNS Zone (shown on the `Server List`) is `traincert.com`, the fully qualified domain name for `proxycli` is `proxycli.traincert.com`. When a computer queries the DNS server for `prox-ycli.traincert.com`, the server returns the IP address 131.107.2.199, from the A record.

A CNAME record (CNAME stands for Canonical Name) provides an alias for a host name listed in the zone. When a computer queries the DNS server for a name listed on a CNAME record, the DNS server returns the IP address associated with the fully qualified domain name aliased to the CNAME. If multiple host names are aliased to the same CNAME, the server provides the Round Robin feature discussed in this section. If, however, only one host name is aliased, that mapping is always returned. For example, let's suppose that Figure 7.15 contains only the first CNAME record (for `proxysrv.traincert.com`). Whenever a client queries for `proxyary.traincert.com`, the DNS server will return the IP address for `proxysrv.traincert.com`, which is 131.107.2.200.

The reason this works is because when a client requests the resource identified by the CNAME, the DNS server returns a list of name-to-IP ad-

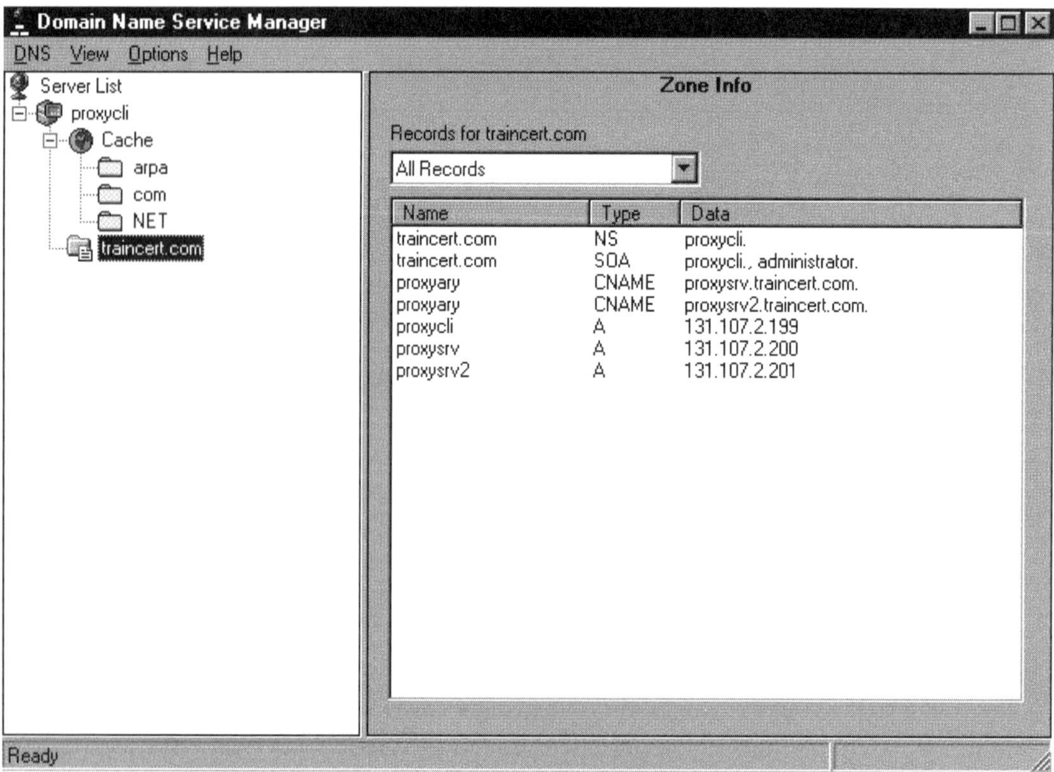

Figure 7.15 *Round robin DNS configuration.*

dress mappings for each resource identified by that CNAME. The client, however, will typically attempt to contact the first IP address on the returned list of mappings. Each time the Microsoft DNS server is called, it rotates the order of the returned name-to-IP address mappings, resulting in a different name on subsequent calls. If, for instance, you use this procedure with Microsoft Internet Explorer, you'll use a different Proxy Server each time you open the browser (not each time you attempt to contact a new resource during the same session).

Study Break

Adding A and CNAME Records

If you have a DNS server in your environment, ask your network administrator if you can add some A and CNAME records to it. If no DNS server is available to you, you may install one on a local computer using the instructions found in Appendix B. (If you install your own DNS make sure you enter the IP address of the DNS server you install in the `DNS Service Search Order` list box on the computer you'll use for the exercise. The `DNS Service Search Order` list box is found by going to the `Control Panel Network` dialog. Select the `Protocols tab|TCP/IP Protocol Properties|DNS` tab.)

Following the example in this section, enter A records (if they are not already present) for your Proxy Server computers and enter a CNAME record aliasing each one to an array name of your choosing. (If you don't have two Proxy Server computers in your network, you may use any two networked machines for this exercise.)

Once the DNS server is configured as outlined above, go to the command prompt and ping the CNAME several times. Do you get different IP addresses each time?

When you have completed this exercise, remove any A and CNAME records you may have added and remove the DNS server IP address from the `DNS Service Search Order` list box (if you entered one during this activity).

Using WINS to Load Balance Proxy Servers

The Windows Internet Name Service (WINS) can also be used for load balancing. To do this, enter a multihomed WINS static mapping for your Proxy Server array. Although multihomed entries are intended for a single computer with multiple network interfaces, you may create a name for the Proxy Server array and enter the IP address for each array member against that name. Although this idea sounds similar to the DNS Round Robin concept, it is functionally different. When a client queries the WINS server for a mapping to the array, it will receive a mapping for a Proxy Server on its subnetwork. If there are no Proxy Servers on the subnetwork, WINS will return a mapping for a Proxy Server on the same network as the client. In the case where more than one Proxy Server is listed for the subnetwork or network, an IP address of one of the machines will be returned at random. If no Proxy Servers are listed on the client's subnetwork or network, WINS will pick a Proxy Server from the WINS list at random.

Although the WINS method of load balancing won't cycle through all of the WINS servers on the list for each client, it has the advantage of providing IP addresses of Proxy Server computers relatively close to the client (subnetwork or network where possible), which will result in more efficient network traffic.

To configure WINS to load balance your proxy servers, launch the `WINS Manager`, select `Mappings|Static Mappings`, and click on the `Add Mappings` button to reveal the dialog shown in Figure 7.16. Select the `Multihomed` radio button and add the appropriate IP addresses against a name you create for your Proxy Server array. As you can see in the figure, we have added the IP addresses of our two proxy servers and named the array `prxyarray`.

If you create such a mapping and test it with the `ping` utility, remember that NetBIOS name resolutions obtained from WINS are entered into the NetBIOS name cache. Multiple `ping`s within a short period of time will consistently return the same mapping unless you clear the cache using `NBTSTAT -R`.

■ Summary

In this chapter we saw we could combine multiple Proxy Server computers in arrays and chains to enhance server caching and bandwidth, provide fault tolerance, and permit load balancing. Proxy arrays are a parallel grouping of Proxy Server machines all running Microsoft Proxy Server 2.0. These machines share configuration information with each other and are able to provide a large combined cache. Since the machines operate in parallel, they provide fault tolerance (if one machine goes down the others pick up the load), and can provide increased bandwidth to the external network. (Remember that actual bandwidth is increased only when each Proxy Server's external interface is *independently* connected to the external network. If Proxy Servers are all connected to the Internet through the same T1 line, for instance, no actual bandwidth increase will be enjoyed.)

Proxy Server chains, in contrast to arrays, feature a serial grouping of machines. Machines grouped in this fashion do not need to run the same ver-

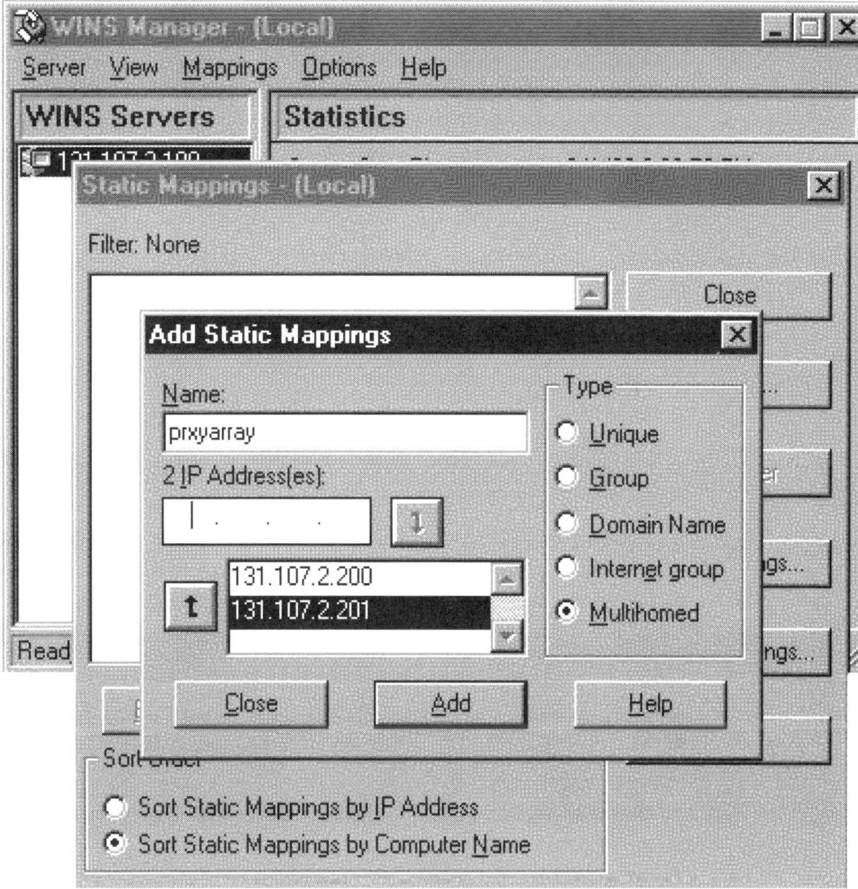

Figure 7.16 *Adding a multihomed static mapping for a Proxy Server array.*

sion of Proxy Server and do not share configuration information. Since the machines are configured serially, no fault tolerance is available unless a backup route is configured. While Proxy Server arrays support all Proxy Server services, Proxy Server chains support only the Web Proxy Service. Proxy Server chains provide hierarchical caching. When a resource is not found in the local proxy server's cache, the request is routed upstream until it is found on an upstream server or until a request is routed to the external network. Proxy Server arrays and chains can both exist on the same network. That is, arrays, not just individual servers, may be grouped hierarchically in chains.

The Cache Array Routing Protocol (CARP) was introduced with Microsoft Proxy Server 2.0. CARP is used to find cached resources within a Proxy Server array and does so by using hash functions to calculate the location of a particular cached resource. This permits Proxy Server to efficiently cache items within an array and quickly react to the introduction or removal of array elements. CARP prevents the duplication of cached information and minimizes network traffic.

Proxy Server arrays are configured from the `Service Properties` tab of any Proxy Server service. The array configuration applies to all Proxy Server services. Arrays are created when two or more machines are designated to join the array. Once joined, arrayed machines share their configuration parameters to permit them to act as a single entity. Because configuration information is synchronized throughout the array, configuration changes should be made to only one machine at a time.

Proxy Server chains are created through the Web Proxy service's routing tab. To configure a Proxy Server to operate as part of a chain, you configure it to use another Web proxy or array for upstream routing.

WinSock Proxy gateways must be statically assigned to each client. This is accomplished through the client's `WSP Client` icon in the `Control Panel`. WinSock Proxy gateways should be assigned based on the capability of the gateway and the usage pattern of the machine's user.

Web Proxy gateways may be statically assigned by configuring the client's Web browser or they may be dynamically assigned through DNS or WINS. Dynamic assignment provides load balancing for arrayed Proxy Server computers. The DNS technique takes advantage of a DNS Server feature called *Round Robin*.

To configure DNS to provide this support, simply enter a CNAME record aliasing all your Proxy Server computers to the same name. Each time DNS is queried for an IP address mapping, it will respond with a list of all the IP addresses that correspond to the CNAME, but will rotate their order for each successive query. WINS can provide load balancing if a static multihomed mapping is entered that lists the IP addresses of all the Proxy Server array members against an array name. The WINS server will provide the IP addresses in a random order, but will respond with only IP addresses on the client's local subnet. If no Proxy Server computers are listed on the local subnet, WINS provides IP addresses of Proxy Server computers on the local network. If no Proxy Server computers are listed on the local network, WINS will provide a random IP address from those listed against the requested name.

▲ REVIEW QUESTIONS

1. *Your network uses multiple Proxy Server computers in an array to provide Internet access. You have just installed a DNS server on the internal net-*

work for name resolution. What is the best way to ensure your Proxy Server computers are load balanced? (Select all that apply)

    A. Create a DNS A record for each Proxy Server computer

    B. Create DNS CNAME records that alias all the Proxy Server computers to the same CNAME and configure Web browsers to use the CNAME

    C. Configure each Web browser to access a Proxy Server computer by the name listed with its DNS A record

    D. Configure each Web browser to use the name listed with the DNS server's SOA record

2. *What does the Cache Array Routing Protocol (CARP) do?*

    A. CARP queries each Proxy Server in an array to determine where a particular item is cached

    B. CARP computes the location of each Proxy Server computer to ensure each computer in the array knows about every other computer

    C. CARP computes the location of cached information so clients and other Proxy Server computers can quickly locate the arrayed computer containing a desired resource

    D. CARP works with DNS to provide efficient Web Proxy load balancing

3. *The Proxy Server computers in your network are combined as a chain. What must you do to ensure an Internet connection will still be possible even when an upstream neighbor fails?*

    A. Configure the WinSock Proxy service to use a server provided by a DNS CNAME record

    B. Select `Use Web Proxy` or `Array` in the Enable Backup Route dialog box on the Web Proxy Service's Routing tab

    C. Select the Use Direct Connection in the Enable Backup Route dialog box on the Web Proxy Service's Routing tab

    D. Proxy Server chains are not fault tolerant; when an upstream machine goes down, the connection is lost

4. *Why would you recommend a Proxy Server array over a single Proxy Server for corporate Internet access? (Select all that apply)*

    A. Higher bandwidth

    B. Better performance

    C. Better fault tolerance

    D. Better security

5. *You want your network to employ Proxy Server computers to provide hierarchical caching. How will you configure your Proxy Server computers?*

    A. Create a Proxy Server array and ensure the `Synchronize configuration of array members` checkbox is unchecked

    B. Install and configure the CARP service to manage hierarchical caching

    C. Ensure each Proxy Server computer is configured to use a Web Proxy or array for upstream routing

    D. Ensure each Proxy Server computer is configured to use a direct connection for upstream routing

6. *Sandy's network employs a Proxy Server array consisting of seven Proxy Server computers, all of which are configured for automatic synchronization. A new custom application was recently installed that requires Internet access. To support the application, Sandy must create a protocol definition for the WinSock Proxy Service. Which Proxy Server computers in the array must she configure?*

    A. All of them

    B. None of them — Proxy Server arrays have nothing to do with the WinSock Proxy service

    C. All Proxy Server computers that have a direct Internet connection

    D. One of them

7. *Tim's network consists of 7,500 computers all requiring Internet access. The company has decided to employ Microsoft Proxy Server to provide secure network access. The company wants to ensure fault tolerance and load balancing in addition to the Proxy Server security features. How should Tim configure the network?*

    A. By installing 15 Proxy Server computers in an array

    B. By Installing one Proxy Server computer on each internal subnet using direct connection for upstream routing and configuring each with a backup route through the other Proxy Server computers

    C. By installing four Proxy Servers to provide hierarchical caching

    D. By installing four Proxy Servers in an array

8. *Proxy Server provides Internet access for your network. What is the easiest way to balance WinSock Proxy access among your network's multiple Proxy Servers?*

   A. Manually configure each client to use a particular Proxy Server computer based on the Proxy Server computer's capability and the user's usage pattern

   B. Configure the client computers to use the automatic load balancing features of Proxy Server arrays

   C. Configure clients to use WINS

   D. Configure clients to use DNS to obtain Proxy Server name resolution from a DNS CNAME record

   E. Configure each Proxy Server computer to use another array member for upstream routing with the last Proxy Server making a direct connection to the Internet

9. *Linda's network has seven Proxy Server computers for Internet access. A DNS server on the internal network provides name resolution and has a host name record for each Proxy Server computer. How should Linda configure her client computers to ensure automatic load balancing across the Proxy Servers?*

   A. Configure each client's Web browser to use WINS for NetBIOS name resolution

   B. Configure each client's Web browser to use the fully qualified domain name of a Proxy Server computer

   C. Configure each client's Web browser to use a DNS canonical name that aliases Proxy Server DNS host name records

   D. Configure each client's Web browser to access a Proxy Server through upstream routing

10. *You have a network with 2000 computers and two T1 lines. What is the best way to configure Proxy Server to provide secure Internet access with maximum bandwidth, fault tolerance, and load balancing?*

    A. Configure 10 Proxy Server computers in two chains with each chain connected to a T1 line. Half the browsers in the network to use one chain and the other half to use the other chain

    B. Configure two proxy servers in an array and connect a T1 line to each Proxy Server

C. Configure five Proxy Servers in an array and configure the array to route upstream to a Proxy Server computer with two external interfaces — one connected to each T1 line

D. Use one Proxy Server computer with a direct connection to one T1 line and a backup route direct connection to the other T1 line

Administering Proxy Clients

This chapter is focused on the Microsoft Proxy *client* service, which includes the WinSock Proxy (WSP), Web Proxy, and Socks Proxy clients. We'll discuss client installation and provide a short review of what to check if something goes wrong. Client settings can be modified during the client or server setup or by using the Internet Service Manager (ISM) or Microsoft Management Console (MMC) on the Proxy Server. We'll discuss client setup, examine the web proxy client applications, Internet Explorer and Netscape web browser clients, and the configuration of SOCKS Proxy clients on other operating systems such as Macintosh and UNIX computers. JavaScript and INS files are discussed using an example, and the chapter finishes with some tips on what items you might need to edit in the proxy client configuration file and how to do so.

By the end of this chapter you will be able to:

- Determine which clients require which proxy services

207

- Configure clients to use the Proxy Server services
- Configure Proxy Server Clients on an IPX-only network
- Understand the Java Script necessary to configure a Web browser
- Modify the Client Configuration in `Mspclnt.ini` to change settings

MCSE 8.1   WinSock Proxy Client Installation and Configuration

In Chapter 4, "Installing Proxy Server," we pointed out that the Proxy Server Setup program creates the `Msp\Clients` folder and shares it as `mspclnt`. The share permissions are set to `Everyone-Read` by default. Inside the msp-clnt share, the folders containing client-specific files await your installation. It is the server installation that creates the share; once it is available, you must next install the client to any of the client machines in the environment. To use proxy services, set up the client computer by using a client Setup program, by using a Web browser, or by running unattended client Setup using Microsoft Systems Management Server. The WinSock Proxy service provides secure, transparent connectivity to Internet resources for client applications that use the Windows Sockets API such as: RealPlayer for streaming real-time audio and video, VDOLive for streaming real-time video, SMTP mail readers for Internet mail, NNTP news readers for Internet newsgroups, and IRC clients for Internet chat sessions.

The WinSock Proxy (WSP) client setup configures a Windows client computer to be a client of the WSP service and makes several additional changes to the client computer:

- The `winsock.dll` file is replaced with the Remote Winsock for the WSP client. The original `winsock.dll` is renamed to `winsock.dlx`.
- The Control Panel is updated with the WSP client applet.
- The Local Address Table (LAT) information that is contained in the `msplat.txt` file is copied to the client. The client regularly updates this file to keep the LAT information current. You can also have a separate local configuration that differs from that of the server if needed.
- The `mspclnt.ini` file is copied to the client; it contains configuration settings for Proxy client applications.

Let's review how to set up the client computer with the WinSock Proxy client setup program. Setting up the WSP client requires you to: connect to the *mspclnt* share and launch *setup.exe*, which is the client setup program:

```
setup [/r] [/u] [/q[1, t]]
```

Appropriate switches are described in Table 8.1.

Table 8.1 *Switches For WinSock Proxy Client Setup*

Switch	Description
/r	Reinstalls Proxy client software (cannot be used with 16-bit clients)
/u	Uninstalls the WinSock Proxy client application but leaves shared components (cannot be used with 16-bit clients)
/q	Runs client Setup in quiet mode. Only progress windows are displayed on the screen, but setup does not prompt the user to approve or modify installation settings.
/q1	Same as the /q option, but also hides the Setup Completion dialog box.
/qt	Same as the /q option, but also hides the progress windows and the Setup Completion dialog box. (This option is not available for 16-bit clients.)

You should run the client setup program from the *mspclnt* share, not from the Proxy Server CD-ROM. This is because the setup program copies files from the server to the client that were modified by the Proxy Server installation. These files will be discussed later in the chapter.

During a silent installation of Proxy client software, the setup program looks for a file named `proxy.ini` in the client distribution shared folder. The client `proxy.ini` file has a single section and entry as follows:

```
[Proxy Setup Install]
Install Dir=C:\Mspclnt
```

This entry is used only for the silent installation of Proxy client and specifies the folder where the proxy client files must be installed. The `proxy.ini` file has no effect on the standard (not quiet) Proxy client setup. If you are installing the proxy client on a dual-boot computer, you will need to remember to run the client setup twice. Each operating system needs to have the proxy client installed, and on each subsequent install after the first you will need to specify a different client installation directory.

The configuration of a WSP client means that any Windows Sockets program is able to transparently use the WSP service. Programs that may need to use this service might include mail or news programs, or real audio. As indicated earlier in the book, you can also install the Proxy Client software using a Web browser. This is a very straightforward task. All you do is connect to the installation page on the server by typing `http://proxyname/Msproxy`, where *proxyname* is the name of the server computer. To complete the installation, simply follow the on-screen instructions.

The Microsoft Proxy Server client Setup program creates a log file each time the Proxy Client software is installed, and it is overwritten with each subsequent installation of the client software. The log is written to the

`C:\Mpcsetup.log` location. If you run into problems with the setup you can check the log file by using any text editor.

Study Break

Using a Production Network

If you are using a production network for your hands-on training, be sure to discuss the following activities with your network administrator before proceeding. Installation of the Proxy Client changes the network environment for the machine being installed. Using the steps outlined in Chapter 4, you must have already installed a Proxy Server on another machine in your network. Once the new Proxy Server is operating, refer to the steps in this section and install the Proxy Client.

1. Using the Windows Explorer (on Microsoft Windows 95/98) or the Windows NT Explorer (on a Microsoft Windows NT machine) connect to the MSPCLNT share point on the Microsoft Proxy Server.
   - Alternatively, you can always connect a drive by launching a NET USE command from a command prompt as follows: `net use x:\\proxyserver\mspclnt`.
   - (HINT: the X: drive can represent any available drive letter.)
   - When the drive is mapped, simply enter x: at the command prompt and you will be using the connected drive.
2. Once the connection is made, select the SETUP.EXE program in the MSPCLNT share. Do not change the directory to the I386 and use SETUP1.exe, as you will get a message returning you to the MSPCLNT share anyway. NOTE: If the proxy client is already loaded to the machine on which you're conducting the installation, you'll be given the additional options of: `Add/Remove`, `Reinstall`, or `Remove All`.
3. If this is a first time installation, you will be taken to a licensing agreement and asked for the location where the proxy files are to be installed. You will then be given the option to select installation. The entire installation takes only a couple of minutes.
4. At the end of the installation you will be prompted to reboot the machine.
5. Experiment by opening your `MSPLAT.TXT` file and the `MSPCLNT.INI` file. What is there that is of interest? Can you identify the information in the LAT?

Local Address Table Consideration

Local Address Table (LAT) entries are copied to the client in a file called `Msplat.txt` and located in the `\Mspclnt` folder. This file contains information about what IP address ranges are "known" and is regularly updated from the server. If the information on the server is incorrect, the client's `Msplat.txt` file can remain incorrect even after you have made manual changes. The reason this is important is because each time a Windows Sockets application on the client tries to make a connection to an IP address, the LAT is used to determine if the address is internal or external. As you can imagine, it is possible for the LAT on the server to be set up incorrectly. Since the server file is used as the source for the copy made to the client, you can end up with your manual changes being overwritten with incorrect data. To get around this problem you can simply create another file called `Locallat.txt`. The client uses both the `Msplat.txt` and `Locallat.txt` to distinguish Internet addresses from local network addresses. In all cases you should carefully review the server LAT to ensure it is set up correctly.

WSP Configuration Considerations

Remember that if you update your operating system with a service pack, you will need to perform a reinstallation of the WSP client software. The update with a service pack or any other software that overwrites the Windows Sockets DLL will need to see the reinstallation of the WSP client software.

A reboot is required each time you reinstall the WSP client software and each time the software is enabled or disabled. You need to perform this reboot for the changes to become effective. HINT: Do not try this on a server in the middle of the day with multiple users attached and using shared files.

The user may be prompted to log on a second time with a domain credentials dialog box if the WSP client software is on a desktop that is capable of using 16 bit applications that conform to the Windows Sockets standard.

Manually Uninstalling the WSP Client

Say you have a machine that is about to be taken out of the proxy environment and you want to remove the WSP client. You should always use the `Setup` program to run uninstall or select `Uninstall` on the program menu bar to remove the client before you perform a manual uninstall. In the case where this is not possible due to file corruption or other error, you can manually uninstall the WSP Client by following the steps that follow below. The control panel icon will also be removed and the machine will be restored to its original non-proxy functionality.

- Delete `c:\mpcsetup.log`
- Delete the `c:\mspclnt` directory and all subdirectories (This will remove all files)
- Delete `wsock32.dll`. If using Win95 also delete `winsock32.dll`

- Rename the `rws.dll` back to `winsock.dll`
- Rename the `rws32.dll` back to `wsock32.dll` (Another way to do this is to copy them from another machine that is non-proxy)
- Remove all proxy entries in the `system.ini` file
- Remove `c:\windows\system\wspcpl32.cpl` (This is what removes the icon in Control Panel)
- Reboot the computer and test it

Using a Mail Client with WSP

In the case where you want to use your mail client in a Proxy Server environment, the first step is to prove that the WSP client functions correctly. One way to accomplish this is to telnet to your server and test. To telnet to a mail server, you first get the IP address of your SMTP server and then start a telnet session using port 25. The exact configuration information needed to complete the telnet session will either be the fully qualified domain name (e.g., `mydiv.mycompany.com`) or IP address and account information such as user ID and password. After you have checked that you can telnet to the SMTP server, check the client to ensure it is correctly configured. Check whether the client is disabled in the `mspclnt.ini`. Outlook and Exchange can both be disabled in the `mspclnt.ini` with the following settings:

```
[mapisp32]
Disable=1
[exchng32]
Disable=1
[outlook]
Disable=1
```

When using Outlook or Exchange, be sure that all of the entries marked "`Disable=`" are set to `Disable=0`.

When working with Netscape Mail, be certain that the Socks entry in the browser's settings is blank. Having a setting for Socks Proxy will cause the mail program to work incorrectly with the WSP client. Typically, the error message that appears in this situation is: "`Host cannot be found.`"

Web Proxy Client Installation and Configuration

Once you have verified proper connectivity between the client and server, and correctly set permissions, you will need to configure your client computers to use the Proxy Server. Although it is possible that either the WSP or Socks Proxy client could be used to browse the web, the Web Proxy client permits this with nearly all CERN compliant browsers on just about any platform. Using the Web Proxy service is a big advantage as browsers are simple to install and maintain. Internet Explorer, Netscape Navigator, and other browsers now exist for many operating systems. Browser availability now provides for near universal support regardless of platform. Protocols supported by the Web Proxy service are: HTTP, HTTPS, FTP, and GOPHER. Although the Web Proxy service does not need extra or special client software, it will not work if the browser is not correctly configured for use with Proxy Server. One item of interest is that there is no need to have DNS set up for the web proxy clients, as the Proxy Server will provide name resolution in all cases.

If you wish to use the Round Robin features of DNS to balance access to multiple Proxy Servers (as discussed in Chapter 7), you will need to configure your Proxy Clients to be clients of a DNS Server on the *internal* network.

Setting up the Web Proxy Client is as simple as installing your chosen browser. Be sure to follow the recommended installation instructions provided with the browser. Next, we look at the browser configuration a little closer, but keep in mind that we are using the Web browser configuration dialog box. To get there you usually need to find the browser's options or settings menu.

Web Proxy Client Using Internet Explorer 4.0 (most versions similar)

To configure the Internet Explorer, open the explorer and select `View|Internet Options`. Click on the `Connection` tab to reveal the dialog shown in Figure 8.1. Once at the properties you will find the connection tab where you will see three boxes: `Connection`, `Proxy  Server`, and `Automatic Configuration`.

If you decide to configure a browser which operates on the Proxy Server computer itself as a Web Proxy client, you will need to use the IP address of the Proxy Server computer's internal network interface in the following steps. You won't be able to use the Proxy Server Computer's DNS or NetBIOS name. This is because when you use the computer name, the IP address returned during the name resolution process may be the external interface, which will be filtered by the LAT.

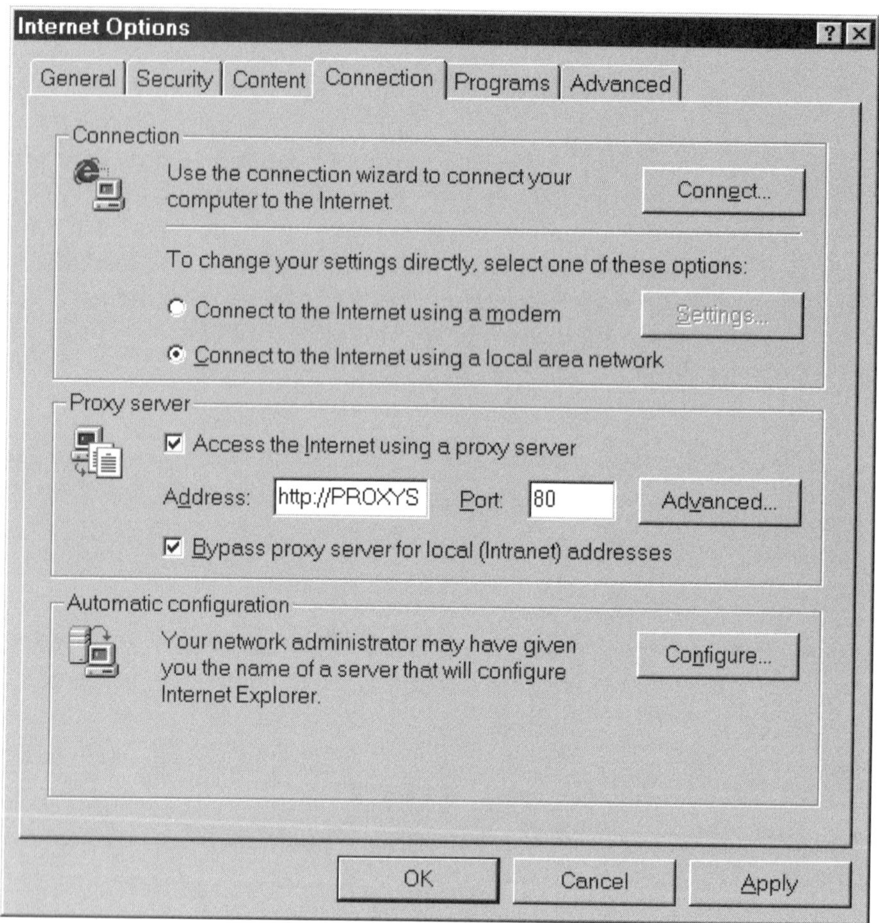

Figure 8.1 *Internet Explorer connection tab.*

For use on a LAN that has a proxy server, select `Connect to the In-ternet using a local area network`. In the area for Proxy Server check the box marked: `Access the Internet using a proxy server`. Next, in the area for the address, type either the IP address or the name of the Proxy Server and make sure you put the port number in. The correct address information will be the IP address, the DNS name, or the NetBIOS computer name (if it is a Windows machine).

The correct port number will be 80 for standard web servers and this must coincide with the settings used in the Permissions tab of the Web Proxy Service Properties dialog box. Be careful — sometimes administrators change port numbers for security reasons — and check the port number if you're not sure. If you are accessing an Intranet web site that does not require a proxy server, also check the box marked: `Bypass proxy server for local (Intranet) addresses`.

The `advanced` button will bring you to the Proxy Settings dialog depicted in Figure 8.2. Here you will be able to configure different Proxy Server and port settings for the most frequently used protocols. There is a place for HTTP, FTP, Secure, Gopher, and SOCKS. If you have dedicated servers performing the different functions, you will be able to configure them separately here. This area permits you to configure settings for all but the Socks Proxy Service as a group by checking the `Use same proxy server for all protocols` checkbox. If there are any Web servers on the local network for which you want to bypass the Proxy Server, type the appropriate host names in the `Do not Use Proxy Server For Addresses beginning with` box. For example, if you do not want to use the proxy server to access the `bad.server.com` Web server on your LAN, type `bad.server.com`.

To do a single step setup, click the `Configure` button in the `Automatic configuration` area of the `Connection` tab to reveal the `Automatic Configuration` dialog depicted in Figure 8.3. Enter the name of a configuration file in the `URL` edit window. (This file must have already been created and placed on a server in the environment.) The configuration file contains information about proxy server, dial-up networking, and other communication settings. Provide the complete URL of the server that contains the file as shown in Figure 8.3. Note that, in the figure, the auto-configuration file is named `myconfig.ins` and it resides in the `Inetpub\wwwroot` directory of computer `proxysrv`. Click the `Refresh` button to reconfigure immediately, otherwise changes won't update until the browser is closed and restarted. (We'll look at an auto-configuration file a little later in this chapter.)

In Internet Explorer version 3.x, the automatic configuration dialog is found on the **Advanced** tab.

Netscape Navigator 4.5 (other versions similar)

The Proxy Server configuration settings for Netscape Navigator are found by selecting `Preferences` from the `Edit` menu. The `Advanced` category must be expanded and the `Proxies` area selected. (See Figure 8.4.)

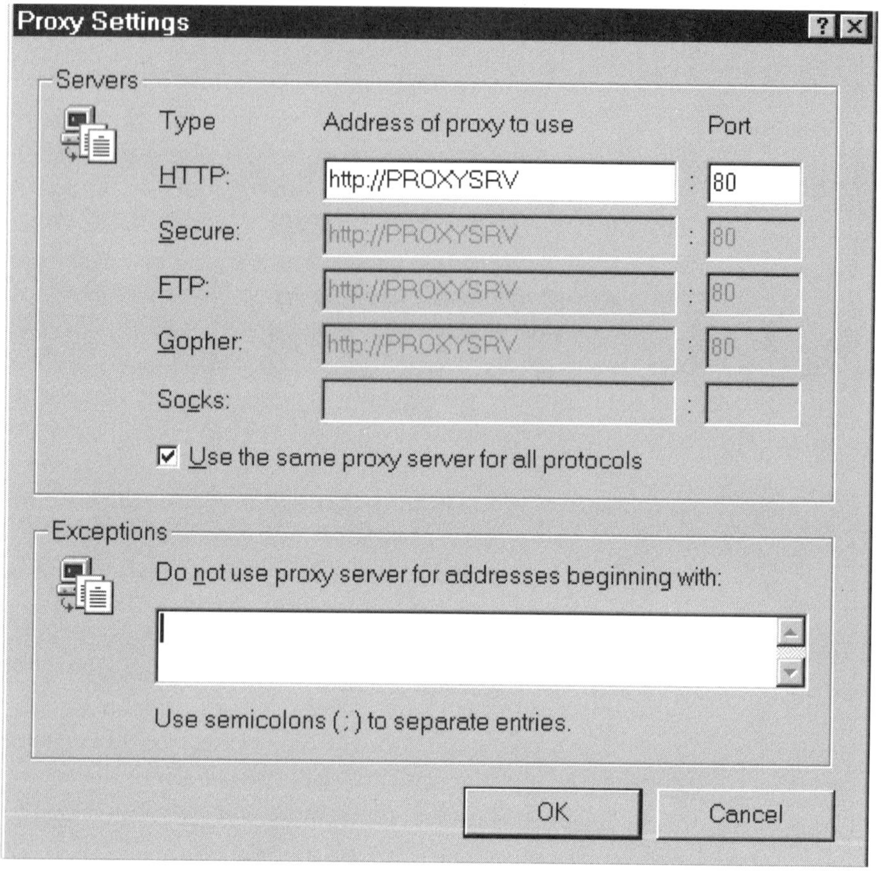

Figure 8.2 *Proxy settings dialog.*

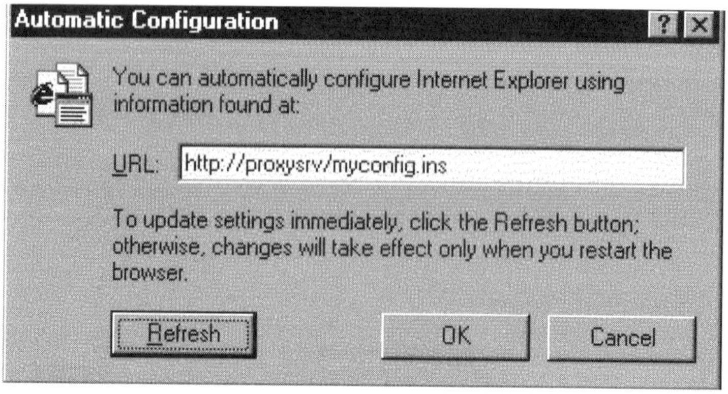

Figure 8.3 *Automatic configuration dialog.*

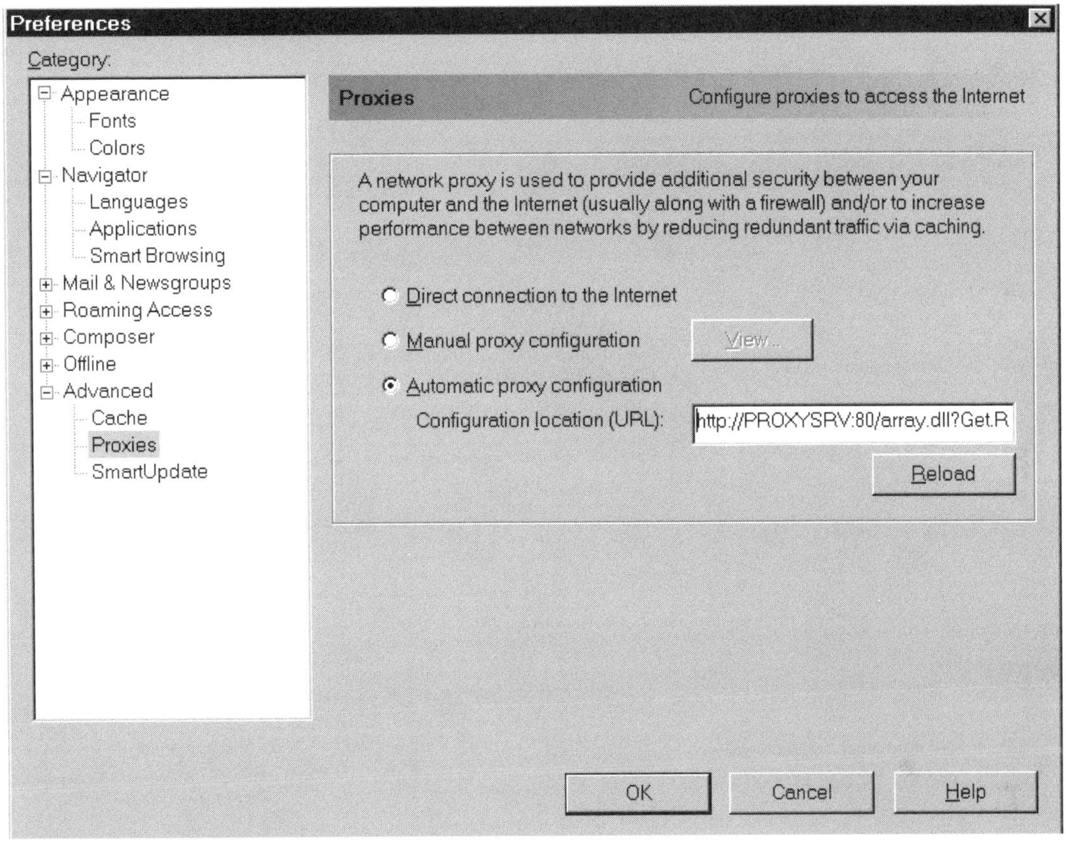

Figure 8.4 *Netscape Navigator preferences dialog.*

Inside the `Proxies` area check the `Manual proxy configuration` radio button and click View to reveal the dialog shown in Figure 8.5.

The IP address or name of the Proxy Server computer must be placed in the `HTTP` edit box to permit the client to function. You should, also, place information in the `Security`, `FTP`, `SOCKS`, `GOPHER`, and `WAIS` locations if you will use these features. In contrast to Internet Explorer, there is no option to use the same settings for all protocols, but each of the options has the same settings by default. The setting for Wide Area Information Service (WAIS) is usually left blank, as this service was used to search cataloged resources and is rarely used except for educational institutions today.

While configuring the Netscape Navigator, note the Exceptions box, a useful option that permits you to block domains that are internal to your organization. It is a way to make the calls to the domain of an Intranet web server so that the request is not sent out to the proxy server (the process for

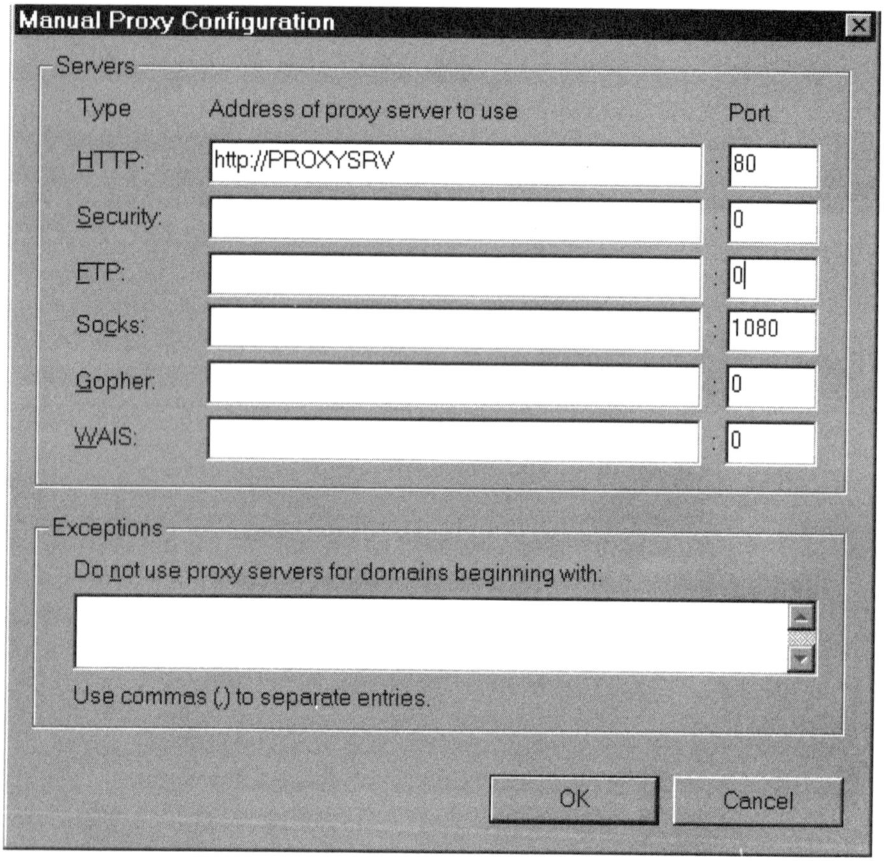

Figure 8.5 *Netscape Navigator manual proxy configuration dialog.*

configuring this option is the same as that described for Internet Explorer 4.0, described in the previous section).

Unless you are going to use the SOCKS service, you can generally leave that entry blank. If, however, you plan to use Netscape messenger (the mail application) you must enter the appropriate SOCKS information. Without it, mail connectivity will fail because the browser will attempt to use the SOCKS service over the WSP client.

Macintosh and UNIX Clients — Web and SOCKS Proxy Services

You may recall our discussion of the Conseil Europeen pour la Recherche Nucleaire, or European Laboratory for Particle Research in Switzerland from Chapter 2 — the organization that lends its acronym to the CERN compliant protocol. You'll remember that HTTP code libraries that were first developed to exploit the HTTP client/server capabilities were developed at CERN, and it was not too long afterwards that the Internet community adopted the use of the CERN-Proxy protocol. Microsoft client and server products are CERN compliant.

Macintosh and UNIX client support is focused in the following two areas: CERN compliant browsers and SOCKS client applications. CERN compliant browsers work with the Web Proxy service. Browser installation and configuration instructions for the Macintosh or UNIX client are similar to other browser installation and configuration procedures.

The SOCKS proxy service supports SOCKS version 4.3a and most SOCKS 4.0 client applications. SOCKS clients work with the SOCKS server to access hosts on the remote network through two operations *connect* and *bind*. The SOCKS client sends the connect request to the SOCKS server when a connection to an application server is required. The application server, on the other side of the SOCKS server, receives the request packet, processes it, and sends a response packet to the client. The response packet contains the status of the request: granted, rejected, or failed. The SOCKS Proxy server redirects API calls in much the same way as WinSock Proxy does. SOCKS, however, does not use true Windows NT Challenge/Response.

Instead, it uses IP addresses and the Identification (Identd) protocol to authenticate SOCKS Proxy clients.

Some SOCKS Proxy service limitations considerations:

- The SOCKS proxy service is dependent on the Web Proxy service. If Web Proxy is disabled or fails, the SOCKS Proxy will not be available.

- The SOCKS proxy service does not support client applications that use the UDP protocol (RealAudio, VDOLive and others).

- The SOCKS proxy service does not support the IPX/SPX protocol.

- All SOCKS client requests are denied by default. To enable SOCKS client request access, you must define SOCKS permission rules on the Proxy Server. Defining a source and destination address, port range, and selecting whether the access is granted or denied makes up a rule (this was covered in detail in Chapter 5).

MCSE 8.2 Configuring a Browser with Scripting

We've mentioned that you can use scripts to configure the browser's proxy settings. Not all types of scripting will work, however, with every type and version of browser. Be sure to check the browser manufacturers published list for compatible scripting types. Scripts are put in a predetermined path that is used to provide requested information for browser configuration. Something that might be a little confusing is that, although the scripts modify the behavior of the browser, the configuration information they change is not always visible in any of the browser's setting areas.

Netscape has software called Mission Control that provides central management for all the Netscape browsers on your network. Microsoft provides this centralized administration through the Internet Explorer Administration Kit (IEAK). In configuring Microsoft Internet Explorer Version 4.0 and later, you will notice that you have the ability not only to use scripts, but also the Internet Communication Settings files. These files have the .INS extension and visibly modify the settings in the browser. Also, there are many options for configuration so they can do more than set up the proxy settings. INS files are just like INI files. Except for the different extension, they look and flow just like the original article. Each section has a name inside of a set of brackets and the information inside is very similar to what you will find in an INI file. Here is an example:

```
[Branding]
Language Locale=en
Language ID=9
Window_Title_CN=
Window_Title=IE 4.0
Toolbar Bitmap=
User Agent=
Platform=2
CabsURLPath=C:\Inetpub\wwwroot
InsVersion=1998.04.10.00
Type=2
[URL]
AutoConfig=1
Help_Page=http://www.alidatrain.com
Quick_Link_1_Name=Internet Start
Quick_Link_1=http://www.alidatrain.com
Quick_Link_2_Name=Dejanews
Quick_Link_2=http://www.dejanews.com
Home_Page=http://www.alidatrain.com
Search_Page=http://www.infoseek.com
AutoConfigURL=http://proxysrv/autocfg.ins
AutoConfigJSURL=
AutoConfigTime=25
[Internet_Mail]
```

```
Window_Title=Outlook Express
[Favorites]
Army=http://www.army.mil
Navy=http://www.navy.mil
AF=http://www.af.mil
Senate=http://www.senate.gov
[Proxy]
HTTP_Proxy_Server=proxysrv:80
FTP_Proxy_Server=proxysrv:80
Gopher_Proxy_Server=proxysrv:80
Secure_Proxy_Server=proxysrv:80
Socks_Proxy_Server=proxysrv:80
Use_Same_Proxy=1
Proxy_Enable=1
Proxy_Override=<local>
[Mail_Signature]
Signature_Text=Visit our web site at http://www.alida-
train.com
Use_Mail_For_News=1
Use_Signature=1
[Signature]
Signature_Text=Visit our web site at http://www.alida-
train.com
Use_Signature=1
```

This should give you a general idea of some of the options, such as standard proxy server settings, favorites, e-mail signatures, and such. The INS file must be in a directory that the IIS service is publishing and it must be addressed in the browser configuration. If you just want to test the file before applying it to your entire environment, you can create the file, put it anywhere on the client machine (like the desktop area), and click on it to configure the browser. The message you receive informs that you are about to reconfigure your browser if you do this.

Scripting languages have generally become more feature-rich and developers must determine the scripting language that is supported by the browser of choice. It is therefore important to know what scripting standards are available for a particular browser. Microsoft Internet Explorer 4.0 supports JavaScript, JScript, and Visual Basic Script. JScript is Microsoft's implementation of the ECMA-262 Script language. ECMA is short for the European Computer Manufacturer's Association.

Study Break

What is ECMA-262?

> The ECMA-262 specification provides for computations and manipulating objects within a host environment, such as the browser. The complete ECMA-262 specification can be found at *http://www.ecma.ch/stand/ecma-262.htm*. If you are interested in locating more information on features and keyword syntax of ECMA-262 from Microsoft, please visit the JScript web site at *http://www.microsoft.com/jscript*.

Both Internet Explorer 4.0+ and NetScape Navigator 3.0+ can be configured through JavaScript. When either browser is initialized, JavaScript is downloaded to the client computer. When a browser attempts contact with a specific site, the script runs to determine the appropriate path for the request. Unlike changes effected through `.INS` files, changes resulting from JavaScript are not visible in the browsers' configuration areas. The main benefit to using JavaScript configuration arises from routing performance when the Web proxy client browser is directly pointed to a Proxy Server array. In cases where the client does not point directly to an array, no significant routing performance will be noted.

MCSE 8.3   Proxy Client and IPX-IP Gateway Support

As you know, Microsoft's Proxy Server 2.0 acts as a firewall or gateway by translating the calls from one side of the connection to the other. The Proxy Server supports both the TCP/IP protocol and NWLINK, the IPX/SPX compatible protocol. In supporting both protocols, it is able to act as an IPX to IP gateway. This is an item worth consideration for those who have Novell NetWare as the primary network operating system (NOS) since that NOS depends on the IPX/SPX protocol. Since the Proxy Server can support either protocol, the client can run Microsoft's NWLINK (Microsoft's 100 percent compatible version of the IPX/SPX protocol), or TCP/IP, or both. Once the Proxy Client is installed on a machine, the Proxy Client icon on the client's control panel will show a selection for forcing the IPX/SPX protocol. Using only one protocol is the preferred method in this case since it offers an additional layer of security. The internal address information has no way to get to the Internet, thus the chance of a network insecurity is nearly eliminated.

You'll remember we discovered in Chapter 4 that even in networks that run IPX/SPX exclusively, we still need to ensure TCP/IP is bound to the internal interface(s) of the Proxy Server computer.

Microsoft Proxy Server 2.0 does not support IPX on Windows 3.1 or Windows for Workgroups 3.11 clients. Both of these clients can use the Web Proxy service by using TCP/IP. Windows for Workgroups clients can use the WinSock Proxy service by using TCP/IP. If the network has IPX/SPX clients, several settings in the `Mspclnt.ini` file may need to be verified or added.

To prevent configuration refreshing or redirection by various Windows NT services running on WSP clients which use IPX/SPX, you should verify or add the following section and entries in the `Mspclnt.ini` file. These entries will disable the WSP client for those services:

```
[Services]
Disable=1
[Spoolss]
Disable=1
[Rpcss]
Disable=1
```

If Novell NetWare servers or IPX routers provide the IPX frame type and network address for the network, a `[Servers IPX Addresses]` section should have been automatically created when the client was installed. Only a single address need be put in this section, formatted as follows:

```
Addr1=(Internal Network Number)-(MAC Address)
```

If there are no Novell NetWare servers, the IPX/SPX client may not autoconfigure the IPX settings correctly. You must open the `Mspclnt.ini` file and add the following section. Or, if the section already exists, replace it with the following information:

```
[Servers Ipx Addresses]
Addr1=nnnnnnnn-000000000001
```

Replace nnnnnnnn with the actual NetWare network number (e.g., 00000001). Be sure you use 000000000001 as the MAC address, regardless of what your internal network adapters actual MAC address is. DO NOT make this modification unless your network doesn't function. If an entry containing the Proxy Server computer's internal network MAC address is present and your clients operate properly using NWLink, the change is not necessary and may prevent proper operation.

To provide IPG Gateway support, Proxy Server should have been installed on a computer already running NWLink and the Service Advertising Protocol (SAP) Agent (as we discussed in Chapter 4). If installation was not completed in this order, it may be necessary to reinstall Proxy Server for the IPX Gateway to work.

Study Break

Using Proxy Server as an IPX Gateway

Now that we've gone over the use of Proxy Server as an IPX gateway, take a few minutes and prove to yourself that the concept works. If you are using the Proxy Server within your corporate network, be sure to discuss this exercise with your LAN administrator before you proceed.

1. Ensure your Proxy Server has NWLink and SAP Agent installed and bound to its internal interface. If no available Proxy Servers are properly configured to use NWLink, you may alternatively install Proxy Server on a server you'll use to access the Internet for your clients.
2. Install NWLink on a computer you will use to access the internet and remove or disable TCP/IP (removing or disabling TCP/IP isn't really necessary since you can prevent its use in WinSock Proxy client configuration, but this will further prove that it is possible to access the Internet using IPX/SPX and a Proxy Server gateway).
3. Refer to the description in this section and ensure the `mspclnt.ini` file on the Proxy Server is updated accordingly. (Again, if you're using the corporate Proxy Server, be sure to discuss this with your LAN administrator.) If the Proxy Server computer
4. From your client computer, access the mspclnt share on the Proxy Server computer and run `Setup`. (If `Setup` was already performed on this machine, select the `Reinstall` option).
5. Still on the client computer, go to the `WSP Client` icon in the `Control Panel` and ensure both the `Enable WinSock Proxy Client` and `Force IPX/SPX Protocol` checkboxes are checked.
6. On Internet Explorer's `Connection` tab, clear the `Access the Internet` using a `Proxy Server` checkbox.
7. Still in Internet Explorer, access a Web site on the external network. By doing so, you have proven that Proxy Server can function as an IPX Gateway to the Internet for a computer not equipped with the TCP/IP protocol.

MCSE 8.4   Proxy Client Connectivity, Permissions, and Configuration Parameters

Whether or not the client is Windows-based, it needs physical access across the network wire to the Proxy Server and the correct permissions to access the resource. Remember to make sure all internal addresses are in the LAT. This is particularly important if you are using the Dynamic Host Configuration Protocol. Before making client or server configuration changes, use the PING utility or look in the Network Neighborhood to ensure you can see the clients and server.

Microsoft Proxy Server and its clients work within the framework of a Windows NT Domain. Proxy Server security is administered at the domain level. If you have configured the components of Proxy Server, such as FTP, Gopher, Secure, or WWW to have their access control disabled, this means the clients do not need to log on to use the services. If you have enabled access control, it means that the clients must have accounts on the Proxy Server (or in the Proxy Server's domain) and the appropriate permissions to access the resources of the Proxy Server.

The permissions available to WSP clients are extensive and more detailed than the other proxy clients. (The protocols are defined through the Protocols tab of the WinSock Proxy Service Properties dialog box on the server covered in Chapter 5).

The Proxy Server client set up creates a log file, `C:\Mpcsetup.log`, that permits you to initiate troubleshooting if you encounter any errors with setup. Keep in mind that the log file will be overwritten each time the client software is installed. Any text editor can be used to view the contents.

Review the connectivity between the client and the server before inspecting issues with the Proxy Server itself. Check the physical connectivity between the client and server. If you do this before modifying permissions and other settings, you are likely to save time and heartache. The first thing that must be done when you suspect a proxy problem is to suspect a connectivity problem and work from there.

Changing Client Configuration Parameters

The client configuration file affects the functionality of the Proxy Client. The client behavior, including how applications connect to the Proxy Server, can be specified so that the client can connect by DNS name, IP address, or by a manually entered array name or group of IP addresses (for an array). If you want to edit the client configuration file, `mspclnt.ini`, you can use any text editor. The file is located in the `Mspclnt` directory on the client computer.

Once the WSP client is installed, the client configuration file is downloaded to the client every time the computer is booted and every six hours after boot-up. The server share paths listed in the `[Master Config]` section of `Mspclnt.ini` determine the path used to update the client with new configuration files. Should you need to make a change to the server copy of `Mspclnt.ini`, you can use any text editor and go to the `Msp\Clients` directory on the server. Although the file also resides on the client, you should always make the changes on the server. If you change the file on the client, all your changes will be overwritten the next time the server refreshes the client files or when the client is rebooted.

Following is a sample `Mspclnt.ini` file:

```
[Internal]
scp=9,10
Build=2.0.372.12
[wspsrv]
Disable=1
[inetinfo]
Disable=1
[services]
Disable=1
[spoolss]
Disable=1
[rpcss]
Disable=1
[kernel32]
Disable=1
[mapisp32]
Disable=0
[exchng32]
Disable=0
[outlook]
Disable=0
[raplayer]
RemoteBindUdpPorts=6970-7170
LocalBindTcpPorts=7070
[rvplayer]
RemoteBindUdpPorts=6970-7170
LocalBindTcpPorts=7070
```

```
[net2fone]
ServerBindTcpPorts=0
[icq]
RemoteBindUdpPorts=0
ServerBindTcpPorts=0,1025-5000
NameResolutionForLocalHost=P
[Common]
WWW-Proxy=PROXYSVR
Set Browsers to use Proxy=1
Set Browsers to use Auto Config=0
WebProxyPort=80
Configuration Url=http://PROXYSVR:80/array.dll?Get.Rout-
ing.Script
Port=1745
Configuration Refresh Time (Hours)=6
Re-check Inaccessible Server Time (Minutes)=10
Refresh Give Up Time (Minutes)=15
Inaccessible Servers Give Up Time (Minutes)=2
Setup=Setup.exe
[Servers Ip Addresses]
Addr1=207.22.36.14
Addr2=207.22.36.20
[Servers Ipx Addresses]
Addr1=55555555-000000000001
[Master Config]
Path1=\\PROXYSRV\mspclnt\
[Inaccessible Servers]
PROXYSVR=2072
```

Table 8.2 describes the entries in the `Mspclnt.ini` file.

Making Changes to an `Mspclnt.ini` File

Although you know you can make changes to the `Mspclnt.ini` file, we caution you that making unnecessary changes can lead to a disorderly environment which is difficult to troubleshoot. Our recommendation is to open the `Mspclnt.ini` file several times and look around to become familiar with what is there. Then, ONLY WHEN NECESSARY, make changes to the configuration and always record your results. Should you make changes that were not intended, be sure to return the file

Table 8.2 *Mspclnt.ini File*

Title	Entry	Explanation
[Master Config]	Path1	A UNC path \\proxyserver\sharename to the shared network directory on the server containing the master copy of the client configuration files; if participating in an array, the paths to the shared network directories of all array members. This is a required section for backward compatibility with Microsoft Proxy Server version 1.0 clients.
[Servers IP addresses]	Name	The computer or DNS name for the Proxy Server computer used by the client; if participating in an array, the DNS name for the array. (This entry does not appear if an IP address is used.)
[Servers IP addresses]	Addr1	The IP address of the Proxy Server computer used by the client; if participating in an array, the IP address of each array member. (This entry does not appear if a computer or DNS name is used.) Additional entries are shown as Addr2, Addr3, and so on. This entry can be used if there is no DNS server on your network.
[Servers IPX Addresses]	Addr1	The IPX address of the Proxy Server computer. If participating in an array, the IPX address of each array member.
[Common]	Port	The port Proxy Server uses for the control channel. This value is rarely changed. If it must be changed, edit the server's master copy of the `Mspclnt.ini` file. NOTE: This should be changed only if there is a conflict with another service on the server. This value should never be edited in the client's copy of the `Mspclnt.ini` file.
[Common]	Configuration Refresh Time	Specified time in hours when the client asks the server to download a fresh copy of the Local Address Table (Msplat.txt).
[Common]	Recheck Inaccessible Server Time	Time, specified in minutes, where the WSP client does not try to redirect a request by using the specific inaccessible server. Default value is 10 minutes.
[Common]	Refresh Give Up Time	Time, specified in minutes, where the WSP client attempts to refresh the configuration if a previous refresh attempt has failed. Default value is 15 minutes.
[Common]	Inaccessible Servers Give Up Time	Time, specified in minutes, where the WSP client does not try to redirect a request if all servers are marked as inaccessible. After this interval, the client tries one of the servers if the `Refresh Give Up Time` has not expired. Default value is two minutes.
[Common]	Set Browsers To Use Proxy	In the `Proxy.ini` file, value set to 1 indicates that the client Setup program will configure the client computer's browser to use the Proxy Server computer defined in the `WWW Proxy` field. Value set to 0 stops the client Setup program from configuring clients to use a Proxy Server computer. This field has no effect on the client's version of the `proxy.ini` file.

Table 8.2 *Continued*

Title	Entry	Explanation
[Common]	Configuration URL	This shows the location of the configuration script that is downloaded to a client browser to use for routing into a particular Proxy Server computer in an array. The URL has the form `http://proxyservername/array.dll?Get.Routing.Script`, where *proxyservername* is the name of the Proxy Server computer that contains the script.
[Common]	LocalDomains	A comma-separated list of suffixes for Domain names that are locally resolved.
[Common]	WWW-Proxy	If `Set Browsers to Use Proxy` is set to 1 in the `Proxy.ini` file, the client Setup program configures client browsers to use the named Proxy Server. This field has no effect on the client's version of the file.
[Common]	WebProxyPort	If `Set Browsers to Use Proxy` is set to 1 in the `Proxy.ini` file, the client Setup program configures client browsers to use the named port. This defines the listen-on port used by the Web Proxy service and should be the same.

to its original state before saving. It is a good idea to copy the file to another location like the \temp directory before starting your work so you can recover the original file if something goes wrong.

Open the `Mspclnt.ini` file with a text editor
Find the Port=
Record what you found ____________________
Find the name of the Proxy Server
Record what you found ____________________
Find the [Servers IP Addresses]
Record what you found ____________________
Find the WWW-Proxy=
Record what you found ____________________
Find Set Browsers to use Proxy=
Record what you found ____________________
Find WebProxyPort=
Record what you found ____________________

■ Summary

This chapter discussed the Microsoft Proxy client services. We looked at the WinSock Proxy (WSP), Web Proxy, and Socks Proxy clients. We discussed client installation and configuration, and how the client settings can be modified. Web Proxy clients, Internet Explorer, and Netscape were touched on as was the configuration of SOCKS Proxy clients on other operating systems such as Macintosh and UNIX.

We looked at various methods for scripting browser configuration. We looked at the construction of INS files and JavaScript and considered JScript and ECMA scripting.

We looked at the configuration that permits IPX/SPX clients to operate on the internal network while using a Proxy Server to provide a gateway to the TCP/IP world on the external network. We saw that using IPX/SPX as the only client network protocol can provide an extra measure of protection against TCP/IP attacks from the external network.

Finally, we looked at some important client configuration issues. We saw that the first areas to consider when problems arise in working with the Proxy Server are actual network connectivity and permissions. We also took an in-depth look at the contents of the proxy client configuration file and discussed some considerations about editing it.

▲ REVIEW QUESTIONS

1. *You have just installed the Netscape Navigator browser on all your network's UNIX-based computers. Your network accesses the Internet through a Microsoft Proxy Server version 2.0. What is the best way to configure the browser to operate with your Proxy Server?*

    A. Nothing. UNIX computers cannot host Netscape Navigator and even if they could a UNIX computer won't work with a Microsoft Proxy Server computer.

    B. Configure the UNIX computers to run Netscape Navigator as a SOCKS application

    C. Configure Netscape Navigator to use Proxy Server for HTTP, FTP, and Gopher requests using the Proxy Server computer's IP address or host name.

    D. Install the WinSock Proxy Service on the UNIX computer and configure the browser as a WinSock client.

2. *Sandy administers an IPX/SPX network (only NWLink is currently installed on her computers). She has just installed a Microsoft Proxy Server computer to act as an Internet gateway for her client computers. How should she configure the server and clients to provide maximum security and smooth Internet access?*

    A. Bind TCP/IP and NWLink to the Proxy Server's internal and external interface; no configuration is required for the clients

    B. Bind TCP/IP to the Proxy Server's internal and external interfaces, bind NWLink to the Proxy Server's internal interface, and configure the WinSock Proxy service on the client to "Force IPX/SPX protocol."

    C. Bind TCP/IP to the Proxy Server's internal external interface, bind NWLink to the Proxy Server's internal interface, and configure the WinSock Proxy service on the client to "Force IPX/SPX protocol."

    D. Bind TCP/IP to the Proxy Server's external interface, bind NWLink to the Proxy Server's internal interface, then bind TCP/IP to the client's network interface but disable it.

3. *You are running a mixture of Internet Explorer versions 3.02 and 4.01 on your local network. All machines are configured for automatic client configuration from the Proxy Server computer, but you wish to disable this feature on some machines for analysis and testing. How can you disable the automatic configuration feature?*

    A. Use the Internet Explorer programs tab.

    B. Uncheck the "Automatically configure Web Browser during client setup" checkbox on the Proxy Server computer.

    C. Use the `Internet Options|Connection` tab on Internet Explorer 4.01 or the `Options|Advanced` tab on Internet Explorer 3.02 and clear the URL Path from the Automatic Configuration dialog box.

    D. Once enabled, automatic configuration can be disabled only by reinstalling the software.

4. *Your Internet Explorer 4.0 browsers are set for automatic configuration through use of an automatic configuration script. What could be downloaded to the browser to effect the configuration?*

    A. A JavaScript script.

    B. The `mspclnt.ini` file.

    C. A Java applet.

    D. A Pearl Script file.

5. *You use a CERN compliant Web browser and access the Internet through your Proxy Server's Web Proxy service. Your computer's* `locallat.txt`

file contains your computer's IP address, but the Proxy Server's Local Address Table does not. What would you expect when you attempt to connect to your local intranet and the Internet?

    A. Successful connection to the intranet but not to the Internet.

    B. Successful connection to the Internet but not the intranet.

    C. Successful connection to both.

    D. Successful connection to neither.

6. *The Macintosh computers on your internal network need to provide graphics support to clients through your Microsoft Proxy Server version 2.0 computer. What services must your Proxy Server computer support?*

    A. CERN Proxy Service.

    B. SOCKS Proxy Service.

    C. WinSock over AppleTalk Filing Protocol (WS/AFP).

    D. Macintosh computers can only use Proxy Server version 1.0.

7. *You need to make some changes to the configuration parameters in your network's* `mspclnt.ini` *file(s). What is the best way to accomplish this?*

    A. Use the `Configuration` tab on your client browser's `Internet Options` menu

    B. Edit the file in each client's `Mspclnt` directory using Notepad

    C. Use the `Mspcled.exe` utility from the Proxy Server's `\Msp` directory

    D. Edit the file in the Proxy Server's `Msp\Clients` directory using Notepad

8. *Your TCP/IP based client computer is unable to access the Internet through the Proxy Server. What is the best thing to check first?*

    A. Ensure your computer's server service is running.

    B. Check that the Proxy Server is properly routed to an upstream server or direct to the Internet.

    C. See if you can Ping the Proxy Server computer from your computer.

    D. Verify the `Mspclnt.ini` file is in your computer's `Mspclnt` directory.

9. *Why would you configure a* `locallat.txt` *file?*

    A. As a backup for the Proxy Server's LAT file.

    B. To supplement the Proxy Server's LAT.

C. To provide a download location for the Proxy Server's LAT.

D. To provide local address information for the SOCKS Proxy service.

10. *Linda's network accesses the Internet through a Proxy Server computer. For security purposes, she has changed the HTTP TCP port from 80 to 300 in the Proxy Server's WWW Service Properties. How should she configure her client computers for successful Internet access?*

A. Configure CERN compliant Web browsers to use TCP port 300.

B. Set the WinSock configuration options in Control Panel to use port 300.

C. Clients must be configured to use SOCKS Proxy service only.

D. The TP port cannot be configured to use port numbers above 255.

Coexistence with Microsoft Proxy Server

This chapter tells you about Proxy Server connectivity issues. We will see how to integrate a Proxy Server computer with a Remote Access Server (RAS) using Point-to-Point Tunneling Protocol (PPTP). We will discuss different scenarios where PPTP enabled computers coexist with Proxy Server. If your network uses Exchange for messaging and you are not sure if it will still work after you install Proxy Server, this chapter will give you the answer. Here also we will point out different scenarios to allow you to accomplish this goal. We will also look at how Proxy Server works with SQL Server, FTP servers, and Telnet servers. You will learn what a "demilitarized zone" is (in the Information Technology context) and will be able to plan sophisticated network configurations with Proxy Server in a mixed environment.

At the end of this chapter you will be able to:

- Explain how PPTP works with Proxy Server
- Plan Proxy and Exchange integration

235

- Explain how SQL Server can publish data though Proxy Server
- Implement Proxy Server connectivity with a wide variety of applications

MCSE 9.1   Proxy Server and the Point-to-Point Tunneling Protocol

Today, many companies utilize the Internet not only for the purpose of gaining access to the information it contains, but also to provide network connections to employees who are out of the office or on the road. It has always been the case that utilizing the public Internet is a much cheaper form of connecting remote locations than using dedicated direct links or long distance phone lines. However, there have always been concerns about transferring confidential or secret information though the public Internet. The solution to this problem is to create a Virtual Private Network based on encrypted tunnels provided by the PPTP.

The idea behind PPTP is based on the encapsulation and encryption of IP packets into a secured tunnel. A tunnel is nothing more that an idea of sending streams of encapsulated packets in secured envelopes that cannot be easily decrypted. Even if somebody captures such an envelope during its travel through the Internet, its contents will not make sense.

A reasonable question in this case is, "How can I combine Microsoft Proxy Server features with the advantages of PPTP?" To answer this question, let's first look at PPTP operation and architecture.

How Does PPTP Work?

Point-to-Point Tunneling Protocol is a network protocol that provides a secure way to transfer data from a remote client to a private server or network by creating a Virtual Private Network (VPN) across TCP/IP-based data networks.

The networking technology of PPTP was created as an extension of the Point-to-Point Protocol (PPP) referred to in RFC 1171. PPTP is a network protocol that encapsulates PPP packets into IP datagrams for transmission over the Internet or other public TCP/IP-based networks. PPTP can also be used in private LAN-to-LAN networking. The PPTP encapsulation technique is based on the Internet standard GRE (Generic Routing Encapsulation), which allows tunneling of protocols over the Internet. (For more information about this you may review RFC 1701 and RFC 1702. You can find RFCs at *www.cis.ohio-state.edu/rfc/* or *http://www.rfc-editor.org.*)

A typical PPTP scenario assumes the remote client already has an Internet connection from its local Internet Service Provider (ISP). Clients may use computers running Windows NT Server or Workstation version 4.0, dial-up networking, and the remote access protocol PPP to connect to an ISP. Being connected to the Internet, the client makes a second dial-up networking call over the Internet connection. Data sent, using this second connection, is in the form of IP datagrams that contain PPP packets. This second call actually creates a virtual private networking (VPN) connection to a PPTP server on the private enterprise LAN — this is referred to as a *tunnel*.

Let's see how the PPTP client creates a packet to send to the PPTP server. For the purpose of our discussion, let's assume that the PPTP client is connected to the Internet using a LAN adapter (the situation changes slightly if the PPTP client uses a communication device such as modem).

The process of encapsulating the data in the PPTP datagrams is illustrated in Figure 9.1.

As you can see, when the application on the PPTP client computer sends a packet to the PPTP server, the data is first encapsulated in the IP datagram using the private IP address — the one that was assigned when the PPTP connection was established. Then the IP packet gets encapsulated into the PPP packet and is encrypted through the PPTP and GRE modules. The encrypted data is then inserted into the IP datagram once more. In this case the real, globally routable IP address is used. The packet is, then, transmitted over the Internet. On the receiving end, the PPTP server reverses the procedure. It receives the packet from the routing network and sends it across the private network to the destination computer. The PPTP server does this by

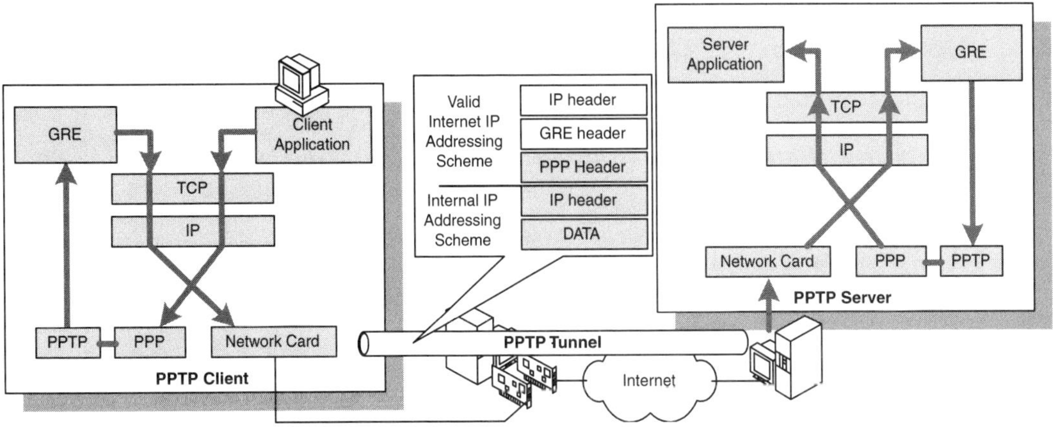

Figure 9.1 *PPTP concepts.*

processing the PPTP packet to obtain the private network computer name or address information in the encapsulated PPP packet.

The key point of this is that packets travel through the Internet in the PPTP tunnel — even if a third party computer in the Internet captures the packet, it will not be able to use the data inside it.

Now that we have a basic idea of how PPTP works, let's ask ourselves a question: "How does this technology work when we add Proxy Server to the picture?" Let's look at what combinations of Proxy Server and PPTP are possible?

Why Can't WSP Clients Use PPTP?

Although you can install PPTP client software on a WinSock client computer, there is no way to make the WSP client redirect PPTP packets though the Microsoft Proxy Server services. The main reason for this is found in the WinSock Proxy Client architecture. When a WinSock Proxy client receives a call from an application, it knows the call needs to be forwarded to a specific IP address and to a specific port. However, the WinSock Proxy client software tricks the application by intercepting packets on the TCP layer and sending them to the Proxy Server's WinSock Proxy service. Looking at PPTP encapsulation once more, we see the data has to cross the TCP layer twice. Since the WinSock Proxy Client software intercepts the packet on the first pass, this data passes the TCP layer only once.

There is a workaround for this issue. If you want a PPTP client or PPTP server to reside in you internal network, you should enable IP forwarding on the Proxy Server computer to let packets reach your internal PPTP client or server. Of course this will also create a significant security problem, since now your internal network is visible from the Internet. You can increase security by enabling packet filters. Microsoft Proxy Server contains predefined packet filters "PPTP call" and "PPTP receive." They should be added to the configuration in order to permit outbound and inbound PPTP connections, respectively.

Since your PPTP enabled computer is on the internal network, you should create a static filter that allows packets to travel to your PPTP enabled computer (see Figure 9.2).

Here, a packet filter for the internal PPTP server is created. The PPTP server is located in the internal network and has an IP address of 195.209.225.15. Note that this IP address should be routable from the Internet. In other words, you cannot use an IP address from the private address space (internal network) here.

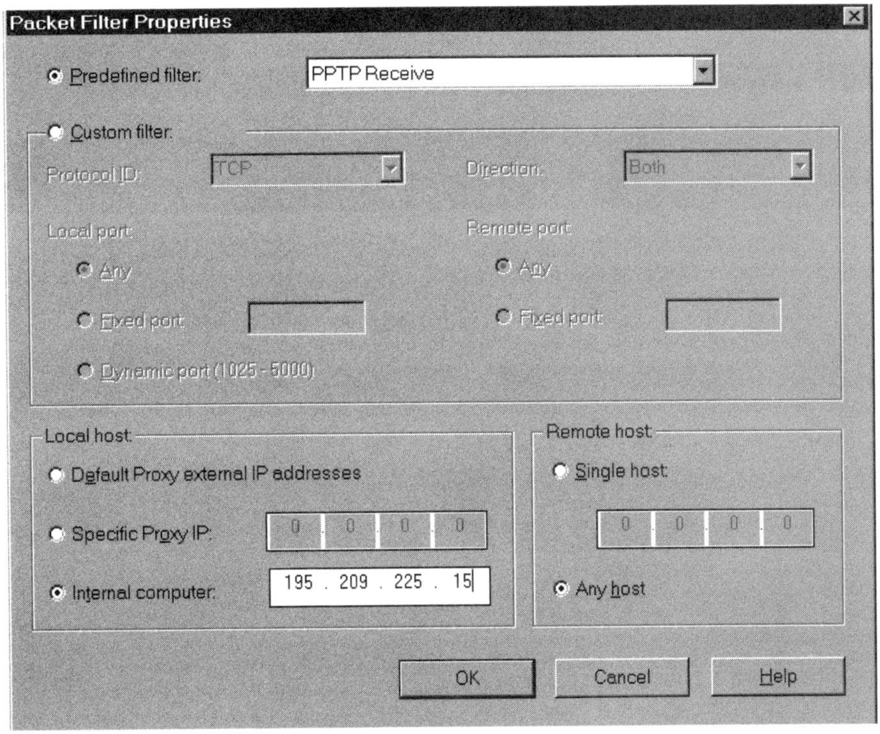

Figure 9.2 *Creating a PPTP filter for an internal host.*

There is a limitation in MS Proxy filtering, however. If you try to set up a custom filter for any computer on your internal network, you will get the message shown in Figure 9.3.

This happens when you create a packet filter for an internal IP address (one that is in the LAT). To solve this problem, you will have to exclude the IP address of that computer from LAT.

When you put a PPTP client or server on the internal network, you must keep in mind that, if IP routing on this computer is enabled, packets from the external network can reach other computers in your internal network. This of course makes the foregoing solution less desirable.

Running PPTP on the Server

It is more desirable to run PPTP server on the Proxy Server. To do this, you should install Routing and Remote Access Server (RRAS) on the Proxy Server computer. If, however, you install the software in the incorrect order,

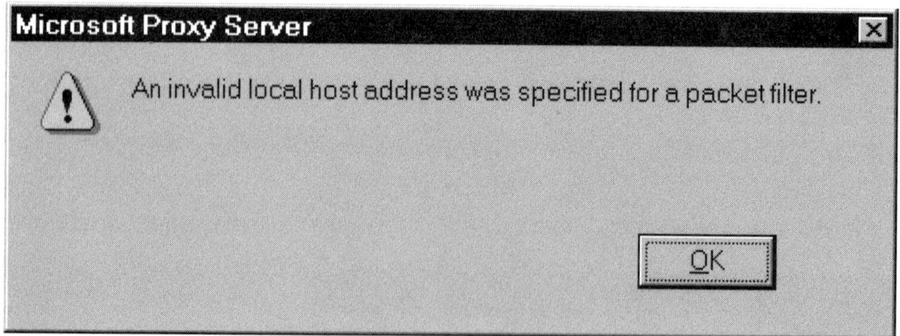

Figure 9.3 *Invalid local host message.*

some services may not start or may fail to function properly. Let's review the recommended installation sequence.

To install RRAS server and Proxy Server on one computer, do the following:

1. Install Windows NT Server 4.0
2. Install all necessary Windows NT Services, Protocols, Network Adapters, and Software
3. Apply Windows NT 4.0 Service Pack 4
4. Install Routing and Remote Access Service
5. Install Internet Explorer 4.01 SP1
6. Install Windows NT 4.0 Option Pack
7. Install Proxy Server 2.0
8. Reapply Windows NT 4.0 Service Pack 4
9. Apply Windows NT Service Pack 4.0 hotfixes. Check Microsoft Web site for any updated PPTP/RRAS fixes.

After all the software is installed, you should check that IP forwarding is disabled in the TCP/IP properties dialog box. If IP forwarding is enabled, your internal network is accessible from the Internet, which could be a serious security problem.

Additionally, you should enable packet filtering and create static packet filters for "PPTP Call" if your computer acts as a PPTP client; and "PPTP Receive" if your computer is a PPTP Server (see Figure 9.4).

There are a couple of other alternative solutions to integrate Microsoft Proxy Server 2.0 and RRAS. These solutions utilize RRAS packet filtering capabilities instead of Proxy Server packet filtering. RRAS packet filtering is beyond the scope of this book. You can find more information regarding this by referring to the RRAS documentation and Microsoft Knowledge Base article Q169548.

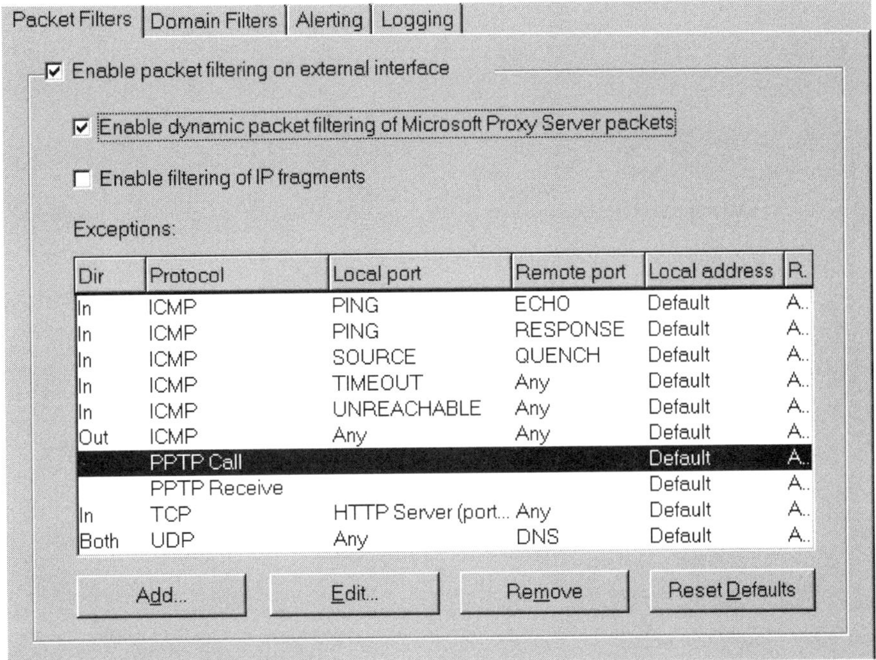

Figure 9.4 *PPTP packet filters.*

Study Break

Testing the Deployment of Proxy Server and the PPTP-Enabled RAS Server

1. To set up the PPTP client in the internal network, go to the `Control Panel` on the internal computer, click `Network`, and go to the `Protocols` tab. Ensure that the `TCP/IP protocol` is installed. Add the `Point-to-Point Tunneling Protocol` (PPTP) and `Remote Access Server`. Set the RAS port to `Dial Out` only. (For more information about installing and configuring Remote Access Server on Windows NT refer to product documentation).

2. Install the PPTP enabled RAS server on the external network. Set the external RAS server to `Receive Calls Only`. In `Control Panel | Network | Services | Remote Access Service | Network` click `Configure` under the `Server Settings` box. Set the static address pool of IP addresses that will be used by the clients of this RAS server. (For more information about setting RAS server refer to Windows NT documentation.)

To configure the Proxy Server computer to pass PPTP requests:

1. In the WinSock Proxy service properties, click `Local Address Table` and exclude the internal RAS client's IP address from the LAT.
2. Click `OK` to close the `Local Address Table Configuration` dialog box. Click `OK` to close the WinSock Proxy service properties.
3. Launch `Control Panel`, double click the `Network` icon, go to the `Protocols` tab, select `TCP/IP properties`, go to the `IP forwarding` tab, and check the box `Enable IP forwarding`.
4. Reboot the Proxy Server computer.
5. After the computer is restarted, launch `Internet Service Manager` and go to the WinSock Proxy service properties.
6. Click the `Security` button and check the `enable packet filtering` checkbox on the external interface.
7. To add a static PPTP filter, click `Add`.
   - In the `Packet filtering properties` dialog box Select `PPTP Call` from the `Predefined filter` drop-down list.
   - To let the PPTP packet go to the specific internal computer, select the `Internet computer` option from the `Local host` box. Input the IP address of the internal PPTP client.
   - Optionally, you can set the packet filter to allow PPTP packets from the specific external PPTP enabled RAS server. To do this, specify the IP address of the external RAS server in the `Single host` field on the `Remote host` box.
   - Click `OK` to close the `Packet Filter Properties` dialog box.
   - Click `OK` to close the `WinSock Proxy service properties` dialog box.
8. If you get the error message "An Invalid local host address was specified for the packet filter," check that the internal PPTP client's IP address is excluded from the Proxy Server LAT.
9. Test the communication by connecting to the external PPTP server from the internal PPTP client.

Proxy Server and Exchange Server

It is impossible today to think of an organization that is connected to the Internet but has no e-mail connectivity. E-mail is still the most commonly used service on the Internet. Many software vendors have developed e-mail server software that allows you to send and receive e-mail messages from the Internet. Microsoft Exchange Server is one of the tools that offers e-mail functionality in addition to other powerful features such as scheduling, storage services, and corporate document flow. The reasonable question at this point is: "How does Exchange Server operate in a Proxy Server environment and what are the configuration steps to make it work?" This question becomes rather difficult when you consider that Exchange Server integrates several different messaging protocols (for example, SMTP, POP3, IMAP4, LDAP, and NNTP).

There are three methods that can be used to allow Exchange Server to coexist with Proxy Server:

- Put Exchange Server and Proxy Server on the same physical computer
- Put Exchange Server on a computer that is connected in parallel with the Proxy Server computer
- Install Exchange Server on a computer that is located in the internal network and configure Proxy Server to propagate incoming requests from the Internet to the Exchange computer

Each solution requires not only installation of the corresponding software products, but also a sophisticated configuration or IP addressing scheme, DNS records, IP routing, and packet filtering.

Installing Exchange Server on the Internal Network

If you decide to install an Exchange computer on the internal network behind the Proxy Server you must use server proxying. Server proxying gives you the ability to listen for the inbound packets destined for a computer located on the internal network (behind the Proxy Server computer). Proxy Server forwards all incoming requests to the internal computer (see Figure 9.5).

In this scenario, the Internet hosts think that Exchange Server is running on the same computer as the Proxy Server computer while, in fact, Proxy Server listens for connections on behalf of the internal server. The Exchange Server computer does not have to have an IP address visible from the Internet — it is treated like a normal WinSock client.

In order to make the Exchange Server work behind Proxy Server, you need to perform the following steps:

1. Install WinSock Proxy Client software on the Exchange Server computer
2. Configure at least one address of an Internet DNS server in the DNS settings of the Exchange Server's Network TCP/IP settings
3. Configure WinSock Proxy service access control
4. Configure Proxy Server packet filtering
5. Configure the Exchange services to use the WinSock Proxy service
6. Update the DNS MX records to point to the Proxy Server's external interface

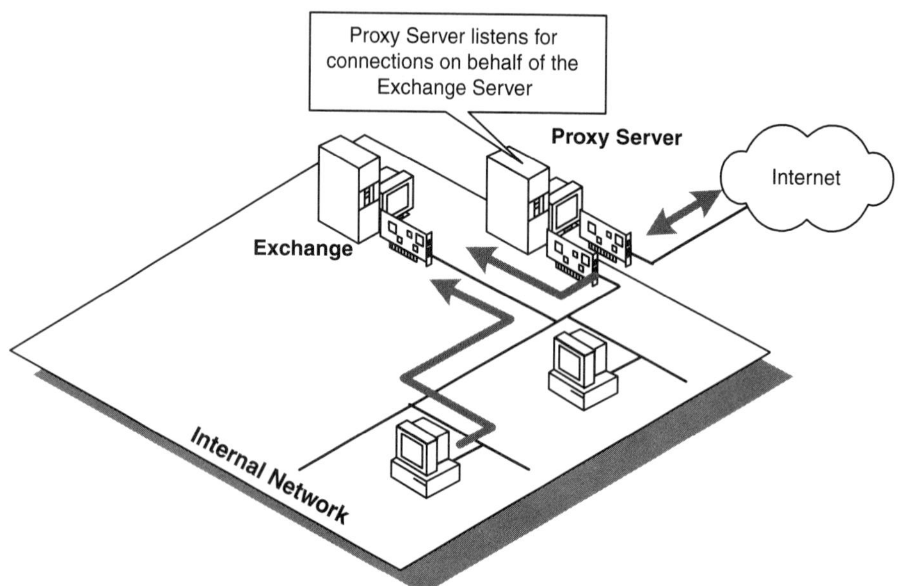

Figure 9.5 *Exchange Server behind a Proxy Server computer.*

Let's now discuss some of these steps in greater detail. Before installing WinSock Proxy client software on an Exchange Server computer, you should select the `Client connects to Microsoft Proxy Server by IP address` option in the `Client Installation/Configuration` dialog of the `WinSock Proxy Service Properties` tab (see Figure 9.6).

After you have specified this option you must install (or reinstall) the WinSock Proxy client software by connecting to the `Mspclnt` shared folder and running `setup`.

You also need to ensure that the Exchange Server computer uses at least one Internet name server for host name resolution. If you don't configure the DNS settings to point to at least one Internet DNS server, your Exchange Server will not be able to properly send e-mail messages to the Internet.

After the WinSock client is installed, it may be a good idea to check its functionality by using a WinSock client application, such as a command line FTP client or a newsreader like Outlook Express.

The next step is to configure the WinSock Proxy service access control. If Access Control is not enabled, no additional steps are required. If you decide to enable Access Control, you must grant access to the Exchange Server service account. This service account must be visible to the Proxy Server computer. In other words, it must belong to the same Windows NT domain

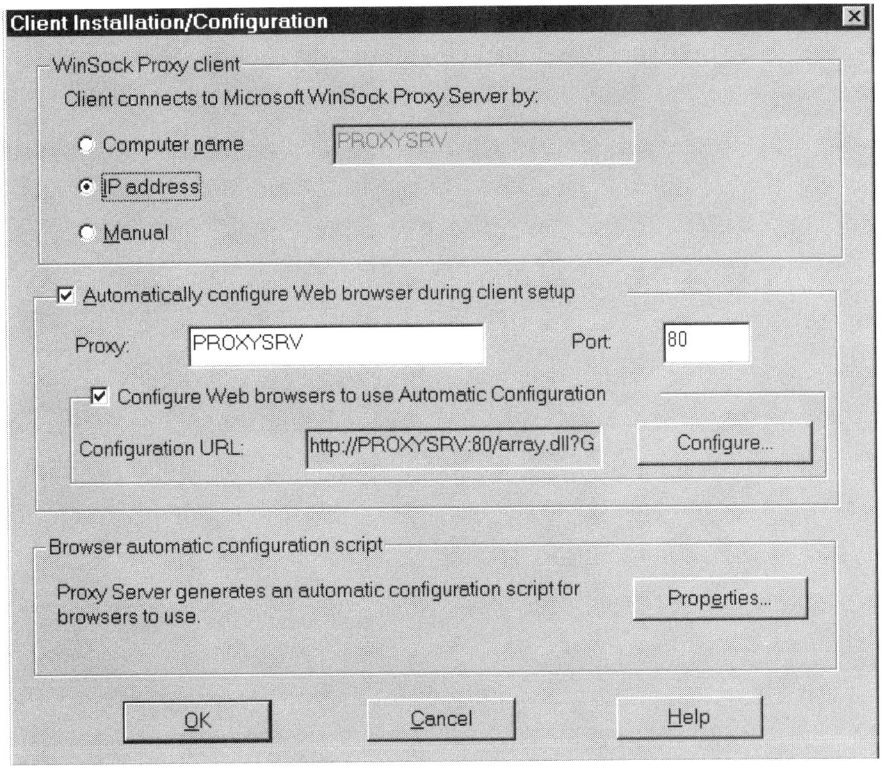

Figure 9.6 *Client computers should connect to Proxy Server by IP address..*

as the Proxy Server or a domain trusted by that domain. You should grant the Exchange service account Unlimited access on the WinSock Proxy service `Permissions` tab.

You must also create two files named `WSPCFG.INI` and place them in the directory where the Exchange Server Internet Mail Service (or Internet Mail Connector for versions of Exchange prior to 5.0) and Information Store reside. These files are used by Exchange Server services to remote requests to the Proxy Server computer.

For the Internet Mail Service the `WSPCFG.INI` file should look like this:

```
[MSEXCIMC]
ServerBindTcpPorts=25
Persistent=1
KillOldSession=1
```

You must place this file to the directory where the Internet Mail Service executable file is located (usually `\EXCHSRVR\CONNECT\MSEXCIMC\BIN`).

This will bind the SMTP Port (port number 25) on Exchange Server computer to the Proxy Server port number 25. Internet hosts will contact the Proxy Server port 25, as it is a well-known port for sending Internet mail messages, and Proxy Server will forward the requests to port 25 on the Exchange Server computer.

If you have Internet Information Server 4.0 with SMTP service running on the Proxy Server computer, you must stop and disable the SMTP service to prevent it from capturing port 25. If you have a third party SMTP service running on the Proxy Server computer, you must disable it as well.

The second `WSPCFG.INI` file is used by the Microsoft Exchange Server Information Store. Create this file in any text editor such as Notepad and place it where the `STORE.EXE` file resides. By default, the `STORE.EXE` file is located in the `\EXCHSRVR\BIN` directory. The `WPSCFG.INI` file for the Information Store should resemble the following:

```
[STORE]
ServerBindTcpPorts=110,119,143
Persistent=1
KillOldSession=1
```

This file specifies that the Exchange Server Information Store should bind Post Office Protocol or POP3 (port 110); Network News Transfer Protocol (NNTP — port 119); and Internet Mail Access Protocol (IMAP) version 4 (port 143) to the corresponding ports on the Proxy Server computer. You can remove any port number from the `WSPCFG.INI` file if you do not need the related service to be visible from the Internet.

After you've created and saved these two files, reboot your Exchange Server computer. Exchange Server should now be listening on the external network interface of the Proxy Server computer. You can now check if Exchange Server can respond to Internet requests. This will not prevent a local client from connecting to Exchange Server using, for example, SMTP or POP3 protocols. Of course, local clients should use the internal IP address of the Exchange Server computer, not the Proxy Server's IP address.

Make sure you've created and saved the WSPCFG.INI files without the TXT extension. When you save files with some text editors (such as Notepad), the default extension may be added to the original file name. In this case you will need to rename the file.

Additionally, if you want to provide outside users with Lightweight Directory Access Protocol (LDAP) connectivity to the Exchange Server, you should add the following lines to the `WSPCFG.INI` file located in the directory containing the Exchange Server Directory Service (`DSAMAIN.EXE`):

```
[DSAMAIN]
ServerBindTcpPorts=389
Persistent=1
KillOldSession=1
```

This means that you must add these lines to the `WSPCFG.INI` file that you have created for the Information Store.

Once you've determined that your Exchange Server responds to Internet requests, you should configure the DNS MX records to point to the external Proxy server IP address. This will permit e-mail to be sent successfully from anywhere on the Internet to your Exchange Server. If DNS records are pointing to the Proxy Server's internal IP addresses or to the Exchange Server IP address on the internal network, Exchange Server will not function correctly. If you are using an Internet Service provider to host your DNS, you must contact them and request that they change or add the MX and A records for your organization.

The MX record is used to identify which server on your network is to receive mail messages from the Internet. In the case when Exchange Server is located behind the Proxy Server and the Proxy Server external network interface has an IP address of w.x.y.z, the DNS records should look similar to the following:

```
A Record     exchs.mydomain.com      IN A w.x.y.z
MX Record    mydomain.com            IN MX 10 exchs.mydomain.com
PTR Record   z.y.x.w.in-addr.arpa    IN PTR exchs.mydomain.com
```

Note that the last entry is not required and should be added to the reverse DNS zone only if you want to provide reverse DNS lookup. The above DNS entries must be included in the DNS server that is used by Internet (external network) hosts, not internal clients.

Once you complete these steps, your Exchange Server should be able to send messages to and receive messages from the Internet. Computers from the Internet will be able to use SMTP, POP3, LDAP, IMAP4, and NNTP to connect to the Exchange Server computer.

To provide additional security, you could enable packet filtering on the Proxy Server computer to permit packets only from specific computers and only to specific services. If Exchange Server is located behind the Proxy

Server computer, you can turn on packet filtering and enable dynamic packet filtering.

If you want to use Outlook Web Access on Exchange Server and put that Exchange Server behind Proxy Server, you will need to implement reverse proxying. You need to redirect certain URLs (which can be used to identify the Exchange Server on the external network) to the Exchange Server. Use the `Publishing` tab in the `Web Proxy service properties` to configure reverse proxying.

Communication with Microsoft Exchange Server or other third-party SMTP servers may be very slow when you install them behind a Proxy Server version 2.0 computer with packet filtering selected (enabled). The mail delivery to and from the Internet may take several minutes or fail completely. **To solve this problem, you must add the predefined filter for `Identd`. For more information about this issue, see Microsoft Knowledge Base arti-**cle Q176947.

For additional information about setting up Exchange Server behind Proxy Server, refer to Microsoft Knowledge Base article Q181420.

Study Break

Multiple Exchange Servers Behind Proxy Server

If you decide to put multiple Exchange Servers behind a Proxy Server computer, you may run into a problem. You may remember that, in order to have multiple machines binding to the same port on the proxy server, the proxy server will have to have multiple external addresses. Multiple addresses can be added to the external interface of the proxy by adding multiple addresses to the same external network card.

To specify which address to bind to on the proxy server, we will need to place additional information in the `WSPCFG.INI` file. You must add the following lines for the application, or service, to specify which external address to bind to on the proxy server:

```
ProxyBindIp=[port]:[IP address],[port]:[IP Address]
```

For example, when an Exchange server needs to listen for port 119 (NNTP) on 207.22.36.1 and port 110(POP3) on 207.22.36.2, the ProxyBindIP line would look like:

```
ProxyBindIP=119:207.22.36.1,110:207.22.36.2
```

To successfully implement this feature, it is highly recommended you install the Microsoft Proxy Server 2.0 combined hotfix. The combined hotfix is described in Microsoft Knowledge Base article Q190997.

Putting Exchange Server on the Proxy Server Computer

You can install Exchange Server on the Proxy Server computer. In this case, Exchange Server is able to serve all client requests from both the internal and external networks. However, if Proxy Server packet filtering is enabled, all communications with Internet mail clients and servers are blocked.

In the previous scenario, we solved the packet filtering issue by enabling the dynamic packet filtering on the Proxy Server computer. Dynamic packet filtering, however, allows WinSock Proxy clients to connect to the Internet when the requests are going through the Proxy Server service software. If you install Exchange Server on the Proxy Server computer, Proxy Server services are not involved when attempting to communicate with the Internet and dynamic packet filtering will not work.

To prevent Exchange Server communications from being blocked by Proxy Server, static filters must be configured and enabled. Exchange Server running on the Proxy Server computer requires two types of static filters: static filters for the client side (so Exchange Server can connect to other mail servers in the Internet) and static filters for the server side (so Internet servers are able to connect to Exchange Server). You need to create static packet filtering for outbound SMTP, POP3, and INETD access. You can do this by choosing the corresponding predefined static filters in the `Packet Filter Properties` dialog box. You also need to create custom static packet filters for inbound access for SMTP, POP3, and LDAP using the description shown in Table 9.1.

Adding Predefined Packet Filters

To add predefined packet filters for Exchange-to-Internet-host communication:

1. In the `Security` dialog box on the `Packet Filters` tab, click `Add`.
2. In the `Packet Filter Properties` dialog box, select the `SMTP` predefined filter.

Table 9.1 *Static Filters For Use With Microsoft Exchange Server*

Name	Dir	Protocol	Local Port	Remote Port	Local Address	Remote Address
SMTP	In	TCP	25	Any	Default	Any
POP3	In	TCP	110	Any	Default	Any
LDAP	Both	TCP	389	Any	Default	Any

- By default, the predefined filters will allow communication to/from any host on the Internet. If needed, modify the `Local host` and `Remote host` settings.

3. Click `OK`.
4. Repeat steps 1 though 3 to add the `IDENTD` filter.
5. Repeat step 1 though 3 to add the `POP3` filter if you are using POP3.

To add predefined packet filters for Internet-host-to-Exchange communication:

1. In the `Security` dialog box on the `Packet Filters` tab, click `Add`.
2. For inbound SMTP connection add the following custom filter:

```
Direction: inbound
Local Port: fixed port: 25
Remote Port: ANY
Local Host: default proxy external IP addresses
Remote Host: any
```

- By default, the custom filters will allow communication to/from any host on the Internet. If needed, modify the `Local Host` and `Remote Host` settings.

3. Click `OK`.
4. For inbound POP3 connection add the following custom filter:

```
Direction: inbound
Local Port: fixed port: 110
Remote Port: ANY
Local Host: default proxy external IP addresses
Remote Host: any
```

- By default, the custom filters will allow communication to/from any host on the Internet. If needed, modify the `Local Host` and `Remote Host` settings.

5. Click `OK`.
6. For inbound LDAP connection add the following custom filter:

```
Direction: both
Local Port: fixed port: 389
Remote Port: ANY
Local Host: default proxy external IP addresses
Remote Host: any
```

- By default, the custom filters will allow communication to/from any host on the Internet. If needed, modify the `Local Host` and `Remote Host` settings.

7. Click `OK`.
8. Click `OK` to close the Security dialog box and click `OK` to close service properties dialog box.

In addition to creating the static packet filters, you may want to change the MX record in DNS point to the Proxy Server external interface.

**EXCHANGE SERVER IN FRONT OF OR IN PARALLEL WITH
THE PROXY SERVER**

Another option of integrating Exchange Server with Proxy Server is to put
Exchange Server outside the local LAN (on the external network). In this
case, no specific configuration to the Exchange Server or to Proxy Server is
required.

You can also install Exchange Server in parallel with the Proxy Server
and disable IP forwarding on the Exchange Server computer to prevent it
from routing packets between the internal and external LAN. (When we say
"in parallel," we mean the Exchange Server will have a network adapter that
connects to the external network as well as one that connects to the internal
network.) This could potentially decrease the load on Proxy Server since
local clients are not required to pass it to reach the Exchange Server.

You should remember that, when the Exchange Server is installed in
front of or in parallel with the Proxy Server, the Exchange Server does not
benefit from any of the network protection afforded by Proxy Server.

Microsoft SQL Server and Proxy Server

If you want Microsoft SQL Server to coexist with Proxy server and respond
to external requests, you again have different methods. The first and easiest
is to install SQL on the same computer where Proxy Server resides. Another
method is to set up SQL Server as a WinSock Proxy client and put it on the
internal network.

In order to make SQL Server visible from the external network, you
need to configure SQL Server to use TCP/IP sockets in its SQL Net Library.
Proxy Server must use IP Address under the WinSock Proxy client configuration (as we did with the Exchange Server). You must install WinSock
Proxy Client software on the SQL Server computer and add the SQL Server
computer's IP address to the Proxy Server's Local Address Table if it is not
already there. If Packet Filtering is enabled on the Proxy Server, Dynamic
Packet Filtering of Microsoft Proxy Server packets should also be selected.

The next step is to create the `WSPCFG.INI` file on the computer running SQL Server. The file should look like the following:

```
[sqlservr]
ServerBindTCPPorts=1433
Persistent=1
KillOldSession=1
```

Place the `WSPCFG.INI` file in the same folder as the `Sqlservr.exe` file. By default this is the `C:\Mssql\Binn` folder. The last step is to restart SQL Server computer.

After you complete the preceding steps, your SQL Server should be accessible to external SQL clients using TCP/IP (clients must be configured to use TCP/IP as their default network library — this is accomplished with the `SQL Server Client Network Utility` that is installed with SQL Server). You must point SQL clients to the Proxy Server's external interface instead of the SQL Server.

Other Internet Services Behind Proxy Server

FTP Server Behind Proxy Server

If you have an FTP server you can place it behind Proxy Server as well. Before we begin our configuration discussion, let's take a brief look at how FTP works. FTP uses two separate TCP connections to communicate between the client and server: a control connection and a data transfer connection. The control connection starts the communication between the FTP client and the FTP server; it is maintained for the duration of the FTP session. The control connection uses port 21 on the server and an open port that is greater than 1023 on the client. The data connection (server port 20) exists only when there is data to be transferred between the client and the server. The data transfer connection closes each time a data transfer is completed. The control connection remains open.

You can configure an FTP service to work with Proxy Server to handle incoming Internet client requests. For the FTP service that is provided with Microsoft Internet Information Server 3.0, for example, you should create a `Wspcfg.ini` file with the settings below and place it in the directory that contains the `inetinfo.exe` file. Note that you should place the `WSPCFG.INI` file on the FTP server computer, not on the Proxy Server computer.

```
[INETINFO]
ServerBindTcpPorts=21
LocalBindTcpPorts=20
Persistent=1
KillOldSession=1
ForceCredentials=1
```

The `ForceCredentials` line is used to specify the user under whom the FTP service interacts with Proxy Server. You should use the `Credtool` utility found on your client machine in the \MSPCLNT directory to specify the user credentials. Credentials should be specified for the account that is used for inetinfo, which is the ftp service executable.

The proper syntax is:

```
credtool.exe -w -n inetinfo -c username domain password
```

where:

inetinfo	specifies the name of the .exe file (in this case "inetinfo").
Username	specifies the user name.
Domain	specifies the local user account on the Proxy Server computer.
Password	specifies the user password.

In addition, if packet filtering is enabled, you must create a static packet filter definition on the Proxy Server computer providing the WinSock Proxy service, with the parameters from Table 9.2.

Finally, in order for Internet users to be able to access your internal FTP by Fully Qualified Domain Name (FQDN), you will have to create an A or CNAME record for your FTP server which points to the proxy server's external address.

Non-Windows Servers Behind the Proxy Server

Non-Windows servers cannot use the WinSock Proxy client and therefore cannot benefit from Proxy Server's reverse hosting and server proxying. The only exceptions to this rule are HTTP servers that can use Proxy Server's Web publishing features and other services that are simply relayed by the third party software installed on the Proxy Server computer (for example, SMTP). In this case, it is reasonable to ask "How can non-windows servers coexist with Proxy Server?"

One of the most popular solutions to this problem is the creation of a so-called *demilitarized zone* (DMZ). This approach provides a secure way for a non-Windows server to publish to the Internet and, at the same time, be available for internal clients.

Table 9.2 *Static Filters For Use With FTP*

Dir	Protocol	Local Port	Remote Port	Local Address	Remote Address
In	TCP	21	Any	Default	Any
Out	TCP	Dyn or Any	Any	Default	Any

The basic idea of the DMZ is to create a third zone in your network that will be accessible to both local and Internet users (see Figure 9.7).

Technically, the DMZ is part of your local area network, but it has valid globally routable Internet addresses. The address space of the DMZ is excluded from the LAT and DMZ is essentially outside your network. The DMZ is routable from the Internet though Proxy Server and can be protected by Proxy Server filtering capabilities. Since servers in the DMZ are not necessarily WinSock-complaint, dynamic packet filters will not work. You must create static filters to allow Internet access to those servers. Note that the routing tables are set so that the DMZ servers can speak to computers in the internal network and vice-versa. Communications from the internal network to the Internet and from the Internet to the internal network must go through the Proxy Server services since the local network is assigned IP addresses that are not directly visible from the Internet.

To implement a demilitarized zone:

1. Install your Proxy Server with three network interfaces. Two interfaces should have valid Internet addresses. One interface should have an IP address from the private address space. Check that your IP addressing scheme does not conflict with general IP addressing rules.
2. Enable IP Forwarding.
3. Make sure your DMZ servers have valid Internet IP addresses.
4. Include IP addresses from the private address range in the LAT. Make sure your LAT does not contain IP addresses from the Internet and from the DMZ.

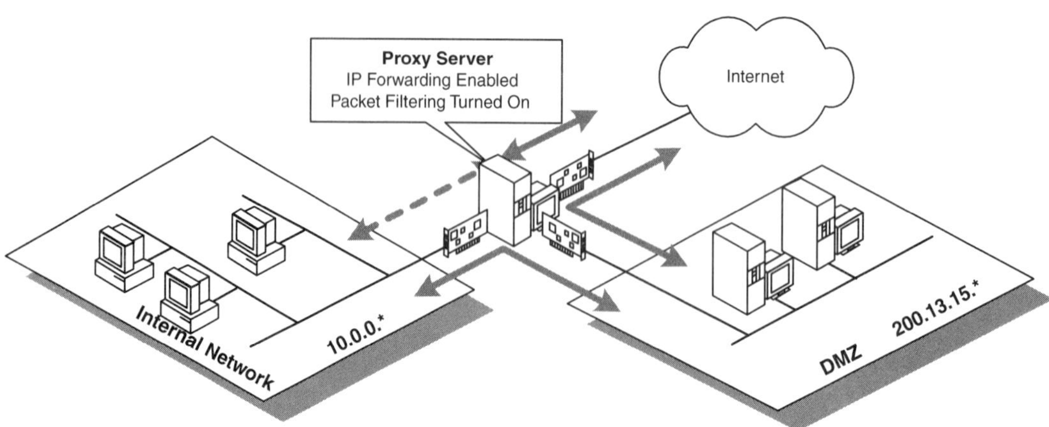

Figure 9.7 *Demilitarized zone.*

5. Make sure you set your DMZ servers to use the Proxy Server computer as their Default Gateway. This is required to allow servers in the DMZ to publish to the Internet and be accessible to local clients.
6. Test your configuration by trying to ping between your DMZ and a computer on the Internet.

Enabling Packet Filtering makes this configuration more secure. Unfortunately, the non-Windows servers in the DMZ do not benefit from dynamic filtering so you will have to create static filters for each of the ports you would like to open for each server. If, for example, you have a Unix-based telnet server in the DMZ at IP address 209.13.15.1, you would need to create the following static filter:

```
Protocol ID: TCP
Direction:   Both
Remote Port: ANY
Local Port:  23
Local Host:  Internal Computer 209.3.15.1
Remote Host: ANY Host
```

You can, of course, change these settings to limit access to specific machines or change the port for different services.

■ Summary

In this chapter we discussed how Microsoft Proxy Server could coexist with other applications in the network. We mentioned that Proxy Server allows you to implement Point-to-Point Tunneling Protocol to provide secure access to your network from the Internet. We discussed different varieties of PPTP and Proxy Server coexistence. You can install a PPTP server or client on the internal network, but you have to enable IP forwarding and ensure that your PPTP-enabled computer is visible from the Internet. The reason for this unsecured solution is that PPTP requests cannot be redirected by the WinSock client software and therefore cannot take advantage of Proxy server proxying. In this scenario, you may want to increase security by implementing Proxy packet filtering. Another option is to install PPTP software along with the RRAS software on the Proxy Server computer. This provides a more secure solution for your network.

We also discussed how an Exchange Server could coexist with Proxy Server. We saw there were several ways to accomplish this. If you install Exchange Server in your internal network, you can take advantage of the

WinSock Proxy service server hosting. The key point in this scenario is the creation of `wspclnt.ini` files. These files are placed in the directories that contain the Exchange Server executable files. They redirect WinSock requests and remote them to Proxy Server. Don't forget that you need to modify your DNS settings to direct Internet clients to the Proxy Server external interface. In this case, Proxy Server acts on behalf of Exchange Server. In this scenario you can also take advantage of dynamic packet filtering.

Alternatively, you may want to consider installing Exchange Server on the Proxy Server computer itself, or install Exchange Server in parallel with the Proxy Server computer. These solutions will also work, but they don't provide the attendant security advantages of putting the Exchange Server behind Proxy Server.

We also looked at how other applications and services can be used in conjunction with Proxy Server. You saw, for example, that SQL server and FTP server can be put behind Proxy without losing their functionality.

Finally, we provided you with guidelines to allow non-Windows servers to coexist with Proxy Server by introducing the concept of a "demilitarized zone."

▲ REVIEW QUESTIONS

1. *You want to implement PPTP in your network to allow users from the Internet to connect to your internal network and access files and folders. Your network is protected by a Proxy Server computer. What is the best way to integrate Proxy and PPTP?*

     A. Install PPTP on the internal computer. Install WinSock Proxy client on the PPTP computer. Disable IP forwarding on the Proxy computer. Configure static PPTP filter for "PPTP receive."

     B. Install PPTP on the internal computer. Install WinSock Proxy client on the PPTP computer. Enable IP forwarding on the Proxy computer. Enable dynamic filtering on the Proxy computer.

     C. Install PPTP on the Proxy Server computer. Enable dynamic packet filtering.

     D. Install PPTP on the Proxy Server computer. Configure static PPTP filter for "PPTP receive."

2. *You placed the PPTP-enabled RAS server in the internal network. On the Proxy Server computer, you enable IP forwarding and decide to configure a static packet filter to let the PPTP packets go to the internal PPTP server. When you try to configure a packet filter, you get an error message saying that an invalid local host address was specified for a packet filter. What should you do to correct the problem?*

   A. Disable IP forwarding.

   B. Exclude the IP address of the PPTP server from the LAT.

   C. Install WinSock Proxy client on the PPTP server.

   D. PPTP cannot coexist with Proxy Server.

3. *You want to set up Exchange Server in the internal network protected by the Proxy Server so the Exchange Server can exchange e-mail messages with the Internet. What steps should you follow after Exchange Server setup is complete? (Select all that apply)*

   A. Install the WinSock Proxy client on the Exchange computer.

   B. Exclude the Exchange Server computer's IP address from the LAT.

   C. Create the `wspclnt.ini` file and place it in the directory where the IMS executable file resides.

   D. Enable IP forwarding on the Proxy Server computer.

   E. Turn on dynamic packet filtering.

   F. Modify the DNS MX records and point them to the external Proxy network interface.

4. *You want to host multiple Exchange Server computers with Internet Mail Service installed behind the Proxy Server. How can you accomplish this in the most secure manner?*

   A. Add several IP addresses to the internal network adapter. Modify the `wspclnt.ini` file and add the ProxyBindIP entry there.

   B. Add several IP addresses to the external network adapter. Modify the `wspclnt.ini` file and add the ProxyBindIP entry there.

   C. Enable IP forwarding. Make sure that all Exchange Server computers are directly accessible from the Internet.

   D. Disable IP forwarding, implement packet filtering. Ensure that Proxy Server has only one external IP address. Bind different Internet Mail services on Exchange computers to different ports on the external Proxy IP address using the ProxyBindIP.

5. *What is the concept of a DMZ? (Select all that apply)*

    A. DMZ is a zone in your network that is accessible to both local and Internet users.

    B. DMZ is a zone in your network that is accessible to neither local nor Internet users.

    C. DMZ is a packet filtering algorithm.

    D. DMZ is a zone in the internal network that has the valid Internet IP addresses.

6. *You want to put a UNIX telnet server behind a Proxy Server. How can you accomplish this?*

    A. Implement reverse hosting.

    B. Implement reverse proxying.

    C. Implement server proxying.

    D. This cannot be done.

    E. None of the above.

7. *You want to put one UNIX-based Web server behind the Proxy Server. How can you accomplish this?*

    A. Implement reverse hosting.

    B. Implement reverse proxying.

    C. Implement server proxying.

    D. This cannot be done.

    E. None of the above.

8. *You want Internet users to access your SQL Server located in the environment protected by the Proxy Server. The only way to accomplish this is to install SQL on the Proxy Server computer.*

    A. True

    B. False

Monitoring and Tuning Microsoft Proxy Server

Now that your Proxy Server is up and running, it is time to learn how to keep it running properly and to make it run as efficiently as possible.

At the conclusion of this chapter you will be able to:

- List available monitoring and optimization tools and explain the use of each
- Explain the use and benefits of Windows NT Performance Monitor as it relates to Proxy Server
- Identify selected Windows NT Performance Monitor objects and counters and explain how they are used to optimize Proxy Server
- Explain the benefits of and procedures for establishing a baseline
- Discuss techniques of searching for bottlenecks

- Outline benefits of and explain procedures for using Network Monitor in support of Proxy Server
- Explain benefits and use of the Proxy Server logs
- Outline procedures for tuning the Proxy Server cache
- Discuss procedures to optimize routing

MCSE 10.1 Available Tools

Proxy Server may be monitored through a number of tools. There are Proxy Server specific tools as well as some Windows NT related tools which will permit you to analyze and optimize much of your Proxy Server's operation. We'll outline the tools in this section and discuss each in some detail later in this chapter.

Windows NT Performance Monitor

The Windows NT Performance Monitor is a very robust tool that can monitor activity within the machine and network. The installation of Proxy Server adds a set of new objects to Performance Monitor's already comprehensive set of tools. With Performance Monitor, you may monitor the server's use of memory, processor, disk, and network resources to ensure the Proxy Server is making the best use of the resources available. Performance Monitor can tell you when it's time to upgrade your server's components and can log data that can form a baseline to help you determine changes in the Proxy Server environment and lead you to decisions on how to reoptimize hardware and software when those changes occur. Performance Monitor can also be configured to send alerts when predetermined thresholds are exceeded.

Network Monitor

The Windows NT Network Monitor can capture individual network packets destined to one or many network interfaces. By intercepting and examining individual network packets, you can determine what type of traffic is passed between the Proxy Server and its clients or between the Proxy Server and the external network. This information can be invaluable when trying to determine why a particular Proxy Server feature is not working as expected and can help you determine how to configure the system to provide the expected functionality.

The version of Network Monitor that ships with Windows NT will monitor only broadcast packets and those sent to or from the computer running Network Monitor. The version available with Microsoft Systems Management Server will monitor all network packets that pass its network interface.

Server Logs

As we indicated in Chapters 5 and 6, Proxy Server logs may be configured to record information for each of the Proxy Server services as well as for packet filtering. These logs display virtually all of Proxy Server's activities and may be used to monitor server use, check for errors in use or configuration, and establish a Proxy Server baseline of activity that can later be used to determine if and how the use of the server has changed.

Current Sessions

Proxy Server's Current User Sessions dialog shows the number of users currently connected to any of the Proxy Server's services at any given time (see Figure 10.1). You can display this dialog by clicking the `Current Sessions` button on the `Service Properties` tab for any of the Proxy Server ser-

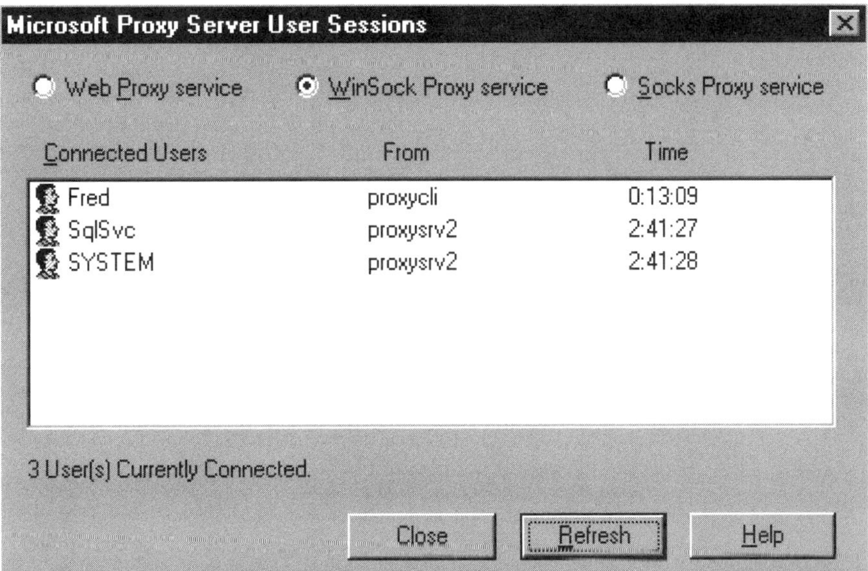

Figure 10.1 *Proxy Server User Sessions dialog showing WinSock Proxy users.*

vices. This is a very useful tool to get an immediate picture of load on your network at any given time. Although Performance Monitor has counters to record *current users* or *active sessions*, the User Sessions dialog provides a quick display of users by name and machine and shows how long an individual user has maintained their session.

MCSE 10.2 Using Performance Monitor with Proxy Server

The Windows NT Performance Monitor will permit you to monitor the operation of many of your system's parts. Performance Monitor uses major categories of data called *objects*. Each of these objects is further divided into specific parameters called *counters*. By selecting the appropriate objects and counters, you can view vital Proxy Server Parameters and determine how the system is operating.

Before you can monitor activity associated with the computer's hard disks (logical or physical), you must enter the following command at the command line: `diskperf -y`. To accomplish this, you must be logged on as an administrator and must restart the computer after entering the command. Enabling disk monitoring will have a non-trivial impact on your computer. When not actually monitoring disk activity, you should disable monitoring with `diskperf -n`.

Performance Monitor Objects Installed with Proxy Server

When Proxy Server is installed, Performance Monitor objects are installed for the Web Proxy Server Service, Web Proxy Server Cache, WinSock Proxy Service, SOCKS Proxy Service, and Packet Filtering. In addition to the new objects, a new Proxy Server menu item (`Monitor Microsoft Proxy Server Performance`) is added (see Figure 10.2). This item launches Performance Monitor with a selection of objects and counters to permit general Proxy Server performance monitoring. (These predefined selections are stored in the workspace file `msp.pmc` in the `\msp` directory.) Tables 10.1 through 10.5 highlight some of the more important counters in these objects.

General Performance Monitor Tools

In addition to the counters and objects supplied by Proxy Server, there are a number of other counters that should be used to monitor your Proxy Server's and overall system's performance. Table 10.6 outlines some of the

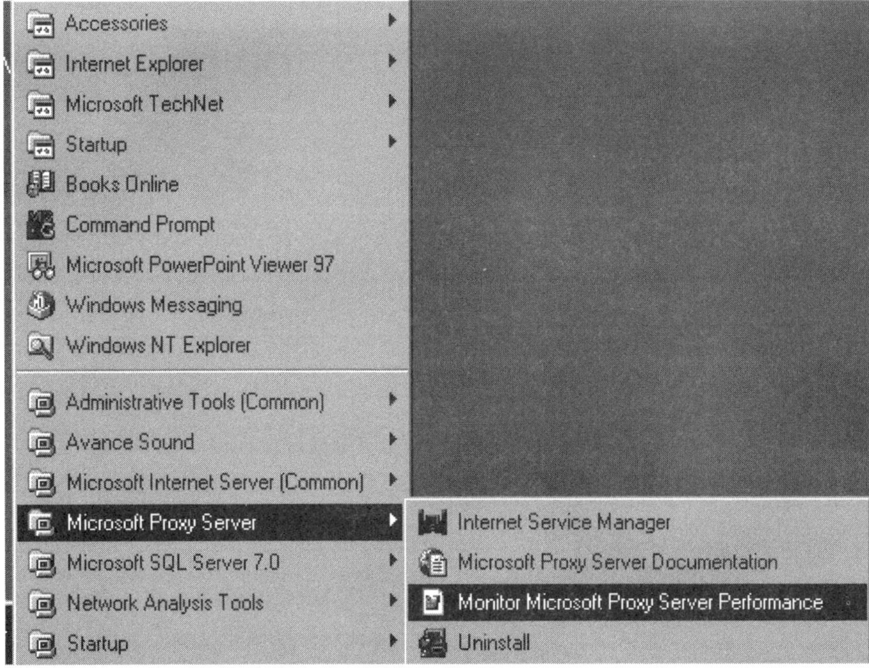

Figure 10.2 *Selecting "Monitor Microsoft Proxy Server Performance."*

additional objects and counters that can be used to monitor your Proxy Server's activity.

Analyzing Server Performance

Now that we've looked at some of the information available from Performance Monitor, we can turn our attention to how to use them to analyze our Proxy Server computer. Performance analysis helps us to determine if our system is properly functioning and, if it is not, how to properly tune the system for better performance. Performance analysis is based on two general activities: establishing a baseline and searching for bottlenecks.

ESTABLISH A BASELINE

Before you can determine changes in your server or environment, you need to know what is "normal" for the installation. To do this you must create a *baseline*. A baseline is nothing more than a representative set of data that you will use to compare with the future state of the network. Using a baseline, you can determine if something has changed and the general area in which

Table 10.1 *Selected Web Proxy Service Counters*

Counter	Definition
Cache Hit Ratio (%)	Shows a percentage of query requests serviced from cached data as compared to the total number of requests to the Web Proxy Service. This reveals how effective your cache is and can be used to help you tune the cache. Your goal should be to get this number as close to 100% as possible. (This counter is set by the `msp.pmc` workspace file.)
Requests/Sec	Shows the number of requests coming into the Proxy Server Service each second. This can be used in establishing a baseline and can help in determining if additional servers are required or if arrays or routes are configured as optimally as possible. (This counter is set by the `msp.pmc` workspace file.)
Current Average Millisecond	Shows the average number of milliseconds required to service a Web Proxy Service request. If this figure climbs, it could mean your server needs increased capacity (from memory, disk, or processor). (This counter is set by the `msp.pmc` workspace file.)
Sites Denied	Shows the total number of Internet sites to which the Web Proxy Service has been denied access. This can show if the limits you have set are working. If this number is unexpectedly high, you may have accidentally blocked necessary sites.
Sites Granted	Shows the total number of Internet sites to which the Web Proxy Service has been granted access. By comparing this with the reading for Sites Denied, you can further determine if your restrictions are working properly. A high number for Sites Denied accompanied by a high number for Sites Granted may indicate proper operation in a high-traffic environment.
Total Users	Shows the total number of users who have ever connected to the Web Proxy Server. This number will give you an indication of the servers use history.
Current Users	Shows the total number of users who are currently connected to the Web Proxy Server. This reveals server usage patterns and can help determine if additional Proxy Server computers are required.
Maximum Users	Shows the maximum number of users who have ever been simultaneously connected to the Web Proxy Server. This reveals server load and can help determine if additional Proxy Server computers are required.
Upstream Bytes Total/sec	Shows the total number of bytes per second processed between the server and the Internet or an upstream chained Proxy Server. This can help determine if you have sufficient bandwidth to the external network. (This was called Inet Bytes Total/sec in previous versions.)

Table 10.2 *Selected Web Proxy Service Cache Counters*

Counter	Definition
Bytes in Cache	Shows the total number of bytes currently in the cache. When this counter approaches the total cache size, it's time to increase the cache size or change your caching options.
Max Bytes Cached	Shows the maximum number of bytes that have ever been cached. When this counter is near the total cache size, you should analyze your network's usage patterns to determine if it's time to increase the cache size or change your caching options. (Note that the default scale on this counter is different from that on the *Bytes in Cache* counter. If you leave them both at the default, it may appear that the *Max Bytes* counter is lower than the *Bytes in Cache* counter.)
Active Refresh Bytes Rate	Shows the number of bytes retrieved from the external network each second to actively update the cache. This counter may be used as a guide to determine if you may increase your active caching or if you should curtail active caching.
Total Actively Refreshed URLs	Shows the cumulative number of URLs that have been actively refreshed from their respective sites. This can provide another guideline for the increase or curtailment of active caching.

Table 10.3 *Selected WinSock Proxy Service Counters*

Counter	Definition
Active Sessions	Shows how many people are using the server at a given time. This can help you determine usage patterns and will help in deciding if additional Proxy Server computers will be required. (This counter is set by the `msp.pmc` workspace file.)
Accepting TCP Connections	Shows the number of TCP connection objects that wait for a connection from WinSock Proxy clients.
Active TCP Connections	Shows the number of active TCP connections — those currently passing data.
Active UDP Connections	Shows the number of active UDP connections — those currently passing data.
Connecting TCP Connections	Shows the total number of pending connections — those awaiting the completion of a session between the WinSock Proxy server and the WinSock Proxy client.
Listening TCP Connections	Shows the number of connection objects that are waiting for a TCP connection from the external network.

Table 10.4 *SOCKS Proxy Service Counters*

Counter	Definition
SOCKS Client Bytes Received/sec	Shows the rate at which the SOCKS Proxy Server is receiving data from the SOCKS Proxy clients.
SOCKS Client Bytes Sent/sec	Shows the rate the SOCKS Proxy Server sends data to the SOCKS Proxy clients.
SOCKS Clients Bytes Total/sec	Shows the sum of the Bytes Received and Bytes Sent counters (above).
SOCKS Sessions	Shows the total number of SOCKS sessions running on the SOCKS Proxy Service.

to look for the change. The baseline will also be helpful in determining if improvements you apply to the system improve performance and by how much. The easiest way to create a baseline is with the Performance Monitor's Log option. You can use Tables 10.1 through 10.6 to select appropriate objects to monitor and create a log of those objects. Create logs during times of representative network workload. One option would be to create logs depicting low, peak, and normal network workloads and store them away for future reference. You may then run Performance Monitor to view the same information during similar periods to compare the baseline with the network's current status. This will help you determine if further network analysis is necessary. When creating a baseline (or analyzing current system performance), it is important to understand that using the Performance Monitor tool may actually have an impact on the machine being monitored. Unless you're measuring network performance, it is a good idea to use Performance Monitor on a remote machine to monitor your Proxy Server computer over the network. This will minimize the impact of monitoring on the data being monitored.

Table 10.5 *Packet Filtering Counters*

Counter	Definition
Frames Dropped Due to Filter Denial	Shows the number of packets rejected because dynamic packer filtering did not allow the data.
Frames Dropped Due to Protocol Violation	Shows the total number of packets rejected because of a protocol impropriety.
Total Dropped Frames	Shows the total number of packets rejected by packet filtering.
Total Incoming Connections	Shows the total number of connections made on the interface(s) protected by packet filtering.
Total Lost Logging Frames	Shows the total number of rejected packets that could not be logged.

Table 10.6 *Performance Monitor Objects and Counters Useful for Proxy Server Analysis*

Object	Counter	Definition
Network Interface	Bytes Total/sec	Shows the number of bytes sent and received by the selected network interface. If this number approaches your network transmission speed, your network is likely becoming a bottleneck. In this case you should upgrade the network (e.g., from 10BaseT to 100BaseT) or divide the network into subnets.
Process	%Processor Time (wspsrv)	Shows the percentage of total process time the WinSock Proxy service is currently using. This will help you determine if other applications are choking the WinSock Proxy service's performance. If you suspect degraded WinSock Proxy performance and this shows a low value relative to other processes, you should consider upgrading the processor or reducing the number of applications running on the Proxy Server computer. (This counter is set by the `msp.pmc` workspace file.)
Process	%Processor Time (inetinfo)	Shows the percentage of total process time the Internet Information Server is currently using. Considerations here are the same as for the previous entry. (This counter is set by the `msp.pmc` workspace file.)
Processor	%Processor Time	Shows the total percentage of the processor's time used to run non-idle threads. If this value is consistently at or above 80–90%, your processor is not able to handle the load and should be upgraded. You can use this value to help determine if low readings from *Process* object counters indicate a processor problem or simply low process activity.
Memory	Available Bytes	Shows the amount of free virtual memory. If this counter stays consistently below 4 MB, paging is occurring and performance is less than optimal.
Memory	Pages/sec	Shows the number of pages read from the disk or written to the disk to resolve memory references to pages that were not in memory at the time of the reference. As a rule, you can assume that if the average of this counter is consistently greater than 10, then memory is probably becoming a bottleneck in the system.
Memory	Page Faults/sec	Shows the number of times per second an item was looked for in memory but actually needed to be retrieved from the page file.

(cont.)

Table 10.6 *Continued*

Object	Counter	Definition
Memory	Committed Bytes	Shows the size of virtual memory (in bytes) that has been committed (as opposed to simply reserved). If this counter is greater than the amount of main memory, it indicates that main memory *may* not be large enough to accommodate all functions of all currently active processes.
Physical Disk	% Disk Time	Shows the percentage of time the disk is actually performing reads or writes. If this counter consistently registers at or near 67%, the physical disk is a bottleneck. This counter is the percentage of elapsed time that the selected disk drive is busy servicing read or write requests, including time waiting in the disk driver queue. (A similar counter is available from the Physical Disk object and may be used to determine if the problem is occurring on a specific partition of the device.)
Physical Disk	Current Disk Queue Length	Shows pending disk operations. If this is consistently greater than 2, significant disk congestion is indicated. (A similar counter is available from the Physical Disk object and may be used to determine if the problem is occurring on a specific partition of the device.)

Although the foregoing discussion implies that baselines are useful mainly when trying to solve problems, the same technique may be used to optimize an already good configuration. When you're pursuing optimization, you can compare logs made after configuration changes to the original baseline. If performance has improved, you can take the new logs as your baseline and continue to seek optimization. If performance has degraded, you should take the changes out and pursue other avenues. When optimizing, it is a good idea to make only one change, analyze it, and make another. By doing this, you won't contaminate the results of one optimization with those of another.

In some cases, configuration changes occur because additional features are added to the environment. When this happens and performance is degraded, it may not be possible to "optimize" performance back to its original level. A good baseline will help you quantify the performance degradation, determine if the impact is significant to your operation, and allow you to decide if additional hardware or network segmentation will be required.

SEARCHING FOR BOTTLENECKS

If you suspect you have a performance problem, the next step is to search for a system bottleneck which may be at fault. A bottleneck search may seem like a never-ending quest. Once a particular bottleneck is located and corrected, another performance degradation may be revealed. The key is to eliminate bottlenecks until your network is returned to the desired performance as indicated by your performance baseline. When you look for bottlenecks, you do so by analyzing performance in four general areas: *Processor*, *Memory*, *Hard Disk*, and *Network*. When dealing with a Proxy Server computer, you should also monitor the performance of the Proxy Server's cache.

Processor • Since Proxy Server is not particularly processor (CPU) intensive, the Processor is not typically a Proxy Server bottleneck. When other applications are running on the Proxy Server computer, however, problems may develop. One key to analyzing processor problems is to view the `Processor|%Processor Time` counter described in Table 10.6. If the counter consistently exceeds 80-90%, the processor may be the bottleneck. ("System % Total processor time" can be viewed for multiprocessor systems.) If this occurs, you need to determine *who* or *what* is consuming the CPU. To determine which process is using up most of the CPU's time, monitor the `Process|%Processor Time` for all of the process instances. If the problem is other processes competing with Proxy Server, you should move them from the Proxy Server computer. If the difficulty appears to be hardware-based, it may be time to upgrade to a more powerful computer or add additional CPUs (if your hardware supports that).

Memory • Memory is frequently the most common cause of system performance problems and, fortunately, usually the cheapest and easiest to correct. (Memory has become relatively inexpensive and installing memory is typically a simple and quick process.) Since Windows NT is a virtual memory system, memory problems may sometimes appear as disk problems when memory shortages result in a great deal of paging. The best way to check for memory problems on a Windows NT server is to determine to what degree paging is occurring. To accomplish this, monitor the `Memory|Available Bytes` counter, the `Memory|Pages/sec` counter, the `Memory|Committed Bytes` counter, the `Memory|Page Faults/sec` counter, the `Memory|Cache Faults/sec` counter, and the `Memory|Commit Limit` counter.

If `Memory|Pages/sec` is consistently greater than 10, then memory is probably becoming a bottleneck in the system — consistently above 20 may actually indicate disk thrashing. If `Memory|Pages/sec` is increasing, but

`Memory|Available bytes` is not decreasing, you may not actually have a bottleneck at all. If this is the case, check for an application that is doing a great deal of disk IO (reads or writes). If the actual size of the page file is greater than its initial size, your system is spending time growing the page file and dealing with page file fragmentation.

If the `Memory|Committed Bytes` counter is greater than the amount of main memory, it indicates that main memory *may* not be large enough to accommodate all functions of all currently active processes — paging is occurring. While some paging *may* be inevitable, you should check `Memory|Pages/sec` and `Memory|Page Faults/sec`. If the `Memory|Pages/sec` is greater than 10 (this number actually varies with disk hardware but 10 is representative) and `Memory|Page Faults/sec` is greater than `Memory|Cache Faults/sec`, your computer is doing too much paging.

When `Memory|Committed bytes` approaches the `Memory Commit Limit` (assuming the page file has already reached maximum page file size), you have run out of pages both in main memory and in the page file. (The `Memory|Commit Limit` is the amount of virtual memory that can be committed without extending the page file.)

Hard Disk • Hard disk performance is particularly important to a caching Proxy Server computer. Since caching is potentially disk-intensive, some performance degradation may be noted here when the hard drive is not up to par. As we mentioned above, poor memory performance may result in a great deal of paging, which may initially appear as a disk problem. It is always a good idea to look at memory before analyzing your hard drives.

To analyze your disk activity you should monitor the `%Disk Time` and `Disk Queue Length` counters from the `Logical Disk` or `Physical Disk` objects. If the `%Disk Time` counter consistently registers at or near 67%, the physical disk is the bottleneck. The counter shows the percentage of time the drive is handling read or write requests — to include time waiting in the disk driver queue. More importantly, if the `Disk Queue Length` (pending disk I/O requests) is greater than 2, it generally indicates significant disk congestion.

Network • Network problems may arise because the network itself is too slow, because network protocols are mismatched, or because the network is handling extraneous traffic. Performance monitor can help you determine if your network is at or near its design capacity. Monitor the `Network Interface|Bytes Total/sec` counter. This shows the number of bytes sent and received by the selected network interface. If this number approaches your network transmission speed, your network is likely becoming a bottleneck. In this case you should upgrade the network (e.g., from 10BaseT to

100BaseT) or divide the network into subnets. You should also monitor the `Web Proxy Server Service|Upstream Bytes Total/sec` counter. This counter shows the total number of bytes per second processed between the server and the Internet or an upstream chained Proxy Server. This will tell you if you have sufficient bandwidth to the external network. If this number is approaching the throughput of your external network connection, you may want to improve your connectivity by installing a faster modem or upgrading to an ISDN, T1, or other high-speed connection. If the preceding values appear lower than you would expect, check the `Network Interface|Output Queue Length` counter. If this counter is consistently greater than 2, your network adapter card is not able to transmit packets as fast as they are provided to it. In this case, you should upgrade your network adapter card, (e.g., replace an 8 or 16 bit card with a 32 bit card).

Before you take any network optimization steps, however, you may wish to analyze the network traffic with Network Monitor and check your protocol configuration to ensure the network traffic is valid (more on this later in the chapter). You should also ensure your Proxy Server caching is optimized.

Proxy Server Cache • The Proxy Server cache is a major feature of Proxy Server. Too much active caching may result in sufficient traffic to saturate your network. Too little caching may result in a high number of calls to the external network to retrieve the same information, which may also saturate your network. Even when insufficient caching has no significant effect on network traffic, the faster user response available from caching makes it important to ensure this feature is properly optimized.

Using the `Web Proxy Server Cache` object, monitor the `Bytes in Cache`, `Max Bytes Cached`, `Active Refresh Bytes Rate`, and `Total Actively Refreshed URLs` counters. The first two counters will the current and maximum number of bytes that have been in the cache. This will help you analyze cache usage patterns and will let you know if your cache is too big or too small. `Active Refresh Bytes Rate` shows the number of bytes going into the cache each second as a result of active caching. Compare this figure with the `Upstream Bytes Total/sec` counter described in the previous section. If external network connectivity is a problem and active caching is taking a large percentage of your throughput, you may wish to curtail active caching. If, on the other hand, you have a great deal of available bandwidth and active caching is only a small fraction of it, an increase in active caching may improve responsiveness.

You should also look at the `Web Proxy Service|Cache Hit Ratio(%)` counter. This counter shows the percentage of query requests serviced from cached data as compared to the total number of requests to the Web Proxy Service. Since servicing requests from the cache is, typically, more efficient than servicing them from the external network, your goal should be to get this number as close to 100% as possible. (We discussed how to configure the cache in Chapter 5 and will discuss some optimization steps a bit later in this chapter.)

Using Performance Monitor to Analyze Specific Server Roles

Although our discussion of performance monitoring may have implied that we could achieve success by monitoring the same counters regardless of the way our Proxy Server computer and network were employed, in practice things aren't quite that monolithic. Server performance must be gauged in respect to the specific operations that will be performed within the network. It is important to understand *if* the Proxy Server will be used primarily to obtain information from Web sites, obtain volumes of file data from FTP sites, be used for reverse hosting, or a combination of these. In some cases, Proxy Server may be servicing many users but will only need to retrieve a relatively small amount of data. In other cases, the server may need to provide a conduit for large volumes of data destined to only a few users. Two typical Internet sessions, HTTP and FTP, are, typically, at opposite ends of this spectrum.

HTTP SESSIONS

An HTTP session will typically result in small amounts of transferred data. In most environments, however, it is likely that many users will want to perform HTTP sessions simultaneously. The number of user sessions will likely be of some interest. In most cases HTTP sessions will be accomplished via a CERN-compliant Web browser and will, therefore, be handled by the Web Proxy service. If caching is employed by the server, you should monitor the cache counters we discussed in the previous section and should pay attention to the Proxy Server computer's hard disk counters. If, during the HTTP session, the user uses web-based applications, the WinSock proxy service counters will also provide some useful information. If, in this case, the user accesses RealAudio or streaming video, the data throughput required of the session might approach that of an FTP session. Under these conditions, Proxy Server memory and processor counters may be of interest. To determine how much of the processor is used for the HTTP request, be sure to monitor the *inetinfo* process also.

Figure 10.3 shows a Performance Monitor screen during a screen refresh for an HTTP session. The counters displayed are from the MSP.PMC

Proxy Server counter selection plus the `Processor|%Processor Time` counter. The highest peaks are found in the `Current Average Millisec-onds/request` counter. The upper horizontal line is `Cache Hit Ratio` and the three lines showing relatively proportional activity are `%Processor Time`, `inetinfo %Process Time`, and `Requests/sec`, respectively.

FTP SESSIONS

In contrast to HTTP sessions, FTP sessions will typically be undertaken by few users relative to the amount of data downloaded. (Although we're discussing FTP, the concepts we're discussing are applicable to any data intensive server application. You can use the same principles when analyzing SQL server activity and, to a lesser extent, activity associated with Exchange Server.) Since the FTP service runs as a WinSock Proxy client, you should monitor the WinSock Proxy object. To get an idea of the load on the system,

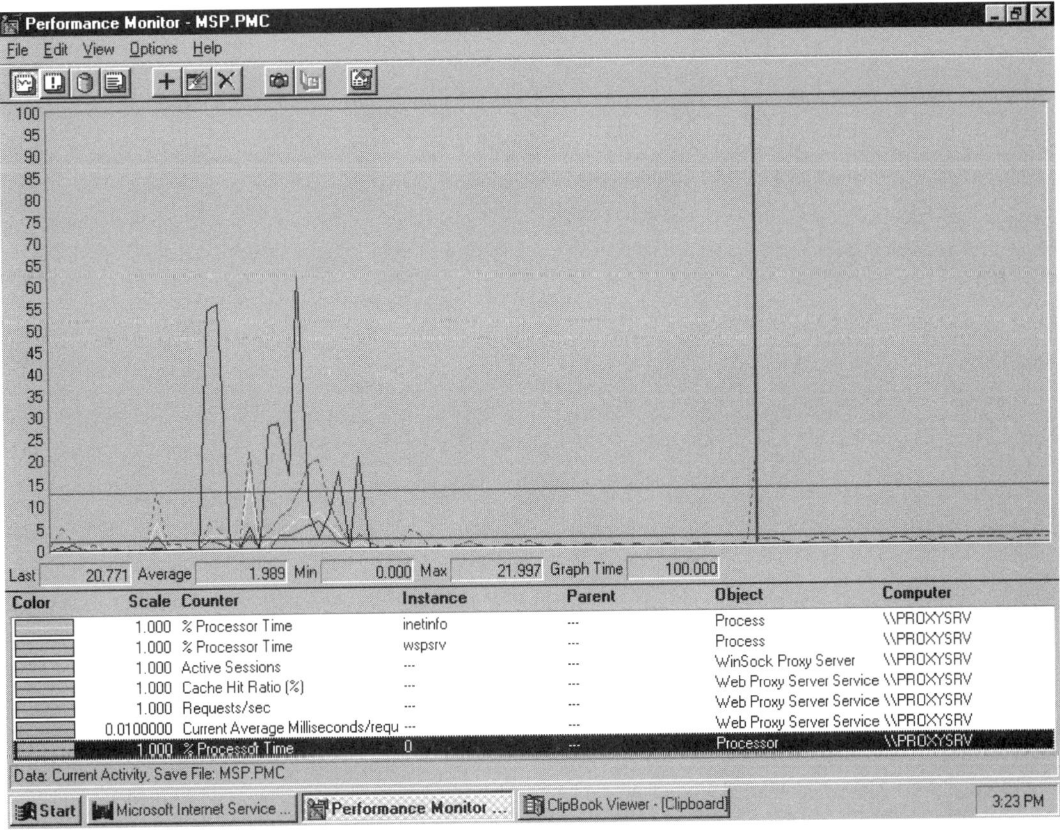

Figure 10.3 *Performance Monitor during an HTTP session.*

look at the processor time counter (be sure to use the `wspsrv process time` counter to determine what impact the WinSock Proxy session has on the overall processor time). Since FTP is more data-intensive than processor-intensive, the processor/process counters won't likely show any dramatic changes. If they do, this should definitely attract your attention. When looking at FTP (or SQL Server) sessions, you should concentrate on data throughput. The `WinSock Proxy Server|Bytes Read/sec` or `WinSock Proxy Server|Bytes Read/sec` counters will show how much data is being transferred during the session. You should also monitor the network counters discussed in the previous section to determine how much of your network bandwidth is used by the session.

Figure 10.4 shows a Performance Monitor screen during a SQL Server data retrieval. The counters displayed are from the `MSP.PMC` Proxy Server counter selection plus the `Processor|%Processor Time` counter and the

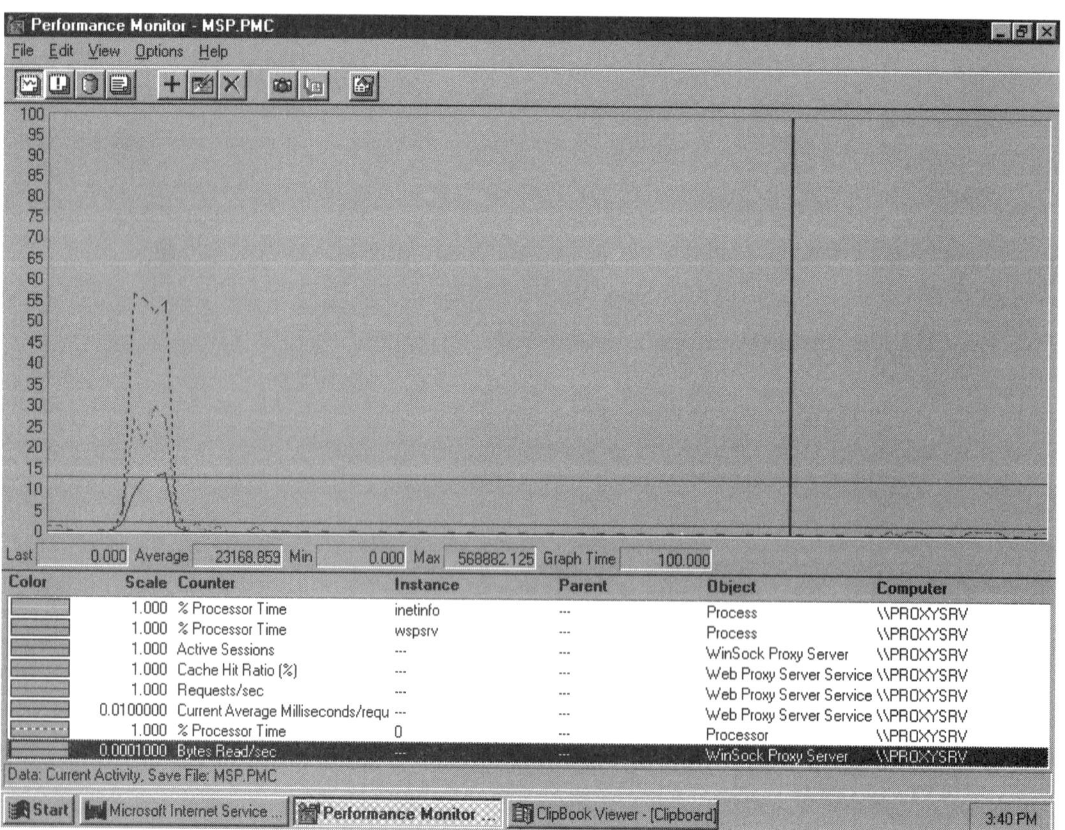

Figure 10.4 *Performance Monitor during a SQL Server data retrieval.*

`WinSockProxyServer|Bytes Read/sec` counter. The three lines showing relatively proportional activity are `Bytes Read/sec`, `%Processor Time`, and `wspsrv %Process Time`, and `Requests/sec`, respectively.

Study Break

Now You Do It

1. Launch Performance Monitor from the `Monitor Microsoft Proxy Server Performance` selection on the Proxy Server menu (as shown in Figure 10.2).
2. Using `Edit|Add` to Chart, add the `Processor|%Processor Time` counter, `WinSockProxyServer|Bytes Read/sec` counter, and any other counters you'd like to monitor.
3. Conduct HTTP and FTP sessions and compare your results to those shown in Figures 10.3 and 10.4.

MCSE 10.3 Using Network Monitor to Perform Network Traffic Analysis

When you need to look "inside the wire," Network Monitor is the right choice. While Performance Monitor will give you a quantitative view of what is going on it the network, Network Monitor can let you know where the traffic is coming from and what kind of traffic it is. This is particularly useful when you're trying to determine if you need to increase your network bandwidth or merely tune the system to eliminate extraneous traffic.

You may remember that Network Monitor will monitor the packets that pass your network interface (in the case of the Network Monitor version that ships with Windows NT, this means *only* packets destined for or sent from that interface, as well as broadcast and multicast packets). Since your Proxy Server computer should have at least two network interfaces, remember you can only monitor one interface at a time. To select the desired interface, select the `Capture` menu and click on `Networks` to reveal the `Select Capture Network` dialog depicted in Figure 10.5. Network monitor will capture packets for whichever network adapter card is highlighted. It the diagram, we'll collect for the network adapter whose hardware address is `0060082931B1`.

When reviewing Network Monitor captures, you should check to see if the network traffic contains the packets you'd expect without a great deal of

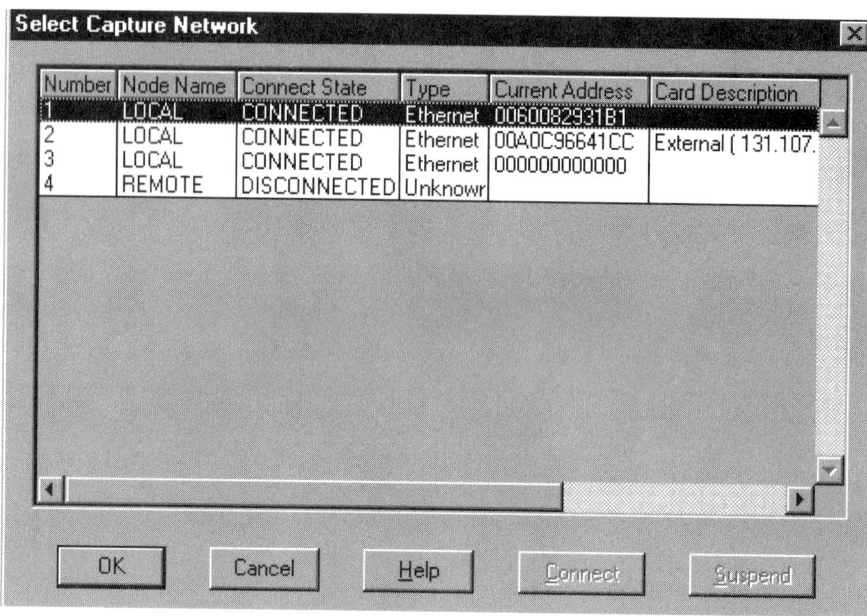

Figure 10.5 *Select Capture Network dialog.*

extraneous traffic. You should always look for both routed and broadcast traffic, since a great deal of broadcast traffic will place a heavy load on your network and is, likely, indicative of a network problem. Figure 10.6 shows a portion of the network capture from an HTTP session. The intercept was taken from the Proxy Server computer's external interface and shows HTTP GET requests from the Proxy Server and responses from the Internet. In addition to the HTTP traffic, you will likely find some TCP acknowledgement and sequencing traffic and may see some DNS traffic when the Proxy Server needs to find sites (or portions of sites) that it hasn't located in a while. While a few DNS calls are expected, if your data shows more DNS calls than HTTP packets, you might suspect a name resolution problem on the external network. Traffic on the internal interface would be similar except that, when Proxy Server is servicing a request from cache, the internal calls will transport more data than the external calls. This is because the external calls will be made only to verify content currency and to update those portions of the session that are not current in cache.

A data-intensive session, such as a SQL Server retrieval, should be a bit cleaner. Figure 10.7 displays a portion of such a retrieval as seen by the Proxy Server internal interface. In this case, an external SQL Server client is

20	4.347	Proxysrv-Ext	ISPRouter	TCP	.A...., len: 0, seq: 99580-99580, ack
21	4.349	Proxysrv-Ext	ISPRouter	HTTP	GET Request (from client using port 1652)
22	4.456	ISPRouter	Proxysrv-Ext	HTTP	Response (to client using port 1650)
23	4.471	Proxysrv-Ext	ISPRouter	HTTP	GET Request (from client using port 1650)
24	4.606	ISPRouter	Proxysrv-Ext	HTTP	Response (to client using port 1641)
25	4.652	ISPRouter	Proxysrv-Ext	HTTP	Response (to client using port 1651)
26	4.664	Proxysrv-Ext	ISPRouter	HTTP	GET Request (from client using port 1641)
27	4.677	Proxysrv-Ext	ISPRouter	TCP	.....S., len: 4, seq: 99586-99589, ack
28	4.685	ISPRouter	Proxysrv-Ext	HTTP	Response (to client using port 1652)
29	4.766	Proxysrv-Ext	ISPRouter	HTTP	GET Request (from client using port 1652)
30	4.847	Proxysrv-Ext	ISPRouter	TCP	.A...., len: 0, seq: 99902-99902, ack
31	4.934	ISPRouter	Proxysrv-Ext	HTTP	Response (to client using port 1650)

Figure 10.6 *HTTP session capture.*

obtaining data from a SQL Server computer on the internal network. You can see the TCP traffic consists of 1460 byte blocks of data from the SQL Server, interspersed with acknowledgement data from the Proxy Server. If we look at a capture from the external interface, we should expect the same general picture with the Proxy Server computer providing the 1460 byte blocks of data to the SQL client. (If the picture looks significantly different here, it is time to look for network problems.)

Some of the most common network problems are found in the area of name resolution. In Figure 10.8, we see the machine Proxycli has had to resort to broadcast name resolution to find the Proxy Server computer PROXYSRV2. This could be a sign that your Windows Internet Name Server (WINS) is not operating or that Proxycli or PROXYSRV2 are not properly configured to use WINS. This could result in excessive broadcast traffic and cause difficulty on your network.

12	8.317	SQLSrv	ProxySrv-Int	TCP	.A...., len: 1460, seq: 15422062-15423521, ack
13	8.318	SQLSrv	ProxySrv-Int	TCP	.A...., len: 1460, seq: 15423522-15424981, ack
14	8.319	ProxySrv-Int	SQLSrv	TCP	.A...., len: 0, seq: 96271-96271, ack
15	8.320	SQLSrv	ProxySrv-Int	TCP	.AP..., len: 1460, seq: 15424982-15426441, ack
16	8.321	SQLSrv	ProxySrv-Int	TCP	.A...., len: 1460, seq: 15426442-15427901, ack
17	8.321	ProxySrv-Int	SQLSrv	TCP	.A...., len: 0, seq: 96271-96271, ack
18	8.322	SQLSrv	ProxySrv-Int	TCP	.A...., len: 1460, seq: 15427902-15429361, ack
19	8.324	SQLSrv	ProxySrv-Int	TCP	.AP..., len: 1460, seq: 15429362-15430821, ack
20	8.324	ProxySrv-Int	SQLSrv	TCP	.A...., len: 0, seq: 96271-96271, ack
21	8.332	ProxySrv-Int	SQLSrv	TCP	.A...., len: 0, seq: 96271-96271, ack
22	8.333	ProxySrv-Int	SQLSrv	TCP	.A...., len: 0, seq: 96271-96271, ack.
23	8.334	SQLSrv	ProxySrv-Int	TCP	.A...., len: 1460, seq: 15430822-15432281, ack
24	8.335	SQLSrv	ProxySrv-Int	TCP	.A...., len: 1460, seq: 15432282-15433741, ack

Figure 10.7 *Capture from SQL Server data retrieval.*

```
104   |50.724 |Proxycli    |*BROADCAST  |NBT  |NS: Query req. for PROXYSVR2    <00>
105   |51.475 |Proxycli    |*BROADCAST  |NBT  |NS: Query req. for PROXYSVR2    <00>
106   |52.226 |Proxycli    |*BROADCAST  |NBT  |NS: Query req. for PROXYSVR2    <00>
107   |69.998 |Proxycli    |*BROADCAST  |NBT  |NS: Query req. for PROXYSRV2    <00>
```

Figure 10.8 *Capture showing broadcast name resolution request.*

Analyzing Traffic

1. If Network Monitor is not running on your system, refer to Appendix B and install it.
2. Using the guidance in this section, configure Network Monitor to monitor your Proxy Server's internal and external interfaces.
3. Execute activity that will utilize the Web and WinSock Proxy Services (e.g., HTTP, FTP, SQL Server sessions) and compare your captures with those in Figures 10.6 and 10.7.

Protocol Binding Order

Although not strictly associated with data obtained from Network Monitor sessions and not Proxy Server-specific, your protocol binding order can have major consequences on the operation of your network. Difficulties are most likely when using Proxy Server with an IPX/SPX internal network. If the machines on your internal network employ more than one protocol, you must ensure the appropriate protocols are installed on all the machines and in the correct order. (Having said that, if you plan to use IPX/SPX on the internal network, this should be the only network protocol installed on the machines unless you have a very good reason to install others. As a general rule, installing more protocols than required results in general inefficiency as well as a vulnerability to the kind of pitfall we're currently discussing.)

Figure 10.9 shows the `Bindings` tab of the Network dialog of a client on an internal IPX/SPX network. You'll notice the Workstation service shows the WINS Client (TCP/IP) protocol bound above the NWLink (remember NWLink is the Microsoft version of IPX/SPX) protocol. This binding order will work fine if all the other machines in the network also have TCP/IP installed. If, however, the other machines are running NWLink only (which would be proper on an internal IPX/SPX network that uses Proxy Server as a gateway to the Internet), an initial call from this machine to another internal network machine will be made using TCP/IP. Since the other machines can't use TCP/IP, there will be no response. Only after that connection attempt has timed out will the client machine resort to NWLink. As

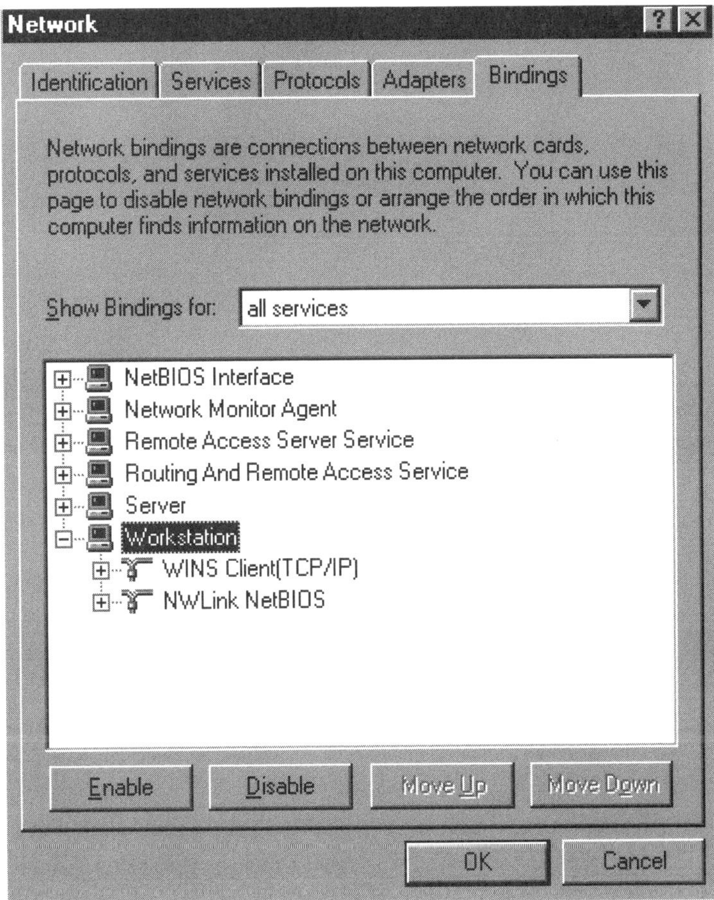

Figure 10.9 *Workstation service bindings.*

you might imagine, such a configuration results in extraneous traffic as well as an unnecessary connection delay each time this client attempts to contact another machine. Remember that it is the Workstation service that determines what protocol will be used first. If you are experiencing mysterious delays in obtaining network connections from a particular client machine, check the workstation protocol binding order and ensure you don't have any extraneous protocols. If you must have use a protocol that is not available to all of the machines on your network, ensure is it not the first one bound to the service.

MCSE 10.4 Using Proxy Server Logs

You may remember that we thoroughly covered Proxy Server logging configuration in Chapter 5. Now that you know how to create logs, let's consider how they can help us.

Text-based Proxy Server logs are difficult to read except for the most basic queries. If you will use Proxy Server logs as part of your Proxy Server monitoring and optimization program, you should seriously consider taking the option to write the data to an ODBC database, such as Access or SQL Server. Once hosted by a database, the data can be sorted, filtered, and presented in a variety of ways (including HTML).

We discussed the value of the Packet Filter log earlier when we covered packet filtering. Figure 10.10, however, shows a custom retrieval from a packet filter log, which was written to a SQL Server 7.0 database. The user of a machine on the external network (192.168.0.143) is complaining that he can no longer reach an application on the internal network. The packet filter log reveals a problem with TCP packets destined for TCP Port 1433. Using this information, you can check your packet filtering and create an exception to permit the user to connect to the application (if appropriate).

In another scenario, several users are complaining that access to the site: *www.alidatrain.com* has become slow over the past several days. A look at a custom retrieval from the Web Proxy Service log reveals the information shown in Figure 10.11.

A quick look at the log indicates the site is always being sourced from the Internet (`Inet` in the `objecsource` column). You check the Web Proxy Service Cache Filters and discover you set the `/pics` directory from this site to "Not Cached" when you meant to set it to "Cached." (More on Cache Fil-

```
select sourceaddress, sourceport, protocol, destinationaddress, destinationport, pflogtime
from pf_log_table
order by pflogtime desc
```

sourceaddress	sourceport	protocol	destinationaddress	destinationport	pflogtime
192.168.0.143	1094	Tcp	192.168.0.181	1433	1999-04-02 16:26:
192.168.0.143	1094	Tcp	192.168.0.181	1433	1999-04-02 16:26:
192.168.0.143	1094	Tcp	192.168.0.181	1433	1999-04-02 16:26:
192.168.0.143	1094	Tcp	192.168.0.181	1433	1999-04-02 16:26:
192.168.0.150	68	Udp	255.255.255.255	67	1999-04-02 16:26:

Figure 10.10 *SQL Server custom retrieval from packet filter log.*

```
select desthost, uri, objectsource, logtime
from web_log_table
where desthost like '%alida%'
order by logtime desc
```

desthost	uri	objectsource	logtime
www.alidatrain.com	http://www.alidatrain.com/pics/button...	Inet	1999-04-06 09:28:
www.alidatrain.com	http://www.alidatrain.com/pics/button...	Inet	1999-04-06 09:28:
www.alidatrain.com	http://www.alidatrain.com/pics/button...	Inet	1999-04-06 09:27:
www.alidatrain.com	http://www.alidatrain.com/pics/button...	Inet	1999-04-06 09:27:
www.alidatrain.com	http://www.alidatrain.com/pics/compas...	Inet	1999-04-06 09:27:
www.alidatrain.com	http://www.alidatrain.com/pics/compas...	Inet	1999-04-06 09:27:
www.alidatrain.com	http://www.alidatrain.com/pics/compas...	Inet	1999-04-06 09:27:
www.alidatrain.com	http://www.alidatrain.com/pics/compas...	Inet	1999-04-06 09:27:
www.alidatrain.com	http://www.alidatrain.com/	Inet	1999-04-06 09:27:

Figure 10.11 *SQL Server custom retrieval from Web log showing no caching for the specified site.*

ters a bit later in this chapter.) You correct the misconfiguration and check the log after your users have accessed the site several times and discover you have resolved the problem (see Figure 10.12).

The previous examples show only two of the myriad of ways you can use the Proxy Server logs for troubleshooting and optimization. After a little practice, you'll be amazed at the things you can learn about your Proxy Server environment from the logs.

```
select desthost, uri, objectsource, logtime
from web_log_table
where desthost like '%alida%'
order by logtime desc
```

desthost	uri	objectsource	logtime
www.alidatrain.com	http://www.alidatrain.com/pics/buttons...	Cache	1999-04-06 10:27
www.alidatrain.com	http://www.alidatrain.com/pics/buttons...	Cache	1999-04-06 10:27
www.alidatrain.com	http://www.alidatrain.com/pics/buttons...	Cache	1999-04-06 10:27
www.alidatrain.com	http://www.alidatrain.com/pics/buttons...	Cache	1999-04-06 10:26
www.alidatrain.com	http://www.alidatrain.com/pics/compas1...	Cache	1999-04-06 10:25
www.alidatrain.com	http://www.alidatrain.com/pics/compas3...	Cache	1999-04-06 10:25
www.alidatrain.com	http://www.alidatrain.com/pics/compas2...	Cache	1999-04-06 10:25
www.alidatrain.com	http://www.alidatrain.com/pics/compas4...	Cache	1999-04-06 10:25
www.alidatrain.com	http://www.alidatrain.com/	Inet	1999-04-06 10:25

Figure 10.12 *SQL Server custom retrieval from Web log showing caching for the specified site.*

Tuning the Cache

As we might have surmised from the last example in the previous section, Proxy Server caching can have a major impact on your operations. Tuning the cache can yield great benefits and may have as much impact on enhancing your system performance as improving network bandwidth. You learned how to configure the cache in Chapter 5, but now that we've learned a bit about how to monitor your system's activities, it's a good time to review cache configuration.

Using the baseline you created with Performance Monitor, you can attempt to forecast your server and cache usage. Using that forecast, you should adjust your caching to best serve the expected usage. Your goal in cache tuning should be to increase your *Cache Hit Ratio* to as near 100% as possible. Some of the things to look at are:

- Is your Passive Cashing sufficiently responsive to the type of data your network typically accesses?
- Is Active Caching as proactive as your network needs?
- Do you have sufficient disk space for cache growth
- Is Time-to-Live (TTL) of HTTP and FTP objects set based on the volatility of data your network typically accesses? (This is in important factor in ensuring your cache is flushed often enough to make way for new objects.)
- Have you limited the size of cached objects to ensure you have room for as many objects as possible?
- Is your cache spread across the appropriate drives to minimize read/write conflict?

The first stop in cache tuning should be the Web Proxy Service's Caching tab (see Figure 10.13). The general active and passive caching policies are set here. This sets some of the parameters in the Advanced Cache Policy dialog and should be used for a "first blush" at setting a cache policy. In the diagram, you'll notice we have selected "Fewer network accesses" for both passive and active caching. This would be an appropriate setting for an organization that typically accessed non-volatile data from the Web. Since the data wouldn't be expected to change frequently, you could depend on the cache for most of your activity. If, on the other hand, you expected to access a lot of news and information services the data is refreshed very frequently, Selecting "Updates are more important" and "Faster user response" would be more appropriate.

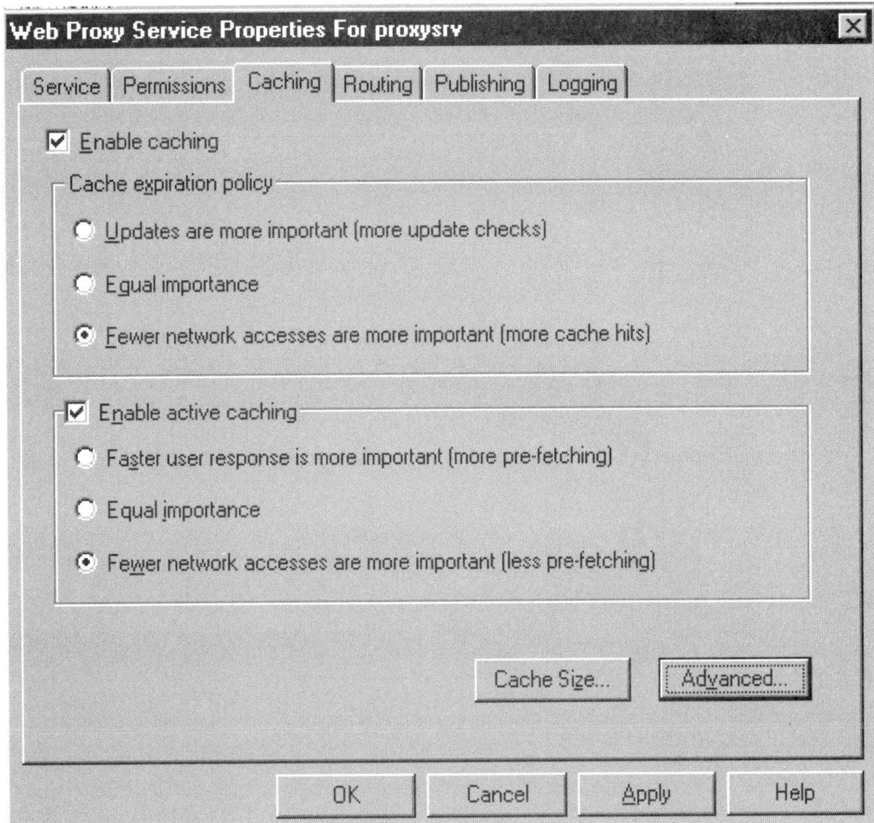

Figure 10.13 *Web Proxy Service caching tab.*

After you check the general policies, click on the Advanced button to reveal the Advanced Cache Policy dialog shown in Figure 10.14. The first checkbox allows you to limit the size of objects you'll cache. It's a good idea to set this slightly above the average size of objects that appear in your cache. (You can determine cache size by looking at the files in the `\urlcache` directory(ies) on your cache drive(s)). By setting this properly, you can allow the objects most typically cached while preventing any really large object that will limit your caching space.

The next checkbox permits you to return objects from the cache, even when the Web site cannot be contacted to verify the object's currency. You should set this to provide information based on the typical volatility of information your network receives. If you download a lot of rapidly changing information, this should be set low or disabled. If, on the other hand, your information changes infrequently, setting this to a high value will permit your users to access the information even when the site cannot be contacted. (This is enabled by default.)

The `Object Time To Live` group permits you to fine tune some of the general settings you made on the `Caching` tab. Here, you can determine if you'll cache HTTP objects, FTP objects, or both. If you select `TTL = 0`, objects in your cache *will not* expire unless the object itself carries an expiration time. This will result in your cache becoming fairly old but will sharply cut your network bandwidth needs. Use this setting if your data is typically nonvolatile. Alternatively, you can select an expiration time based on a percentage of the object's age. If you select this, you also must enter the minimum and maximum you wish to apply to the object. Selecting the correct values here is, again, dependent on your data volatility. Use higher numbers for less frequently changing data. Under FTP caching, enter the number of minutes you wish to keep FTP data in the cache.

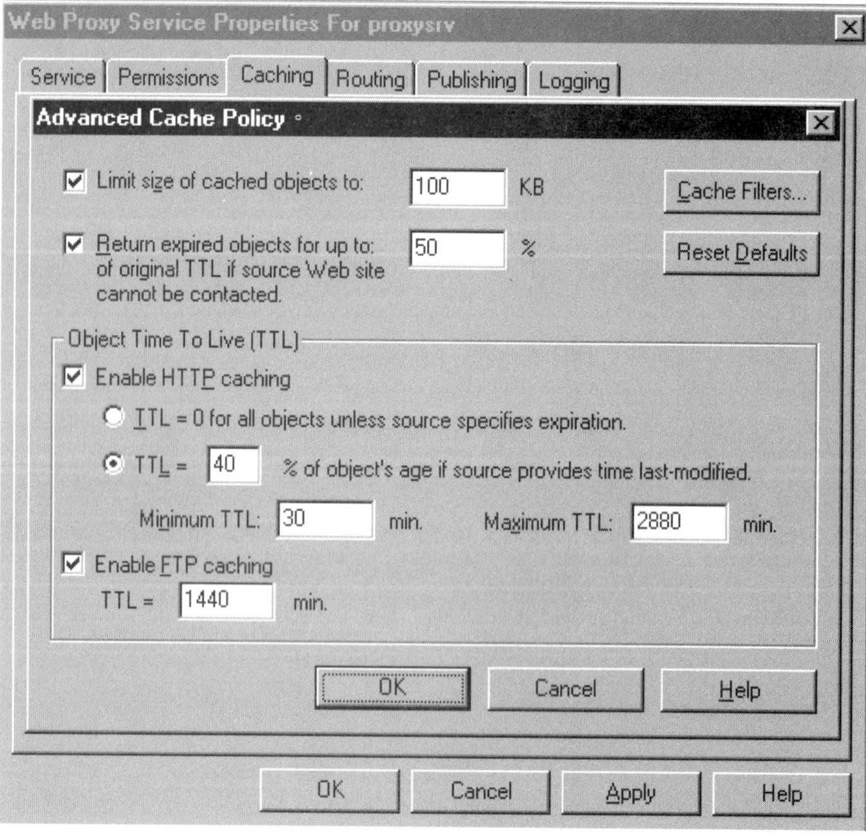

Figure 10.14 *Advanced cache policy dialog.*

Cache Filters

It may be useful to ensure some information is kept out of the cache while guaranteeing other information will always be cached. Some sites may be accessed only infrequently and should not be placed in the cache. Other sites may, on the other hand, be frequently accessed but their data is so volatile that trying to have the cache keep up with them would be a waste of time and resources. To create cache filters, click on the `Cache Filters` button on the `Advanced Cache Policy` dialog (see Figure 10.14). This will reveal the `Cache Filter` dialog as shown in Figure 10.15. Referring to the diagram, you'll notice `www.alidatrain.com` is set as `Not Cached`. This was done because information on the site changes so rapidly, we decided not to cache it. Unfortunately, as we discovered in the previous section, the diagrams in the site's `/pics` directory take longer to load than we'd like. Since

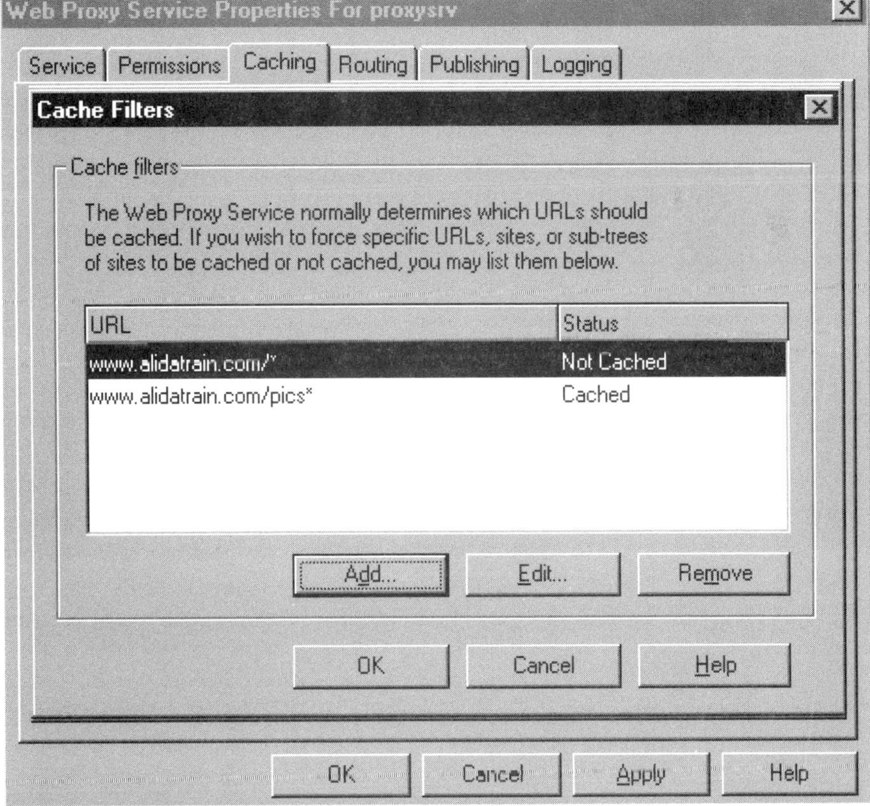

Figure 10.15 *Cache filter dialog.*

these don't often change, we'd like to be able to cache just those items. We have, therefore, entered *that* directory as `Cached`. In this way, we set an overall caching policy for the site and then created exceptions to that policy.

To create or edit a cache filter click the `Add` or `Edit` button on the `Cache Filter` dialog to launch the `Cache Filter Properties` dialog, shown in Figure 10.16. Once in the dialog, enter the desired path in the `URL` edit box and select `Always Cache` or `Never Cache` as appropriate. Note that you must include a path and may use the asterisk (*) wildcard character. For example, entering `www.alidatrain.com/*` includes the entire site. Placing the asterisk at the other end (e.g., `*.alidatrain.com`) would refer to `www`, `ftp`, and `gopher` sites.

If reviewing Web Proxy Service logs shows your internal users are consistently accessing particular URLs, you can improve your cache hit ratio by creating cache filters that guarantee those URLs will always be cached.

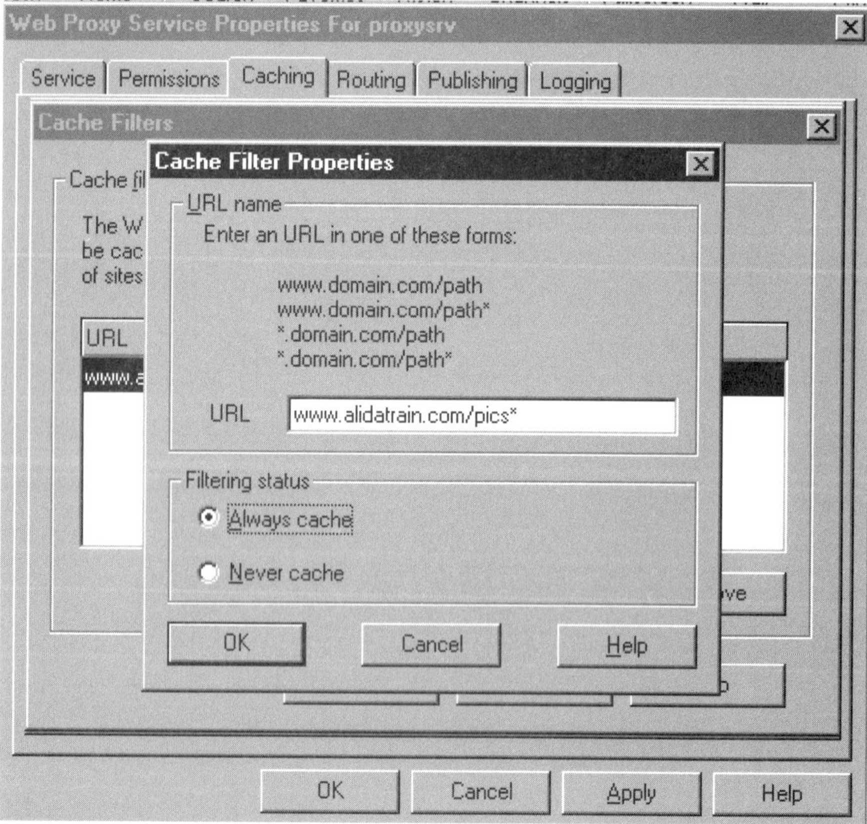

Figure 10.16 *Cache filter properties dialog.*

Optimizing Cache Drives

Cache drives and sizes are originally configured during Proxy Server installation. Once caches are set up and loaded with data, they may be administered through the `Proxy Server Cache Drives` dialog (shown in Figure 10.17). To access this dialog, depress the `Cache Size` button on the service properties `Caching` tab (see Figure 10.13). To change the size of the cache (or to create a cache) on a particular drive, highlight the drive, enter the desired size in the `Maximum Size (MB)` edit window, and click the `Set` button. You should create caches of sufficient size to handle your current and forecast caching needs. Caches should be neither too big nor too small. It is a good idea to place caches on physical drives that do not contain the Windows NT system or boot partitions or the Windows NT page file. (Depending on the number of physical drives on the server, this may or may not be possible.) It is important to note that reducing the size of an existing cache may result in

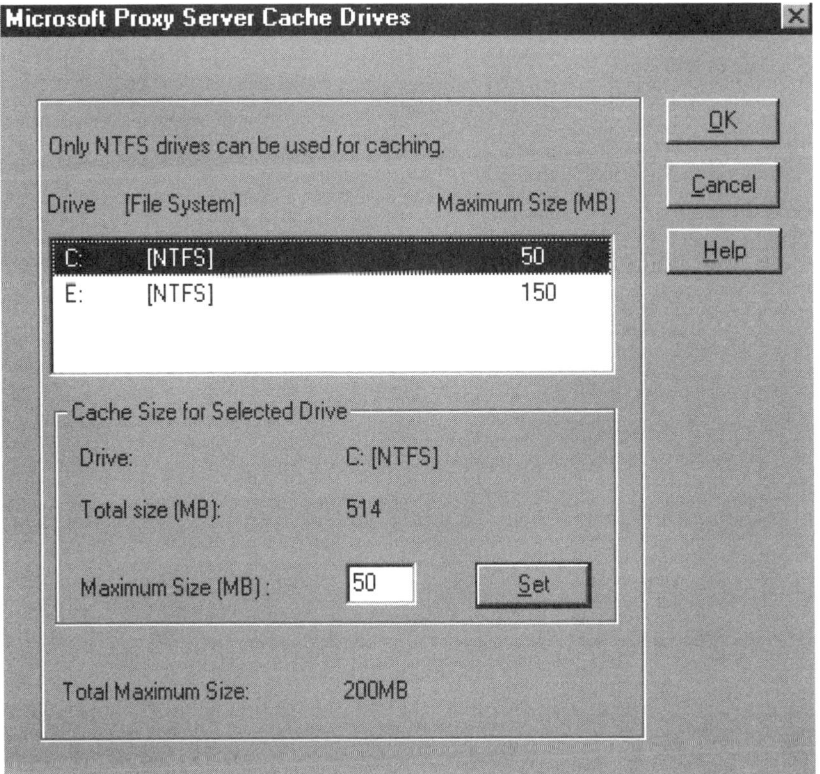

Figure 10.17 *Cache drives dialog.*

data loss, while expanding the cache has no effect on the current data. If you reduce the cache size to zero, all data in the cache will be deleted.

> A cache integrity check is accomplished during Proxy Server startup. The duration of the check is proportional to the size of the cache and the number of objects it contains. If you attempt to change the cache size before the check is complete, you'll receive an error message. When this happens, simply close the Web Proxy Service Properties dialog and wait until the check is complete.

As you may have surmised, most of cache optimization must be done incrementally. That is to say, you would make a cache configuration change, determine if it helps or hurts your system's operation, and then make another change. Using this technique, you can effectively gauge your cache's size requirements as well as the volatility of typically accessed information.

MCSE 10.5   Optimizing Routing

You can take a number of steps to optimize routing and network throughput. Most of these involve increasing cache efficiency. You should ensure good caching is available as close to your users as possible. If you have users on different network segments who access a unique set of Web resources frequently, it is a good idea to place a Proxy Server within their environment. The local Proxy Server would route to an upstream server, but would be able to maintain the unique information within its local cache. When your network is protected by an upstream firewall or Proxy Server, you may be interested in using the local Proxy Server in a cache-only role. The cache-only Proxy Server would use all of its network interfaces to handle requests from clients and upstream routing. To configure a machine for cache-only, simply ensure that the Local Address Table (LAT) contains all IP addresses that will use the Web Proxy Service cache. If the server is already protected by a firewall, it is permissible to use the LAT range of 0.0.0.0 to 255.255.255.255, essentially placing everything that can access the Proxy Server in the internal network.

Additional routing and network optimization may be realized by further strengthening caching. You may increase the cache size to ensure all desired information is cached, enable active caching to keep the cache optimally updated, and increase object TTL to minimize cache purging and refreshing. When choosing which applications to promote on the network, you may want to minimize those using WinSock and Socks Proxy services in favor of those which use the Web Proxy service (since only the Web Proxy service employs caching). Remember, however, the benefits achieved from some of these techniques depend on the volatility of the information your users typically retrieve. By lengthening the amount of time data remains in the cache, you may run the risk of increasingly outdated information.

■ Summary

This chapter showed us the myriad of tools available to keep Proxy Server running as efficiently as possible. We saw the Windows NT Performance Monitor provided a capability to monitor many machine, network, and Proxy Server functions. Performance Monitor provides a graphic representation of system functions that may be saved in a log. It can also be set to send alerts when parameters exceed preset limits. We discovered that Network Monitor can intercept and display network activity on a packet-by-packet basis and will provide an accurate picture of information on each packet filtering the Proxy Server computer's network interfaces. Proxy Server logs provide a full set of information from each of the Proxy Server services, as well as a summary of packets dropped by packet filtering. Finally, the Proxy Server Current User Sessions dialog provides an accurate picture of users currently using Proxy Server and how long they've been connected.

Performance Monitor receives a number of Proxy Server-specific objects when Proxy Server is installed. The new objects provide counters for each Proxy Server service as well as the Web Proxy Cache. These objects should be employed in addition to general Windows NT Performance Monitor objects to monitor and optimize your Proxy Server. The first step in using Performance Monitor to optimize Proxy Server is to select appropriate counters to establish a performance baseline. Counter information may be saved in a Performance Monitor log and used to compare to Proxy Server operation after environmental changes or optimization attempts. Baseline readings should be made during a period (or periods) of typical load. Further analysis centers around a search for performance bottlenecks in the system's processor, memory, hard disk, network, and Proxy Server cache. Analysis should be made in view of typical server roles. Environments characterized by HTTP sessions, for instance, may feature many users accessing a relatively small amount of data. Activities will be centered around the Web Proxy Service. FTP, SQL Server, or other data-intensive activities may be undertaken by fewer users but with larger amounts of data. These sessions may show a significant utilization of the WinSock Proxy service.

Network Monitor will show us actual network traffic (packets) at each of the Proxy Server computer's network interfaces. Viewing actual network data will permit us to determine if our network has extraneous traffic caused, perhaps, by name resolution problems, protocol binding mismatches, or other network difficulties.

Proxy Server logs provide a great deal of information on the actual operation of the Proxy Server computer. It is useful to configure the logs to write to a database, which permits to sort, format, and view data of interest in solving particular problems. We also looked at packet filtering and caching examples in the chapter.

The Proxy Server cache is the backbone of the Web Proxy service. Whenever we attempt to optimize Proxy Server, we need to take a close look at caching. Our cache tuning goal should be to make the *Cache Hit Ratio* as close to 100% as possible. Cache tuning centers on activating active and passive caching and adapting it to the volatility of the data your network typically works with. Caches should be placed across appropriate drives to minimize read/write conflicts and where sufficient space is available for predicted growth. Additionally, object size and Time-to-Live may be adjusted to allow for as may objects as possible in the cache. It is possible to prevent the caching of certain portions of Web sites by creating cache filters.

Routing may be optimized. The key to efficient routing is to place Web caches as close to the users as possible. Some Proxy Server computers may be configured as caching-only servers when they will operate behind the protection of an upstream Proxy Server or firewall. Additional routing optimization involves cache tuning to minimize network traffic.

▲ REVIEW QUESTIONS

1. *Sandy wants to determine how to improve the cache hit ratio of the Proxy Server computer that services her network. Of the tools listed below, what is the best one to use?*

    A. Network Monitor

    B. Web Proxy service logging

    C. WinSock Proxy service logging

    D. Server Manager

2. *What Performance Monitor objects should you select when monitoring HTTP activities? (Select all that apply)*

    A. Web Proxy Service

    B. WinSock Proxy Service

    C. Browser

    D. Socks Proxy Service

3. *If you wish to determine if bandwidth availability is creating a bottleneck, what Performance Monitor counter should you view?*

    A. Network Interface: Current Bandwidth

    B. Network Interface: Bytes Total/sec

    C. Network Interface: Output Queue Length

    D. Network Interface: Packets/sec

4. *Tim suspects a bottleneck in his system. Network Monitor shows the Network Interface: Bytes Total/sec counter well under his network's bandwidth capacity and the Network Interface: Output Queue Length counter shows a value between 3 and 5. What would you suggest Tim do?*

    A. Upgrade hard drives

    B. Upgrade memory

    C. Upgrade the network, the Current Disk

    D. Upgrade the network interface

5. *Sylvi has a Proxy Server computer that has a single CPU and hard drive. She monitors a number of Performance Monitor counters and discovers the %Processor Time is consistently 75%, Current Disk Queue Length is 3 to 5, and the Cache Hit Ratio is at 90%. Based on these counters, what, if any, devices may be causing a bottleneck? (Select all that apply)*

    A. CPU

    B. Memory

    C. Hard Disk

    D. All readings appear normal

6. *While reviewing your Proxy Server's Performance Monitor logs, you notice the following counter readings: Memory: Pages/sec, 4; Processor: %Processor Time, 96; Cache Hit Ratio, 92; Network Interface: Output Queue Length, 1. Where should you suspect bottlenecks? (Select all that apply)*

    A. Memory

    B. Processor

    C. Network

    D. Hard Drive

7. *Your network accesses the Internet through a Proxy Server computer. In an attempt to increase overall throughput, you decide to configure the Proxy*

Server to update its content cache during off-peak hours when the greatest amount of bandwidth is available. How should you configure the server?

    A. Enable Active Caching

    B. Reduce minimum TTL under the Advanced Cache Policy

    C. Create cache filters that permit caching only during evening hours

    D. Increase the size of cached objects in the Advanced Cache Policy dialog

8. *Proper placement of chained Proxy Servers will result in more optimum routing. What function of this chain results in more efficient routing?*

    A. Chained Proxy Server computers permit the shortest route to the external network

    B. Chained Proxy Servers can bring the cache closer to the users

    C. Chained Proxy Servers permit use of Socks Proxy to increase Web access

    D. Chained Proxy Servers limit proxy operation to the WinSock Proxy Service, which is more efficient than the Web Proxy Service

9. *Suspecting a network problem, Linda wants to monitor traffic on her Proxy Server's external interface. What would you recommend she use?*

    A. Performance Monitor

    B. Packet Filter Logs

    C. Network Monitor

    D. Windows NT Diagnostics

10. *You review your Proxy Server Performance Monitor log and discover the following average information: %Processor Time, 45%; Cache Hit Ratio, 45%; Current Disk Queue Length, 1; Memory: Pages/sec, 6. What should you do to improve your Proxy Server's performance?*

    A. Nothing, everything is within limits

    B. Upgrade the CPU

    C. Increase the size of the page file

    D. Increase the content cache size

11. *You are interested in the length of time your users are connected to the Internet through your Proxy Server. What tool should you use to determine this?*

Troubleshooting

This chapter provides help on what to check if something goes wrong. With Microsoft Proxy Server, perhaps more than with any other product, you will need to follow a systematic process to resolve issues. You will find it helpful to write down the changes that are made to the environment settings before proceeding. Keeping a log of what is configured is the first step in ensuring continued functionality should something change. If you are testing different configurations it is likely that something will change.

Think of troubleshooting as a process that includes several steps. These steps, done in logical order to first narrow the possibilities and then solve the problem, are as follows:

1. problem identification
2. diagnosis
3. testing the hypothetical solution
4. verification that the problem was solved by the proposed solution

In this discussion we focus our efforts to solve problems by considering both client and server side, viewing troubleshooting as a process, and elaborating the steps in creating a hypothesis, testing, recording the outcome, developing a new hypothesis, testing, and coming to a resolution. Throughout the chapter we will review much of what you already know about Microsoft Windows NT considerations and TCP/IP, and we delve into the registry keys that make up the Proxy Server. You should, of course, use registry changes only as a last resort.

By the end of this chapter you will be able to:

- Resolve Proxy Server and Client installation and access problems
- Resolve Proxy Server and Client computer problems
- Resolve security problems
- Resolve caching problems
- Troubleshoot a WINS server to provide client access to Proxy Servers
- Troubleshoot hardware-related problems such as network interfaces and disk drives
- Troubleshoot Internet/intranet routing hardware and software such as RRAS

MCSE 11.1 Resources for Troubleshooting

We would be frustrated much too easily without knowing about the available troubleshooting resources. In other chapters we have pointed out how the client and server work together and detailed many settings for each. We will not repeat each of the settings. Before spending a day of troubleshooting on the Proxy Server, a realistic rule to follow is to consider checking every setting once more. Look for obvious or easy problems that may be present.

When you think of troubleshooting, think of the entire system, which includes both the client and the server. Break this apart and start at one end or start in the middle, but do not make changes unless you are certain of what the outcome of the change will be. This means that you need to get your ideas around the entire client-server system and everything that makes it up, including the cables, switches, hubs, network cards, RAS or RRAS services, modems, and the individual configuration parameters of each piece of software. Each time you consider making a change, be sure to document what you changed. If you make a change and the problem remains, return the setting to its original value and proceed. If you forget to do this you may end up with less functionality than you started with and it will take a great deal longer than necessary to fix the problem.

If an installation has not worked from the start, ask "What is the most likely cause?" If the installation was working and suddenly stops working, ask "What changed?" The answer to these questions is not always obvious, but will get you headed in the right direction.

Because troubleshooting is the most complex and difficult challenge you will face in an environment that contains Proxy Server, it must be approached as a process. The approach we outline below works well; try it out with your next problem.

1. Establish a relative priority for this problem.
2. Collect and document sufficient information to achieve correct problem identification.
3. Develop a list of the possible causes.
4. Provide an appropriate level of system diagnosis.
5. Do everything possible to isolate the cause.
6. Attempt to create a reasonable hypothesis.
7. Test and retest the hypothetical solution, and
8. Verify that the problem was solved by the proposed solution. If the problem was NOT SOLVED then you should reset any changed parameters, return to the problem isolation, and create another workable hypothesis.

Problem identification is somewhat straightforward, but you must be certain that you have identified the correct problem. Start by capturing your observations and ask questions of users.

- Has the installation ever worked properly?
- Is this a first or just another problem in a series?
- If the difficulty is connecting to any large site, ask "Has the distant end been contacted?" If not, then contact the distant end and see if there is a problem with their location.
- Have you checked with the Internet Service Provider to help localize the problem?
- Is your Internet Service Provider experiencing outages upstream?
- Is the DNS working properly?
- Are the DNS records changed (Use NSLOOKUP)?
- Can you PING the router and the remote host?
- Are multiple users having problems or just one?

- If just one user is having the problem, has a setting on the network interface card changed?
- Is the problem on the client or the server?
- Is the problem random or can it be reproduced?
- Is the problem similar to a previous problem you have experienced?
- Has any hardware or software been reconfigured recently?
- Has anyone else attempted to fix this problem? If yes, what's been done already?
- Was any new application installed on the user's machine?
- If using RAS:
  - Have the modems been tested separately?
  - Have the phone lines been checked out separately?
  - Has the error code been reviewed in TechNet CD?
- If using ISDN or T-1, has the phone company checked the line?
- Are the hubs working fine otherwise?
- Has any change been made to the cabling?
- Are the connectors secured?
- Is there any new equipment on the network?
- Any other recent change such as a gateway, router, switch, or bridge?
- Has any new protocol been added for use with a mainframe or other OS?
- What are the security issues involved? Use of NTFS on drives?
- Is there one domain or are multiple domains involved?
- If there are multiple domains involved, is there a trust issue?
- What direction were the trusts established in?
- Is the trust working properly?
- Is there an account issue?
- Was an account removed or changed?

Notice that the list above only starts you asking the questions. Your own skills should be such that you can come up with many more to ask. Ask the right questions and you will start toward the right issue. Narrow the issue down to a single point if you can.

Proper diagnosis of the problem can be much more difficult. Before you start to create a hypothesis about what to test, you will want to become familiar with, and use, every available tool at your disposal. Diagnosis of the exact problem can take from minutes to hours to perform depending on the nature and severity of the issue. What clues are present? What is known about the problem? What history does it have? Where can you go to ask about this type of issue — newsgroups? Listserv? TechNet CD?

There is an on-line version of the Microsoft Knowledge Base that is used by the Microsoft Support engineers to diagnose and troubleshoot problems with customer installations. There are also software wizards and support files that are available from Microsoft, such as drivers for many types of hardware. You can locate the Microsoft Knowledge Base at *http://support.microsoft.com* or you can purchase the Microsoft TechNet CD subscription, which has the Knowledge Base included.

The Microsoft Proxy Server home page provides a great deal of information on the Proxy Server. It is located at *http://www.microsoft.com/proxy;* it is a good idea to check this page frequently as new information is listed here on a regular basis. Most of the Proxy Server information is also available on the Microsoft TechNet CD. Microsoft Proxy Server comes with a set of on-line documentation that provides a lengthy tutorial to the features and functionality that is put on your local machine during installation. This includes information about the installation of the Proxy Server and clients, configuration of both, and the registry entries and event messages for the Proxy Server. Read the supplied on-line documentation.

Some of the other tools and resources you need to be familiar with include:

- Microsoft Proxy Server Help files, which will give you a starting point
- (to access these files click the F1 key while inside the MMC)
- newsgroups at *msnews.microsoft.com* such as *microsoft.public.proxy*
- several good mailing lists such as: NTSYSADMIN-list
- web sites such as: *www.ntinternals.com*
- Frequently Asked Questions (FAQ and FAQ97), which can be found via the search engines, and
- Microsoft TechNet CD, which is available by subscription from Microsoft

Most of us install the product and reconfigure only what needs to be done when asked. Gaining experience with diagnosis and troubleshooting isn't always easy, so let's look at the Proxy Server and Proxy Client components to get an idea of what some of the likely error messages might be. Document everything to minimize troubleshooting time. If your network environment is not documented, start the process now and keep it up to date.

Administrators sometimes feel that there isn't enough time to document and have to spend more time than necessary learning what should have been written down to start with.

Although it goes without saying, we believe you should check to make sure you have recently done and recorded a normal backup. Do not proceed to make any changes if you don't have a solid backup. Also, check to see if you can restore from the tape. This should be done as a test on a frequent basis. Finally, try not to make many changes at one time. If you do, it will be much more difficult to find out which change fixed the problem. Documenting what fixed the problem will help you and others in your environment figure out what has been done and what works.

MCSE 11.2 Troubleshooting Utilities for Proxy Server

To troubleshoot utilities for Proxy Server start with the Microsoft Windows NT event viewer logs, as this tool displays information useful to troubleshoot problems that occur with Microsoft Proxy Server. There are many event messages; our intent is not to list them all. Of the several classes of messages, some are better at helping to determine the source of the problem, which enables us to more quickly move along to the solution.

The Proxy Server event messages are grouped into sections such as:

- Server Setup event messages
- Web Proxy service event messages
- Web Proxy cache event messages
- Web Proxy array and chain event messages
- WinSock Proxy service event messages
- Socks Proxy service event messages
- Packet filtering event messages
- Logging event messages
- RAS event messages
- Miscellaneous event messages

The Proxy Server will write viewable events that are similar to other services in the following format:

```
Messagetext Errornumber
```

where:

Messagetext provides an explanation for the event.
Errornumber provides a Windows NT error code number.

Not all error messages follow this format. For information about Windows NT error codes, see your Windows NT Server documentation.

These events can be found in the Microsoft TechNet CD, and an explanation of the solution usually accompanies the error. An example of the contents of the event viewer is shown in Figure 11.1.

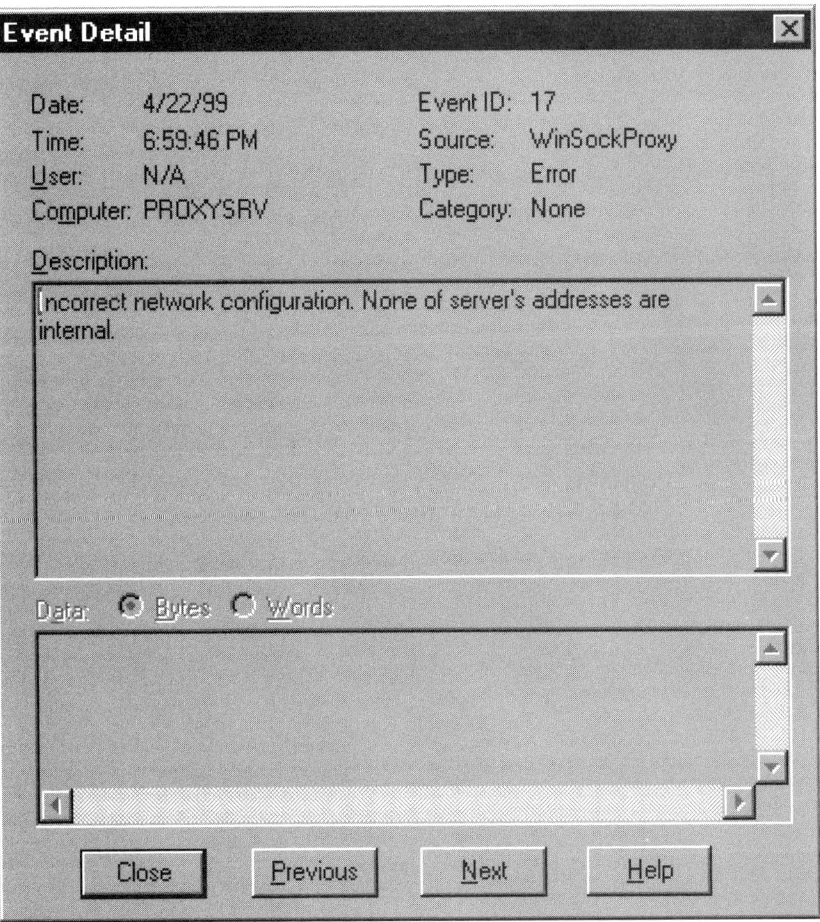

Figure 11.1 *A Proxy Server error.*

Use of the Microsoft Windows NT Event Viewer

The Microsoft event viewer is easy to use. To view the logs:

1. Select `Start`
2. Select `Programs`
3. Select `Administrative Tools (Common)`
4. Select the `Event Viewer`.

To be certain that you are viewing the system events be sure to select the `Log` pull-down menu and select `System`. If you want to view the details of any specific event, double-click the `event` message and a dialog box with the information will appear.

Using the Server Diagnostic Utility

The Microsoft Proxy Server compact disc contains the `Mspdiag` utility, located in the \Msproxy directory. This utility helps detect common configuration problems on the server computer. If Proxy Server is not yet installed, or if there were problems installing Microsoft Proxy Server, the `Mspdiag` utility can be installed to the C:\Msp directory on your Proxy Server computer. If you have already successfully completed server Setup, the utility is automatically installed for you. `Mspdiag` checks for several conditions such as:

- verifies the version of Proxy Server that is installed
- verifies that Windows NT Server 4.0 or later is installed
- verifies that Internet Information Server (IIS) 3.0 or later is installed
- verifies that Windows NT Service Pack 3 or later is installed
- verifies that the SAP agent is installed when IPX/SPX is configured
- verifies that valid IP addresses are assigned in the LAT
- checks the status of the IIS WWW service
- checks the status of the Proxy services
- checks to see if you have administrator privileges on the server computer
- checks to see if IP forwarding is disabled
- checks to see if there is only default gateway specified
- checks the settings in the `Mspclnt.ini` file against the server computer's configuration settings

To run the server diagnostic utility: on the Proxy Server computer, from a command prompt, change to the Msp directory. Next, type `mspdiag`.

Server Setup Event Messages

Microsoft Proxy Server Setup creates its own log file in C:\Mpssetup.log. This log gives you information about the setup and overall installation process. Should you ever need to get the Microsoft Technical Support Team involved with the troubleshooting of your installation, this log should be available. The log can be accessed with any text editor and you will notice that it has information beyond the error messages that are displayed to users. A listing of the error messages that you may encounter can be found in Appendix C.

Study Break

Running the mspd1ag Utility

Using the guidance in the preceding sections, run the server diagnostic utility (`mspdiag`). What did it tell you about your server?

MCSE 11.3 Troubleshooting Proxy Clients

Service event logs provide valuable information when a problem occurs with Microsoft Proxy Server. You can use the following list of event messages to determine the source of a problem and obtain suggestions for resolution. Client event messages and problems are grouped into the following sections:

- Client Setup event messages
- Web Proxy client event messages
- WinSock Proxy client event messages
- IPX client problems
- Client performance problems

Using Event Viewer

Microsoft Proxy Server client event messages are displayed at the client computer as pop-up messages, or they are registered in the Windows NT system event log. The Windows NT system event log can be viewed by using Event Viewer.

To view event messages with Event Viewer:

1. From the server's desktop, click `Start`, point to `Programs`, point to `Administrative Tools (Common)`, and then click `Event Viewer`.
2. On the `Log` menu, click `System`.
3. To view event detail, double-click the event message.

Client Setup Event Messages

The Microsoft Proxy Server client Setup program creates a log file on the client computer, C:\Mpcsetup.log, with information about the Setup process. If you call your support provider for assistance, have this log file available for review. It contains valuable information beyond messages that are displayed to users. A listing of the Client Setup error messages that you may encounter can be found in Appendix D.

IPX Client Problems

Running IPX on your internal network may cause your clients to experience connectivity problems. In order to diagnose Windows NT clients check the network configuration. In `Control Panel`, double-click the `Network` icon. Once you are in the `Network` dialog box, click the `Configuration` tab, and select the `NWLink IPX/SPX Compatible Protocol`. It is imperative that you check and verify that the frame type on the client and server match, or that they both are set to `Auto Frame Type Detection`. If this is not the case, make the necessary change and continue checking the configuration.

Next, verify that the Internal Network Number is 00000000. NOTE: If you change this setting, it can cause problems with connectivity to other IPX-enabled servers on your network. If you want to show the IPX network settings, go to the command prompt and type `ipxroute config`. If you want to show all information, type `ipxconfig /all`. These commands look and work similar to the `ipconfig` used to show the client TCP/IP settings. If you are trying to diagnose Windows 95 clients, the process is similar. In the `Control Panel`, double-click the `Network` icon. Once in the `Network` dialog box, click the `Configuration` tab, and select the `NWLink IPX/SPX Compatible Protocol` icon. There you must verify that the frame type on the client matches what you have already set at the server. If you are not sure, go to the server and check. If there is no frame type listed, both client and server must be set to `Auto Frame Type Detection`. Caution: You should NOT USE `Auto Frame Type Detection` if you have multiple frame types on your LAN. One easy check is to test and verify that you can connect your clients and servers with ONLY the IPX protocol running on the client.

Next, check the `Mspclnt.ini` file on the server. Make sure that the correct information is contained in the file. It should contain one IPX address, and make sure the IPX address is for the network adapter on the internal side of the network. If you find more than one IPX address in the `Mspclnt.ini` file, one is almost certainly to be for the external adapter. You should disable the IPX bindings on the external adapter, and then reinstall the Proxy Server so that the `Mspclnt.ini` file is setup correctly.

IPX clients exhibit behaviors that are common and can be corrected. Examples of connectivity problems and errors are included in the following sections.

- Cannot Connect to Another ISP after Installing the WinSock Proxy Client

The WinSock Proxy client is using the internal network. When you connect to another Internet service provider (ISP), you are now on a different network and the WinSock Proxy client must be disabled.

Once the WinSock Proxy client software installed, it can use Windows Sockets applications to access Internet sites through Proxy Server on the corporate network. The client cannot use Windows Sockets applications to access any Internet sites through a dial-up connection to a private ISP because the client now *requires* the Proxy Server. This error will happen frequently when a user in your environment has a computer that travels between work and home, and attempts to access a local ISP from home (without going through a Proxy Server). To correct this problem, simply turn off the WinSock Proxy client by using WinSock Proxy Client in Control Panel. When the user returns to work, the inability to use the proxy will show up and you will need to turn the WinSock Proxy client back on in the same manner.

- Failure to Refresh Configuration Files or Failure to Connect to the Server

This error happens when there is a problem connecting to the Mspclnt share on the Proxy Server computer. This share must remain available all the time so that Proxy Server clients can refresh their configuration files. Also, check to make sure that the client has permissions to the share. If the client is not a member of the same domain as the Proxy Server computer, or if the Proxy Server computer is a stand-alone server, you need to enable the Guest account on the Proxy Server computer and give it permission to the share, or you need to create an account on the Proxy Server computer that matches the user name and password of the user on the client computer.

For IPX clients, this error message can indicate that the TCP/IP protocol is installed on the client computer but TCP/IP is not enabled on the internal network adapter for the Proxy Server computer. Some IPX clients might also require TCP/IP to be installed for certain applications, or some clients might have Remote Access Service (RAS) installed for modem connections with TCP/IP bound to the RAS adapter. There are two workarounds for this type of problem: remove TCP/IP from the client computers, or force the clients to use only IPX for all WinSock Proxy connections. This can be done by editing the `Mspclnt.ini` file on the Proxy Server computer. Remove the [Servers Ip Addresses] section. The Proxy clients refresh their configuration automatically so it is not necessary to refresh all of the clients manually.

- Internal Subnetwork Cannot be Reached Through a WinSock Proxy Client Application

Check that the subnetwork address ranges are included in the Local Address Table (LAT), C:\Msplat.txt. If there are internal subnet addresses missing from the LAT, add the missing IP address pairs to the server LAT file (C:\Msp\Msplat.txt) so that these address changes are propagated to all clients when the next table update cycle is performed by Microsoft Proxy Server.

- Prompts to "Enter Domain Credentials" Each Time a New Windows Sockets Application is Launched

Each time a Windows Sockets application is launched and another Windows Sockets application is not currently active, the domain credentials will be required. When leaving a Windows Sockets application open and minimized, there is no need to resupply domain credentials.

- The WinSock Proxy Service Has Problems with Other Third-Party TCP/IP Stacks

Third party TCP/IP stacks, or protocol software built by an external company, is not likely to have been tested with Proxy Server and can produce unpredictable results.

- Windows for Workgroups Clients That Use IPX are not Able to Access the WinSock Proxy Service for Proxy Server

IPX is supported only for Windows 95 and Windows NT clients.

Client Performance Problems

Sometimes connections between client and server are impossible — the user might not be able to get to external WWW sites, WinSock clients might be seeing slow connections, or the network might be bogged down.

- Browsing Internal Web Sites Works, But External WWW Sites Do Not Appear in User Browse Lists

Try to ping the server IP address for Microsoft Proxy Server from the command prompt on the client. Check for client address resolution including DNS and WINS if the response is "Bad IP address." Also, check the TCP/IP configuration carefully and check that your machine name is not duplicated on the network.

- Connection is Slow from a Client that uses a Windows Sockets-Connected Application on a Local Network

If only certain local addresses appear to be slow, you may be having the WinSock Proxy service attempting to redirect a local connection. To keep this from happening, make sure that the computer you are trying to reach is properly defined in the Local Address Table (LAT). Be sure to check the client LAT, which is located by default in the file C:\Mspclnt\Msplat.txt.

- Internal Network Performance is slow for all Clients Accessing the Same Server

If all performance is slow for the WinSock Proxy client requests to certain servers on the internal network, check that the server IP addresses are in the Local Address Table (LAT). If the internal server is not in the LAT, the WinSock Proxy clients try to redirect connections to it through Proxy Server. For every machine that runs Proxy Server on your network, verify the IP address ranges listed in the `Construct Local Address Table` dialog box. Add the IP address ranges or individual IP addresses as required. As a last resort, you can edit the Msplat.txt file in the C:\Msp\Clients folder on every computer that runs Proxy Server.

Resolving A Client Installation Problem

You've just found that the problem is with the client installation but you are unable to get to the server to make any changes. Although you know that you can make changes to the

`Mspclnt.ini` file, we will caution you that making unnecessary changes can lead to a disorderly environment, which may be difficult to troubleshoot. Our recommendation is to work with the `Mspclnt.ini` file and make changes *only when necessary*. Once you make changes to the configuration always record your results. Should you make changes that were not intended, be sure to return the file to its original state before saving. TIP: Copy the file to another location like the \temp directory before starting your work and you should be fine. Take ten minutes and open the server LAT and review the entries there. Also, open the client LAT and review the entries there. This is *only* to review information, not to make changes. Once you are familiar with the information, edit the file or remove the file altogether and note the result.

MCSE 11.4 Resolving Cache Problems

Most cache problems occur because of hard disk corruption or because the hard disk drive is full. If caching fails to occur in general, check the available disk space on the caching drive. You may want to increase the cache size using the Web Proxy service properties dialog box or allocate an additional drive for caching.

Each time the Web Proxy service starts, the cache performs an integrity check and other tests. If the cache occupies a significant amount of disk space these checks can take some time. If caching problems are still reported, the hard drive may be the problem. You may a want to use the `chkdsk` utility to analyze the drive. Use `chkdsk  /r` if you suspect cache errors. This utility tries to locate disk errors and recover readable information for the drive. If errors still persist you may need to replace the drive.

There are three particular messages that may appear in the System Event Log to indicate cache problems. Let's take a brief look art each.

```
"W3Pcache corrected a corrupted or old format URL cache by
removing all or part of the cache contents"
```

This error message means that some of the cache objects have been deleted from the cache. If this message recurs, you may want to run the `chkdsk` utility to check for disk errors.

```
"W3Pcache failed to initialize the URL Cache on disk"
```

This error message could indicate cache configuration problems. Use good troubleshooting techniques to solve this problem. Try to stop the Web Proxy service and correct cache parameters by selecting `Reset  the defaults` from the `Caching` tab. Then restart the Web Proxy service. If the initialization fails again, you may need to run Proxy Server setup with the `Reinstall` option.

Even after the reinstall the problem might remain for several reasons. If this is the case, run `chkdsk /r` to recover from possible hard drive errors. You may also consider relocating cache directories to another drive. You can also try to delete Web Proxy service caching directories and have Web Proxy service recreate them on its startup.

You must stop the WWW service to delete the contents of the caching directories.

```
"W3Pcache initialization failed due to incorrect configu-
ration. Please use the administration utility or manually
edit the registry to correct the error and restart the
service."
```

In this case try to stop the WWW service in the Internet Service Manager and then use the `Reset the Defaults` button in the Web Proxy service properties to reset Web cache parameters. Restart the WWW service. If initialization fails again try reinstalling Proxy Server. If the problem persists after the reinstallation, check the hard disk drive for errors and consider erasing the Web Proxy cache and then reinstalling Proxy Server.

When you are troubleshooting cache problems remember that Web Proxy cache can be located on NTFS volumes only.

MCSE 11.5 Troubleshooting a WINS Server to Provide Client Access to Proxy Servers

If your users are complaining that they cannot access Proxy Server, you may want to check network connectivity and network name resolution. For example, Web Proxy clients such as Internet Explorer and Netscape Navigator use host name resolution to find Proxy Server. If the host name resolution sequence does not work, Proxy clients are unable to find Proxy Server in the network.

The host name resolution methods are the following:

- Hosts file
- Domain Name System (DNS)
- Windows Internet Name Service (WINS)

- Broadcast name resolution
- Lmhosts file

To test name resolution, try to ping Proxy Server by computer name. If ping fails, check the name resolution methods that are used in your internal network. Most internal networks use WINS for name resolution. If WINS is the only name resolution method used, the WINS server becomes a critical point of your network to communicate with the Internet. Although WINS is not used for Internet name resolution, the client cannot find the Proxy server if the WINS server is down.

If you have the WINS issue, you may want to check that the WINS server is up and running and that client computers are configured to use WINS. If you created static multihomed mappings for Proxy Servers to implement load balancing, ensure that these mappings are correct.

If you are using other name resolution methods, such as DNS, check that they are functional and perform resolution to the right IP address.

MCSE 11.6 Miscellaneous Troubleshooting Issues

In many cases the source of the problem lies outside the scope of Proxy Server software. For example, if there is a hardware problem due to the malfunctioning of the modem or the network adapter card used by the Proxy Server, communication will not be possible. If you suspect hardware-related problems, check that other services and functions that are not related to Proxy Server work. For example, you may want to try pinging the Internet from the Proxy Server computer. If you cannot ping, then you have a communication problem.

With packet filtering enabled, the ping packet can be blocked even when you ping from the Proxy Server computer.

If you suspect a hardware-related problem, check that your modem cable is plugged in the computer tight and the network adapter is connected to the network. If you just installed an operating system on this computer, check that all IRQ numbers are correct and there are no device conflicts.

Many problems with Proxy Server are connected with other services. For example, if you are using Proxy Server with RAS or a RRAS server, you may encounter the problem when Proxy Server AutoDial fails to disconnect from the Internet. If this happens, check that one or more of the following conditions are applicable:

- A Winsock application on a client is open and connected to the Internet
- A Web Proxy client (Web Browser) is left open and connected to a Web Page that contains a refresh tag
- The active caching feature of the Web Proxy service is updating the cache
- Other TCP/IP traffic is present on the modem connection from the Internet. For example, some Internet service providers may send router messages (such as ICMP or IGMP messages) to your server while it is connected to the Internet. (A network trace utility such as network monitor can be used to verify that this is the cause of the problem. It may be necessary to contact your Internet service provider to correct this problem.)

■ Summary

This chapter discussed the process of troubleshooting. Remember the strong recommendation to document everything and check when something goes wrong. The systematic process to resolve issues was spelled out as follows:

- problem identification
- diagnosis
- testing the hypothetical solution
- verifying that the problem was solved by the proposed solution

In the larger sense we discussed the resources available to you for use with your troubleshooting. We talked about the utilities that are used to troubleshoot the Proxy Server. We mentioned the common server and common client problems and solutions to those problems. We also provided the overview of resolving WINS issues, hardware-related issues, and Internet / Intranet issues using RRAS.

▲ REVIEW QUESTIONS

1. *You have found a problem with the Server installation. You should*

    A. Check C:\Mpcsetup.log,

    B. Check the LAT

    C. Check the CD

    D. Review the documentation on Client Installation

2. *You have found a problem with the Client installation. What should you check to determine what went wrong?*

    A. Mpcsetup.log

    B. TCP/IP settings

    C. WSP Icon in the control panel

    D. Event Viewer Security Log

3. *After Proxy Server successfully worked for more than two months you notice that the Web Proxy cache on drive D: is corrupt. What utility should you use to work around this problem?*

    A. CONVERT D: /FS:NTFS

    B. CHKDSK D: /R

    C. Format D: /Q

    D. Setup /r

4. *You are using DNS and WINS in your internal network for local name resolution and Proxy Server load balancing. At some point you start to notice that initial connection to Proxy Server is successful but takes approximately 1 minute. What should you check first?*

    A. Check that WINS server is up and running

    B. Check that DNS server is up and running

    C. Check the hosts file

    D. Check lmhosts file

5. *You install Proxy Server in your network. During the installation you specify that clients will connect to Proxy Server using the computer name. You do not currently use DNS in your local network name resolution. You install WINS for computer name resolution and make Proxy Server a WINS client. After installing Proxy Client software, some of your clients cannot gain access to the Internet. Others can access the Internet fine. What must you do to solve this?*

    A. Install DNS server in your LAN and make all client computers use this DNS server. Since Internet access is required, DNS is a must.

    B. Check that all computers are WINS clients

    C. Rerun Proxy Server setup and specify that all client computers must connect to Proxy Server using the IP address

    D. Check that the WINS server is up and running

6. *Your company has a dedicated T1 line to the Internet. You set up Proxy Server computer, but after the setup program is completed and the Proxy Server computer is restarted, no one is able to access the Internet. You suspect that the external network adapter is malfunctioning. How can you check this?*

    A. Ping the internal network adapter IP address from the Proxy client computer

    B. Ping the external network adapter IP address from the Proxy client computer

    C. Ping the Proxy Server default gateway from the Proxy client computer

    D. Ping the Proxy Server default gateway from the Proxy Server computer

7. *You configure Proxy Server AutoDial. You set up dial-up client software to disconnect after 10 minutes of idle time. However, when 10 minutes pass, the connection is not dropped. What could be the reason for this?*

    A. Proxy Server does not work with the auto disconnect feature

    B. Active caching is in progress

    C. The system time is set incorrectly

    D. The modem is locked up

8. *Your Proxy Server accesses the Internet through a modem. You discover that you cannot reach your Internet service provider and suspect the modem is malfunctioning. What is the best first step in analyzing this problem?*

    A. Remove and reseat the modem card in the computer

    B. Reinstall TCP/IP

    C. Check that the modem cable is connected

    D. Run the `ChkMODEM` utility

Answers to Chapter Review Questions

Chapter 1

1. C; When Proxy Server stores Web pages it is called caching.
2. B, C, D, E; Proxy Server caches Web content, can block inbound and outbound Web access and provides packet filtering.
3. C, D; Proxy Server is installed on Windows NT Server.

Chapter 2

1. C; Since all users have CERN-compliant browsers, the Web Proxy Service is the best choice. There is no "CERN Proxy Service."
2. C, D; The question does not tell us that all browsers in use are CERN-compliant. For those that are, the Web Proxy Service will be able to collect the desired information. Browsers that are not CERN-compliant can run as WinSock applications. Since the WinSock Proxy service also has a logging feature, selecting these two options provides the best capability.
3. C; Content caching is available only through the Web Proxy Service which works only with CERN-compliant browsers. It is necessary, therefore, to ensure each client has a CERN-compliant browser.
4. D; Although the Web Proxy Service handles client requests from CERN-compliant Web browsers, when those browsers use helper applications that rely on UDP the WinSock Proxy Service comes into play. UDP-dependant applications include Real Audio and VDOLive.

5. C; Since Internet Explorer is a CERN-compliant browser, it will be able to use the Web Proxy Service which features a logging mode. Using the Proxy Server audit log won't work since this feature cannot track URLs accessed through a Proxy Server.

6. B, C; The SOCKS Proxy Service can support any TCP/IP application that uses the SOCKS 4.3a standard. The Web Proxy Service will support any CERN-compliant browser without regard to the system upon which it is operating. Since Netscape Navigator is CERN-compliant, this service will function with the Macintosh computers, also.

7. A, C; The Web Proxy Service works with CERN-compliant browsers regardless of the platform upon which they operate. HTTP and FTP are both supported by the Web Proxy Service. The UDP protocol would need to work with the WinSock Proxy Service, which is not available for the UNIX operating system.

Chapter 3

1. B; Setting protocol permissions
2. Depending on existing network: A, C H, I
3. Depending on existing network: A-D, F-J
4. Depending on existing network: A-J
5. Depending on existing network: A-J
6. D; Analog Modem satisfied minimum requirement
7. D; 300 to 2000 clients requires an Intel Pentium 166 MHz and 64MB RAM

Chapter 4

1. A, B, D, F, G; Hardware requirements for Microsoft Proxy Server 2.0 include Intel® 486 or faster processor, 24 MB of RAM (32 for RISC systems) and an adequate free space on hard disk drive for the Web Proxy cache. The Web Proxy cache cannot reside on FAT volumes, so an NTFS volume for the Web Proxy cache is a requirement. Additionally, Internet Information Server 3.0 (which is included in Windows NT Server Service Pack 3) or higher must be installed on the computer.

2. A, B; Proxy Server Administration Tools and Documentation can be installed on Windows NT Server and Windows NT Workstation. Proxy Server services can be installed on Windows NT Server only.

3. D; Since the local network uses IPX/SPX only, you should bind IPX/SPX to the internal interface. For security reasons you should unbind IPX/SPX from the external interface. TCP/IP must be bound to

the external interface but, additionally, the Local Address Table (LAT) must have at least one IP address that is assigned to one of the Proxy Server network interface cards. The local address table can contain only IP addresses from internal network cards which, by definition, means TCP/IP must be bound to the internal network adapter also.

4. A; The LAT information is stored in the *msplat.txt* file in the Clients subdirectory.

5. C; If access control is enabled, only those clients that have been explicitly assigned permissions are able to use the service. That means that you must specifically assign permissions to users in the Proxy Server Administrator program before they will be able to use these services.

6. C; You can choose only NTFS formatted disks for caching; FAT volumes will appear dimmed in the dialog box.

7. B; To set up the client computer using the client setup program, connect to the *mspclnt* share and launch *setup.exe*. You should run the client setup program from the *mspclnt* share, not from the Proxy Server CD-ROM.

8. B; Because of differences in content caching procedures, the contents of the cache is deleted during the upgrade and the cache is created anew.

9. D; Installing and uninstalling the Proxy client software each time you switch between office and home will be inconvenient. Microsoft Proxy client software allows you to disable the WinSock Proxy client.

10. B; The Proxy Server Local Address Table (LAT) must contain IP address ranges that cover all internal IP addresses of the internal network. LAT must not have extra IP addresses that are not a part of the internal network.

11. B; The Microsoft Proxy Server Setup program creates a log file: C:\Mps-setup.log. If you encounter problems during Proxy Server setup, you can review this file with any text editor.

12. A, B, C, E; The Proxy Client setup program updates the Control Panel, the WinSock Proxy client applet, copies the LAT information, replaces the standard Winsock.dll, and attempts to configure the Web browser on the client computer, if you specify so during Proxy Server setup.

13. D; A Proxy Server license is required for each installation of Proxy Server. Proxy Client software does not require licensing, however, and no client access licenses are required by Proxy Server.

Chapter 5

1. B; When Internet Information Server is installed, a default anonymous user account named IUSR_*computername* is created, where *computer-*

name is the name of the server computer. This account is used by the Web Proxy service to grant access permissions.

2. A, B; Permissions for the HTTP and HTTPS protocols are the same. If a user is assigned permissions to the "WWW" protocol, he will have access to secure SSL Web (HTTPS) pages as well as to standard HTTP Web pages.

3. B; The permissions Tab in the WinSock Proxy service properties dialog box is used to designate which users or groups can use the particular protocol to access the Internet through Proxy Server. It is recommended that you assign Proxy Server permissions for groups of users and then regulate group membership to grant or deny permissions for a specific user.

4. A; You are not limited to these predefined protocol definitions, nor are you restricted to Windows Sockets applications that work with these predefined protocol definitions. You may use the `Protocol` tab to add protocol definitions that support additional Windows Sockets ports.

5. D; The WinSock Proxy service uses Windows NT challenge/response authentication only to provide secure communication for Windows Sockets applications. The WinSock client application does not have to support the Windows NT challenge/response authentication — authentication is done by the WinSock Proxy service client software.

6. B; Socks Proxy service cannot be used to provide support for applications that utilize the UDP protocol such as RealAudio, streaming video, or NetShow.

7. B; Domain filtering applies to all users who access the Internet through the Proxy Server. There is one exception to this rule: Domain filtering does not affect WinSock Proxy service users who have been granted unlimited access in the Permissions tab.

8. False; The Socks Proxy service permissions tab displays the ordered list of entries where each entry specifies a source, destination, port number, and whether the request using these parameters should be granted or denied. By default, all requests are denied, so if no entry is found that corresponds to the client request, the request is denied.

9. B; By default, all information is logged to a text file. After installing Proxy Server, you can set configuration parameters for either logging to a text file or logging to a database.

10. E; To set up logging information to an ODBC-compliant database you must complete the following steps: Install the database application; Install the ODBC driver for the database you are using; Create a system Data Source Name (system DSN) for the database; Create a table in

your database application with the necessary fields; and Configure the log for the database.

11. B; Domain filtering is used to grant or deny access for specific Internet sites for Web Proxy, WinSock Proxy, and Socks Proxy services. Domain filtering affects all users except those who are granted unlimited access for the WinSock Proxy Service.

12. A; The WinSock Proxy service Protocols tab is used to configure protocol definitions. Protocol definitions determine which WinSock applications can be used to access the Internet. By defining protocols for the WinSock Proxy service you can regulate access to the Internet using these protocols.

13. B; After Proxy Server is installed, the Web Proxy cache contains data and it should be administered using Internet Service Manager. Do not use the Proxy Server Setup program to change the cache properties after Setup is completed. You can change the cache size and location after Proxy Server is installed by using the Cache Size button in the Caching tab.

14. D; Active caching automatically goes out to the Internet for an object, without client prompting. Proxy Server performs active caching based on the object popularity. Active caching reduces time that users have to wait while browsing popular Internet sites.

15. B; In the Web Proxy service caching properties dialog, you can limit the maximum size of cached objects.

16. B; You can increase or decrease the cache size, specify additional drives for caching, and even set the cache size to zero. If you set the cache size for a selected drive to zero, all cached data is deleted and the drive is not used for caching anymore.

17. A; RemotMsp is primarily used to configure and administer remote Proxy Server computers. For example, the RemoteMsp utility can be used to load and save Proxy Server configuration, stop and restart services, and set server configuration options.

18. C; On the Services tab, there is the Current Sessions button. By pressing the Current Sessions button, you can view the lists of all connected users that are currently using Proxy Server services.

19. C; If reverse DNS lookup is configured for the filtered domain, additional domain filtering by IP address is not necessary. However, many network administrators do not configure reverse DNS lookup for their domain. To ensure that the undesired domain is reliably blocked from access, you should configure domain filters for both domain names and IP addresses.

20. A; When you select the option "Faster User response is more important," Proxy Server performs more Internet retrievals and provides users with fresher information.

21. A, C, D; The Proxy Server AutoDial feature requires a Windows NT RAS client and a valid RAS Phonebook entry. Additionally, you need to configure Remote Access properties to use Auto Dial.

22. C, D; If the client computer Microsoft Internet Explorer is not configured to use Proxy Server, then Proxy Server AutoDial will not occur when the client attempts to access the Internet. If Internet Explorer is not configured to use Proxy Server, but WinSock Proxy client is installed, then the client computer uses WinSock Proxy service; and AutoDial must be enabled for this service as well. Since AutoDial is performed by the Proxy Server but not by an individual user, special AutoDial permissions are not needed.

23. E; The following configuration parameters are not rolled back during a partial restore: size and location of Web Proxy service cache, location for all service logs and the packet filter log, packet filtering configuration, AutoDial configuration information, server alias used in the "Http Via" header for routing, Server intra-array IP address, and Proxy Server registry keys that cannot be configured through the user interface.

24. B; Reverse hosting maintains a list of internal servers that can publish to the Internet, thereby allowing Proxy Server to listen and respond on behalf of multiple servers that are located behind it. Reverse proxying allows you to place a single Web server behind Proxy Server. Server proxying is the technology used for placing non-Web Servers to be put behind Proxy.

25. B; To find those users who are using newsgroups, we would examine the WinSock Proxy logs to see who is using the NNTP protocol.

Chapter 6

1. B; Alerting is configured in the Proxy Server Security properties dialog. While packet filter logging will permit you to view the dropped packets, this step will not provide an alert.

2. C; Under dynamic packet filtering, a port must be opened for inbound access. Disabling dynamic packet filtering will require filter exceptions for both inbound and outbound access. Enabling Packet Forwarding will allow access to the internal network, but at the expense of the protection provided by the Proxy Server.

3. B; Packet filtering will protect your Proxy Server computer by preventing unwanted access from the outside. If no inbound access is required,

dynamic filtering will ensure that all ports remain closed until an internal client needs to open one for outbound access.

4. C, D; By creating a filter exception that permits only the designated user to access the designated machine, you allow only very limited external access to your network. For further protection, you can exclude the file server's IP address from the LAT.

5. D; When the Web server operates on a port other than the default port 80, a custom filter exception must be configured. As long as dynamic filtering is configured, internal applications can obtain outbound access, but filter exceptions are still required for inbound access from the external network.

6. A; Selecting Rejected Packets will trigger a warning when the rate of rejected packets exceeds a predetermined threshold. Selecting Protocol Violations causes Proxy Server to report only when the rejected packets that appear to be potentially malicious exceed the threshold. The question specified any attempt against a closed port, not just those appearing malicious.

7. D; Packet filtering will prevent packets not specifically excepted from passing through the Proxy Server external interface.

Chapter 7

1. A, B; You can use the DNS Round Robin feature by entering an A record for each DNS server and aliasing all the A records to the same CNAME record. Configure browsers to use the CNAME record.

2. A; CARP uses hash functions to compute a unique location within the array for a particular cached resource. The location of other array members is critical to CARP's operation, but is not a CARP function.

3. C; By configuring a backup route that makes a direct connection to the external network you can still get Internet access (assuming you have an external interface that can connect to the Internet).

4. B, C; A Proxy Server array will provide fault tolerance and its load balancing and increased cache capability will increase performance. An array, however, provides the same measure of security as a stand-alone server. Higher bandwidth is not correct in this case because the question doesn't indicate that each server has its own independent Internet connection. Without an independent connection, adding additional servers will not increase bandwidth since each one must still compete for a common Internet connection. Better caching will, however, increase available bandwidth by reducing the frequency of Internet calls to retrieve resources that can be read from the cache.

5. C; Hierarchical caching is a function of Proxy Server chains. By configuring upstream routing to use a Web Proxy or array, you create a Proxy Server chain.

6. D; When arrayed computers are configured for automatic synchronization, settings not specific to a particular Proxy Server computer are automatically replicated to other array members. WinSock Protocol definitions are automatically synchronized.

7. C; Only a Proxy Server array will provide fault tolerance and load balancing. It is recommended one Proxy Server array member be installed for each 2000 computers so four arrayed computers would be sufficient. Hierarchical caching and upstream routing are features of Proxy Server chains, not arrays.

8. A; Unlike the Web Proxy service, WinSock Proxy clients should be assigned gateways manually. Distribute the assignments based on server capability and the users' usage patterns.

9. C; You can use the DNS Round Robin feature by entering a host name (A) record for each DNS server and aliasing all the A records to the same canonical name (CNAME) record. By configuring browsers to use the CNAME record, they will get the IP address of a different Proxy Server each time.

10. B; Proxy Server arrays provide load balancing and fault tolerance. When each array member has an independent connection to the external network (in this case the Internet), bandwidth is increased. Since one Proxy Server computer array member is recommended for each 2000 computers, a two-machine array will perform well in this scenario.

Chapter 8

1. C; UNIX machines can run Netscape Navigator and operate with Proxy Server computers. Although UNIX machines can make use of the SOCKS proxy service, Netscape Navigator is a CERN-compliant browser and, as such, can use the Web Proxy service to take advantage of Proxy Server caching.

2. B; Proxy Server can be used as an IPX/SPX gateway. The Client WinSock Proxy service should be configured to "Force the IPX/SPX Protocol." The Proxy Server computer must have TCP/IP on its external interface to communicate with the Internet. It needs IPX/SPX (NWLink) on the internal interface to communicate with the clients. Proxy Server also needs to have TCP/IP on the internal interface for proper operation (even if no client uses this protocol).

3. B; To disable automatic configuration, select the Internet Options|Connection tab on Internet Explorer 4.01, or the Options|Advanced tab on Internet Explorer 3.02, and clear the URL Path from the Automatic Configuration dialog box. Unchecking the "Automatically configure Web Browser during client setup" checkbox on the Proxy Server computer will cancel automatic update on all your network computers.

4. A; Internet Explorer 4.0 and later browsers may be automatically configured through a JavaScript, Jscript, VBScript script, or an INS file.

5. C; The Web Proxy service does not depend on local address information — this is WinSock Proxy service configuration information.

6. B; Macintosh clients use the SOCKS Proxy Service for application support. Although Macintosh CERN-compliant browsers can use the Web Proxy service, the question asks about application support.

7. D; Mspclnt.ini may be edited using any text editor (such as Notepad). You may edit the file either on the clients or on the server. Editing the file server allows you to make one set of changes that will propagate throughout the network. Changes made to clients will be overwritten when the server updates client files from its own mspclnt.ini.

8. C; The first thing to check is connectivity. If you can ping to the Proxy Server, you know you have connectivity with the Proxy Server. If this check fails, you can concentrate on network connectivity problems rather than Proxy Server configuration.

9. B; You manually create a locallat.txt file on a client computer when that computer needs to recognize a particular set of IP addresses not included in the LAT as local.

10. A; The TCP port settings in the WWW Service Properties dialog affects CERN-compliant browsers under the Web Proxy service. If the port number is changed, a corresponding change must be made to the browser configuration.

Chapter 9

1. D; It is more desirable to run PPTP server on the Proxy Server. After all the software is installed, you should check that IP forwarding is disabled in the TCP/IP properties dialog box. If IP forwarding is enabled, your internal network is accessible from the Internet, which could be a serious security problem. Additionally, you should enable packet filtering and create static packet filters for "PPTP Call" if your computer acts as a PPTP client and "PPTP Receive" if your computer is a PPTP Server.

2. B; If you try to set up a custom filter for any computer on your internal network, you will get the *Invalid Local Hosts* message. This happens

when you create a packet filter for an internal IP address (one that is in the LAT). To solve this problem, you will have to exclude the IP address of that computer from LAT.

3. A, C, E, F; In order to make the Exchange Server work behind Proxy Server, you need to perform the following steps: install WinSock Proxy Client software on the Exchange Server computer; configure at least one address of an Internet DNS server in the DNS settings of the Exchange Server's Network TCP/IP settings; configure Proxy Server packet filtering; configure the Exchange services to use the WinSock Proxy service by creating the wspcfg.ini files; and update the DNS MX records to point to the Proxy Server's external interface.

4. B; In order to put multiple Exchange Servers behind a Proxy Server computer, the proxy server external interface must have multiple external addresses. To specify which address to bind to on the proxy server, you need to place a ProxyBindIp entry in the WSPCFG.INI file.

5. A; The idea of the DMZ is to create a third zone in your network that will be accessible to both local and Internet users.

6. E; Server hosting works for WinSock clients only. Reverse hosting and reverse proxying work for the HTTP protocol. A UNIX telnet server can be placed behind Proxy Server using the concept of DMZ.

7. B; Reverse proxying is the ability of Proxy Server to listen to incoming requests for an internal Web server computer and respond on behalf of that server. HTTP requests from the Internet are forwarded *downstream* to the Web server located behind the Proxy Server computer.

8. B; Microsoft SQL Server can be put in the internal network behind Proxy Server. In order to make SQL Server visible from the external network, you need to configure SQL Server to use TCP/IP sockets, install WinSock client software, and create a WSPCFG.INI file.

Chapter 10

1. B; The cache hit ratio can be improved by increasing caching. By reviewing the Web Proxy service log, Sandy can determine which sites are most utilized by her network's users. With this information she can create cache filters to ensure the most popular information is cached.

2. A, B; While most of your HTTP session will be covered by Web Proxy Service counters, if you access any Web based applications (e.g., RealAudio), you will also use the WinSock Proxy Service. The Browser object gathers data concerning the Windows NT network browser service and has nothing to do with Web browsers.

3. B; Bytes Total/sec shows the number of bytes sent and received by the selected network interface. If this number approaches your, network transmission speed your network is likely becoming a bottleneck.

4. D; When the Network Interface: Output Queue Length consistently exceeds two and the Network Interface: Bytes Total/sec is under nominal network bandwidth, the problem typically is that the network interface card is unable to transmit packets as fast as they arrive.

5. B, C; When the Current Disk Queue Length exceeds two, the hard drive is participating in excessive input/output. This could be a sign that the hard drive should be upgraded with a faster drive or drives. Excessive disk activity could also be indicative of excessive paging, which would imply a memory problem. (To verify a memory problem, check the Memory: Pages/sec counter. If it consistently exceeds 10, you likely have a memory problem.) CPU problems are usually indicated when the %Processor Time consistently exceeds 80–90%; in this case the CPU is within normal parameters.

6. B; When the Processor: %Processor Time value exceeds 80–90% you should suspect a processor bottleneck. Memory and hard disk appear within limits as noted by the Memory: Pages/sec and Network Interface: Output Queue Length counter values. No counter value was provided to give a clear picture of hard drive health.

7. A; Active caching results in a pro-active caching program that can make use of unused bandwidth and increase your overall throughput. Reducing minimum TTL actually causes the cache to fill with information that expires quickly. There is no time setting for cache filters. Increasing the cached object size will reduce the overall number of cached objects and make the cache less useful in increasing throughput.

8. B; Properly distributed Proxy Server chains can bring the cache closer to the user for increased efficiency. Because of its caching features, the use of the Web Proxy Service is preferable to use of the WinSock Proxy Service for increased efficiency.

9. C; Network Monitor will monitor network traffic on a packet-by-packet basis on each interface.

10. D; Except for Cache Hit Ratio, all readings are within limits. Your goal with Cache Hit Ratio should be to make this value as close to 100% as possible. Increasing the cache size will permit more caching and should raise this value.

11. C; The User Sessions Dialog Box is the only listed tool that can show time users have been connected to the service. There is no Web Sessions Log.

12. C; A high Cache Hit Ratio is a good thing! A Current Disk Queue Length that exceeds two, however, is usually an indication of a disk

problem. The only available choice to improve disk performance is to spread the cache over multiple drives. Since logical drives may or may not all be on the same physical unit, there is no way to tell from the question if choice D will be of any value.

13. D; Baselines should always be accomplished under typical load conditions.

14. B; The Performance Monitor provides Web Proxy Service: Current Users, WinSock Proxy Service: Active Sessions, and Socks Proxy Service: SOCKS Sessions counters to provide this information.

15. A; This shows the cumulative number of URLs that have been actively refreshed from their respective sites. This can provide another guideline for the increase or curtailment of active caching.

16. B; Using Performance Monitor's Packet Filtering: Total dropped frames, Frames dropped due to filter denial, or frames dropped due to protocol violations will record the number of dropped frames. By setting a Performance Monitor alert, Vickie can be quickly notified when rejected packets exceed a set number. Using the Proxy Server Alerting tab will track dropped frames but it won't send an alert except through SMTP mail or by writing to the event log. Both options require a manual check to get the information.

17. B; To configure a machine for cache-only, simply ensure the Local Address Table (LAT) contains all IP addresses that will use the Web Proxy Service cache. There is no Caching Only checkbox on the Web Proxy service properties caching tab.

Chapter 11

1. A; Microsoft Proxy Server Setup creates its own log file in C:\Mpssetup.log. This log gives you information about the setup and overall installation process. Should you ever need to get the Microsoft Technical Support Team involved with the troubleshooting of your installation, this log should be available.

2. A; The Microsoft Proxy Server client Setup program creates a log file on the client computer called Mpcsetup.log. The log contains valuable information beyond messages that are displayed to users.

3. B; If caching problems are reported, the hard drive may be the problem. You may want to use chkdsk utility to analyze the drive. Use chkdsk /r if you suspect cache errors. This utility tries to locate disk errors and recover readable information for the drive.

4. B; If you are using name resolution methods such as DNS, check that they are functional and perform resolution to the right IP address. If

DNS server is unavailable, the timeout that the client waits before trying other name resolution methods is approximately 1 minute.

5. B, D; In order ro Proxy clients computers to access Proxy Server in the WINS environment, WINS server must be up and running and Proxy Client computers must be configured as WINS clients.

6. D; If you suspect hardware-related problems, check that other services and functions that are not related to Proxy Server work. For example, you may want to ping the Internet from the Proxy Server computer. Since Proxy Server does not work with ICPM packets that are used by the PING utility, pinging the Internet from the Proxy Client computers will not help.

7. B; If Proxy Server active caching is in progress, Proxy Server AutoDial will not disconnect from the Internet until active caching if completed.

8. C; The best and easiest first step is to ensure you have connectivity. Checking that all cabling is properly connected should always be accomplished first. There is no ChkMODEM utility.

Additional Installation Instructions

Installing a DNS Server

Before you install the DNS server it is critical that TCP/IP be properly configured on the machine on which you will do the installation. The machine *must* have a static IP address. This means it shouldn't be a DHCP client or, if it is, it should have a client address reservation. Additionally, you should check the DNS tab of the TCP/IP properties dialog to ensure host and domain names are properly specified. If these entries are present, SOA, A, and NS records for the server will be automatically created during the installation. If they're not present, only the SOA record will be created. If your network is a stand-alone, training-only affair and doesn't have an Internet domain, you may make up whatever domain information you like (e.g., mydomain.com).

Installing the Service

Once we're sure our TCP/IP data is correctly configured, we can proceed to the actual server installation. DNS installation is very similar to that of any other TCP/IP service. The first step is a visit to the (Control Panel) Network dialog's Services tab. Select Add and highlight Microsoft DNS Server. (Remember to have the installation CD-ROM handy — the system will need to copy files from it.) Once the appropriate files are copied, close out of the Network dialog and you'll be prompted to restart the computer. Accept the restart and the DNS service will start automatically.

Configuring the DNS Server

Now that your DNS server is installed and running it needs to be configured to do some work! Right now it is running as a caching-only Internet name server because it has only the Internet root information it has found in the default cache file and knows nothing about the network on which it operates. Although there are a myriad of configuration options, configuring a DNS server boils down to a few relatively simple steps:

- Add Server to DNS Manager
- Create primary and/or add secondary zones
- Add resource records (as required)

The first step in DNS configuration is to add your server to the Domain Name Service Manager. You can launch the DNS Manager from the *Administrative Tools (common)* program group. Once you have the DNS Manager running select DNS from the menu bar and click on New Server. This will bring up the Add DNS Server dialog box in which you should enter the name or IP address of the computer on which you just installed the DNS service.

ADDING ZONES

In order for your server to service your network, you'll need to determine the hierarchy for your DNS domains and zones and ensure they're properly identified in the server. If your network is a stand-alone, training-only affair and doesn't have an Internet domain or a DNS zone, you can make up whatever domain and zone you like (e.g. mydomain.com). You can add a primary zone to the server by highlighting the server name and selecting New Zone from the DNS menu. This starts the Zone Wizard — select New Zone.

Click Next and enter the name of the zone you wish to create. If you press the TAB key, the DNS manager will fill in the name of the database file.

Click Next and Finish and the DNS server creates the zone and adds SOA, NS, and A records for the DNS server computer. Your DNS server is now installed and configured!

Installing Microsoft Network Monitor

You must be a member of the Administrators group to install Microsoft Network Monitor on Windows NT Server 4.0.

To install Network Monitor:

1. Log on as Administrator.
2. Launch Control Panel. Double-click the Network icon and select the Services tab.
3. Click Add. The Select Network Services dialog box appears.
4. Select Network Monitor Tools and Agent from the Network Service list. Click OK.
5. You may be asked to provide the path to the Windows NT Setup files. Type the full path to the Windows NT distribution point and click Continue.
6. Click Close to exit the Network dialog box.
7. Click Yes to restart the computer.

After the computer restarts, you will be able to use Microsoft Network Monitor.

Server Setup and Run-Time Event Messages

Setup Messages

The Proxy Server Setup program returns the following event messages, which are listed alphabetically:

- **Could not identify disk drive configuration.**
  - This indicates that Setup was not able to recognize your current disk drive configuration. Check all cables, check to ensure the controller can see the drive(s), and, if necessary, contact your technical support team for further assistance.

- **Either the logged account is not permitted to modify the system file: *filename*, or the file is locked by another application.**
  - This is displayed when another Internet service is currently active on the server, or the account you are using does not provide administrative access. In this case you should stop all of the other Internet services and be sure that you are an administrator with proper rights before trying to restart Setup.

- **Failed to initialize Service Manager. Error=errornumber.**
  - This error indicates that the Microsoft Proxy Server cannot be installed with your existing server configuration. Be sure that your configuration meets the recommended hardware minimums and, if necessary, consult your support provider if you require further assistance. The information found in the Mpssetup.log file would be helpful as well.

333

- **Failed to wait for process termination.**
  - This indicates a process was ended unexpectedly by the system. In this case you will want to get more help from the support team and be sure to have the Mpssetup.log file available when you call.
- **Load of dynamic-link library filename failed returning value.**
  - This happens when a .dll file is either missing or failed to load. The best practice here is to check that the .dll file is located in the Setup share path and run Setup again. If the file is missing altogether, you will need to get another copy of the Setup files.
- **Out of memory.**
- In this case, you have insufficient memory on the server to run Setup. Check the minimum required memory and, if you have enough memory installed, simply restart the computer and close down all other applications. Normally, all applications should be shut down before installing Proxy Server or any other software.
- Proxy Server Setup requires administrator privileges.
  - This happens when you attempt to install the Proxy Server using an account that does not have administrator privileges. Simply log off and log on as an Administrator before running Setup again.
- **Setup cannot access the environment variable: *variablename*.**
  - This error indicates that an environment variable was not defined or needs to be reset. This may be overcome by restarting the machine and attempting to run the Setup program again. Otherwise, you will need to contact technical support for more help.
- **Setup cannot access the file: *filename*.**
  - This error indicates that a file could not be updated during Setup. Check to ensure no files are being held open by other programs and try to run the Setup program again. If this happens again, contact technical support.
- **Setup cannot create the file: *filename*.**
  - This error indicates that a file could not be created during Setup and you should attempt the Setup program again. If this problem continues, contact technical support.
- **Setup cannot access the Registry value: *valuename*.**
  - This error occurs because the Registry could not be updated. It is possible that the Registry entry was not there, but if this continues, contact technical support.

- **Setup cannot create the share:** *sharename.*
  - This error relates to a problem in creating a share on the drive you have chosen. Here you should check all the basics (space, rights, etc . . .) and attempt the Setup again. If this problem continues, contact technical support.
- **Setup cannot delete the Registry entry:** *entryname.*
  - This error occurs when the Registry does not get updated properly by Setup, possibly due to one of the following:
    - An earlier version of Microsoft Proxy Server was installed on the server.
    - There are problems with the Registry itself.
    - Your logon account has limited or restricted access to the server.
  - Be sure that you are using an Administrator account with the right privileges. If the Microsoft Proxy Server 1.0 or 2.0 was previously installed, run Setup again and select Remove All. This will remove all components completely and then you can run the Setup program again. If the same error message appears, check TechNet CD and the Windows NT Server documentation for more information on Registry problems.
- **Setup cannot load protocols to the Registry.** *Error=errornumber.*
  - This happens when the file called Proto.bin is removed from the Setup installation path or when the path suddenly can't be found. This error is only present when you run the Proxy Server Setup from a network share path created by using files copied from the Proxy Server compact disc. The solution is to copy the file Proto.bin to the network share point right from the Proxy Server compact disc.
- **Setup cannot open or create the Registry entry:** *filename.*
  - This error occurs when the Registry does not get updated properly by Setup, possibly due to one of the following:
    - An earlier version of Microsoft Proxy Server was installed on the server.
    - There are problems with the Registry itself.
    - Your logon account has limited or restricted access to the server.
  - Be sure that you are using an Administrator account and the proper rights are in place on the drive you have selected for the install. If Microsoft Proxy Server version 1.0 or 2.0 was previously installed, run Setup again and select Remove All. This will remove all components completely and then you can run the Setup program again. If the same

error message appears, check TechNet CD and the Windows NT Server documentation for more information on Registry problems.

- **Setup cannot set the Registry value: *registryvalue*.**
  - This error occurs when the Registry does not get updated properly by Setup, possibly due to one of the following:
    - An earlier version of Microsoft Proxy Server was installed on the server.
    - There are problems with the Registry itself.
    - Your logon account has limited or restricted access to the server.
  - Be sure that you are using an Administrator account with the right privileges. If Microsoft Proxy Server 1.0 or 2.0 was previously installed, run Setup again and select Remove All. This will remove all components completely and then you can run the Setup program again. If the same error message appears, check TechNet CD and the Windows NT Server documentation for more information on Registry problems.
- **Setup cannot write to the file: *filename*.**
  - This happens when a file could not be updated during Setup. Check and shut down running applications and try to run the Setup program again. If this problem continues, contact technical support.
- **Setup could not access the service *servicename*. Error=*errornumber*.**
  - This error happens when the Microsoft Proxy Server Setup is not able to complete because of problems in accessing other installed Internet services. Contact technical support and have the Mpssetup.log file available when you call.
- **Setup could not configure the name service.**
  - This error happens when Microsoft Proxy Server Setup was not able to configure a specific service. Check the TechNet CD for the service in question. Determine if the named service should be running or if it was used for another application that was shut down to accomplish the installation. If necessary, contact technical support with the information from the Mpssetup.log file.
- **Setup could not create the directory *directoryname*. Error=*errornumber*.**
  - This is likely when Setup cannot create a specific directory and usually indicates that the disk drive is full. Check and make sure you have sufficient available disk space.

- **Setup could not create link to *name. Error=errornumber.***
  - This error is found when Setup cannot create the named link, likely when the disk drive is full or when there are other file system errors or inability to write to the drive. Check and make sure you have sufficient available disk space and ensure the integrity of the drive or RAID Array. Consult the TechNet CD and, if necessary, contact technical support.
- **Setup could not create the name service.**
  - This error is the result of Microsoft Proxy Server Setup's inability to create the named service. Contact your support provider for further assistance. Be sure to have information from the Mpssetup.log file available when you call.
- **Setup could not delete the name service.**
  - This error happens when Microsoft Proxy Server Setup is not able to delete the named service. Contact your support provider for further assistance. Be sure to have information from the Mpssetup.log file available when you call.
- **Setup could not find the IIS virtual root Scripts directory.**
- This error happens when the default Scripts directory that is created by Internet Information Server (C:\InetPub\Scripts) gets removed or renamed. In order to fix this, go to the Management Console or Internet Service Manager and in the WWW service of IIS, on the Directories tab, click Add, and in Directory, type the directory name. Under Virtual Directory, in Alias, type Scripts. Under Access, be sure you have selected the Execute check box.
- Setup could not open the *name service.*
  - This error happens when Microsoft Proxy Server Setup is not able to open the named service. Contact your support provider for further assistance. Be sure to have information from the Mpssetup.log file available when you call.
- **Setup could not start the service *servicename. Error=errornumber.***
  - This happens when the Microsoft Proxy Server Setup cannot start another Internet service. Check to be sure that the service has not been disabled and try to start the service manually using the Management Console or the Internet Service Manager. Check the TechNet CD and try to run the Setup program again. If this does not solve the problem, contact technical support.

- **Setup could not stop the service *servicename* because dependent services are running.**

  - This happens when the Microsoft Proxy Server Setup cannot stop an Internet service that is dependent on another active Internet service. This sometimes happens when services become unstable and can sometimes be overcome by simply rebooting the server. Check to be sure the service can be controlled manually by shutting it down using the Management Console or the Internet Service Manager. Check the TechNet CD and try to run the Setup program again. If this does not solve the problem, contact technical support.

- **Setup could not stop the service *servicename*. *Error=errornumber*.**

  - This happens when another Internet service is active and cannot be stopped by the Microsoft Proxy Server Setup. Check to be sure the service can be controlled manually by shutting it down using the Management Console or the Internet Service Manager. Check the TechNet CD and try to run the Setup program again. If this does not solve the problem, contact technical support.

- **Setup has identified a newer version of Microsoft Proxy Server (*versionnumber*) installed on this computer in *sharename*. To install an older version you must first run *versionnumber's* Setup program and choose Remove All.**

  - This happens when you try to install an earlier version of Microsoft Proxy Server than the version that is installed. You will need to run Setup, select Remove All, and reboot the machine before you can install an earlier version of Microsoft Proxy Server.

- **This software can only be installed on a computer with an Internet Information Server installation that includes the WWW service.**

  - Microsoft Proxy Server requires that the WWW service for Internet Information Server (IIS) version 2.0 or higher be installed. You must run Internet Information Server Setup. Once IIS is installed, you will be able to install Proxy Server by running the Microsoft Proxy Server Setup again.

- **This software can only be installed on Windows NT Server version 4.0 build *buildnumber* or later.**

  - This happens when you have attempted to install Microsoft Proxy Server onto a preliminary release of Windows NT Server 4.0 that does not support this release of Microsoft Proxy Server. First be sure that Windows NT Server 4.0 is the current release and run Microsoft Proxy Server Setup again.

- **This software can only be installed on a computer running Windows NT Server version 4.0 or later.**

  - This happens when you have attempted to install Microsoft Proxy Server onto an earlier version of Windows NT Server. Here, you must first install or upgrade to Windows NT Server 4.0 and run Microsoft Proxy Server Setup again.

- **Unattended Server Setup failed.**

  - This error happens when you incorrectly enter the compact disc key number on the command line or use improper command syntax. Check TechNet CD for the correct format such as: stpwrapp /sms /k "CDkeynumber." If the problem persists, the key number may not be recognized as valid. Contact Microsoft Technical Support to obtain further assistance or a new key number.

- **Use of dynamic-link library filename failed returning *value*.**

  - This error occurs when the named .dll file failed an operation. The file may be not be present or may be corrupt. Here you will need to make certain that the named .dll file is found in the Setup share path for Microsoft Proxy Server. If the file is in the path then try to run the Setup program again. If the problem persists, you should contact technical support.

- **WSA Startup failed. *Error=errornumber*.**

  - This error happens when there is an error in the TCP/IP services initialization. You will want to review the TCP/IP configuration and make sure that the settings are valid. Also check the TechNet CD.

Run-Time Messages

Web Proxy Service Event Messages

Web Proxy Service event messages, including those for Microsoft Proxy Server arrays and chains, are in the Windows NT system event log under the source names WebProxyServer and WebProxyLog.

The Web Proxy service returns the following event messages:

- **HTTP/1.0 500 server error (an attempt has been made to operate on an impersonation token by a thread that is not currently impersonating a client).**

  - This error occurs when changes are made to the home directory properties for the WWW service and the Web Proxy service is also in use. If the home directory setting is changed to specify a remote UNC path name (that is, \\servername\sharename), and not a currently mapped local drive path (such as D:\InetPub\Wwwroot), all requests made through the Web Proxy service fail.

- To correct the problem, stop and restart the WWW and Web Proxy services by using Internet Service Manager. An alternative is to create a virtual directory entry instead of altering the default local drive path for the home directory when adding directory names that use remote UNC path names.

- **HTTP/1.0 500 server error (-*number*).**

  - This error occurs when Windows NT challenge/response authentication is used on Microsoft Proxy Server to validate Web proxy clients. Microsoft Proxy Server uses the password authentication specified by the WWW service to validate Web Proxy clients. Check the form of password authentication in use for the WWW service by using Internet Service Manager. As a temporary alternative, select Basic (cleartext) authentication and report the error to your support provider.

- **HTTP/1.0 500 server error (the specified module could not be found).**

  - This error occurs when certain Proxy Server binaries are not installed in the correct directory for Proxy Server scripts. Verify the location of your IIS scripts directory. Make sure there is a Proxy subdirectory under this directory location.

- **115 — W3Proxy failed to start because the system time is incorrect.**

  - The date and time on the server's system clock are not correct and must be adjusted before the service can be restarted.

  - Reset the time and date for the server using the Date/Time application. You can double-click the time display located on the Taskbar or, in the Control Panel, double-click Date/Time.

- **116 — W3Proxy failed to start because the Microsoft Proxy Server RC program expired on date. Please contact Microsoft about this product.**

  - You are using a release candidate version of Proxy Server. Contact Microsoft Technical Support to obtain the final version.

- **118 — The Web Proxy service was halted. The 60-day free evaluation period has expired.**

  - You are using the 60-day evaluation version of Proxy Server. Contact Microsoft to obtain the full version of Proxy Server.

- **125 — The Web Proxy service received number requests from the Internet port during the past number seconds while Internet publishing was disabled.**

- If Proxy Server publishing is disabled, this error message displays the number of requests from the Internet during the specified time, in seconds.
- **126 — The Web Proxy service configuration has been modified *number* time(s) during the past *number* seconds.**
  - The number of times the Web Proxy service configuration has been changed during the specified duration.
- **129 — The Web Proxy service is continued.**
  - The Web Proxy service has been successfully restarted.

Web Proxy Cache Event Messages

Web Proxy service cache event messages are in the Windows NT system event log under the source name WebProxyCache.

The Web Proxy service returns the following cache event messages. They are in numerical order:

If caching fails to occur, check that the available disk space on the cache drive is sufficient and that the disk drive allocated for caching is not full. If necessary, increase the disk cache space.

- **111 — Web Proxy cache initialization failed due to an incorrect configuration. Please use the administration utility or manually edit the Registry to correct the error and restart the service.**
  - Use Internet Service Manager to stop the WWW service. This also stops the Web Proxy service. To correct the cache settings in the Web Proxy service, on the Caching tab, click Advanced, and then click Reset Defaults. Restart the WWW service. If initialization still fails, run Setup and select the Reinstall option.
  - If the problem continues, repeat the previous steps to stop the WWW service again, and then delete the cache directories before running Setup and selecting the Reinstall option.
- **112 — Web Proxy cache corrected a corrupted or old format URL cache by removing all or part of the cache's contents.**
  - Some cached objects have been deleted or removed from the cache and no further action is required. If the message reoccurs, you can type chkdsk /r at the command prompt to locate disk errors and recover readable information for the disk drive.

- **113 — Web Proxy cache failed to initialize the URL cache on disk.**
  - Use Internet Service Manager to stop the Web Proxy service. To correct the cache settings in the Web Proxy service, go to the Caching tab, click Advanced, and then click Reset Defaults. Restart the Web Proxy service. If initialization still fails, run Setup and select the Reinstall option.
  - If the problem continues, you can also try typing chkdsk /r at the command prompt to recover readable information, or delete the cache directories and move the cache to a different drive location.
  - You must stop the WWW service before you can delete Web Proxy cache directories.
- **114 — The hard disk used by the Web Proxy server to cache popular URLs is full. Space needs to be freed, or the Web Proxy cache needs to be reconfigured to resume normal operation.**
  - Delete cached objects from the hard disk.

Web Proxy Array and Chain Event Messages

Proxy Server array and chain event messages are in the Windows NT system event log under the source names WebProxyServer and WebProxyLog.

The Web Proxy service returns the following Proxy Server array and chain event messages. They are in numerical order:

- **130 — The Web Proxy service detected that the upstream proxy *servername* is down.**
  - An upstream Proxy Server computer is unavailable. Use Internet Service Manager to determine the reason the upstream server is unavailable and restart the server if necessary.
- **131 — The Web Proxy service detected that the upstream proxy *servername* is back up.**
  - The upstream Proxy Server computer is available.
- **132 — The Web Proxy service detected that the array member *servername* is down.**
  - A Proxy Server array member computer is unavailable. Use Internet Service Manager to determine the reason the array member computer is unavailable and restart the server if necessary.
- **133 — The Web Proxy service detected that the array member *servername* is back up.**
  - The Proxy Server array member computer is available.

- 139 — Proxy Server *servername* requires proxy-to-proxy authentication. Proxy Server *servername* is not configured with this type of authentication.

  - If there is an array of Proxy Server computers, or if they are chained, they must authenticate communication between servers.

- **Configure the identified Proxy Server computer for authentication.**

WinSock Proxy Service Event Messages

WinSock Proxy service event messages are in the Windows NT system event log under the source names WinSockProxy and WinSockProxyLog.

   The WinSock Proxy service returns the following event messages. They are in numerical order:

- 1 — **The WinSock Proxy service failed to initialize. The data is the internal error code.**

  - The service was unable to process the client request, possibly because of missing system files or configuration settings.

  - Use Internet Service Manager to restart the WinSock Proxy service. If this message appears again, run Setup and select Reinstall to restore missing files and settings.

- 2 — **The WinSock Proxy service failed to initialize the network. The data is the error.**

  - The service was unable to process the client request, possibly because of missing or corrupted network settings.

  - Stop and restart the network and all other Internet services on the computer running the WinSock Proxy service. If the condition persists, check for physical problems, such as cabling or termination faults on the local network segment.

- 3 — **The WinSock Proxy service started.**

  - Self explanatory

- 4 — **The WinSock Proxy service cannot initialize due to a shortage of available memory. The data is the error.**

  - The Proxy Server computer cannot initialize the service because of lack of available memory on the server.

  - Check for available memory and memory usage on the server. To view server memory usage, click Start, point to Administrative Tools (Common), click Windows NT Diagnostics, and then click the Memory tab. If available memory is low or if further memory errors occur, close all applications that are not required on the server or consider adding memory to the server computer.

- **5 — User username at host hostname has timed out after number seconds of inactivity.**
  - The WinSock Proxy service discontinued the listed connection because no response was received within current time-out limits.
  - If you are using the WinSock Proxy service with Remote Access Service (RAS), try increasing the RAS time-out parameters. For more information on increasing time-outs or configuring RAS parameters, see your Windows NT Server 4.0 documentation.

- **6 — The WinSock Proxy service cannot initialize performance counters. The data is the error.**
  - System dynamic-link libraries (DLLs) needed for performance monitoring of the service may be missing or cannot be located on the system.
  - Check that the required DLL, Wspsperf.dll, is available in the Windows system directory, usually C:\Winnt\System32. If it is missing, run Setup and select Reinstall to repeat the last installation, restore the missing DLL file, and reinitialize service settings.

- **7 — The WinSock Proxy service has failed due to a shortage of available memory. The data is the number of connections.**
  - The Proxy Server computer cannot support additional connections for the server because of a lack of available resources. Check the number of connections in use on the server and server memory usage.

- **9 — The performance counters DLL for the WinSock Proxy service failed because the function *functionname* failed. The data is the error.**
  - System DLLs needed for performance monitoring of the service are missing or cannot be located on the system.
  - Confirm that the required DLL, Wspsperf.dll, is in the Windows system directory (usually C:\Winnt\System32). If it is missing, run Setup and select Reinstall to restore the missing DLL file and reinitialize service settings.

- **10 — The WinSock Proxy service failed to initialize because of missing or corrupted Registry settings. The data is the error.**
  - The WinSock Proxy service was unable to process the client request, possibly because of missing or corrupted Registry settings.
  - Use Internet Service Manager to restart the WinSock Proxy service. If the error continues, run Setup and select Reinstall to restore miss-

ing files and settings. If the condition persists, restore the Registry or affected keys on the server.

- **11 — The WinSock Proxy service failed to bind its socket to unknown port *portnumber*.**

  - The requested service port is already in use, or data loss might have resulted from a large number of packet collisions on the local network segment.

  - Monitor the application service that failed for the server and the client. You can also monitor traffic on your internal network.

- **12 — Client from unknown attempts to access WinSock Proxy service by using control protocol version *versionnumber*. The server supports version *versionnumber*.**

  - Control protocol version specified is not supported by Proxy Server.

- **13, 14 — The WinSock Proxy service requires Windows NT 4.0 Server.**

  - The WinSock Proxy service cannot run on previous versions of Windows NT Server (including 4.0 Beta versions).

  - You must have Windows NT 4.0 Server with Service Pack 3 or later installed on your computer before you can install Proxy Server version 2.0.

- **15 — The WinSock Proxy service failed to load security DLL.**

  - The server requires a security DLL to be loaded and active in order to process clients. The required DLL is missing or cannot be found.

  - Check that Security.dll is located in the Windows NT system directory, usually C:\Winnt\System32, and then restart the WinSock Proxy service.

- **16 — The WinSock Proxy service failed to determine network addresses.**

  - The IP addresses used to establish a connection cannot be located on either the internal or external network.

  - Verify that the Local Address Table (LAT), C:\Msp\Msplat.txt, is correct. Confirm that there are no discrepancies between the LAT that is in use for the server and the LAT in use by the client by manually copying the LAT from the server to the client. If the error persists, verify that the correct IP address settings are in use for the client.

- **17 — Incorrect network configuration. None of the server's addresses are internal.**

- An IP address configured for the internal network adapter for the server needs to be included within the LAT for the server.
- Replace or modify the LAT by using the Local Address Table Configuration dialog box or by editing the file C:\Msp\Msplat.txt. It is recommended that you use Internet Service Manager to make changes to the LAT.

- **18 — The WinSock Proxy service failed to start because the system time is incorrect.**

  - The date and time on the server's system clock are not correct and must be adjusted before the service is started.

- **19 — The WinSock Proxy service failed to start because the Microsoft Proxy Server RC program expired on *date*. Please contact Microsoft for details about this product.**

  - You are using either a beta or a release candidate version of Proxy Server. Contact Microsoft for information on how to obtain the final version.

- **20 — Warning: the Microsoft Proxy Server RC program expired on *date*. Please contact Microsoft for details about this product.**

  - You are using either a beta or a release candidate version of Proxy Server. Contact Microsoft for information on how to obtain the final version.

- **36 — Address *address* is missing from the configuration file.**

  - If you are managing this file manually, you need to add the missing IP addresses. If you are not managing this file manually, rebuild your addresses by using the Local Address Table Configuration dialog box in Internet Service Manager.

In addition to the Windows NT system event log messages, you might experience the following problems with the WinSock Proxy Service:

- Inability of a user to access or administer different protocols for the WinSock Proxy service.
  - By default, the Administrator user logon account is the only account that can access any port, regardless of port configuration. To allow other users to access or administer protocols or assigned ports:
    - Check the LAT to make sure that the user computer's IP address is included.
    - Use Internet Service Manager to check that the protocol has been added.

- Use Internet Service Manager to check that the user (or a group the user belongs to) has been granted permission to use the protocol.

- **Ping and Tracert fail to work reliably with the WinSock Proxy service.**

  - Ping and Tracert are two standard utilities used to assist in troubleshooting TCP/IP-related problems on your network. Because the Ping and Tracert utilities operate at the transport layer by using Internet Control Message Protocol (ICMP), which does not use Windows Sockets, they cannot be redirected by the Proxy Server computer. If you use Ping or Tracert to test Proxy connections, the results might be invalid.

  - Ping uses Windows Sockets only when looking up the domain host name of the server you are trying to ping. Once the Domain Name System (DNS) name lookup has completed, Ping uses ICMP for connection. If you have an internal DNS server, make sure its IP address is contained in the Local Address Table (LAT), C:\Msp\Msplat.txt. Also, check your Ping utility program. If you are using an application to ping that requires the use of a third-party Windows Sockets DLL, ICMP ping results may be unpredictable.

- **The WinSock Proxy service has problems with other third-party TCP/IP stacks.**

  - Currently, Proxy Server has not been tested with other third-party TCP/IP implementations. Use of a third-party stack may produce unpredictable results.

- **Server domain name lookups fail on the local network.**

  - The WinSock Proxy Service redirects all DNS lookups to the computer running Proxy Server. If you have an internal DNS server, make sure its IP address is contained in the LAT, C:\Msp\Msplat.txt. Domain names that do not contain dots are considered internal names to Proxy Server.

Socks Proxy Service Event Messages

The Socks Proxy service creates two log entries for each successful connection: one when the connection is established and one when the connection is terminated. When a connection is terminated, the number of bytes sent and received is recorded. Normal and abortive connection termination have individual result codes so you can determine the reason for the termination.

Socks Proxy service event messages are in the Windows NT system event log under the source names SocksProxy and SocksProxyLog.

Packet Filtering Event Messages

Packet filtering event messages are in the Windows NT system event log under the source name PacketFilterLog.

Event messages 125 through 134 are Proxy Server event messages for administration only. They are in the Windows NT system event log under the source name MSProxyAdmin.

- **134 — The proxy PF log cannot allocate memory.**
  - There is not enough memory in the computer to transfer information into the packet filtering log. Check for available memory and memory usage on the server. To view server memory usage, click Start, point to Administrative Programs (Common), click Windows NT Diagnostics, and then click the Memory tab. If the available memory is low or if further memory errors occur, close all applications that are not required on the server or consider adding memory to the server computer.
- **135 — The proxy PF log service cannot fetch the log contents.**
  - The packet filtering log service cannot find the logs on the computer. Check to see that logging is configured properly and that the correct name of the log file is entered.

Logging Event Messages

The following event mlessages pertain to logging for all the Proxy Server services. They are in numerical order:

- **102 — The server cannot load Odbc32.dll for SQL logging due to the following error: number. The data is the error code.**
  - The specified dynamic-link library (DLL) cannot be located in the current system path.
  - Verify the existence of the Odbc32.dll file in the Windows system directory, usually C:\Winnt\System32.
- **103 — The server cannot open the ODBC Data Source *sourcename*, Table: *tablename*, under User Name: *username*. The ODBC error is: *number*. The data is the error code.**
  - The ODBC specified data source cannot be opened because it does not exist or because the table and user name information are incorrect.

- Use Internet Service Manager to verify that information in ODBC Data Source Name, Table, User name, and Password is correctly entered on the Logging tab for the Web Proxy, WinSock Proxy, and Socks Proxy services. Check that the ODBC database is ready to accept logging.

- **104 — The parameters specified for logging are too long. Field: *fieldname*, Data Given: *data*.**

  - The database table used for service logging requires an adjustment. Either the field is not long enough to contain the data, or the field type is incorrectly set in the database design.

  - Check the database configuration to see that the table fields and data types declared for each field are entered correctly.

- **106 — The server failed to create a log context. The data is the error code.**

  - Information for configuring logging may be missing or incorrect.

  - Verify that logging information is entered correctly in the Service Properties dialog box by using Internet Service Manager. On the Logging tab, verify that the database is using the same settings for data source name, table name, and user name.

- **107 — The server failed to log information. The log object was never created, possibly due to the wrong configuration.**

  - Information for configuring service logging may be missing or incorrect.

  - Using Internet Service Manager, verify that the logging information is correctly entered on the Logging tab in the Web Proxy, WinSock Proxy, and Socks Proxy services. Also verify that the database is using the same settings for data source name, table name, and user name.

- **108 — The server was unable to find the log file directory *directoryname*. The data is the error code.**

  - The log file directory is either missing or incorrectly set for the Web Proxy, WinSock Proxy, or Socks Proxy services.

  - Use Internet Service Manager to verify the log file directory is set correctly on the Logging tab. Verify that the specified directory exists and re-create the directory if necessary.

- **109 — The server cannot continue request logging due to failure indicated by the error code in the data. Additionally, the server received error message: *number*.**

- An error in service logging occurred for the Web Proxy, WinSock Proxy, or Socks Proxy service.
- Contact Microsoft Technical Support for further assistance. Be sure to note the exact message text and the number returned with the message.
- **110 — The server resumed request logging.**
  - The server resumed service logging without intervention.
  - No further action is required.

RAS Event Messages

The following event messages pertain to the Remote Access Service (RAS) and Proxy Server Auto Dial. They are in numerical order:

- **136 — Proxy dialout connection failed.**
  - Check that AutoDial and RAS are configured properly.
- **142 — A dialout to the Internet failed.**
  - The Remote Access Service cannot dial out to the Internet. Either a chained Proxy Server computer is unavailable, or the connection to your Internet service provider (ISP) is unavailable.

Miscellaneous Event Messages

The following event messages are of a miscellaneous nature, and may also apply to the WWW, FTP, and Gopher services of Internet Information Server (IIS).

- **100 — The server cannot log on to the Windows NT account *accountname* due to the following error: number. The data is the error code.**
  - The server cannot log on to the Windows NT user account. Check that the user name and password are correct and try again.
- **101 — The server cannot add the virtual root *rootname* for the directory *directoryname* due to the following error: number. The data is the error code.**
  - The directory name is not recognized for the server volume specified in the virtual root mapping.
  - Check that the directory name entered for drive mapping is correct.

- 105 — The server cannot register the administration tool discovery information. The administration tool may not be able to see this server. The data is the error code.

  - The server failed to register on the network. Check for a server name conflict on the Internet.

- 117 — Warning: The Microsoft Proxy Server RC program expired on date. Please contact Microsoft for details about this product.

  - You are using either a beta or a release candidate version of Proxy Server. Contact Microsoft for information on how to obtain the final version.

- 137 — Some of this information may be out of date because of network problems.

  - If the network has been unavailable, some of the Proxy Server configuration information may be out of date.

Client Setup Messages

This section shows event messages returned by the Proxy Server client Setup program. Messages are listed in alphabetical order.

- **Call to LoadString with ID *Number* failed.**
  - An unexplained error in Setup occurred.
  - If you see this error message consult with your technical support team or network administrator for further assistance. Be sure to have the information from the Mpssetup.log file.

- **Call to LoadString with ID *Number* failed. Error=*ErrorNumber*.**
  - An unexplained error in Setup occurred.
  - If you see this error message consult with your technical support team or network administrator for further assistance. Be sure to have the information from the Mpssetup.log file.

- **Instances of Winsock DLLs appear in both the System and Windows directories. Setup cannot proceed until there is only one TCP/IP installation.**
  - You see this message if setup found multiple copies of Winsock.dll. Only one copy of this file can be located within the Windows or System directory.
  - To correct this problem you may want to delete or rename the additional copies of this file from the Windows and System directories and rerun Setup. If you have multiple TCP/IP installations on this

computer, contact your technical support team or network administrator for assistance.

- **Please set a description of the internal network.**
  - This message shows that the Local Address Table (LAT) file is not present on your computer. This file is named Msplat.txt and is typically installed in C:\Wspclnt.
  - If you see this message, make sure you have sufficient disk space. Also ensure the logon account you are using is permitted to write to C:\Wspclnt\Msplat.txt. Also, ensure this file has at least one valid range of address pairs that identify internal IP network clients.
- **Setup cannot create the file:** *Filename.* **Error=***ErrorNumber.*
  - This error message means that the file cannot be copied onto your computer.
  - Check for available disk space and permissions, or contact your technical support team for further assistance.
- **Setup cannot locate the Microsoft Internet Explorer 1.***x* **location.**
  - You see this message if the installed path to your browser application cannot be located.
  - This is not a critical error — you can continue running Setup, but you need to manually configure your browser for use with the Web Proxy service.
- **Setup cannot locate the Microsoft Internet Explorer 2.0 location.**
  - The installed path to your browser application cannot be located.
  - This is not a critical error — you can continue running Setup, but you need to manually configure your browser for use with the Web Proxy service.
- **Setup cannot locate the Netscape Navigator location.**
  - The installed path to your browser application cannot be located.
  - You can continue running Setup, but you need to manually configure your browser for use with the Web Proxy service.
- **Setup cannot set the INI value:** *Initialization Value.*
  - This error means that one of the .ini files might be corrupted or missing on this computer.
  - If you see this error message, try running Setup again. If the problem continues, contact your technical support team or network administrator.

- **Setup could not access System.ini. Error=*ErrorNumber*.**

  - The System.ini file might be missing.

  - Make sure that the System.ini file exists. If necessary, consult with your technical support team or network administrator. Be sure to record the error number displayed with this message and have information from the Mpssetup.log file available when you call.

- **Setup could not close file handle to System.ini. Error=*ErrorNumber*.**

  - This error might be caused by insufficient file handles.

  - If you see this message, you might be able to solve the problem by increasing the number of file handles in the FILES= statement in Config.sys. You need to restart the computer and rerun the Setup again.

- **Setup could not delete the file *File Name*.**

  - This error message can indicate that the file is in use by another application or system resource.

  - Close all other applications and run Setup again.

- **Setup could not delete the file *File Name*. Error=*Error Number*.**

  - The named file might be in use by another application or system resource.

  - Close all other applications and run Setup again.

- **Setup could not find the file Wsock32.dll on your system. Please consult the documentation for your system.**

  - If you are using Windows NT clients, make sure that the Wsock32.dll file is located in C:\Winnt\System32.

  - For further details on Wsock32.dll, consult your Microsoft Windows documentation or contact your technical support team or network administrator.

- **Setup could not rename the file *FileName1* back to *FileName2*.**

  - This message is generated if setup cannot complete a system file update that is needed for installation to continue. Critical system files might be missing, corrupt or incorrectly named.

  - If you encountered this error message, run Setup and click **Remove All** to completely remove all components of the previous version. The rerun the Setup program again. If the message still occurs, try renaming the following files in the Windows System directory:

    - For Windows 95 or Windows NT clients, rename _msrws32.dll to Wsock32.dll.

- For Windows 3.1 clients, rename _msrws16.dll to Winsock.dll.
- Run Setup again.

- **Setup could not rename the file *FileName1* to *FileName2*.**
  - Setup cannot rename a file that is needed for installation to continue.
  - Try running Setup again. If that fails, contact your technical support team or network administrator.

- **Setup could not save the Local Address Table.**
  - The LAT file cannot be saved to disk on the computer. The file is named Msplat.txt and is installed in C:\Wspclnt.
  - If you see this error message make sure that this file is not already installed and in use by another application (such as a text editor). Make sure you have enough disk space and that that you have appropriate permissions to write to C:\Mspclnt\Msplat.txt.

- **Setup failed creating the temporary file.**
  - This error is caused if Setup cannot create a file needed temporarily for installation, possibly because of temporary files left from a previous installation attempt.
  - To work around this issue, delete temporary files and then run Setup again. If this fails, delete all files starting with an underscore (_) in your Windows and System directories, and run Setup again.

- **Setup failed to create a process. Error=*ErrorNumber*.**
  - Setup failed to create a process and might require system program files that are not present on this computer.
  - If you see this error on a Windows NT client, check that the files Router.exe, Lodctr.exe, and Unlodctr.exe are present in the System directory. The Setup program requires these files.

- **Setup failed to set Microsoft Internet Explorer 1.*x* proxy settings. You need to do this manually.**
  - This message means that your browser was not updated properly.
  - You must manually configure your browser for access to the server.

- **Setup failed to set Microsoft Internet Explorer 2.0 proxy settings. You need to do this manually.**
  - This message means that your browser was not updated properly.
  - You must manually configure your browser for access to the server.

- **Setup failed to set Netscape Navigator proxy settings. You need to do this manually.**

- This message means that your browser was not updated properly.
- You must manually configure your browser for access to the server.

- **Setup failed to examine the System directory.**
  - This message appears when the Setup program cannot examine or locate the Windows or Winnt system directory on the computer.
  - To solve this problem contact your technical support team or network administrator for further assistance.

- **Setup failed to examine the Windows directory.**
  - The Setup program cannot examine or locate the Windows or Winnt directory on the computer.
  - Contact your technical support team or network administrator for further assistance.

- **Setup failed to write a line to _mssetup.bat.**
  - This error indicates Setup cannot write needed changes to your Windows configuration files. This could be because these files are currently in use by another application, or because of lack of disk space.
  - To solve this problem, make sure all other applications are closed and that there is enough disk space.

- **Setup failed to write a line to Win.ini.**
  - You see this message when Setup is unable to write changes to your Windows configuration files. This could be caused by running applications which lock these files or because of lack of disk space.
  - Make sure all other applications are closed and that there is enough disk space before you run Setup again.

- **You must reboot to complete the previous installation before running Setup again.**
  - This message is shown when you try to run the setup program for the second time immediately after proxy client installation. A restart of the computer is required to complete the installation.
  - Restart the computer to complete the previous client Setup. You might also need to run Setup again to resolve errors or complete updates to system configuration settings.

- **Your system may be in an inconsistent state. Please run Setup again.**
  - This error indicates that Setup cannot complete file updating that is needed for installation to continue. System files might be missing or incorrectly named.

- To work around this problem, run the Setup program and click Remove All to completely remove all components of the previous version. If the message still occurs, try renaming the following files in the Windows System directory:
  - For Windows 95 or Windows NT clients, rename _msrws32.dll to Wsock32.dll.
  - For Windows 3.1 clients, rename _msrws16.dll to Winsock.dll.
  - After you rename the files, run Setup again.

Client Run-Time Errors

Winsock Proxy Client Errors

After you install the client software, you will notice a WinSock Proxy diagnostic utility in the Mspclnt directory on the client. This utility gives you the configuration information that is useful when you troubleshoot WinSock Proxy problems. The 32-bit version of this utility is called Chkwsp32. For computers running 16-bit operating systems the utility name is Chkwsp16.

To run the WinSock Proxy diagnostic utility:

- On the client computer, from a command prompt, change to the Mspclnt directory.

- In the command prompt type chkwsp32 -f.

- Chkwps32 checks connectivity with the Proxy Server computer. If the connection succeeds, the "Client control protocol matches the server control protocol" message is displayed. You can use FTP or Telnet for further testing.

- Should you receive a message that the client is not installed properly, you may want to check the following issues:
    - Check that the configuration information is present in the System.ini file in the [Microsoft Proxy Service] section, "Configuration Location" key.
    - Check that the WinSock DLL can be found, and that this is the file installed by the client Setup program. Check that you have only one

copy of the WinSock DLL. It must be located in the Windows directory.

The following event messages are from the WinSock Proxy service:

- **The WinSock Proxy service has denied client authentication.**
  - This occurs if the account password or user name is incorrect or has expired.
  - If you encounter this problem, verify that the user name and password are correct. Additionally, check that the password never expires in User Manager for Domains. If the password is allowed to expire, the service or server application does not work through the Proxy Server.
- **The WinSock Proxy service client authentication has failed.**
  - This error message means that the client authentication process was terminated on the client side.
  - To troubleshoot this problem you should create a section in the Wspcfg.ini file on the computer running the problem service. In the Wspcfg.ini file, use the ForceCredentials entry to override the default user. Use the Credtool command-line utility that is provided with Proxy Server to store the alternative user credentials in local security storage. The credentials stored apply to the account that is used for authentication between the server application and Proxy Server.
- **The WinSock client application requires NTLMSSP.**
  - This error message tells you that a Windows NT service running as a WinSock Proxy client application is dependent on running the Windows NT LM Security Support Provider (NTLMSSP) service.
  - You can create a dependency on the NTLMSSP service by using the Service Controller (SC) command line utility. For information on the SC utility, see your Windows NT Resource Kit documentation.
- **A cross-device link exists.**
  - This error message means that a device on the remote server system that is required for this operation cannot be accessed for the current connection.
  - To troubleshoot this problem verify that the device is available and not already in use by other sessions.
- **A data source on the remote server could not be obtained.**
  - If you see this message the data source is incorrectly configured or not available.

- To troubleshoot this problem check that the data source has been correctly configured and has not been renamed or relocated. Consult with your database administrator to verify that the remote database server is available.

- **A resource deadlock would occur.**

  - The operation cannot be completed because sufficient resources do not exist or are not available on the system.

  - Close other programs to free resources or restart the system. If the problem continues, contact your technical support team to check your computer's configuration.

- **Accessing a corrupted share.**

  - This error message indicates that there might be disk errors on the remote drive. In some cases, the file system might be of an unrecognized or unsupported type for the current application or platform.

  - You may want to check that the remote disk drive is not corrupted, and review the installation requirements for the current program.

- **Address is already in use.**

  - This error message indicates an addressing conflict. This means that the requested address cannot be obtained because it is used by another system in the network.

  - To work around this problem, check the network address settings for the client. You may try to assign a different fixed network address to the client. If the problem persists, contact your network administrator for resolving address duplication on the local network.

- **Address family is not supported by the protocol family.**

  - If you see this message the network address provided is not correct or is not supported for the local network.

  - Make sure that the address is in the correct format. If the problem continues, report the problem to your network administrator.

- **Advertise error encountered.**

  - You see this message because network or routing problems prevent the shared resource to be properly advertised. Packet filtering may also cause this error.

  - Check that the network is on-line. The next step is to verify that any required routing advertising protocols, such as Routing Information Protocol (RIP) or Service Advertising Protocol (SAP), are implemented. You can use other utilities to verify that the shared resource can be accessed or browsed from the network.

- **An error in type registration occurred.**
  - This error indicates that a software error occurred.
  - It is recommended that you contact your technical support team and report the problem.
- **An interrupted system call was received.**
  - This error means that the current proxy connection was interrupted, and the socket operation did not complete as expected. The problem might be the current program or a temporary problem or condition on the network.
  - Check the network connection for the computer or try reconnecting. If the problem continues, report the problem to your network administrator. If other network functions are stable and working, report the problem to the supplier of the current program.
- **An invalid exchange was made.**
  - This error means that there may be an error in the data, or an exchange between the remote server and the client has been attempted that is not allowed within the software.
  - Reenter the data and retry the operation. If the problem continues, contact the supplier of the current program to report the problem and obtain a fix or workaround.
- **Argument list too long.**
  - This error means that the requested operation contained additional information or parameters that cannot be processed correctly through the current connection.
  - Retry the request. If the problem continues, contact the software supplier for the current program or report the problem to your technical support team.
- **Attempting to execute a shared library.**
  - This error means that an incorrect file type was specified for execution on the system, possibly because a required shared library is missing.
  - If you know or can check the specific .DLL files needed for the program you are trying to run, verify them. Otherwise, try reinstalling the current program to restore missing libraries or components. If the problem continues, contact the software vendor for an update, patch, or workaround.
- **Attempting to link in too many libraries.**
  - This error means the current operation is attempting to link in libraries that are not permitted by the system or program.

- Check that the hardware platform in use for the software program meets the manufacturer's requirements for installation and that any special additional software and configuration changes have been followed, including updates, patches or workarounds. If the problem continues, contact the software supplier for the current program to obtain an update, fix, or workaround for the problem.

- **Bad address encountered.**

  - This error means that the network address used for the remote server is invalid for the current network.

  - Check to see that the address is typed correctly and that your computer can reach the distant network address from within the local network. If this problem continues, report the problem to the distant end network administrator for resolution.

- **Bad file number encountered.**

  - This means that an error occurred in the software or in accessing the file system.

  - Retry the operation. If the problem continues, report it to the supplier of the current program.

- **Bad font file format used.**

  - This error means that a font file contains incorrect format information or is outdated.

  - Report this problem to the software vendor and obtain an updated font file or workaround.

- **Bad network address encountered.**

  - This error means that the network address used for the remote server is invalid for the current network.

  - Before retrying, check to see that the address is typed correctly, and that you can reach the remote network address from the local network. If the problem continues, report the problem to the network administrator for the remote server.

- **Bad protocol option used.**

  - This error means that the software program has selected an unsupported protocol for use with this operation.

  - First, check the software program for protocol settings. Next, review the documentation included with the program on how to check or change the current protocol settings. If this problem continues, contact the supplier of the software program.

- **Can't access a needed shared library.**
  - This error means that the software components installed or called by the current program are missing or corrupted, or that there might be hard drive errors.
  - First, retry the operation; if no change in the error is found, then re-install the software program and retry the operation. If the problem continues, contact the software vendor to obtain an update, fix, or software workaround.
- **Cannot assign requested address.**
  - This error means that a request for a server-provided address was not honored. The address might already be in use elsewhere on the network, or there might not be addresses left to assign for the local sub-network.
  - To correct this error first check the network address configuration to verify that the client is configured for dynamic addressing, or assign a different address for the client. For networks using Dynamic Host Configuration Protocol to assign addressing to client computers, review the scope and make sure that there are spare addresses remaining in the address pool.
- **Channel number is out of range.**
  - This error happens when a port or protocol error has occurred in the program or network environment.
  - To correct this error, check that all ports that provide services are correctly defined for the software program and for the WinSock Proxy service. If the problem continues, contact the software vendor.
- **Communication error in sending.**
  - This error happens when an error occurs in sending information between the remote server and the local client.
  - Retry the requested communication. Restart the application and check for network errors. If the problem continues, and no significant errors on the network are found, report the problem to the software vendor.
- **Computer is not on the network.**
  - This error occurs when the local computer is not connected to the network.
  - To fix this issue, make the necessary connection to the network. The connection must first be made before any requests can be processed.

- **Connection refused.**
  - This error occurs when the remote server refused a connection. This means the server is busy or that excess traffic is on the network.
  - To fix this issue, simply try again. Sometimes trying again later is the easiest method of solving this; otherwise, if the connection is still refused, contacting your network administrator will be required.

- **Connection reset by peer.**
  - This error occurs when the current connection has been closed by another peer user or peer server process.
  - To fix this issue you should first attempt to reestablish the connection. Report the problem to your network administrator, or check the connection logs for other servers on the network for more information.

- **Connection timed out.**
  - This error occurs when a connection cannot be placed between the client and the remote server within the preset time allowed for a response. No connection was opened.
  - This means that you should verify that the remote server and client are present on the network and that they are properly configured. You should try to increase the connection time-out interval for the current client or software program if there are controls built in that support adjusted time-out values.

- **Cross-mount point achieved.**
  - This error occurs when an error in accessing a device used for the current operation occurred, or the device is already linked elsewhere.
  - To fix this, first restart the system and try that operation again. If this error continues you should contact the software vendor for an update, fix, or workaround.

- **Current version is not supported.**
  - This error occurs when the software program is using a third party or later version of Windows Sockets, which is not supported.
  - First, check to see if the program is using the remote procedure calls that are compatible with Windows Sockets 1.1. Then, if not in use, simply install and use an earlier version of the software program that does support the Windows Sockets 1.1 calls.

- **Destination address required.**
  - This error occurs when either no IP or DNS network address resolution for the remote server was provided.
  - This can sometimes happen when DNS is not available. To resolve, you will need to enter the correct address for the remote server and resubmit the remote command request.
- **Device is not a stream.**
  - This error message occurs when there is an error in the data, or an exchange not allowed within the software has been attempted between the remote server and the client.
  - To fix this issue you would reenter the data and try the operation again. If the problem persists, you will need to report the problem to the software vendor, and obtain a fix or workaround.
- **Directory is not empty.**
  - This error occurs when the Directory cannot be removed. It still contains other files or subdirectories.
  - To fix this, simply move or delete the other remaining files or subdirectories and try the operation again.
- **Disk quota exceeded.**
  - This error occurs when the operation requires the use of additional disk space that is not authorized by the server.
  - To fix this, first cancel the request that caused the error. Once the current disk operation is shut down, next change the file share permissions to allow more space for the current user.
- **EPROCLIM returned.**
  - This error indicates that a software error occurred.
  - First, exit the current software program and restart it. If the problem continues, report the problem to the software vendor.
- **ESTALE returned.**
  - This error occurs when there is an unexplained service error in the current environment.
  - Exit the software program and restart. If the problem persists, report the problem to the software vendor.
- **EUSERS returned.**
  - This indicates a software error.
  - Exit the software program and restart it.

- **Exchange is full.**
  - This indicates an error in the data, or an exchange between the remote server and the client has been attempted that cannot be completed. The system might be too busy to process the request at this time.
  - Retry the operation later. If the problem continues, report the error to the software vendor and obtain a fix or workaround.
- **Executed format error.**
  - This indicates a software error has occurred.
  - Retry the operation later. If the problem continues, report the error to the software vendor and obtain a fix or workaround.
- **Failure in streams buffer allocation.**
  - This indicates that there is insufficient buffer space available to maintain the currently streamed connection.
  - Increase the space allocated for streams buffers on the server.
- **File already exists.**
  - This error occurs when there is an attempt to create or save a file on the remote server that cannot be completed because a file using the same name already exists.
  - Save the new file under a different name, or either delete or rename the old file.
- **File is too large.**
  - This error occurs when a disk restriction did not permit the file operation to be completed. A disk quota might be set for the destination directory, or there is a lack of available space on the targeted drive.
  - Ensure that sufficient hard drive space is available and that no disk quota or write permission restrictions are in effect for the directory.
- **File table has overflowed.**
  - The current operation has exceeded available disk capacity or other resources on the system.
  - Verify that sufficient hard disk space and resources are available on the local system before retrying.
- **Host is down.**
  - The remote host cannot be reached at this time or has been shut down.
  - Verify connections. Contact your network administrator to confirm status of the remote host.

- **Host is unreachable.**
  - The remote host cannot be reached at this time or has been shut down.
  - Verify connections. Contact your network administrator to confirm the status of the remote host.
- **Host was not found.**
  - The requested remote server cannot be located.
  - The server might be off-line, renamed, or relocated. Try again later, or check with the server administrator to see if the server is off-line or relocated under a different network name or address.
- **ICMP network is unreachable.**
  - A routing failure has occurred.
  - Investigate configuration of routers on local and remote networks to see that they are active and properly configured.
- **ICMP port is unreachable.**
  - The remote server port is not responding.
  - You might be unable to reach the remote server port because hardware has failed or because a nonexistent address was specified. Confirm that the address entered for the connection is correct and retry the operation. If the problem persists, contact the network administrator for the remote server.
- **ICMP protocol is unreachable.**
  - The remote server is not responding.
  - You might be unable to reach the remote server because hardware has failed or because a nonexistent address was specified. Confirm that the address entered for the connection is correct and retry the operation. If the problem persists, contact the network administrator for the remote server.
- **Identifier removed.**
  - Some identifying information for the connecting socket is missing or was parsed in communications transfer or operation. The cause might be a software problem or an intermediate device used to service the connection.
  - Retry the operation. Report the issue to the software vendor for a fix or workaround. Use of network analysis tools to troubleshoot the network may be helpful. Check for invalid packet errors on network data communicating equipment. If unusual numbers of errors are occurring, interference such as electromagnetic interference or radio fre-

quency interference (EMI/RFI) on cabling or data lines may be present.

- **Illegal seek performed.**
  - There is an error in shared file permissions or possible errors in the file table.
  - Verify that the appropriate permissions are set. Verify the hard disk integrity through the use of CHKDSK and/or SCANDSK.

- **Inode is remote.**
  - Input for the current operation cannot be obtained from a remote source.
  - Report the issue to the software vendor and obtain a solution or workaround.

- **Invalid argument.**
  - The requested operation contained additional information or parameters that cannot be processed correctly through the current connection.
  - Retry the request. Report the issue to the software vendor or technical support and obtain a solution or workaround.

- **Invalid Ethernet packet in use.**
  - There is a problem with packet formation or possible configuration problems with a router.
  - Verify that the selected frame type matches on both client and server on the LAN. Verify the router configuration for packet-length settings or use a packet analysis tool to further investigate packet framing that is being used on the LAN.

- **Invalid request code used.**
  - The requested operation is not recognized or supported by protocol services in use between the remote server and the client.
  - Confirm that the protocol and port types are correctly configured for the WinSock Proxy service for use with the current program; specifically any port types (UDP or TCP), port initial direction (inbound or outbound), and port numbers in use for the connection. Report the issue to the software vendor and obtain a solution or workaround if the issue cannot be traced to port settings or if it continues.

- **Invalid request descriptor used.**
  - There is an error in the data, or an exchange between the remote server and the client has been attempted that is not allowed within the software.

- Reenter the data and retry the operation. Report the issue to the software vendor and obtain a solution or workaround.

- **Invalid slot used.**

  - Hardware configuration error has been detected and applied by the current operation.

  - Verify hardware device settings for the software being used to ensure they are correct. Reset as necessary; may require use of EISA utilities.

- **I/O error encountered.**

  - The problem might be caused by instability in the local system environment.

  - Exit the program and perform a COLD BOOT restart of the computer. Try the operation again. Note: shutting the power down is recommended, as it will reset the hardware. A warm restart does not always do this on all hardware. Report the issue to technical support and obtain a solution or workaround if it continues.

- **IP subnet table is full.**

  - The address table for routing hosts on the network indicates that all addresses on this subnetwork are in use.

  - Rebuild routing tables for affected hosts, or assign the host to a new subnetwork with available address space.

- **Is a directory.**

  - A directory object has been selected for the current operation where a file was expected.

  - Select a file to complete this operation, or cancel the operation.

- **Is not a directory.**

  - A file object has been selected for the current operation where a directory was expected.

  - Select a directory to complete this operation, or cancel the operation.

- **Is not a typewriter.**

  - The current configuration does not support the attempted method of input.

  - Verify that you are using the correct syntax and switches. Retry the operation. Report the issue to the software vendor and obtain a solution or workaround.

- **Level 2 halted.**

  - A problem has occurred at the data-link level, or the link connection has been cleared.

- Check for errors logged for data link or data communications hardware devices. Network analysis tools may be required to go further. Report the issues with this line to your appropriate service provider for further assistance in resolving the problem.
- **Level 3 halted.**
  - The network has been stopped. The current connection probably failed.
  - This is a serious error and you should check for errors logged for network connections. Check the client network connection or have the client reconnect to the network. If several clients are having the same difficulty, check network cabling, termination, and other network devices. Also check that network hardware or software has not been stopped.
- **Level 2 is not synchronized.**
  - There is a data line problem for the current connected operation, possibly because of noise or interference on the line itself.
  - Check for performance problems or further errors on the line. Use of network analysis tools to check for EMI/RFI may be necessary. Report the line to the appropriate service provider for further assistance in resolving the problem.
- **Level 3 reset.**
  - The current connection failed and the network has been reset, probably because an intermediate network host servicing the current connection, such as a router, was reset.
  - Reestablish the remote connection. If the issue returns, note network errors or excess traffic on the network.
- **Library section in code file corrupted.**
  - Software components installed or called by the current program are missing or corrupted, or there might be disk errors.
  - Check the hard disk for errors by using CHKDSK or SCANDISK, and reinstall the software if warranted. Report the issue to the software vendor or technical support and obtain a solution or work around if the issue persists.
- **Link number is out of range.**
  - The link is broken and the number specified for linking is invalid.
  - Re-create the link by using the options within the program. Report the issue to the software vendor or technical support and obtain a solution or work around if the issue persists.

- **Log name used is not unique.**
  - The service is attempting to name a log by using a file name that is already in use within the path the service uses for logging.
  - Rename or delete the previous log file or select a different name for the new log file.
- **Math argument used.**
  - The input for the current operation was of an invalid type or unexpected for the current program, possibly because of an error in the data or software-based restrictions.
  - Re-enter the data. Report the issue to the software vendor or technical support and obtain a solution or work around if the issue persists.
- **Message is too long.**
  - The message length exceeds current limits for the program. This can indicate an incorrect protocol setting, or that a mismatched port type is configured between server and client.
  - Verify that the selected transport is the same on both client and server and that it is valid for the software. Report the issue to the software vendor or technical support and obtain a solution or work around if the issue persists.
- **Mount device or directory is busy.**
  - The remote server drive is unavailable or is out of space.
  - Verify that there is sufficient space on the remote drive and retry the operation. If no space is available on the remote drive, contact the administrator for the remote server.
- **Multihop attempted.**
  - The remote connection attempted to cross an excessive number of intermediate routes between devices. If the connection has multiple routers available for forwarding, this might indicate a problem in other network forwarding devices, such as routers or bridges on the network.
  - Verify that the maximum number of hops allowed for the protocol service with this connection is sufficient. Check statistics on bridges or routers by using network-monitoring tools to see if excessive hop counts have been obtained. Report the issue to technical support if the issue persists.
- **Name entered is too long.**
  - Incorrect name entered or name has too many characters.

- Check validity of the name entered. Retype the name and check that no added characters were included.

- **Network is down.**
  - Current connection has failed and problems maintaining a connection to the local network exist.
  - Verify that the client has a network connection and have the client reconnect to the network. If errors occur for multiple clients, verify correct network cabling, termination, and other hardware. Check that the network hardware or software has not been shut down.

- **Network was reset.**
  - The current connection has failed, which indicates that an intermediate network host servicing the current connection, such as a router, has been reset.
  - Reestablish the remote connection. If the problem persists, check for errors or excess traffic on the network with a network analysis tool.

- **No anode exists.**
  - There is an error in the data or an exchange between the remote server and the client has been attempted that is not allowed within the software.
  - Reenter the data and retry the operation. Report the issue to the software vendor or technical support and obtain a solution or workaround.

- **No buffer space is available.**
  - There is no buffer space available to maintain the current streamed connection.
  - Allocate sufficient space for stream buffers on the server. For more information on setting TCP or UDP buffer size for clients by using the Registry on the server, see Help for .

- **No buffer space is supported.**
  - The software requires the use of buffer space on the remote server to buffer connection throughput.
  - Verify sufficient buffer space has been allocated at the server. For the WinSock Proxy service, you may want to increase the server Registry entries for UDP or TCP buffer size.

- **No children exist for parent object.**
  - A program call to a referenced code library cannot complete normally. The program might be missing components needed to complete the request.

- Report the issue to the software vendor or technical support and obtain a solution or workaround.

- **No CSI structure is available.**

  - The software cannot complete the operation because a required specialized component is missing.

  - Report the issue to the software vendor or technical support and obtain a solution or workaround.

- **No data was found.**

  - No data was available to complete the operation.

  - Reenter the data to retry the operation. If the issue persists, ensure that the network is still connected.

- **No data record is available.**

  - No data is available at the specified location or the remote source is empty.

  - Verify that the path to the data is correct and that the location contains data.

- **No message of desired type exists.**

  - The software does not support messages of this type or a message cannot be located.

  - Check to see whether the message exists at the expected source location. Review the software documentation. If a message exists, report the issue to the software vendor or technical support and obtain a solution or workaround.

- **No space is left on device.**

  - Indicates insufficient space on destination hard disk to complete a file copy operation. Usually this happens as a result of a disk quota being set for the destination directory path.

  - Verify sufficient free space on the destination hard disk, and that disk-space restrictions such as quotas are not in effect for the directory.

- **No such device exists.**

  - Device name not found on the network.

  - Verify that the device name was entered correctly and that the specified device is operational and properly configured on the client computer.

- **No such device or address exists.**

  - Device or address entered not found on the network.

- Verify that the device name or address was entered correctly and that the specified device is operational. Check that the address can reply to test utilities such as Ping and is active on the network, or contact the network administrator for the remote device and report the problem.
- **No such file or directory exists.**
  - The requested file or directory does not exist on the remote server.
  - Create, rename, or modify the requested file or directory accordingly.
- **No such process exists.**
  - The remote server does not recognize the requested operation. The operation might be the result of errors in data or invalid user input.
  - Retry the operation. Report the issue to the software vendor or technical support and obtain a solution or workaround if the issue persists.
- **Nonrecoverable error encountered.**
  - A fatal error was encountered by the WinSock Proxy service.
  - Attempt to restart the WinSock program on the client and initiate a new connection.
- **Not enough memory is available.**
  - Insufficient memory is available on the local system to support the current operation.
  - Shut down all non-essential software and retry. If the issue persists, COLD BOOT the computer, which will free memory resources, then try the operation again.
- **Not owner.**
  - You have insufficient permission or ownership rights to access the remote shared resource.
  - The network administrator for the remote resource must add you to the permissions list for proper access.
- **Operation is in progress.**
  - Indicates that the attempted operation is still in progress.
  - The new attempt should be cancelled and the previous command must be allowed to complete.
- **Operation is not supported on socket.**
  - The current operation is not supported for Windows Sockets with the current program.

- Verify software settings and, if the issue persists, report the problem to the software vendor.
- **Operation would block one in progress.**
  - The requested operation would prevent an operation already in progress from completing.
  - Either cancel the current operation before retrying or wait for the system to complete the processing of the current operation.
- **Package is not installed.**
  - The requested feature is not currently installed.
  - Reinstall the program or upgrade to install the missing program. Review the software documentation for more details.
- **Permission denied.**
  - The remote server refused access to the requested resource.
  - Contact the administrator for the remote server and report the problem or request permissions to access this shared resource.
- **Pipe has broken.**
  - The current operation was suspended because of the data or connection in use, possibly caused by a failing network connection or errors on the network.
  - Reconnect to the remote source and attempt the operation again. If the issue persists, you may need to check using network analysis tools for errors or excessive traffic on the network.
- **Protocol driver is not attached.**
  - There is no driver for a supported protocol bound to the network adapter on the local computer.
  - Verify proper network configuration for the local computer. For Windows NT or Windows 95, use the Network dialog (in Control Panel) to view or modify current driver and protocol settings. To review the current bindings for the adapter, click the Bindings tab in the Network dialog box. Verify that at least one supported network protocol for the WinSock Proxy service (either TCP/IP or NWLink IPX/SPX) is bound to the network adapter.
- **Protocol error encountered.**
  - A protocol error has occurred in the program or network environment.
  - Verify correct service ports are defined for the software and that the WinSock Proxy service is correctly configured. Report the issue to

the software vendor or technical support and obtain a solution or workaround if the issue persists.

- **Protocol family not supported.**
  - The protocol is not defined for use with the WinSock Proxy service.
  - Add the protocol to the WinSock Proxy service.

- **Protocol is not supported.**
  - The protocol selected for use with the current program is not supported by the WinSock Proxy service or has not been defined for the service.
  - Check that the protocol used by the software has been added and correctly defined for use with the WinSock Proxy service.

- **Protocol is wrong type for socket.**
  - The program requires a socket call that is not supported by the current protocol settings for the client program.
  - Verify the software settings for the protocol type in use for the remote connection. Ensure that if TCP or UDP protocol support is used for the software it is properly configured for use with the WinSock Proxy service.

- **Read-only file system is in use.**
  - The file system that is selected for a file copy or transfer operation does not allow write modification. Permissions may be prohibiting write access, or the drive media might be of a type that does not permit write access.
  - Verify that the drive is using a media type that supports write access, and that write permissions are properly assigned and in effect.

- **Remote address changed.**
  - The remote server network address was changed.
  - This requires that you reconnect to the remote server, or contact the administrator for the remote server to obtain more information about this problem.

- **Result is too large.**
  - The output for the current operation was invalid for the system or program, possibly because of an error in the data or because of software-based restrictions.
  - Reenter the data and report the issue to the software vendor or technical support and obtain a solution or workaround if the issue persists.

- **Server mount error.**
  - The server is advertising on the network, but a resource on the server is not mounted or is otherwise unavailable.
  - Verify that the requested server resource is mounted and available on the network. Check to ensure there has been no hardware failure on the remote server.
- **Service cannot send after socket shutdown.**
  - The connection for this program has been closed, which precludes the operation from completion.
  - Restart the software or establish a new connection before retrying the operation.
- **Socket is already connected.**
  - The current operation is unnecessary because a socket already exists between the client and the remote server.
  - Try reconnecting, or open a connection to the remote source using the software.
- **The current operation cannot be completed because the remote connection has been lost or was not made.**
  - This indicates that an error caused by the software occurred in socket creation.
  - Report the issue to the software vendor or technical support and obtain a solution or workaround if the issue persists.
- **Linked libraries for Windows Sockets are not initialized properly for client configuration.**
  - Sockets library is not initialized.
  - Exit and restart the software. Report the issue to the software vendor or technical support and obtain a solution or workaround if the issue persists.
- **Socket operation attempted on a nonsocket.**
  - The selected operation indicates that an error caused by the program software occurred in socket creation.
  - Report the issue to the software vendor or technical support and obtain a solution or workaround if the issue persists.
- **Socket type is not supported.**
  - The current configuration does not support the attempted socket operation.

- Verify that the correct transport protocol (TCP, UDP) is selected for use with the software and with the WinSock Proxy service as well.
- **Software caused connection to abort.**
  - Another software process has caused the current connection to fail.
  - Exit and restart the original program, then reconnect. Report the issue to the software vendor or technical support and obtain a solution or workaround if the issue persists.
- **Subnet module not linked.**
  - A required software component is missing or not configured.
  - Verify the client configuration settings. If necessary, try reinstallation of the software. Report the issue to the software vendor or technical support and obtain a solution or workaround if the issue persists.
- **System call interrupted.**
  - The current proxy connection was interrupted, and the socket operation did not complete as expected. The problem might be the current program or a temporary problem or condition on the network.
  - Verify the network, all connections, and the local computer configuration. If nothing has changed and it was working earlier, try reconnecting. Report the issue to the software vendor or technical support and obtain a solution or workaround if the issue persists. Escalate to software vendor only if there are no LAN issues.
- **System is not ready.**
  - The WinSock Proxy service is not active or is still in the process of starting.
  - Verify that the WinSock Proxy service is running. Stop and restart the service by using Internet Service Manager, or from a Windows NT command prompt by issuing the following set of commands:
    - net stop wspsrv
    - net start wspsrv
  - Should the error continue, shut down all services on the Windows NT Server and restart the machine.
- **System is out of streams resources.**
  - Insufficient streams buffers are available, or a buffer overrun has occurred.
  - Increase the buffer count for streaming protocol (TCP) or modify the connection rate.

- **The link has been severed.**
  - The current connection has been broken.
  - Exit the software and check for related communications hardware and software failures on the local computer. Restart the program and try to reconnect. If the problem continues, check for other failures on the network or verify that the remote server has not been shut down or removed from the network.
- **The object is remote.**
  - The attempt to perform an operation on a remote object failed because it is not local.
  - Report the issue to the software vendor or technical support and obtain a solution or workaround if the issue persists.
- **Timer has expired.**
  - The operation failed because the time-out allowed for this operation expired.
  - Increase the time-out parameters for this operation within the program or within your network client configuration to allow a longer delay in responding.
- **Too many levels of symbolic links.**
  - A software error occurred.
  - Report the issue to the software vendor or technical support and obtain a solution or workaround if the issue persists.
- **Too many links used.**
  - You have reached the maximum number of links that can be opened.
  - Close other connections or programs and retry. Report the issue to the software vendor or technical support and obtain a solution or workaround if the issue persists.
- **Too many open files.**
  - The system does not have enough available file handles to proceed with the current operation. An excessive number of files are currently open or in use by other programs on the system.
  - Close other programs and/or increase the number of file handles before retrying. Report the issue to the software vendor or technical support and obtain a solution or workaround if the issue persists.
- **Too many references used.**
  - The requested operation contained additional information that cannot be processed correctly through the remote connection.

- Retry the request. Report the issue to the software vendor or technical support and obtain a solution or workaround if the issue persists.
- **Try again.**
  - The server may be too busy so it was temporarily unable to process the current request.
  - Try reentering the request, or renewing the connection to the server now or at a later time. Report the issue to technical support to obtain a solution if the issue persists.
- **Trying to read unreadable message.**
  - The message input has errors or is of an incorrect type to be processed by this operation.
  - Check the message data for errors. Report the issue to the software vendor or technical support and obtain a solution or workaround if the issue persists.
- **Unknown error number encountered.**
  - A software error occurred.
  - Report the issue to technical support and obtain a solution or workaround. If the issue persists report the problem to the software vendor.
- **Unknown I/O control call.**
  - A software error occurred.
  - Report the issue to the software vendor or technical support and obtain a solution or workaround if the issue persists.

Web Proxy Client Errors

Internet Information Server (IIS) services return the following event messages, which can be viewed by Web Proxy clients. These messages can appear during Web Proxy connections to FTP, Gopher, or World Wide Web (WWW) services. Some messages are general in nature and are common to all IIS services. The service that returns the message is noted with each entry in brackets, such as:

[Gopher Service]

where the message is specific to a Web Proxy connection accessing Gopher services for IIS. Note that Gopher Service is not supported by IIS 4.0.

For HTTP browser messages, all client messages are in the form:

The Proxy Server has encountered an error. **MessageText**

where MessageText is a brief explanation of the error message. MessageText explanations are described in the following list:

- **A connection with the server could not be established.**
  - [IIS – All Services]
  - The specified server is not responding or not available.
  - Verify that the server name was entered correctly, and that the server has available connections.
- **A Gopher protocol error occurred.**
  - [Gopher Service]
  - Verify that the server supports the same version of Gopher protocol used by the client. Protocol errors between a server supporting only standard Gopher and a client that uses Gopher Plus can occur.
- **A protocol with the required capabilities was not found.**
  - [IIS - All Services]
  - Microsoft Proxy Server does not support the requested protocol.
  - Retry the request after verifying that the protocol is a supported type such as HTTP, FTP, or Gopher.
- **Access is denied.**
  - [WWW Service]
  - HTTP Error 5. A security or permissions violation has occurred for the browser client. The server has been configured to deny access to the requested URL site.
  - Change *only* the effective permissions to permit required access.
- **An error was detected while parsing the data.**
  - [Gopher Service]
  - Likely there is an issue with trying to access the Gopher server remotely.
  - Try again later and verify that the server supports the same version of Gopher protocol used by the client. In some cases, protocol errors can occur between a server that supports only standard Gopher and a client that uses Gopher Plus.
- **An internal error occurred in the Proxy Internet extensions.**
  - [IIS - All Services]

- A software error occurred for a Proxy Internet extension program that is needed for the current operation.
- Report the issue to the software vendor or Microsoft technical support and obtain a solution or workaround.

- **FTP using Netscape Navigator shows all files as plain text when attempting to download.**
  - This problem occurs for some versions of Netscape Navigator that are configured to use the Web Proxy service of Microsoft Proxy Server. When Netscape Navigator sees the HTTP document-type header, it attempts to display the FTP contents on screen without examining the header.
  - Workaround for when you click the link to download a file is to hold down the SHIFT key.

- **HTTP error 5 occurred.**
  - The connection was refused for a client browser. If anonymous logon is allowed for IIS, then Microsoft Proxy Server uses the IUSR_computername account to authenticate clients. Microsoft Proxy Server checks that client users have access to a requested service.
  - Check that the IUSR_computername account is listed on the Web Proxy service Permissions tab for the requested service (FTP, HTTP, and so on) that is being affected. If using IIS version 4, check to ensure that the password has not been changed for the IUSR_computername account.

- **HTTP error 12 occurred.**
  - Internal network is running TCP/IP protocol and the Local Address Table (LAT) is configured to specify the server's internal IP address, which is located on the local network.
  - Check that the IP address assigned for the server's internal network adapter card is included in the LAT.

- **HTTP error 18 occurred.**
  - This error can occur when you attempt to use a browser for FTP service that is configured for the Web Proxy service and the FTP directory on the remote computer is empty. (WinSock Proxy FTP does not return this error if the directory is empty.)
  - Check the contents of the remote directory or report the issue to the network administrator.

- **No more Internet handles can be allocated.**
  - [IIS - All Services]
  - The Internet server does not have enough available resources to support the request for service at this time.
  - Try again later. Report the issue to the software vendor or technical support and obtain a solution or workaround if the issue persists.
- **The access code is invalid.**
  - [WWW Service]
  - HTTP error 12. This error occurs when a client attempts to connect by using the Internet port, and access to the Proxy Server computer is invalid. The error might be caused by a LAT configuration problem.
  - Copy the Msplat.txt file to the client directory from the share source path on the Proxy Server computer (typically C:\Msp\Clients). Once copied, verify functionality.
- **The connection with the server was reset.**
  - [IIS - All Services]
  - The connection was cleared at the server, or the server was shut down.
  - Reconnect to the server and retry to complete the request.
- **The connection with the server was terminated abnormally.**
  - [IIS - All Services]
  - The server or the network was stopped without warning.
  - Reconnect to the server and retry to complete the request.
- **The destination host is too busy.**
  - The destination host (on the Internet) is currently not available.
  - A network link in the path to the destination host is not available.
- **The FTP session was terminated.**
  - [FTP Service]
  - The connection was closed, either because of a possible attempted security violation or a time-out on the remote server.
  - Reconnect to the server or check for server availability.
- **The length is incorrect for the option type.**
  - [IIS - All Services]
  - The length, in bytes, of the specified option is incorrect.

- Reselect the current option and type the data again. Verify that you did not mistype by adding or subtracting characters and that the value typed is within the allowed length range.
- **The locator is invalid.**
  - [Gopher Service]
  - The locator used is not valid for the remote Gopher server.
  - Verify that the correct path was used to locate the requested file by browsing the directory.
- **The locator must be for a file.**
  - [Gopher Service]
  - The URL entered is for a directory location and not a file.
  - Browse the directory listing to locate the file and enter a Gopher URL that contains a file name.
- **The locator type is incorrect for this operation.**
  - [Gopher Service]
  - A file name or directory name might be applied incorrectly.
  - Verify that the name used for specifying location is a file or directory name and is correctly matched for the operation.
- **The locator type is not recognized.**
  - [Gopher Service]
  - An incorrect Gopher type was used or the Gopher type used is not supported.
  - Verify that the name used for specifying location is a file or directory name and is correctly matched for the operation.
- **The logon request was denied.**
  - [IIS - All Services]
  - The Internet server logon request was denied. The logon account might have been disabled or logon information might have changed.
  - Verify that the information used was entered correctly and retry the logon. If the problem continues, report the problem to the administrator of the Internet server you are requesting.
- **The object or file requested is not referenced correctly or has been removed from the linked location.**
  - [IIS - All Services]
  - Usually indicates that a link to another document is incorrect or no longer valid.

- Inform the administrator of the remote server about the returned message.
- **The operation has been canceled.**
  - [IIS - All Services]
  - The client or the server canceled this operation.
  - Retry the operation.
- **The operation timed out.**
  - [IIS - All Services]
  - The remote server did not respond within the time allowed.
  - The server may be unavailable. Try again later or report the error to the remote server administrator.
- **The password was not allowed.**
  - [IIS - All Services]
  - The password specified in the URL is not allowed. The password might have been changed or typed incorrectly.
  - Retry entering the password. If the problem continues, contact the remote server administrator to report the problem.
- **The request for an HTTP header is invalid.**
  - [WWW Service]
  - The remote server does not recognize a header contained within the URL request.
  - Contact the server administrator for the Web site to confirm that your browser is supported.
- **The request must be for a Gopher Plus item.**
  - [Gopher Service]
  - The server and client do not support the same version of Gopher protocols.
  - The client must be modified or upgraded to use Gopher Plus.
- **The requested attribute was not found.**
  - [Gopher Service]
  - The requested attribute is supported for Gopher Plus servers and was not found on the server.
  - Reconfigure the client to use standard Gopher protocol and resend the request.

- **The requested header was not found.**
  - [WWW Service]
  - The requested URL contained source information that cannot be located by the server.
  - Refresh the document from the Web browser.
- **The requested operation is invalid.**
  - [IIS - All Services]
  - The requested operation entered in the URL is not allowed or is not recognized by the remote Internet server.
  - Retry the URL or select a different operation.
- **The server does not support the requested protocol level.**
  - [WWW Service]
  - The protocol type specified in the URL request is not compatible with WWW, Web Proxy services, or the requested resource.
  - Verify that the proxy service supports the protocol you requested (such as FTP, Gopher, or HTTP).
- **The server name or address could not be resolved.**
  - [IIS - All Services]
  - Find out if DNS, WINS, or DHCP services are in use on the local network. This message might indicate an error in client or server configuration settings for any of these services that are actively in use.
  - Review the TCP/IP Protocol properties by using Network Icon in the Control Panel for all of these services. Further information can be found in the *MCSE Study Guide: Internetworking TCP/IP with Microsoft Windows NT 4* by Kostya Ryvkin, Dave Houde, and Tim Hoffman.
- **The server returned an invalid or unrecognized response.**
  - [WWW Service]
  - The server cannot fully or correctly interpret the HTTP request. The request might have been corrupted by transmission errors.
  - Try reloading the document in your Web browser to correct the problem. If the problem continues, contact your Microsoft support provider.
- **The server returned extended information.**
  - [IIS - All Services]

- The remote server that might interfere with local processing of the client request returned status information about the current connection.
- Review the request output for more detail. Report the issue to the software vendor or technical support and obtain a solution or workaround if the issue persists.
- **The specified option is invalid.**
  - [IIS - All Services]
  - The current configuration does not support the requested option.
  - Clear the message and select a different option.
- **The specified option value cannot be set.**
  - [IIS - All Services]
  - The server does not support this value, or the value was typed incorrectly.
  - Check spelling and retry the operation. If this persists, ask your network administrator to check the status of the remote computer.
- **The supplied HTTP header is invalid.**
  - [WWW Service]
  - The remote server does not recognize a header contained within the URL request.
  - Contact the server administrator for the Web site to confirm that your browser is supported.
- **The URL does not use a recognized protocol.**
  - [IIS - All Services]
  - The protocol is not supported or the request was not typed correctly.
  - Confirm that a valid protocol is used, such as HTTP for a Web request.
- **The URL is invalid.**
  - [IIS - All Services]
  - The request was not typed correctly.
  - Type the correct URL and try again.
- **The user name was not allowed.**
  - [IIS - All Services]
  - The user name that was specified in the URL is not allowed to log on.
  - Check the spelling and try again or try a different name.

- **There is already an FTP request in progress on this session.**
  - [FTP Service]
  - Only one FTP session can be active at one time.
  - Wait until the current request has been completed, or disconnect and then reconnect to the FTP server to check for server availability.
- **There is no more data.**
  - [Gopher Service]
  - No more data exists beyond the last block of data returned from the server.
  - Stop the request for additional data by canceling the operation in progress.
- **Windows Internet Extension support has been shut down.**
  - [IIS - All Services]
  - An Internet Extension program is required to complete the current operation.
  - Open the required Internet Extension program and reselect the command option.

cbt
systems

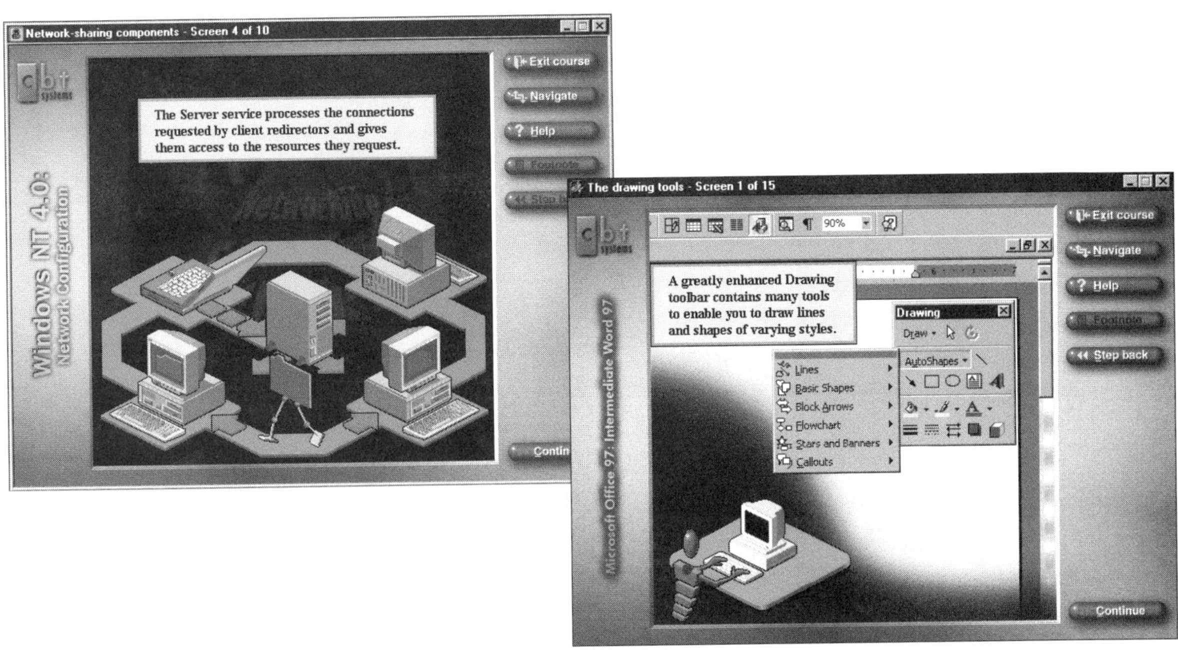

Other curricula available from CBT Systems:

- Cisco
- Informix
- Java
- Marimba
- Microsoft
- Netscape
- Novell

- Oracle
- SAP
- Sybase
- C/C⁢+
- Centura
- Information Technology/ Core Concepts

- Internet and Intranet Skills
- Internetworking
- UNIX

To order additional CBT Systems courseware today call 800.789.8590 or visit www.clbooks.com/training/cbt.htm

At Scholars.com our certified Learning Advisors are available for online personalized mentoring when your students need it most — 24-hours-a-day, 7-days-a-week.

OPENING MINDS WITH PERSONAL SUPPORT.

Scholars.com introduces flexible self-paced study with the added benefits of expert help. With CBT Systems' award-winning courseware, Scholars.com works closely with students for personalized assistance through every step.

OPENING THE DOOR TO ONLINE LEARNING.

As Microsoft and Novell's largest online training provider, Scholars.com offers the only 24-hour online support in the world. Our team of Learning Advisors assists through online chats, discussion groups and help desk scenarios. Proactive mentoring also provides daily e-mail and answers to students' questions within 6 hours.

OPENING THE SECRETS TO CERTIFICATION.

CBT Systems courseware is Microsoft and Novell approved, and Scholars.com Learning Advisors are Microsoft and Novell certified. So you get help from mentors who know firsthand what it takes to pass certification exams.

Our dedication to the most effective I.T. training keeps us up nights. So don't let another 24 hours pass without online mentoring, visit our web site today.

Scholars.com — A new way to learn.

Try a FREE course — Microsoft: Administering Windows NT 4.0: Managing Users and Groups. Or Novell: Introducing Novell Netware 4.11. Register now at **www.scholars.com**

scholars.com

A CBT Group Company

CBT SOFTWARE LICENSE AGREEMENT

IF YOU DO NOT AGREE WITH THESE TERMS AND CONDITIONS, DO NOT INSTALL THE SOFTWARE.

This is a legal agreement you and CBT System Ltd. ("Licensor"). The licensor ("Licensor") from whom you have licensed the CBT Group PLC courseware (the "Software"). By installing, copying or otherwise using the Software, you agree to be bound by the terms of this Agreement License Agreement (the "License"). If you do not agree to the terms of this License, the Licensor is unwilling to license the Software to you. In such event, you may not use or copy the Software, and you should promptly contact the Licensor for instructions on the return of the unused Software.

1. **Use.** Licensor grants to you a non-exclusive, nontransferable license to use Licensor's software product (the "Software") the Software and accompanying documentation in accordance with the terms and conditions of this license agreement ("License") License and as specified in your agreement with Licensor (the "Governing Agreement"). In the event of any conflict between this License and the Governing Agreement, the Governing Agreement shall control.

You may:

a. (if specified as a "personal use" version) install the Software on a single stand-alone computer or a single network node from which node the Software cannot be accessed by another computer, provided that such Software shall be used by only one individual; or

b. (if specified as a "workstation" version) install the Software on a single stand-alone computer or a single network node from which node the Software cannot be accessed by another computer, provided that such Software shall be used by only one individual; or

c. (if specified as a "LAN" version) install the Software on a local area network server that provides access to multiple computers, up to the maximum number of computers or users specified in your Governing Agreement, provided that such Software shall be used only by employees of your organization; or

d. (if specified as an "enterprise" version) install the Software or copies of the Software on multiple local or wide area network servers, intranet servers, stand-alone computers and network nodes (and to make copies of the Software for such purpose) at one or more sites, which servers provide access to a multiple number of users, up to the maximum number of users specified in your Governing Agreement, provided that such Software shall be used only by employees of your organization.

This License is not a sale. Title and copyrights to the Software, accompanying documentation and any copy made by you remain with Licensor or its suppliers or licensors.

2. **Intellectual Property.** The Software is owned by Licensor or its licensors and is protected by United States and other jurisdictions' copyright laws and international treaty provisions. Therefore, you may not use, copy, or distribute the Software without the express written authorization of CBT Group PLC. This License authorizes you to use the Software for the internal training needs of your employees only, and to make one copy of the Software solely for backup or archival purposes. You may not print copies of any user documentation provided in "online" or electronic form. Licensor retains all rights not expressly granted.

3. **Restrictions.** You may not transfer, rent, lease, loan or time-share the Software or accompanying documentation. You may not reverse engineer, decompile, or disassemble the Software, except to the extent the foregoing restriction is expressly prohibited by applicable law. You may not modify, or create derivative works based upon the Software in whole or in part.

1. **Confidentiality.** The Software contains confidential trade secret information belonging to Licensor, and you may use the software only pursuant to the terms of your Governing Agreement, if any, and the license set forth herein. In addition, you may not disclose the Software to any third party.

2. **Limited Liability.** IN NO EVENT WILL THE Licensor's LIABILITY UNDER, ARISING OUT OF OR RELATING TO THIS AGREEMENT EXCEED THE AMOUNT PAID TO LICENSOR FOR THE SOFTWARE. LICENSOR SHALL NOT BE LIABLE FOR ANY SPECIAL, INCIDENTAL, INDIRECT OR CONSEQUENTIAL DAMAGES, HOWEVER CAUSED AND ON ANY THEORY OF LIABILITY., REGARDLESS OR WHETHER LICENSOR HAS BEEN ADVISED OF THE POSSIBILITY OF SUCH DAMAGES. WITHOUT LIMITING THE FOREGOING, LICENSOR WILL NOT BE LIABLE FOR LOST PROFITS, LOSS OF DATA, OR COSTS OF COVER.

3. **Limited Warranty.** LICENSOR WARRANTS THAT SOFTWARE WILL BE FREE FROM DEFECTS IN MATERIALS AND WORKMANSHIP UNDER NORMAL USE FOR A PERIOD OF THIRTY (30) DAYS FROM THE DATE OF RECEIPT. THIS LIMITED WARRANTY IS VOID IF FAILURE OF THE SOFTWARE HAS RESULTED FROM ABUSE OR MISAPPLICATION. ANY REPLACEMENT SOFTWARE WILL BE WARRANTED FOR A PERIOD OF THIRTY (30) DAYS FROM THE DATE OF RECEIPT OF SUCH REPLACEMENT SOFTWARE. THE SOFTWARE AND DOCUMENTATION ARE PROVIDED "AS IS". LICENSOR HEREBY DISCLAIMS ALL OTHER WARRANTIES, EXPRESS, IMPLIED, OR STATUTORY, INCLUDING WITHOUT LIMITATION, THE IMPLIED WARRANTIES OF MERCHANTABILITY AND FITNESS FOR A PARTICULAR PURPOSE.

4. **Exceptions.** SOME STATES DO NOT ALLOW THE LIMITATION OF INCIDENTAL DAMAGES OR LIMITATIONS ON HOW LONG AN IMPLIED WARRANTY LASTS, SO THE ABOVE LIMITATIONS OR EXCLUSIONS MAY NOT APPLY TO YOU. This agreement gives you specific legal rights, and you may also have other rights which vary from state to state.

5. **U.S. Government-Restricted Rights.** The Software and accompanying documentation are deemed to be "commercial computer Software" and "commercial computer Software documentation," respectively, pursuant to FAR Section 227.7202 and FAR Section 12.212, as applicable. Any use, modification, reproduction release, performance, display or disclosure of the Software and accompanying documentation by the U.S. Government shall be governed solely by the terms of this Agreement and shall be prohibited except to the extent expressly permitted by the terms of this Agreement.

6. **Export Restrictions.** You may not download, export, or re-export the Software (a) into, or to a national or resident of, Cuba, Iraq, Libya, Yugoslavia, North Korea, Iran, Syria or any other country to which the United States has embargoed goods, or (b) to anyone on the United States Treasury Department's list of Specially Designated Nations or the U.S. Commerce Department's Table of Deny Orders. By installing or using the Software, you are representing and warranting that you are not located in, under the control of, or a national resident of any such country or on any such list.

7. **General.** This License is governed by the laws of the United States and the State of California, without reference to conflict of laws principles. The parties agree that the United Nations Convention on Contracts for the International Sale of Goods shall not apply to this License. If any provision of this Agreement is held invalid, the remainder of this License shall continue in full force and effect.

8. **More Information.** Should you have any questions concerning this Agreement, or if you desire to contact Licensor for any reason, please contact: CBT Systems USA Ltd., 1005 Hamilton Court, Menlo Park, California 94025, Attn: Chief Legal Officer.

IF YOU DO NOT AGREE WITH THE ABOVE TERMS AND CONDITIONS, SO NOT INSTALL THE SOFTWARE AND RETURN IT TO THE LICENSOR.

The enclosed CD contains the following computer-based training (CBT) course module:

Implementing and Supporting Microsoft Proxy Server 2.

The CD can be used on Windows 95, Windows 98, or Windows NT systems. To access the CBT course, launch the SETUP.EXE file. For further information about installation, read the README.TXT file on the CD. At the Start menu, select Run and type in D:/readme.txt (where D is your CD-ROM drive).

Technical Support

If you have a problem with the CBT software, please contact CBT Technical Support. In the US, call 1-800-938-3247. If you are outside the US, call 3531-283-0380.

Prentice Hall does not offer technical support for this software. However, if there is a problem with the media, you may obtain a replacement copy by e-mailing us with your problem at:
disc_exchange@prenhall.com.